D0754110

PRIVATE MORALITY
IN GREECE AND ROME

SOME HISTORICAL ASPECTS

MNEMOSYNE

BIBLIOTHECA CLASSICA BATAVA

COLLEGERUNT

W. DEN BOER • A. D. LEEMAN • W. J. VERDENIUS

BIBLIOTHECAE FASCICULOS EDENDOS CURAVIT

W. J. VERDENIUS, HOMERUSLAAN 53, ZEIST

SUPPLEMENTUM QUINQUAGESIMUM SEPTIMUM

W. DEN BOER

PRIVATE MORALITY
IN GREECE AND ROME

SOME HISTORICAL ASPECTS

LUGDUNI BATAVORUM E. J. BRILL MCMLXXIX

PRIVATE MORALITY
IN GREECE AND ROME

SOME HISTORICAL ASPECTS

BY

W. DEN BOER

Professor of Ancient History
in the University of Leiden

LEIDEN E. J. BRILL 1979

4-8-81 (3x9 ATCT

50975

HN
10
R7
B63

ISBN 90 04 05976 8

Copyright 1979 by E. J. Brill, Leiden, The Netherlands

All rights reserved. No part of this book may be reproduced or
translated in any form, by print, photoprint, microfilm, microfiche
or any other means without written permission from the publisher

PRINTED IN THE NETHERLANDS

CONTENTS

PREFACE

Morality is not a modern thing currently en vogue. A moral point of view, past or present, may often be regarded as prejudice. It is profitless to argue about this. On the other hand, it would be extremely harmful to our understanding of the past if we were to do no more than call morality simply 'prejudice'.

There is a great deal of morality in the past, by no means all of it recorded in religious or legal definitions. Most of it is to be found as a framework of human society, preached and lived, often existing simply as an invisible and almost indefinable 'moral standard' (*taxis tōn ethōn*), sometimes hard and inexorable in determining human behaviour. Because of the lack of any written and publicly determined code, it has been called 'private morality'.

Although it is unwritten, however, the code certainly exists and has always existed. Because of it people may live in a state of tension often far more powerful than the tension exerted by written laws of morality. The code is unwritten, but it is seldom or never felt as higher, as is usually of course the case with unwritten laws. Quite often it is a result of strong emotions.

In this book, I am principally concerned with the code of behaviour in everyday life and not with the state or the gods, whose laws were sometimes quite different. This code was binding and often tyrannical. It was also a very personal code of behaviour following a uniform standard. The questions discussed in this volume have, then, to do with personal behaviour determined to a great extent by the threat of retribution exercised by gossip among neighbours. Although it strikes modern man very often as meaningless or ridiculous, it was always taken very seriously by people in the past.

During the years I have been working on this book I have learnt much from many scholars—far too many to mention them all individually—and among them the late Professor Bolkestein, with whose work I sometimes found myself in disagreement, but whose stimulating publications have extended many scholars' horizons.

The translation of this book was, as in all such cases, a demanding task. I should like to thank the publishers and the translators

for their careful work. My friend Geoffrey Woodhead read part
of the typescript and made a number of helpful comments.

It was a year's study-leave at the Netherlands Institute for
Advanced Study (NIAS) in Wassenaar (1974-75) that made the
writing of this book possible. I am most grateful to all those involved in running this centre of research.

Netherlands Institute for Advanced Study (Wassenaar) 1974-75
Leiden, 22 August 1976

LIST OF ABBREVIATIONS

AC	L'Antiquité classique
AJA	American Journal of Archaeology
AJPh	American Journal of Philology
An Gr	Anecdota Graeca, ed. Bekker, 3 vols 1814-1821
A f R	Archiv für Religionswissenschaft
BCH	Bulletin de correspondance hellénique
BiOr	Bibliotheca Orientalis
BSA	Annual of the British School at Athens (= ABSA)
CAH	The Cambridge Ancient History
CLE	Carmina latina epigraphica, ed. Buecheler
CPh	Classical Philology
CQ	Classical Quaterly
CR	Classical Review
D. or DK	Fragmente der Vorsokratiker, ed. H. Diels — W. Kranz [6]
FGrHist	Fragmente der Griechischen Historiker, ed. F. Jacoby
GGA	Göttingische Gelehrte Anzeigen
GGR	Geschichte der Griechischen Religion (M. P. Nilsson)
HSCPh	Harvard Studies in Classical Philology
HTR	Harvard Theological Review
IG	Inscriptiones Graecae
Jahrbuch AntChr	Jahrbuch für Antike und Christentum
JHS	Journal of Hellenic Studies
JRS	Journal of Roman Studies
LCL	Loeb Classical Library
LSJ	Greek-English Lexicon (H. G. Liddell — R. Scott)
Med. Kon. Ned. Akad. van Wetenschappen	(also MKNAW) Mededelingen van de Koninklijke Nederlandse Akademie van Wetenschappen
Mnem.	Mnemosyne
Mus.	Museum. Tijdschrift voor Filologie en Geschiedenis (1895-1959)
OCD	Oxford Classical Dictionary
Philol.	Philologus
RAC	Reallexicon für Antike und Christentum
RE	Paulys Real-Encyclopädie der classischen Altertumswissenschaft
REA	Revue des études anciennes
REG	Revue des études grecques
Rh.Mus.	Rheinisches Museum
Riv. Filol. Class.	Rivista di Filologia e d'Istruzione Classica
RVV	Religionsgeschichtliche Versuche und Vorarbeiten (= RGVV)
SIG	Sylloge Inscriptionum Graecarum ed. W. Dittenberger

SEHRE	The Social and Economic History of the Roman Empire, M. Rostovtzeff
SVF	Stoicorum Veterum Fragmenta, ed. H. von Arnim
TvG	Tijdschrift voor Geschiedenis
TLL	Thesaurus Linguae Latinae
TLS	Times Literary Supplement
ThWNT	Theologisches Wörterbuch zum Neuen Testament (G. Kittel — G. Friedrich) 1928-1973
Vig. Chr.	Vigiliae Christianae

CHAPTER ONE

MORALITY AND SOCIAL RELATIONSHIPS

In any study of the Greeks *sub specie morum*, most attention is, not surprisingly, given to their philosophers. A great deal was written by Plato, Aristotle, Epicurus, Zeno and countless others about human relationships. A very great deal indeed was written about relationships between men and other men, rich and poor, men and women, servants or slaves and freemen, citizens and aliens. It is, however, only here and there that anything was said in the enormous literature about these relationships in practice, and even then this information is often to be found in hidden corners. In the literature of this period, strictly logical thought was always respected and there was a strong inclination to philosophize and speculate. There was also a clear preference for what was special and impressive (a preference shown generally, of course, throughout history). This inevitably resulted in less attention being given to what was ordinary and could be taken for granted. This is again a well known phenomenon in literature and history. Ordinary everyday life lay outside the sphere of interest of Greek historians. They were not necessarily conscious of this nor, initially at least, consistent about it. This is clear, for example, from the Histories of Herodotus. This author often did do full justice to 'ordinary' life, mainly because it provided him with the opportunity for a good story or a striking illustration. But historians as different from one another as Thucydides and Polybius give the distinct impression of preferring the great and the important as decisive in the making of history. It was this characteristic of the history writing of those times which once made a young student exclaim 'I would exchange Thucydides any day for a recording of a conversation between a couple of ordinary Athenian women'.

This is, of course, a very one-sided comment, but it is a challenging one and it draws attention very clearly to the fact that the objects of Greek historiography are great men and important events. The little man, his needs, his way of life and his relationships with his fellow-men in everyday life—these are not, or hardly at all, to be found. But it is precisely my object in this book on Greek morality. I am not in search of great thoughts, but of small scale practice. It will emerge in the course of this book where the latter can be found.

This opposition between the philosophical treatment of morality and practice in the life of middle-class Greek society has already been noted. In his work on this subject, Bolkestein made a distinction between 'lived' morality, which was the object of his study, and 'preached' morality, that of the philosophers. At first sight, his distinction seems correct—an ideal is preached, but people do not measure up to it in their day to day lives. The same kind of opposition can be made out in talk of democracy. We can speak from the point of view of the high ideals, or theory, underlying democratic practice or from the point of view of practice itself, which always falls far short of the theory. If two people known as democrats are compared, there is a danger that the theory of Person A may be contrasted with the practice of Person B, because Person B is disliked and the need is felt to justify prejudice with evidence. The opposite can also occur. The theory of Person B is contrasted with the poor practice of Person A. Can we, however, apply to moral theory and practice a classification that may be quite correct in the case of political institutions? I very much doubt it, for psychological as well as historical and practical reasons. Let us take the psychological objections first.

To choose a fairly arbitrary example, in the relationship between parents and children, something forbidden by the parents is often ignored by the children, but only the most hardened would show no sign of awareness in their behaviour of not carrying out their parents' wishes. Every individual is much more powerful than any political body in a democratic state, and his actions are often determined by his conscience. A child who has done wrong will enter the room with an appearance of guilt. But the state as a political body, in my view, hardly ever betrays any noticeable sense of guilt. In the individual sphere, on the other hand, it is almost always possible to see evidence of a personal sense of guilt in the relationships between people. In other words, there is a close link between what a person does and what he is permitted to do. Even when he goes against what he is permitted to do, the moral imperative is still clear to him. In collective political action taken by members of a state or their representatives, the constitution (which in this case is the moral imperative) is by no means always clear. It is not

surprising, then, that collective political behaviour is different, because the individual in his actions, is always confronted by other
individuals who judge him from day to day according to the imperative of preached morality and he is not in this respect independent: the democratic state, on the other hand, *is* independent. In
the case of ancient Greece, at a time when no international law or
at the most only very rudimentary international rights existed,
there was no opportunity to judge and certainly none to condemn
a people's behaviour or statements. (The people in this case, of
course, were the whole community or the state). It was only in the
case of very important international issues, as, for example, whether
or not the whole of Athens was to be destroyed at the end of the
Peloponnesian War in 404 B.C., that public opinion ever really
played any part. In the case of the individual within the state, on
the other hand, public opinion was always present. What acted as
the norm for this public opinion was *nomos*. This *nomos* was originally the same as usage or custom. When it became written custom, it
then became law.[1]

The concept of conscience is nowadays heavily laden with a
Christian content, but this has not necessarily been always and
everywhere the case. A striking example is provided by Julian the
Apostate, whose conscience troubled him when, as a Christian, he
abandoned the pagan religion of his ancestors. Both public opinion
and conscience clearly play a part in morality. They very often
determine the individual's attitude and also frequently provide a
reason for that attitude. The latter is important, because it can
show that the contrast between lived and preached morality is by
no means as simple as Bolkestein suggested.[2] Indeed, it is clear
that preached morality sometimes leads to lived morality or, to
express this in another way, that lived morality is a result of or a
putting into practice of the moral imperative in question.

For this reason in particular there has been in recent years a
general movement away from theories denying that the written
sources of preached morality have any historical value, because their
moral precepts were never in fact applied. In the case of Israel, the
theory put forward by Wellhausen, who regarded the biblical laws

---

[1] According to E. Schwartz, *Ethik*, p. 43, note 2: 'νόμος should not be
translated as "law". It did not become "law" until γεγραμμένος was added.
The Romans would have translated it as *mos maiorum*'.

[2] H. Bolkestein, *Wohltätigkeit und Armenpflege im vorchristlichen Altertum*
(1939), preserved this distinction as the basis of his thesis.

concerning debt, for example, as Utopian, is still to a great extent
dominant, although it is nowadays applied with considerable caution
and viewed rather sceptically.[3] In other words, it is now believed
that the Old Testament statutes governing debt were not as a rule
Utopian, but that they were at certain times in the history of Israel
carried out in their entirety.

In the case of Greece, it is nowadays again generally accepted
that such lawgivers as Charondas and Zaleucus were historical
figures, preaching morality in Catana in Sicily and at Locri in Italy
respectively. This is in contrast to the hypercritical view of scholars
of the preceding generation, who claimed, on insufficient evidence,
that these figures, who emerged at a fairly late period, were popular
personifications of lawgivers, rather than the historical persons they
are now thought to have been. I have deliberately not used the
Spartan lawgiver Lycurgus as an example, because the tradition
here is much less clear. Elsewhere I have tried to show that Sparta
received a set of laws or a constitution at a certain period in its
history and that one person must have provided the impetus for
this. Whether this lawgiver was called Lycurgus or not is of no
particular importance in this context. If the lawgiver in a given
case was a historical figure, then it is certainly possible that there
was really a set of laws given by that person. (I would go no further
than claim it as a possibility.) The differences of opinion among
scholars are not so great on this last point, since laws are generally
classified under the heading of texts for lived morality by critics
of existing sets of laws which are thought to have been given by
one person.[4]

We must now look at the historical and practical objection to the
classification proposed by Bolkestein. My objection is based on the
written sources of Bolkestein's lived morality (p. 68 ff). These are:

1. ἀραὶ βουζύγιοι, imprecations on those who have violated the
   sacred laws of the community. We have evidence of imprecations

---

[3] V. Tcherikower, 'Jewish Religious Influence in the Adler Papyri',
HTR 35 (1942), p. 28 ff.

[4] For Charondas and Zaleucus, see F. E. Adcock, 'Literary Tradition and
Early Greek Code-Makers', *Cambridge Historical Journal* 2 (1927), p. 95 ff.;
M. Mühl, in an article on these two lawgivers published in *Klio* 22 (1929),
pp. 105 ff., 432 ff. For Zaleucus' first codification, see also Ehrenberg, who
dated this to about 650 B.C. and assumed that the *ius talionis* also occurred
in his code of laws OCD² (1970) *s.v.*

of this type dating from the fourth century B.C. to the third century A.D. Examples are: it is forbidden to sacrifice a plough-ox, it is forbidden to leave a dead body unburied, fire must be given to anyone asking for it, water must be shared with others, the way must be shown to anyone who has lost it. Those who break these and similar laws are cursed.

2. Various laws, especially those given by or ascribed to Solon, because he was a historical figure; later laws were attributed to Solon, but were not his. The so-called Prayer to the Muses is certainly his. In this poem, shame and guilt are associated. Solon prays that he may have a good name among men. He does not want to be everyone's friend. On the contrary, he prefers to be bitter towards his enemies. Towards his friends, however, he intends to be αἰδοῖος. Here, then, αἰδώς is the feeling that he inspires among his friends. He wants respect, not contempt, and he is on his guard against their *nemesis* or disapproval. This, however, brings him under the influence of guilt, since he says that he hopes in later life to have possessions, but is not prepared to acquire these in an unjust way. Thus he comes to the essential point, namely that the law will find him out if he does not act justly: πάντως ὕστερον ἦλθε δίκη. It is here that the curse on later generations, which can cause men suffering even though they have done neither good nor evil, makes its appearance.

3. Proverbial wisdom in collections such as those by Demetrius of Phalerum, known as χρεῖαι. Some of these were included in Stobaeus' Anthology: Δημητρίου Φαληρέως τῶν ἑπτὰ σοφῶν ἀποφθέγματα. Another collection of such excerpts, attributed to Sosiades (one hundred and forty-seven in all), was also preserved by Stobaeus. I do not think, however, that proverbial wisdom, any more than any philosophical precept, can be classified under the heading of lived morality. A proverb such as 'honesty is the best policy' can be preached morality and can also be quoted by any cheat.[5]

4. Funeral inscriptions. It is certain that we can learn about certain special virtues from these inscriptions, but can we ever be certain that these virtues were not highly coloured?

---

[5] For proverbs, see L. Bieler, 'Die Namen des Sprichworts in den klassischen Sprachen', *RhM* (1936), p. 240 ff.; R. Strömberg, *Greek Proverbs. A Collection of Proverbs and Proverbial Phrases which are not listed by the Ancient and Byzantine Paroemiographers*, Göteborg (1954).

5. Funeral orations. My objection to these as examples of lived morality is even greater. Were they not a form of preaching that was often even further from the reality of life? [6]

6. Prose biographies. The classical example of this form is, of course, Xenophon's *Agesilaus*, but to what extent is this work lived morality? And to what extent is Ischomachus' wife in the *Oeconomicus* an example of lived morality? Is there no preaching at all, either in the case of Xenophon himself or in that of his characters? He has, after all, freqently been included among the philosophers.

My provisional conclusion, then, must be that these six groups of sources refer not only to lived morality, but also to preached morality. The Jewish Book of *Ecclesiastes* is perhaps the best example of both.

What is the situation with regard to Bolkestein's other group of sources, those which reveal preached morality? Are they really exclusively examples of preached morality or do they also contain an important element of practical, lived morality? In this context, Bolkestein mentions five great philosophers: Pythagoras, Democritus, Socrates, Plato and Aristotle. This is not all, however. In addition to the works of these great forerunners, he also includes the writings of various moralists (most of the laws of various non-Athenian lawgivers come under this heading), the Cynics, Epicurus and the Epicureans, and the Stoics.

It cannot, of course, be denied that philosophers preach morality, but their precepts have, in my opinion, a clear connection with reality. Although this connection is sometimes negative, because the precept is not lived, it is usually positive.

My chief objection to Bolkestein's classification, however, is concerned with the third group, because a proverb is as much preached morality as a moral sermon. Any moral admonition is full of proverbs and proverbial sayings. But in either case it may be rooted in life or it may not. Sometimes the proverb is lived and sometimes the admonition is preached, but it may be the other way round, or also both may be the same. In other words, there is a difference, but neither form of precept is exclusively preached or lived.

The variety of the different kinds of morality can perhaps be

---

[6] Poets include Phocylides and Theognis, and among prose orators the name of Isocrates at once comes to mind.

illustrated by an example. What I have in mind is a fairly frequently quoted *skolion* or drinking song.[7]

The third line of this poem is clearly a precept with a moral content. The poet wants prosperity, but insists that it must be honestly acquired. Is this lived or preached morality? It is both, though there are rogues both in practice and in theory.

This *skolion* is also interesting because it places health in the foreground: *nostrorum sanitas*! External appearance and youth with its attractive form are also stressed—it is well known that an ugly, misshapen body was despised in ancient Greece. In the fourth line there is a direct reference to being young with one's friends and therefore to drinking parties and also perhaps to old age. There is an implicit aversion to the latter and possibly an indirect reference to the poet's contemporaries and the frequent deaths among them. When old men gather with their friends, they talk about their illnesses. It is only the young who can enjoy the gaiety of drinking parties.[8]

To be healthy was certainly to be exceptionally blessed. This conviction is expressed in a short poem contained in the Nicomach. Ethics of Aristotle which is said to have been inscribed on the sanctuary of Leto on the island of Delos:

Κάλλιστον τὸ δικαιότατον, λῷστον δ' ὑγιαίνειν.
Πάντων δ' ἥδιστον, οὗ τις ἐρᾷ, τὸ τυχεῖν.

'The most beautiful is what is most righteous, the most pleasant
    is to be healthy.
The sweetest of all is to gain what one desires'.

The man who had this inscribed at the entrance of the temple, τὴν ἑαυτοῦ γνώμην ἀποφηνάμενος, was in fact summarizing in these few words his wisdom (that is, his preaching) and his experience of

---

[7] No 8 Bgk = Athenaeus XV, 694 E:
'Υγιαίνειν μὲν ἄριστον ἀνδρί,
δεύτερον δὲ φυὰν καλὸν γενέσθαι,
τὸ τρίτον δὲ πλουτεῖν ἀδόλως,
καὶ τὸ τέταρτον ἡβᾶν μετὰ τῶν φίλων.

'To be healthy is best for a man;
second best is to possess an attractive exterior;
third, to be honestly rich;
and fourth, to be young with one's friends'.

[8] W. J. Verdenius made a similar comment in discussing Schwartz' *Ethik*; see *Erasmus* 6 (1953), pp. 804-807.

life. No clear distinction can be made here between preached and lived morality.

These lines from the Eudemian Ethics have often been wrongly interpreted. The first phrase, 'the most beautiful is the most righteous', has frequently been thought to mean that the most righteous is what arouses moral striving (this was the interpretation of 'the most beautiful'). It is, however, precisely the other way round. The subject has been interpreted as the predicate and the predicate as the subject. The poet was in fact saying the opposite—that justice in the full sense of the word was for him the most beautiful thing in the world. The idea of moral striving is not as such contained in the first word of the first line of this poem ('the most beautiful'). What is expressed is the satisfaction that the righteous man is able to feel when he contemplates justice. According to Greek thought, the righteous man is entitled to rejoice in his own justice. There is no implication of sinful pride in this.

It is obvious that this ethos is extremely personal and individual, but this does not mean that collective responsibility is completely absent. This is most clearly expressed in the third precept of the *skolion*: 'to be honestly rich'.

As we have seen, the attitude of the individual towards what is and what is not permissible was determined by public opinion on the one hand and by conscience on the other. On the basis of these two concepts, public opinion and conscience, E. R. Dodds made a clear distinction among the Greeks between a shame-culture and a guilt-culture.[9] He is not responsible for the fact that this distinction has enjoyed an enormous popularity for twenty-five years and has therefore perhaps been taken too seriously. Let us go back, then, to the origin of this distinction in Dodds' book, since it is only in this way that we shall be able to do full justice to the scholar himself.

What did he mean by 'shame-culture'? This existed in a community in which there were no feelings of guilt about evil actions and no consciousness of shortcomings but in which only the judgement of other individuals was regarded as important. The disapproval of the members of the group or community was known as *nemesis*. This disapproval was the most important guiding principle in human life. Wrong action was the result of blindness. Agamem-

---

[9] E. R. Dodds, *The Greeks and the Irrational*, Berkeley (1951).

non, for example, was blind when he took the slave-girl Briseis, who formed part of Achilles' booty, from the latter. Because of this blindness, Agamemnon later experienced shame, αἰδώς, and the story of his quarrel with Achilles is at the root of the difference between the two forms of culture.

A criminal was not burdened with guilt or accursed and even a murderer was able to begin a new life in a different environment without being regarded as defiled or criminal by the one who offered him hospitality. The conclusion that Dodds and others have drawn from this example is that, at least in the early Greek period of the epic, the feeling of personal or collective guilt did not exist or hardly existed. It was only gradually that the idea of collective guilt emerged, leading to the blood-feud, in which all the members of a tribe were branded as guilty if one of them had shed blood. Later, personal guilt made its appearance in society and only the one who had committed the crime was regarded as guilty, not his family.

In collective guilt, there is a residual element of *nemesis*, the collective disapproval of the community. This collective guilt is also clearly present in the blood-feud, in which the whole clan or family is held responsible. The transition from shame to guilt has often been explained by a decline in the close ties of the family, with the result that only the individual was regarded as guilty. To be fair to Dodds, he is not rigid or absolute in his insistence on the division between shame and guilt; he is indeed very cautious in his treatment of the two phases, and we must be grateful to him for that. Nonetheless, I believe that certain fundamental objections can be made to his argument.

In the first place, the idea of guilt is not in any sense absent from the Homeric epic. Dodds states: 'I find no indication in the narrative of the Iliad that Zeus is concerned with justice as such' (*op. cit.*, note 32). He limits this statement by saying that he himself has not encountered the concept of justice in the story *at least in connection with Zeus*. It is, however, undeniable that justice has a certain part to play in the Homeric simile (as we shall see below, Iliad 16. 384 ff.).

Later authors have tended to place too much emphasis on the fact that the Greek word that is usually translated as 'good' (ἀγαθός) has no moral significance in Homer. On the other hand, those scholars who, because of this, do not accept morality in Homer's writing in the sense that we regard it also forget that a word meaning 'just' or 'righteous' (δίκαιος) occurs quite frequently in Homer and gives emphasis to the distinctively epic orientation of the work.[10]

An example that comes to mind at once is the question of the misdeeds of Odysseus' companions, for which they were put to death. They had slaughtered the cattle of Helios and eaten the meat. Other examples are the punishments in the underworld (Od. 11), the death of Penelope's suitors, who were bold enough to want to compel her to marry again, and the case of Aegisthus at the beginning of the Odyssey. Even the case of the murderer who went elsewhere and began a new life cannot be used to support Dodds' hypothesis, because this passage is basically a description of the impression made by Priam on Achilles (Il. 24. 480). The *tertium comparationis* here is the amazement caused by the old king and also by the murderer. And the word 'amazement' (θάμβος), of course, has a religious significance.[11]

When this murderer entered the company of the men whose protection he was seeking, he caused consternation among them and could only interpret this effect as the fear and terror that is aroused by any man who has laid violent hands on another,[12] and he was dumbfounded to realise how his own fate affected the whole community which he was entering. The amazement involved in the experience of the old man himself is as effective as the terror of the men whose protection was being sought by the murderer. I am bound to stress the word 'terror' here, because it indicates that the murderer's arrival caused a profound as well as a natural reaction within the community in which he was living.

Finally, guilt is certainly involved in another case, in which Zeus is shown to be angry with the men who drove out the goddess of justice, Dike. He punished them by sending his thunder, which was, of course, regarded as a sign of his wrath. Guilt clearly plays a part here (Iliad 16. 384-388) and we cannot speak in this context of a 'reflex of later conditions' (Dodds, p. 32), simply because the situation presents us with a difficulty. There is a close association between this passage and the ideas expressed by later poets such as Hesiod.

---

[10] This has been stressed again and again by Hugh Lloyd-Jones in his book *The Justice of Zeus*, Los Angeles (1971) and more recently in an excellent study of 'Homer and Mr Gladstone', in *The Times Literary Supplement* (3 January 1975), pp. 15-17.

[11] See A. J. Festugière, *Vig. Chr.* III (1949), p. 204; E. Peterson, Εἰς θεός (1926), p. 193.

[12] I have myself also pointed out in the past (*Hermeneus* 16, 1944-1945, p. 84) that the meaning of θάμβος might to some extent be weakened here.

If it were in fact possible to establish a distinction between Homer and later writers with regard to morality, then this would surely be attributable not to a difference between the cultural stages in the society in which they were living and writing, but rather to the social differences between various sections of Greek society. The Greek nobility, for example, valued its own honour very highly indeed and had its own code to which everything was subjected. Many scholars have reacted so strongly to this as to conclude that there was no morality as such and indeed no religion.[13] But would it not be better to regard this in the same light as the so-called guilt-culture? Dodds himself correctly (p. 49) insisted on the totally religious aspect of envy, in other words, of being jealous of one's honour, of the ancestral curse which bears down on later generations and of the absence of a moral imperative in the demand for absolute subjection to the sovereign will of the gods. This last case can be compared with two biblical examples. The first is Paul's view concerning divine election. The second is the 'hardening of heart' of the pharaoh who refused to allow the Israelites to leave Egypt for their promised land. This comparison can only be made if it is a question of divine action not linked to any morality.

In this context too, we may point to Sophocles, whom Dodds has called 'the last great exponent of the archaic world-view'.[14] In his writing, the action of the deity is not linked to any morality. Again, a New Testament comparison is made—Dodds correctly points to the Lord's Prayer and especially to the words 'lead us not into temptation', which show that temptation was regarded as coming from God. In this supra-ethical view, we are clearly concerned with a very primitive religious strand in human thought.

The concept of honour in the so-called shame-culture was also a primitive religious category of the same kind. Honour was indeed more closely connected with a very specific morality than many scholars have suspected. It was not reflected in the behaviour of the man who was self-inflated and wanted to be more than he in fact was. On the contrary, it was intimately connected with the divine element. Both gods and men had their *timē*. In Christian

---

[13] These scholars have been briefly discussed by Dodds on p. 2 of his book.

[14] *Op. cit.*, p. 49 and note 112, in which Dodds quotes from K. Latte's well-known article *A.f.R.* 20, p. 275. See also Rudolph Otto, who particularly emphasizes the supra-ethical element in religion in his book *Das Heilige*, as does W. B. Kristensen in *Symbool en werkelijkheid* (1954), pp. 36-48, especially p. 45 ff.

teaching too, God has his honour—this is illustrated by Paul's
demand that tasks have to be carried out 'for the honour of God'. A
common Judaeo-Christian idea was that 'God may come to his
honour', and whether we can accept this now or not is really irrelevant. The *timē* of the gods (Il. 4. 158) is paralleled by the honour
of God in the Bible, even though they may have been different
for the reader of the Bible and the Greek who read or heard
Homer.[15]

---

[15] This was quite clear to people at a later period. Solon (fr 1D) linked
shame and guilt. He was therefore more 'Homeric' than many scholars have
in the past been prepared to admit. See above, p. oo.

CHAPTER TWO

MORALITY AND RELIGION

In the previous chapter I observed more than once that in Greek thought certain moral ideas were connected with religion, appearing in this context as guilt. Although some scholars have accepted this more or less unquestioningly, most specialists, the foremost among them, have not. Schwartz, for example, begins his argument with an explicit rejection of any link between ethics and religion. I do not intend to challenge his position here—I have already done this in 1973 in the *Harvard Studies in Classical Philology* and there is no need to return to the question. At the same time, it is important to question both the view that ethics were completely independent in ancient Greece and the related one that they had no connection with religion there because they applied both to men and to the gods. Ethics were certainly not an independent reality, because we know from the findings of anthropology that for primitive man life was a totality within itself.[1] As for the second opinion, it is true that the ethical laws that applied to man were sometimes, but by no means always, applied to the gods. It was one of the characteristics of the divine in Greek thought that it was able to break through the human. Hades is man's friend and his enemy. Zeus is gentle (*meili-*

---

[1] See de Buck's inaugural address on the religious significance of sleep and the whole of Kristensen's work, in which he emphasized that men's lives in relationship to each other were not lived independently of their lives in relationship to the gods. De Buck expressed this interconnection in the case of ancient Egypt in the following way: 'We have quite effortlessly moved from an everyday, secular object such as the support for the head or pillow (the Egyptian *weres*) to religious ideas about creation and resurrection. The decoration of this product of applied art seemed to be very meaningful and was connected with fundamental ideas about the origin of all things. Sleep and death gave access to infinity and in awakening and resurrection were revealed the same creative power that had been active at the genesis of the cosmos. The support for the head was an amulet, but at the same time it also fitted harmoniously into a whole of theological speculations embracing the world and the life of men. This is what I mean by the unity of Egyptian civilization', A. de Buck, *De godsdienstige opvatting van den slaap inzonderheid in het Oude Egypte*, Inaugural address Leiden, Leiden (1939), p. 21. These ideas of de Buck were obviously inspired by his teacher, W. B. Kristensen, and especially by the latter's work, *Het leven uit den dood* (1925).

khios), but he is also evilly demonic (*maimaktes*). The Eumenides
are the avenging demons for whom ethical considerations are alien.
Demonically incalculable is the character of the god, whose law is
not the law of man, the god of universal life and wisdom. His way
of acting is supra-ethical and arbitrary. Since, then, the gods are
not subject to human laws, but above them, ethics cannot be separated from religion simply because of the (mistaken) view that
ethics in ancient Greece applied also to the gods.

H. J. Berman has recently and very persuasively demonstrated
that the law and morals have a religious dimension.[2] 'The traditional aspect of law', Berman argues, 'cannot be explained in purely
secular and rational terms'. I would agree with him in this, but I
cannot accept the reason he gives for it, namely that the law
'embodies man's concept of time, which itself is bound up with the
trans-rational and with religion'.[3]

It is clear, of course, that Berman owes a great deal to Mircea
Eliade here, and especially to the latter's book on the myth of the
eternal return. In this work, Eliade distinguishes between two categories of time. On the one hand, there is the archaic concept of time
which was based on a religion of periodic redemption taking place
in cyclical form and beyond history. On the other hand there is,
it is claimed, a Judaeo-Christian concept of time which is progres-
sive (in other words, historical), includes continuity, does not contain a return and is based on a religion which affirms an ultimate
redemption at the end of time.

It is not difficult to understand why Eliade links this concept of
time with human justice. He points to the fact that justice based
on the concept of law has a heavenly and transcendent model in
the cosmic norm. (This was called *themis* by the Greeks). In archaic
societies (these are sometimes called 'traditional'), human law is
seen as a repetition of divine or cosmic justice which first appeared
in the obscurity of sagas or in a mythical past. It was, in other
words, situated outside the temporal sphere, that is, outside time as
we know it, beginning with the period that can be verified. On the
other hand, in the monotheistic revelation of Judaism, Moses received the law at a definite time and at a definite place, and this

---

[2] H. J. Berman, *The Interaction of Law and Religion*, Cambridge, Mass.
(1974).
[3] *Op. cit.*, p. 34. Berman quotes from the English translation of M. Eliade,
Cosmos and History: The Myth of the Eternal Return, New York (1959).

law was supplemented from time to time by expositions which were added to it.

What can we say about this connection between cosmic world-views and time? The most important comment that can be made is that it bypasses our problem as such. Let us formulate that problem once more. It is that, in contemporary thought, religion and morality are wrongly separated. Eliade was right to insist that they cannot be kept separate, but his argument is obscured by his linking it with the two concepts of time outlined above. These have, in my opinion, nothing to do with the problem of law. I do not deny that there were two concepts of time in the ancient world, linear time in which a later point never returns to an earlier point, (in other words, time seen in a straight line), and cyclical or circular time, in which everything returns again and again. I am convinced, however, that concepts of the law that are linked to a revelation of God or gods are not connected with either of these concepts of time. Both societies—those which believed in a cyclical form of time and those familiar with a linear concept of time—may have derived their idea of law from a divine revelation.

When this confusion of time and law in human society has been disentangled, something of great value still remains and it is with this that Berman is concerned in his book. He says: 'In all societies, even the most sophisticated, there are shared beliefs in transcendent values, shared commitments to an ultimate purpose, a shared sense of the holy; in all societies, even the most rudimentary, there are structures and processes of social ordering, established methods of allocating rights and duties, a shared sense of the just. These two dimensions of social life are in tension: the prophetic and mystical sides of religion challenge, and are challenged by, the structural and rational sides of law. Yet each is also a dimension of the other. Every legal system shares with religion certain elements—ritual, tradition, authority and universality—which are needed to symbolize and educate men's legal emotions. Otherwise law degenerates into legalism. Similarly, every religion has within it legal elements, without which it degenrates into private religiosity'.[4]

It is therefore worth while repeating that my point of departure is morality linked to religion. This point of departure is in no sense doctrinaire. It is, on the contrary, based on the data provided by

---

[4] H. J. Berman, *op. cit.*, p. 49. His references to Eliade will be found in *Cosmos and History*, p. 150. note 13; cf. p. 34.

the ancient writers themselves. I am convinced that the contemporary attitude towards religion of philologists and historians specializing in ancient Greece, namely that it must be separated from morality, has led us seriously astray. Having obtained a certain personal 'freedom' by dissociating their own behaviour and that of their contemporaries from religion, they were conscious of a need to project their own experience back into Greek society. One of the intentions of this book is to demonstrate how this attitude has resulted in failure.

In the previous passage, we saw how the gods were above human laws and how this was a reason for not separating religion from morality, since morality applied also to the gods. How, then, did Schwartz and Dodds succeed in making their division between religion and morality? Schwartz's reasoning is quite clear. The gods are the object and man is the subject of religion. Anything in which the gods are both subject and object cannot be religion. According to Dodds, the fact that the gods experienced *phthonos*, which was originally not a moral concept, that they were, in other words, jealous of human happiness, made it possible to claim 'that religion and morals were not initially interdependent, in Greece or elsewhere; they had separate roots. I suppose that, broadly speaking, religion grows out of man's relationship to his total environment, morals out of his relation to his fellow-men'.[5]

The reconstruction which Dodds prefers is as follows. There is no *phthonos* or envy, and generally speaking no morality, in a shame-culture.[6] In a guilt-culture, on the other hand, there was originally no morality, but awareness of human deficiency and submissiveness. This was followed, so it is alleged, by a period in which men suffered and became conscious of social justice. This gave rise to the need for evil-doers to be punished and good men to be rewarded.

This is a very doubtful reconstruction. We have already found the antithesis between shame and guilt cultures questionable in itself, since in both cases ethics are separated from religion. If this is so, the separation is not important for our problem. One central

---

[5] *Op. cit.*, p. 31. Schwartz refers, in *Über das Verhältnis der Hellenen zur Geschichte, Gesammelte Schriften* I (1938), p. 57, to 'religious faith' as opposed to 'thinking ethics'. These adjectives point to an unscientific prejudice on the author's part.

[6] This is, as we have seen, very dubious, since there is a code of morals that applies both to the gods and to men, although it is a very primitive code, rather similar to that of an open-minded child.

objection does, however, remain; that is that Dodds was greatly influenced by the nature of his sources. He insisted that ethics and law originated in social suffering and its accompanying sense of injustice. These latter, however, are not easy to find in the Iliad and indeed, according to many scholars, they are completely absent. The argument used here is, in my opinion, a dangerous *argumentum a silentio*. Is it really possible to conclude, on the basis of the fact that suffering and injustice are not stressed, that they did not exist in Homeric society or that they were not important? I think that the real reason is to be found elsewhere—in other words, that these particular aspects of life were not prominent in the environment in which the epic was set. But they were not entirely absent. Achilles' complaint about the farm-worker is clear enough, even if it is to be found in the Odyssey. Iros the beggar is also a figure from the other world that is not often considered in the epic.

The main objection to this separation between morals and religion, however, is based on a faulty assessment of human relationships. There can be no doubt that social injustice as such existed and was condemned during the epic period. One of the most important pieces of evidence pointing to its existence is the treatment given to children as soon as their parents ceased to belong to the privileged class.

The most important datum of all, however, indicating a close relationship between morality and religion is to be found in the utterance of the deity. The law regulating human relationships was from a very early period indeed regarded as divine. The early word for 'law' was ῥήτρα, meaning 'word' or 'oracle' (cf. Hebrew *dabhar*).[7] The law was what was pointed out. There was, in this respect, no essential difference between the Greeks and the Jews in their attitude towards the law. Nothing could be added to or taken away from the law. The Oresteia can be regarded as a drama in which man is not permitted to take anything away from the law. There is also evidence here that it is the shame-culture that introduced the blood-feud and that this form of revenge also existed in such a culture. An example of this is the revenge of Patroclus' death. The gods speak, giving the laws, but thereafter these laws are human, although their divine origin functions as a guarantee that they will not be violated and a new oracle is required if a law is to be changed.

---

[7] In German 'das Geweisde' or 'die Weisung'.

It is probable that the people of the archaic state of Sparta continued to consult the oracle for the longest period of time whenever a slight change had to be made in the law. It is not possible to speak here exclusively of a sanction given by the god whose oracle was consulted. On the contrary, the oracle itself was the law. This is what Plutarch says in Chapter VI of his life of Lycurgus.

CHAPTER THREE

THE EARLIEST GODS AND MORALITY

The earliest of the Greek gods were undoubtedly nameless. When he visited the sanctuary of Zeus at Dodona, Herodotus heard that the Pelasgians prayed there to gods without names (2. 52). According to the story of Epimenides' purification of the city of Athens, there were 'nameless' altars there.[1]

Kern made a detailed study of these data.[2] There is, however, one fact that is worth noting in the epic period. Zeus is invoked in Iliad 16. 232 as the Pelasgian god of Dodona and this clearly reveals him as a very early god. It is obvious that very early traditions were preserved at Dodona. Herodotus stressed that all the detailed descriptions of divine power and of individual divine figures were of a later date and must therefore have been imported.

However that may be, these nameless gods are certainly the earliest divine figures that we can approach. If it can be shown that they were in any way associated with ethics, then any theory concerning the division between morality and religion will at once be thrown open to doubt. It might then be possible to maintain on philosophical grounds that such a division had existed, but it would no longer be possible to do so on historical grounds. In Eleusis, τὼ θεώ—an identification of Demeter and Kore or Asclepius and Hygieia—are originally nameless. This can be compared with τὼ σιώ in Laconia, identified, although at a later period, with the Dioscuri. A feeling of awe was, of course, often experienced when the gods were called by name and this accounts for the frequent occurrence of the prohibition against calling them by their names. The word δαίμων was used for the nameless demons, often when they appeared in a strange form, such as that of a horse. This has often been regarded as pre-Greek.

To this very primitive group belong those gods who were called by what German scholars have termed *Lallnamen*, words taken from the language of children. Examples of these names are Μᾶ Δᾶ and perhaps also πόποι, which became known later in the expression

---

[1] Diog. Laert. 1. 110.

[2] O. Kern, *Die Religion der Griechen* I (1926), p. 125 ff.

ὦ πόποι. Mother figures such as the Great Mother were worshipped with such *Lallnamen*.

As Kern has pointed out, 'The moral evaluation of the gods did not occur at such a late period as is generally believed. Some of the deities invoked without names point clearly in the direction of morality and the most holy feelings existing between men on earth'.[3] This is, as Kern has shown, especially so in the case of the nameless mother goddess, the earth as a mother figure: 'Whoever worshipped the earth as mother gazed up at her, like a child looking up at its own mother who gives strength and embodies everything that is good. The group of mother and daughter . . . teaches both maternal love and the love felt by the child'.[4]

From the fact that a number of teachers appeared who practised purification and preached repentance, such as Epimenides of Crete, it is clear that a moral teaching in religion emerged at a very early stage. An outstanding example of the enormous importance of the law in this very early period is the treacherous attempt made by Cylon, a young man of noble descent, to seize power in Athens.

Details of Cylon's life and his attempted revolution can be found in at least four important authors. Herodotus mentioned it (5. 71), as did Thucydides (1. 126). Aristotle spoke about the event in his Constitution of Athens (c. 14) and Plutarch devoted a whole chapter to it in his life of Solon (c. 12). Herodotus does not provide many details, but this is not surprising, since the event took place in the distant past. There is no certainty about the date of Cylon's *coup d'état*. According to one tradition, it occurred very soon after a victory won by him in the Olympic Games. According to another tradition, these were the thirty-fifth Games. (It was not until a fairly late stage that the Games were numbered). Cylon may therefore have tried to seize power in 640 B.C., although no one knows for certain.

It is worth recording this story for reasons that will emerge later. The attack took place and was frustrated by other noblemen of Athens, especially members of the family of the Alcmaeonidae and their retainers. We are not told what Cylon's fate was, but his followers had fled and sought refuge in the temple of Athena, placing themselves under the protection of the goddess. They were, however, dragged from the sanctuary and massacred by the Alcmaeo-

---

[3] Kern, *op. cit.*, p. 133.
[4] Kern, *op. cit.*, p. 134.

nidae, who in this way committed an act of impious violence that had
to be expiated.

For a long time after this event the Alcmaeonidae were regarded
as tainted in the party strife of political passions among the Athenians. Pericles, the great leader of the fifth century, who was descended
on his mother's side from the Alcmaeonidae, was also accused by his
opponents of being tainted and accursed. Since he was such an important figure in Greek history, later writers wrote a great deal
about the curse of the Alcmaeonidae.

From our point of view, however, what is of importance in this
story is that men who believed that they were safe in the holy place
were killed and that the killers had to expiate this and be purified.
The rite of purification was performed by Epimenides, a miracle-
worker and medicineman from Crete who had experience in carrying
out such ritual acts as the purification of whole communities.

Epimenides purified the city of Athens, using an action reminis-
cent of the purification by the scapegoat in Israel. He thus made
the inhabitants of the city capable of avoiding the effects of divine
wrath. The importance of this event is always stressed by those who
believe that life together in a community had a religious significance
for the Greeks. It was an unwritten law that the guilt due to the
shedding blood had to be purified again and again. The Alcmaeonidae were, in this case, guilty of the death of Cylon's followers and
they never disputed the legal validity of the rite of purification in
later generations. The most that they did was to question the guilt of
their ancestors and whether they ought to be held responsible for it.

What is of great interest to us, however, is that a common practice such as the purification of the community in fifth-century
Athens was deeply rooted in the past—a past that had by that time
become very vague and almost unknown. We should moreover not
lose sight of the fact that the case in question was one of personal
power as opposed to the power of the community as a whole, and
that what was applied here was a rule that was maintained by the
community, a rule which was opposed, though never in its theoretical basis and only for some practical end, by individuals or
politicians. It must be stressed that the Alcmaeonidae never questioned the legal validity of the decision of the purification, as I
pointed out above. (The fact that many important men, such as
Solon, were linked with this case does not concern us here).[5]

---

[5] Plut. Solon, c. 12 and context.

Several attempts have been made by scholars to invalidate the data concerning Cylon's followers, especially in view of the fact that a fairly late date was given to the tradition concerning the tainted family. I shall not discuss these attempts in details here, but confine myself to data given in our earliest source, Herodotus' History.

Firstly, Cylon was a champion in the Olympic Games. Secondly, he was eager for tyrannical power. Thirdly, he had a band of followers of his own age with whom he collaborated. Fourthly, it is not clear whether he made a direct attack against the Acropolis. Fifthly, his followers established themselves as suppliants on the Acropolis. Sixthly, his followers were misled by negotiations. (This may have been intended as an attempted reconciliation). Seventhly, the case was placed, for adjudication, in the hands of an ancient college, of which no more is heard, the 'leaders of the ship owners'. Eighthly, the guilt for the execution of the suppliants was imputed to the leader of the political opponents. Ninthly and finally, Herodotus dated the whole affair to a time before that of the tyrant Pisistratus, a fact that shows clearly how uncertain the historian was in his attempt to clarify the chronology of the episode.[6] There are, however, many events in ancient Greece which cannot be defined chronologically, and to throw doubt on the event itself simply because it cannot easily be dated would be very rash. What is more, it would be wrong to think that Herodotus invented the court, simply because no more is heard of it. The word translated as 'leaders' or 'presidents' indicates that it was an ancient institution.[7]

Thucydides was not a writer who attached any importance to gossip and yet it is clear that he took the story of the taint or curse of Pericles' family very seriously. He also took Cylon's attack itself seriously, describing how the young man was of a noble family and that it was his ambition to achieve power with the support of his father-in-law, the tyrant of Megara. It is indisputable that this was a historical event. In our context, however, that is not the most important element. For us, it was an event that revealed the law in its earliest form as fulfilling an unusual and very important function, that of a decree of divine origin.

---

[6] The known stemma of the Alcmaeonidae would be a reasonable guide, *plus* the connexion with Theagenes.

[7] πρυτάνιες τῶν ναυκράρων; for various (questionable) theories about this, see F. R. Wüst, *Historia* 6 (1957), pp. 176-197.

We may conclude this discussion by pointing to what an expert in this field, M. P. Nilsson, has said in this context. He has argued that morality formed part of the unwritten laws protected by Zeus in the earliest Greek society, that is, before Homer, but also in Homer's poems, and that it was not until later that morality and the law became separated.[8]

---

[8] G.G.R., I², p. 418. I am not appealing to Nilsson in this point because he is on my side and opposed to those who insist on a division between religion and morality in ancient Greece (actually he is not). My only reason is because I think it important to show that Nilsson too believes that unwritten laws can hardly be based exclusively on human endeavour, and that legal order of the kind maintained by unwritten laws cannot continue to exist without the gods.

CHAPTER FOUR

THE EMOTIONAL LIFE OF THE GREEKS

Its Influence on their Moral and Religious Disposition

What is permissible and what is not permissible is always closely connected with the emotions of the people to whom these rules apply. The striking example of κάθαρσις τῶν παθημάτων can be used to introduce this question. In a well known passage on tragic catharsis, Aristotle says that the effect of tragedy can be seen as δι' ἐλέου καὶ φόβου περαίνουσα τὴν τῶν τοιούτων παθημάτων κάθαρσιν.[1] The person watching the play, in other words, experiences pity and terror and sympathetically shares in what is happening on the stage. Catharsis arises from this experience. What, then, is this catharsis? There are two contrasting views—that it is a sublimation of the emotions and that it is a purgation. The first is commonly accepted today—we are, as it were, exalted by the tragedy, raised above ourselves and thus purified. I would call this the romantic view of catharsis. This view is, from the philological standpoint, not tenable, because a very special meaning is given to a word which in almost every other context was used in connection with sick parts of the body. The stomach or the bowels were purified or were the objects of purification. When we are freed from the suffering of our emotions, the latter are separated from our bodies and tragedy brings about a purification through pity and terror. (This purification of the emotions is, of course, a purification of the soul). By shuddering and crying, the person watching the play experiences a feeling of relief. Catharsis, then, is a homeopathic cure that brings about a sense of relief from oppressive emotions and is also associated with pleasure.[2] The most striking effect of tragedy is cathar-

---

[1] Aristotle, Poet. 1449ᵇ 28. Since J. Bernays' famous *Grundzüge der verlorenen Abhandlung des Aristoteles über Wirkung der Tragödie* (1857) κάθαρσις as a medical term has become the basis of modern interpretations (Nietzsche and Freud), see A. D. Momigliano, *Quinto Contributo* (1975), p. 143-145.

[2] This is how Verdenius expressed it in a passage in a paper read to the Societas Philologica. See also his article Κάθαρσις τῶν παθημάτων in *Autour d'Aristote, Recueil d'Etudes offert à Monseigneur A. Mansion* (1955) p. 367. C. W. van Boekel, *Katharsis*, provides a good summary of the various interpretations of Aristotle in this case and a philological reconstruction of Aristotle's views of the emotional life in his dissertation (Nijmegen), published in Utrecht, 1957.

sis. Weeping and shuddering are aspects of the southern, Mediterranean temperament. The accolade and the loud, boisterous quality of conversations are examples of this, together with the directness of expression that characterizes the Greeks. Other classical examples are Phrynichus' play about the taking of Miletus by the Persians and the poet's prosecution for it, or Sappho's lyric poetry and Solon's reaction to it. This fierceness also had its effect on relationships with one's fellow-men, but, to my knowledge, there has in recent years been no comprehensive study of the Greek temperament.

In addition to this direct reaction displayed in a primary emotion, the Greeks were also capable of a reserve or even a distrust, which often had the effect of banishing spontaneity. This too was an aspect of human life based on experience, influenced at times, especially in intellectual circles, by sophistry. Popular emotion, however, always remained important and liable to overwhelm personal and thinking self-control. An example of this is the trial of the Hermocopidae. Other examples can also be found of that later reflection which could hardly hold popular emotions in check, and others could be found of the occasions when spontaneity and directness prevailed.[3]

In our culture, it is children who are the most spontaneous in their expression and the most direct in their morality and emotions. The emotional and moral reactions of many Greeks can be compared, in a sense, to those of children, who are also direct, cruel, hard, and 'logical'.

Guilt and Punishment

In the moral and religious temperament of the Greeks, there was a certain attitude towards the sinner and his punishment or purification which it is difficult for modern man to accept. This is because of a rooted objection to all religious forms in which the sovereign deity coerces and, it is believed, humiliates the creature. The Bible contains examples which arouse human sympathy, a well-known one being that of the first king of Israel, Saul. In the Greek tradition too, there were figures who were cherished by their fellow-men and passionately acquitted of guilt or, if acquittal was not

---

[3] E. C. Stevens, 'Some Attic Commonplaces of Pity', *AJPh* 65 (1944), p. 1 ff; this study was cited by Heichelheim in *Erasmus* (1949) against Bolkestein, *Armenpflege*, p. 68, note 1.

possible, made acceptable morally by extenuating circumstances. An example of such a figure is Prometheus, who served mankind and revolted against the absolute power of the supreme god, but had to expiate this sin. (His expiation is generally felt by modern man to be unfair).

In very early Greek literature, there are also the examples of Tantalus, Sisyphus and the Danaids. All of these were condemned to be punished in ways that strike us now as inhuman. Tantalus was eternally tortured by hunger and thirst, although with food and drink in view but out of reach. Sisyphus's eternal punishment was to roll a stone uphill and the Danaids had eternally to fill a leaky jar with water.

Here, we shall confine ourselves to these three examples of guilt and punishment. There have been countless interpretations in which the hope has been expressed and, in some cases, the prospect has been accepted that those who were condemned to such pitiless and unending punishments in fact reached the end after a period of purification and were able to begin a new life, either in this world or in the next. The terms 'catharsis' or 'purifying effect' have been used in connection with this suffering, which, it has been suggested, would eventually end.

This is, in my opinion, a pious wish and tells us more about the moral and religious attitude and the sense of justice of the modern scholars who have suggested this interpretation than the Greeks who created these myths. The latter were in fact expressing a spontaneous and direct attitude towards human guilt, which was regarded as absolute and incapable of being erased. In the view of twentieth-century man, then, the Greek sense of justice is unacceptable, because it is not in accordance with his own moral and religious temperament. If the modern scholar were really objective, however, he would suppress his own feelings and let the texts speak for themselves.

A recent attempt has been made to review the cycle of stories about the Danaids.[4] Danaus' daughters had murdered their husbands and were therefore doomed to fill a jar without a bottom. The task of filling this *pithos* was to last for ever. The author of this recent study has interpreted the various attributes associated with the many illustrations of the task imposed on these unfortunate

---

[4] E. Keuls, *The Watercarriers in Hades: A Study of Catharsis through Toil in Classical Antiquity*, Amsterdam (1974).

women that were made throughout the whole of classical antiquity, mainly on vases. This led her to assume first that this was a catharsis or purification and secondly that it was not an unending punishment, but a return of and a liberation from the doom to which these women were subject, following their purification.

What is particularly striking in this context is that the concept of catharsis does not occur in any of the data concerning the Danaids. When relief follows catharsis, this can be seen as the removal of an obstacle or as a purgation from objections and what is hostile. To apply this original significance of catharsis to the myth or story of the Danaids would be absurd. There is no reason to suppose that these women experienced any relief or liberation. There can therefore be no question of catharsis in the sense of Aristotle's famous passage.

Is it, however, possible to say at all that the idea of purification is found in the classical data concerning the Danaids? Here too, a negative answer is inescapable. The attributes on the vases illustrating the story of the Danaids cannot be cited here, although, in a different context, they were certainly used for the purpose of purification. The pithos or jar was used either for washing or for purification. The cleansing of man's soul from guilt was also given the name of *katharmoi*, purifications. Those who were purified in this way, however, were received into a circle of initiated persons, so that Plato, for example, mentioned the *katharmoi* in the context of the hereafter, a place where men underwent punishments that erased guilt. In the case of those who were doomed and had to suffer eternal punishment, there was no ultimate erasure of guilt. Purification was not granted to such people. The only possible reason for this is that it satisfied the reaction of spontaneous and irreconcilable anger to which these myths bear witness. If man violates the law of the gods, he must be punished. This precept formed a part of all teaching for centuries in Greece. This is why I have stressed the importance of a childlike, spontaneous reaction in determining the whole moral and religious attitude of the Greek, as well as his emotional temperament.

The possibility always exists, for certain groups of men only, to have their guilt erased. There have, however, always been cases in which the expiation of guilt was impossible and the Greeks clearly thought that Tantalus, Sisyphus, and the Danaids were such cases. Who, then, determined whether it was possible or not possible for

50975

guilt to be erased? The only one who could decide this was the sovereign and immortal deity. The adjectives used here are sufficient to point to the importance of the deity, since man is neither sovereign nor immortal. His activity is always an activity that is conditioned by time. There is no trace in ancient Greece of catharsis achieved through labour, toil, or sacrifice. Such a view of toil would be a contradiction of everything that we know about ancient life and thought.

Toil as a Punishment

Both in Jewish and in Greek thought, toil or *ponos* was a sign of human shortcoming. In the curse and banishment from paradise in Genesis, the human race was condemned to toil. In the Greek world, *ponos* is the peasants' doom, to farm the land in order to produce the bread that they need to keep alive. It is clear that this is in no way related to the later ethos of the toil that is socially necessary and therefore valuable. It is a further example of the Greek's moral and religious temperament, according to which toil was not a duty performed by the blessed, but a task carried out by mortals during their existence on this earth.

This attitude to work should also not be judged from the twentieth-century point of view of the scholars study. All over the world, agrarian communities have tended to regard toil as something that had to be done because it was the will of the deity or deities. The fruit no longer grew on the tree as it had in the distant past, nor did the corn come of its own accord in the ear, as it had before. All the Utopian ideas that have preoccupied, delighted, and sometimes disturbed later mankind have been inspired by the weight of everyday experience and practical living. This too is basically a childlike and spontaneous idea. Utopia is the counterpart of toil without an end in sight. There is no end either to toil or to Utopia, which is, in every society, an ideal situation that will last for ever.

These ideas should not, however, be regarded as a historical heritage concerning a historical situation, but rather as projections of human thought made during a period of man's existence that I prefer to call spontaneous and childlike. There may, of course, be objections to these terms, but I have deliberately chosen them because they express in the best possible way the fact that these ideas have no history, no development from poverty to a better life. There is no hope for the Danaids.

For those who prefer a 'milder' explanation of their myth, the jars of the Danaids, their *pithoi*, are hopeful signs for a better future. The pithoi were, generally speaking, the symbols of life when they appeared on tombs. They often contained sacrificial gifts of food and drink, thus symbolizing food, which, after death, was the guarantee of eternal life.[5] We must, however, reject the suggestion that every illustration showing women with jars is a reference to the myth of the Danaids. Generally speaking, the function of the jar was to contain food. So that the dead person could take food, a *pithos* was often placed in the ground with a hole in the bottom. This shows that there was another function associated with the *pithos* apart from punishment—it had to be filled to provide the dead person with nourishment. Those who explain the toil of the Danaids as 'purification through hard work' have not taken into account this other function of the pithos, which was indeed very widespread.

The *pithos* was used for so many purposes that it cannot be claimed exclusively as an illustration of the punishment of the Danaids and a fortiori as a symbol of the purifying effect of toil and its ability to free man from a curse. This is something that does not occur in the Greek attitude. It is a modern explanation which has arisen because of difficulties in accepting the harshness of the Greek moral and religious attitude, so that scholars have looked for something milder and more modern. The historian is bound, however, to have certain reservations about this approach.

As we have already said, this is an example of a very primitive conception of the relationship between the deity and man. The deity acts arbitrarily and often does things that cause us displeasure today. We inevitably react by thinking that it could never have been the gods' intention that man's toil should have been so cruelly monotonous and useless and last eternally.

The reality, however, is quite different. In ancient Greece, the gods were regarded as sovereign in their authority over man. This sovereignty was closely connected with that of kings. As Kristensen has pointed out: 'If we think that we have found the origin of kingship purely and simply in a strong man with his stick (sceptre) forcing his compatriots to obedience, it is not history which such "common sense" has taught us, but the less worthy side of our own

---

[5] See W. B. Kristensen, *The Meaning of Religion*, pp. 95, 98 ff.

nature. This is the point to which our theories of development invariably bring us'.[6] This view of the ruler and of kingship can also be applied to the myth of the unending toil of Sisyphus and the Danaids.

Another theme, in which the Greek moral and religious disposition is either not taken into account at all or else only considered very little is that of the action that is not understood. This occurs both in epic poetry and in tragedy. What happens to the hero often seems to be completely contradictory to our own rational moral and religious attitude, with the result that we find ourselves intellectually opposed to the poet's or dramatist's presentation of the events. Certain examples spring at once to mind—Oedipus' suffering, Prometheus' destruction, and Antigone's death. These are often regarded nowadays as intolerable and described as cases of tragic morality. It is worth investigating this question a little further.

Inevitability in Human Situations

The concept of tragic morality has been applied to the Iliad, but this is based on an interpretation of the Greek temperament which is not founded on their sense of reality. When Achilles sees his enemy Priam broken, he refers to the thread spun by the gods for mankind, while those gods go on living a carefree life. The poet expresses this idea in the image of the two jars, one containing good gifts and the other evil gifts. Some people receive a mixture of good and evil from the gods, others receive only evil gifts and go through the world in a state of torment, 'unregarded by gods and men' [7] (οὔτε θεοῖσι τετιμένος οὔτε βροτοῖσιν).[8]

Man is in agreement with the gods in this case. There can be no question of mankind revolting against this decision, which is determined by fate, so that mutual sympathy has no part to play. The clearest example of a change in the situation in society is the fate of Hector's son Astyanax, who lost his father and whose fate was to be banished from the circle of his little friends. A child living today would say: 'I'm not going to play with you any more; my mother says you're a good-for-nothing'. However movingly and sympathetically the poet's telling of this story may be, the protest

---

[6] W. B. Kristensen, op. cit., p. 98.
[7] Dodds, op. cit., p. 29.
[8] Il. 24. 525-533.

against this inhuman treatment remains unheard. The rules of the game had to be observed.[9]

The attitude towards sport is very similar. Children are not natural sportsmen and the same applies to the Greeks in the Iliad. The gods help their favourites among the combatants in the most treacherous ways. A beggar, for example, who does not satisfy the generally accepted norms of physical beauty and appearance, is regarded as a clumsy person and is beaten again and again. Any unattractive man is always a coward and it can cause no surprise that he has five sisters; in other words, he is a person with whom everything is bound to go wrong. Sophocles' Ajax is another example of this. The goddess Athene plays a cat and mouse game with the tormented hero of the drama, in which the sovereign will of the gods, who behave as they want to, is clearly in evidence. A final and even more powerful example is Oedipus.[10]

Self-interest, then, was taken for granted in Greece and this emerges strikingly in the fighting scenes in the Iliad. Hector is a better example for us to take here than Achilles, who was unreasonable, inflexible, and fierce, a man full of resentment (μῆνις). Hector, on the other hand, gives the impression of being a nobleman. He was the 'holder' or protector of the city, with a strong sense of duty. Yet, despite the fact that he is morally of high standing, an ideal picture of Greek manhood, there is another side to his character.[11] Verdenius has argued with some truth how, at certain times, Hector behaves as an egoist, telling those who fight with him that it is not ignominious to die in defence of the fatherland, since one's wife and children can continue to live and one's home and property remain intact.[12] This is, however, not egoism, even though it may not be an attitude of commitment to the people. It is clear that the family is in this instance more important.

Another concept, that of τιμή or honour, occurs in various forms, but certainly reflects an attitude that is quite different from our own; the egoism is also painful for many of us today. There is the

---

[9] Il. 22. 490. See also below, pp. 38 and 44. W. Burkert, *Zum altgriechischen Mitleidsbegriff*, Diss. Erlangen (1955), p. 136, mentions this passage in passing and says that sympathy with the poor and oppressed is very seldom expressed in the Iliad. (He mentions Il. 22. 494).

[10] For Oedipus, see below p. 84 ff.

[11] Il. 15. 496-498; cf. 17. 423-424. See Verdenius' discussion of Hector in his inaugural address, *Hector* (1947).

[12] Il. 6. 476-481.

well-known scene in which Hector says good-bye to his wife Andromache before returning to the battlefield. He says that he hopes
that the son will be more successful than the father in battle and
in killing the enemy. Inner worth is clearly unthinkable without
external success—a materialistic point of view [13] that can be compared with the advice given by the father of the young Achilles to
his son to control himself and behave in a friendly fashion so that
the other Greeks will honour him more. Like a child, a grown up
Greek is here publicly admitting that a certain type of behaviour
should be followed so that personal benefit will be gained from it.
Success is clearly the aim. Those who cannot accept this Greek view
of life should not forget that it has been common at all times and
in all places and not usually exclusively among children. The only
real difference between this attitude among ancient peoples and
the same attitude among our contemporaries is that the latter do
not usually declare their appetite for success so publicly.

A related theme is the desire to receive gifts, something that is
found especially in the Odyssey. Odysseus tells his host Alcinous,
for example, that he would like to stay longer with the Phaeacians
in order to acquire even more gifts. The reason for this is that he
would gain more respect when he returned home.[14] Back in Ithaca,
his first thought is for the treasures that he has accumulated and
his first action is to count them.[15]

The Homeric hero lived in a world where great store was set by
marks of honour. Armour taken as booty was a common mark of
honour. Triumph, which must be regarded as something contrary
to man's nature, does not occur in the Homeric epic, although
trophies or signs of triumph (τρόπαιον) are frequently mentioned
in the historical texts. In Thucydides, for example, the word occurs
fifty-seven times.

This attitude on the part of the Homeric heroes is a persistent
one, although it changes according to circumstances. A sign of
honour was set up for the slightest blessing. 'The desire for personal
success and a tangible mark of honour is a dominant theme in Homeric
military operations'.[16] Competition was regarded as a form of self-
expression and growth; the Greeks felt a need to excel one another.

---

[13] Il. 9. 255-258.
[14] Od. 11. 357-360.
[15] Od. 13. 215-219.
[16] Verdenius, op. cit., p. 18.

Opinions differ very greatly indeed about the question as to whether Homer disapproved of cruelty and cruel actions. On the one hand, it is thought that he did in fact pass ethical judgements. On the other hand, there is the view that ethical judgements of this kind would be in conflict with the uncommitted nature of the epic. I do not wish to enter into this question here, but would like to point out that, in my opinion, Verdenius has gone too far in his view of the 'objective' quality of the epic and of the poet as someone who never condemns. At the same time, it seems to me to be a superficial assessment to think of the poet as a judge of human behaviour. To substantiate this claim, I would point to two texts which I believe certainly have an ethical connotation. In the first the poet objects to human sacrifice and in the second he expresses disapproval of Achilles' dragging of the body of Hector behind his chariot.[17]

The Moral and Religious Attitude of Pericles

Pericles' speech on the subject of the fallen warriors is passionate and noble with regard to what Athens, the 'school of Hellas', had achieved and full of pride in the real and potential qualities of her citizens. His words addressed to the parents, widows and children of the fallen warriors, however, are at a much lower level. It has been suggested that this is fully in accordance with Pericles' character, or at least with the way in which many of his contemporaries saw him. In this, Pericles was quite different from Pisistratus, who was not in any sense 'a man of the people', and poured out his feelings to the public not differently from his political enemy, Cimon, who led the people before him, or his fateful successor Cleon.[18]

What would strike us today as unseemly in this speech, however, is Pericles' attempt to console the parents among his audience with the hope of other sons, not their older or younger sons who had not died, but new sons, and this was, of course, a remote possibility indeed for parents whose sons were soldiers. This statement has nothing to do with Pericles' reserve; modern opinion is bound to find it tasteless and insensitive. Was Pericles alone in expressing this kind of hope or was it something that his audience appreciated?

---

[17] Il. 23. 24; cf. lines 175-176; for Hector's corpse, see also Il. 24. 22.

[18] See A. W. Gomme's commentary on Thuc. 2. 44. 3-45; see also P. Walcot, 'The Funeral Speech. A Study of Values', *Greece and Rome* 20 (1973), pp. 111-121.

I believe that the latter is the case. We should not forget that for the Greek citizen the city was all-important.

The Greek attitude towards widows is very similar to this attitude towards parents, which we cannot help finding distasteful. Gomme has observed in this context that Pericles' 'explanation of the whole matter is not only priggish, but advice, not consolation, and advice that is most of it not called for by the occasion'. Pericles' words are: 'Great will be your glory if you live up to your own proper nature and if neither good nor evil is said of you by men'. Gomme here remarked, rather mischievously: 'Pericles at this time married Aspasia'.[19]

In my opinion, however, Gomme's observation is not really to the point. There is no question here of an explanation. It is a speech, intended above all to give consolation, with the result that there is a difference in the atmosphere and even in outlook. It is quite possible that the widows were pleased by these words spoken by the city's leader and that their suffering was thereby raised above the personal level of individual loss and bereavement. If this is the case, what Pericles says in this speech may perhaps mean more than we can understand now. Those who specialize in the study of changing attitudes throughout history have devoted a good deal of attention recently to attitudes towards death in various civilizations and they may be able to show us that women have not always reacted in the same way throughout history to the loss of close relatives. The attitude towards mourning may, in other words, have undergone several changes. This question can be considered here first in the particular case of widows.

Widows

As Bolkestein has pointed out,[20] some of the Greek city-states were concerned for the fate of widows, but, as we shall see, this care was very incomplete. Women who had lost their husbands were

---

[19] A. W. Gomme, *Commentary* II (1956), p. 143, where both quotations (here in Rex Warner's translation) are to be found. See also his study, 'The Position of Women in Athens in the Fifth and Fourth Centuries B.C.', which was first published in *CPh* 20 (1925) and was republished in *Essays in Greek History and Literature* (1937), pp. 89-115. For a long time, this article determined attitudes in scholarly circles, but there have recently been reactions in the U.S.A. against Edwardian liberalism; see especially S. B. Pomeroy, *Goddesses, Whores, Wives and Slaves*, New York (1975), especially p. 59. See also below, p. 243.

[20] H. Bolkestein, *Armenpflege*, p. 281.

generally classified under two headings—those who had children and those who were childless. Childless widows had to return to the house of their Kyrios (κύριος), who would then be given back his bridal gift. Widows with children had the choice of remaining in their dead husband's house or of returning to their lord's house. If a widow chose to remain in her husband's house, she had to be supported by her sons or, if these were under age, by guardians. Those who looked after her received the bridal gift.[21] An expectant mother who became a widow was placed under the special protection of a magistrate. According to Dem. 43. 75, for example: ὁ ἄρχων ἐπιμελείσθω τῶν ὀρφανῶν καὶ τῶν οἴκων τῶν ἐξερημουμένων, καὶ τῶν γυναικῶν, ὅσαι μένουσιν ἐν τοῖς οἴκοις τῶν ἀνδρῶν τῶν τεθνηκότων. The sequence is worth noting—the woman is mentioned last—and the terminology shows clearly that the widow is unimportant and that only the children count. Even in the case of the latter, only the boys matter. The only girl who has any status is the one who can inherit, in other words, a daughter who is the only child.

Widows were not supported by the state, even if they were war widows. This deficiency may have been offset by the duty of children to support their parents, although it would not apply in most cases to wives whose husbands had died as soldiers at a relatively early age. Such women were usually younger than their husbands and probably had no grown-up children to look after them. Another mitigation may have been applied in the case of the support of the parents of the fallen.[22] Wilamowitz wrongly took this support as given to all parents who were without a near relative to care for them. Nothing can be found in the source quoted to say this.[23]

In the ancient sources, the only data are those dealing with the parents of men killed in war. Thus it inevitably strikes us today as even more painful that widows are not mentioned, only parents and children.

One word—χηρωσταί—points in the direction at least of those

---

[21] J. H. Lipsius, *Das attische Recht* II ², p. 495.

[22] See, however, Plato Menex. 248E: καὶ ἰδίαι καὶ δημοσίαι γηροτροφήσουσι. This passage refers to the children and parents of those who had been killed. This is clear from the context.

[23] Wilamowitz, *Plato* II, p. 138; this view is supported by Bolkestein, p. 282, note 4; [Dem.] Epitaph. 32: γονεῖς περίβλεπτοι γηροτροφήσονται. The keyword is περίβλεπτοι: they are parents of repute, of 'status', who were admired because their sons were killed in battle.

whose task was to look after the interests of widows.[24] This basis
is, however, far too narrow. Zimmern has mentioned that Thucydides suggested that such women were able to live by prostitution:
'It was one of the few recognized ways in which a Greek woman
could earn a livelihood'.[25] The author is clearly referring here to
Pericles' words concerning the women of Athens.[26] These words
have been variously assessed by different scholars, but it seems almost impossible that prostitution is intended. By analogy with
ὀρφανισταί, the word χηρωσταί has been interpreted as those whose
function was to take care of the interests of widows, since the first
word is probably to be translated as those with the task of caring
for orphans. Very little importance is attached, however, by modern
scholars to this interpretation, which stresses *care* of widows, since
there is no hint in any tradition of any such care of the widows of
the fallen. The word χηρωσταί probably points to the fact that certain people had oversight of the way in which widows brought their
children up.

In Thuc. 2. 46, we read that widows have to make sure of a safe
refuge and then be silent and not give trouble. We should not, however, be too hard on the Greeks. Christians, following Paul, were
not much better. The social problem is clearly recognized in 1 Tim.
5. 3-14 and the word here (χήρα) has a technical meaning, namely
the widow who is supported by the church. Several groups of widows
can be distinguished. The first group were those who were supported
by their children, the second those who lived a life of lasciviousness
licentiousness and the third—for us the most interesting group—
were those who had a social service function in the church. Ordinary
widows without any position in society had to be supported by
their relatives. A final group of widows consisted of those above
the age of sixty. If these had a clean sheet of conduct they could
be accepted for spiritual work with hope in God and the practice of
prayer.

It is clear from this passage that widows had a very humble role.
One of their tasks, to wash the feet of fellow Christians, was an act
of extreme humility. Widows without a family and below the age
of sixty had only one chance—they could remarry and have more

---

[24] This word was discovered by Bolkestein in Eustath II, V, p. 404.
[25] A. E. Zimmern, *Solon and Croesus* (1928), p. 141, referring to a well-
known passage, 2. 46. 2, in the *Funeral Speech*; see also above, p. 33.
[26] See above, p. 33.

children, something that is not easy for women between the age of forty-five and sixty. But Paul did not find women of that age suitable for the function of community widows.[27]

Orphans [28]

According to most modern scholars, orphans were usually cared for because the state regarded this as a duty. Among oriental peoples, and especially the Jews, orphans were dependent on charity, which was usually private. Care of orphans in Greece was never care of the poor, as it was in the East. Many scholars have therefore concluded that the Greeks had a better organization for social care than the oriental peoples. It is our task here to investigate whether this is the case or not.

Both in Greece and in Rome, the orphans in question were descendants of freeborn citizens. The law was not concerned with other orphans. There was, however, no law determining the way in which orphans should be cared for. They were given guardians by the civil judge. The name for this guardian was *epitropos* in Greek and *curator* in Latin. According to Xenophon (*Poroi*, 2. 7), there were also special magistrates to whom the care of orphans was entrusted. In none of these cases, however, is there any sign of a law concerning orphans or their care. All that emerges is that a certain control was exercized over those who had orphans in their charge within the family.

Orphanages providing accommodation for all orphans, irrespective of their origin, first appeared in Christian times. Such an orphanage was known either as βρεφοτροφεῖον or as an ὀρφανοτροφεῖον. The words have different meanings. The first was for foundlings of un-

---

[27] See Dibelius' commentary in *Handbuch zum NT*, 1 Tim. 5. 3, 9; see also W. Bauer, *Wörterbuch zum NT* (1952⁶), under χήρα; J. de Zwaan, *Commentaar op de Heilige Schrift*, p. 1153; G. Stählin, *ThWNT* IX (1973), under χήρα; by the same author: *Das Bild der Witwe* (Ein Beitrag zur Bildersprache der Bibel und zum Phänomen der Personifikation in der Antike), *Jahrbuch An. Chr.* 17 (1974), p. 5-20. All these provide bibliographies.

[28] See Bolkestein, *Armenpflege*, p. 127 ff, 275. Although I often disagree with this author, I respect his treatment. For a complete summary of the passages from the early tradition, his work can safely be consulted. More recent summaries will also be found in *ThWNT* V (1954), under ὀρφανός (Seesemann); A. Dorjahn, *R.E.*, s.v. ὀρφανοί. For Athens new evidence has been published by R. S. Stroud, 'Theozotides and the Athenian Orphans', *Hesperia* 40 (1971), p. 280-301. See also p. 54 ff. below.

known origin, the second for the children of freemen.[29] The Christian orphanage was a kind of asylum or poorhouse and not an orphanage in the generally accepted sense of the word, since children of poor or destitute families were accepted in them.

Let us now consider the literary texts illustrative of the Greek attitude towards orphans, in the first place the epic. In the Iliad, the fate of the orphan is depicted in very strong colours. The little Astyanax was banished from the circle of his friends because his father no longer belonged to the club.[30] Actions singled out by Hesiod as characteristic of bad men are the ill-treatment of strangers, parents, and orphans.[31] The text is to be found in a passage in which the rich are criticized. In the Iliad, those who act without restraint are threatened with punishment by the gods. (In the case of Andromache, Astyanax' mother and Hector's widow, this is a bitter acquiescence and she does not blame the gods, who will protect her son). A certain doubt has been felt from time to time regarding the historical accuracy of these data, but this is in my view unfounded. The fate of the orphan is very much what one would expect to find in Greek society and the child's status is derived from that of his father. Aphrodite cared for the daughters of Pandarus, who had become orphans, and this shows that the goddess did what the family of the Trojan archer did not do.[32]

Both the literary and the legal data show that there was no system of guardianship in the Greek world in the epic period. From Gortyn in Crete a legal code has been preserved, probably dating back to the fifth century B.C. and containing very early legal provisions, some of them referring to *orphanodikastai*. These were state officials with the duty of protecting the rights of heiresses in the male line if there were no men in the male line of the family itself to perform it. These officials constituted a new element in society and R. F. Willetts was in my opinion right when he concluded: 'We can therefore assume that the *orphanodikastai* were a late development whose existence could modify the earlier arrangements'.[33] The previous arrangements referred to in this quotation

---

[29] Daremberg and Saglio, *Dictionnaire des Antiquités*, under Orphanistai; for Xenophon (Poroi 2. 7), see G. Bodei Giglione, *Xenophontis de Vectigalibus*, Florence (1970), LXIV.

[30] See above, p. 31.

[31] Op. 330.

[32] Od. 20. 68.

[33] R. F. Willetts, *Aristocratic Society in Ancient Crete*, London (1955), p. 206.

were not based on the state, but on the family, so that they were not an official guardianship.

It is not pure coincidence that practices concerning orphans should only be found in legal provisions affecting the *epiklèros* or heiress. The persons involved in these laws were girls whose fathers had died and whose rights had to be safeguarded. The measures taken to do so had nothing to do with the so-called matriarchate. On the contrary, they were concerned with the fact that such cases, both those of young children described in the Iliad and those of a later date, were frequently of orphans in a situation without rights and therefore at the mercy of grasping relatives. State intervention was greatly to be desired, among other things in cases where a daughter was to be married. The marriageable age in Gortyn was, in my opinion precisely for this reason, twelve (for girls). Among the Spartans, and in Dorian society generally, girls married late. Gortyn was also a Dorian city and therefore forms a remarkable exception to the general pattern of Dorian life. By marriage the family was rid of the daughter problem, since she became the responsibility of the husband; early marriage was therefore desirable. It is possible that this legal enactment of the marriageable age was late, but it may well have been based on an existing practice.

A boy brought up as an orphan by his uncle had at least a piece of land or κλῆρος that he could later manage for himself. There were, however, difficulties even here. According to Demosthenes, who had some painful experiences, all kinds of astonishing things could happen even in a civilized state with adequate legislation.

A girl could also be at the mercy of her husband's family. There was not much danger on the mother's side, but the girl could be subjected to abuse by the patriarchal clan and was more defenceless from the latter. Many problems could arise in connection with the distribution of the inherited piece of land and its use. I do not propose to discuss these details here, but merely note that the Gortyn law seems to confirm that the care of orphans was originally a private matter in other words the responsibility of relatives. It is also clear from the Iliad and Hesiod that the relatives did not always do their duty by the orphan. This is, of course, a phenomenon that has been prominent throughout history. A nineteenth century parallel is not hard to find, for instance in the novels of Jane Austen.

It is generally accepted that the state began to protect orphans because the fortune had to be safeguarded and the care of orphans could not be equated with the care of the poor.[34] We know very little about arrangements for the care of orphans outside Athens, however, and for this reason must confine ourselves to a consideration of these.

Certain citizens were appointed in Athens as guardians, either by the father in his will or by the state if there was no will. When the state intervened, it was the archon who appointed the guardians in accordance with certain laws (κατὰ νόμον). There is therefore a difference between ἐπίτροποι καταλελειμμένοι and a κατάστασις ἐπιτρόπων. The father and the archon were free to choose the guardians and to decide their number. There was no need for them to be members of the family. This, I believe, indicates an abrogation of family rights, which may have caused a good deal of distress. These guardians were called epitropoi (ἐπίτροποι) or when they formed a college (ὀρφανισταί) as in the Dorian cities, then almost exclusively ὀρφοβοταί. This last word is known to us only from a lexicon and we are bound to ask whether it refers to an office of state or a family guardian. If it is compared with a word such as ἱπποβοταί, then the latter seems more probable.

The duty of the epitropos was to ensure the subsistence (σῖτος) of orphans not yet of age, to provide for their education and to represent them legally. They were in loco patris in fact. They also had to manage the estates of orphans not yet of age and hand them over when they came of age. The best example of a guardian is perhaps that of the Spartan Lycurgus who, according to tradition, brought up Charilaos, who later became king.

The archon too had some duties towards orphans (ἐπιμελείσθω τῶν ὀρφανῶν), a clear assumption of responsibility by the state. According to the law as quoted by Demosthenes (Dem. 43. 75), he was evidently required to receive complaints about ill-treatment of orphans. Two kinds of offence are mentioned. The first was more general, allowing a complaint to be laid against any citizen charged with κάκωσις ὀρφανῶν. Secondly and more specifically, guardians could be brought to trial if they had committed any offence against the estate of the orphan in their charge (κάκωσις οἴκου ὀρφανικοῦ). Orphans who had come of age could also bring their guardians to law for mismanagement (δικὴ ἐπιτροπῆς). Besides the archon there

---

[34] Bolkestein, op. cit., p. 276 ff.

was a special college of guardians of orphans (ὀρφανοφύλακες). This college is mentioned by Xenophon (Poroi 2. 7). The historicity of this college has rightly not been called in question, mainly because a parallel occurs in Plato's Laws (924 B). And though, as we shall see later, the Platonic parallel is no real guarantee that such colleges existed, we may conclude for the present that the state did take charge of orphans and regarded it as an important duty and that two other bodies existed in addition to the guardians.

Orphans in Plato's Laws and Other Works

We have already alluded to the important question of the position of orphans in Plato's Laws. We must now consider in greater detail the extent to which the philosopher's teaching can be traced to rules that were already in force in Athens.[35]

In his Laws, Pluto writes of the need to appoint four guardians, two on the father's and also two on the mother's side (924 B). Later in the same passage (926 E), he names the custodians of the law whose duty it was to watch over orphans and protect them from other members of their family who might threaten their interests. In the first text (924 B), a college is mentioned in which three men were appointed over the guardians and alternated in their duties with twelve other custodians of the law. The members of this triumvirate were known as custodians of the guardian (ἐπιτρόπου φύλαξ; 928 A).

Plato's Republic also has some relevant passages. One of the reasons for the existence of a plutocracy is said to be the criminal behaviour for which guardianships of children provide the opportunity. I agree with Bolkestein that we here have evidence of the "pre-capitalistic" nature of the Athenian state. (I also think the word 'pre-capitalistic' is too highly charged and modern, but that is beside the point). The main question is whether these guardianships or ἐπιτροπεύσεις were offices of state or private institutions. They were presumably the latter. There were certainly many orphans and, according to Plato's theory, it was the state's duty to prevent injustice from being done to orphans. If so, then Plato's view seems to me in complete accord with what really took place

---

[35] Bolkestein, *op. cit.*, p. 278, note 4 and pp. 279-280; I owe a great deal to this passage in Bolkestein's work, although my conclusions are different from his.

in the private sphere, although he himself wanted to institutional-
ize the practice.

The fact that the state was concerned does not mean that it
provided complete protection for orphans. There is no evidence for
Bolkestein's claim, made elsewhere, that state concern (in Greece)
was morally superior to private care of orphans (in the East). We
do not know, for instance, whether the care provided by the state,
which must, of course, have been carried out by people, was better
than private care. Nor is it certain whether all the guardianships
were in private hands, so that we cannot draw far-reaching conclusions or make too many distinctions between state intervention
and private guardianship.

It is, I believe, misplaced to put an exclamation mark, as Bolkestein does, after Plato's statement that criminal actions were en-
couraged by the system of guardians. By so doing he deprives the
philosopher's pronouncement of all its seriousness. Presumably
Bolkestein meant to suggest that private guardians were rogues
and that the neutral state was preferable. But we are bound to ask
whether he was not going too far. It was certainly not Plato's purpose
to make general rules or laws to hinder private persons from keeping
their inheritance, especially if they belonged to the highest class in
society. These texts in the Laws and other works of Plato do not
really have so much bearing on the case of orphans except perhaps
in a negative sense. But they do require us to take account of a
historical fact of general importance, that orphans were protected
in Athens. Moreover Bolkestein himself attached considerable importance to them, since he quoted an entire passage from his *Econo-
misch Leven* (pp. 236-237) in his *Armenpflege* (p. 280): 'great estates
acquired in three ways: the accumulation of landed property which
was possible because everybody had an unlimited right to buy and
sell it; lending money at interest to young people who led extrava-
gant lives; theft or misappropriation, for which the management of
orphan estates tended to give special opportunities'.

What is striking here is that Bolkestein, who insisted on a sharp
distinction between lived and preached morality, did not always
apply this distinction in the case of care of the poor.[36] According
to him, it was clear from Plato's writings 'that the legislator as
moralist had immersed himself with warm concern in the fate of

---

[36] Bolkestein, *op. cit.*, pp. 129 and 184.

the orphan' (p. 129). 'Warm concern' is modern wishful thinking. It is also simply not true that in Athenian practice care was given only to wealthy orphans or that orphans were confined to the social class of their parents. Orphans in Athens were given a full suit of armour (panoply) and served in the army—but not simply by virtue of the private property they possessed. These examples have been adduced as evidence of the desire to confine orphans to the class to which their parents belonged. What is more, in the maintenance of war orphans, special care was given to the fourth class of citizen, the *thetes*. The idea underlying all this practice was that orphans should, if possible, be raised above their class. Members of the fourth class could not afford their own weapons or armour. In giving this privilege to orphans of that class, a certain social mobility was achieved and dissatisfied citizens were enabled to move up to a highei class. This practice is not to be found in Plato. He does not mention poor orphans at all, at least not in this context.[37] Bolkestein's conclusion here is correct: 'that Plato is almost exclusively concerned with orphans of the property-owning classes'. My only objection to his conclusion is his use of the word 'almost', but in view of this statement, it is strange to speak of Plato's 'warm concern' for orphans. In Greek society it was regarded as important to look after one's own affairs. In this matter of military equipment alone, the lawgiver was expected to give help.[38]

Outside Athens, we have Charondas' legislation at Catana. Charondas provided that there should be epitropoi on both the father's and the mother's side with the respective duties managing the orphan's estate and supervising his education.[39] There was also a college of ὀρφανοφύλακες in Gorgippia on the Black Sea and another in Delphi.[40]

Hippodamus of Miletus, the town planner who built Piraeus and Thurii, also tried to bring orphans, at least theoretically, into his legislation. He drafted a constitution with three classes of citizens—artisans, peasants, and soldiers—and three kinds of land—temple, state, and private land. This threefold division resulted in three

[37] It is possible that the question is raised in Phaedo 116[B].

[38] Aeschines, *Against Ctesiphon*, 154, was clearly referring to a legal provision in the past. For the 'parade of the orphaned children in full armour', see A. Pickard-Cambridge, *The Dramatic Festivals of Athens*, Oxford (1953); see also below, p. 46 ff.

[39] Bolkestein, *op. cit.*, p. 277, note 4.

[40] Bolkestein, *op. cit.*, p. 278, notes 7 and 8.

kinds of laws and three categories of elected leaders, who were entrusted with the care of orphans as part of their responsibilities.
Bolkestein has spoken in this context of 'civil matters'. The task
of these leaders with regard to strangers and orphans is described
in Aristotle's *Politica* (1268 A 14) as τοὺς δ' αἱρεθέντας ἐπιμελεῖσθαι
κοινῶν καὶ ξενικῶν καὶ ὀρφανικῶν. This can be compared with Plato's
Republic (500 C ff.).

It is often forgotten in discussing this question that the care of
orphans was not necessarily a public matter and was kept distinct
from τὰ κοινά. It is my contention that the care of orphans was
treated primarily as a private responsibility.

Returning now to Hippodamus, it seems to me that he may have
favoured this legislation because he had personally experienced the
effects of war and its aftermath of orphaned children. He may even
have been thinking here of a war in Athens or at least a war in
which Athens was involved. Whether this is the case or not, I cannot
believe that he based his recommendations on something which was
already a general rule. As Newman correctly observes in his commentary on Aristotle's *Politics*, the philosopher had something quite
different to say about the competence of magistrates in 1299 B 10 ff.
This should not cause us any surprise, since Aristotle regarded
Hippodamus' ideas as fantastic.[41]

Bolkestein treated Hippodamus' measures, however, as public
even though they were purely theoretical and therefore more on
the level of what Bolkestein himself would call preached morality.
I must say that I find his interpretation of Hippodamus rather
one-sided. On the one hand, he credits Hippodamus with giving a
practical formulation of what he conceives as the humane spirit of
Greek legislation. On the other, he dismisses the shocking treatment
of the orphaned Astyanax, as described in the Iliad, as standard
public behaviour of no special significance. In the same way, he
says that Hesiod's exposure of the treatment of orphans and the
behaviour of parents as an offence against the children [42] referred
merely to a period when guardians did not exist, as though guardianship were any real guarantee that children would be treated justly!
As for Homer, Bolkestein's comment on Andromache's shocking
account of the wretched life of a beggar and outcast awaiting her

---

[41] R. E., *s.v.* Hippodamus for the references.
[42] Bolkestein, *op. cit.*, p. 276, where Hesiod's words are discussed (Hesiod,
Op. 330).

fatherless son is that these words cannot in fact tell us very much about the real situation of either mother or son. But how can any modern scholar know this with any certainty? If it is borne in mind how immensely popular the poems of Homer were in ancient Greece, we are bound to assume that educated Greeks must have been familiar with the treatment of children in the situation of Hector's orphaned son. We need not even limit the observation to educated Greeks, since many others must have known Homer through recitals and thus been quite familiar with the passage.

Hippodamus' proposed law was, on the other hand, successful. The period at which he formulated it certainly seems to have been one when war was being waged or in prospect so that the expectation of many new war orphans was high. I base this assumption on Aristotle's statement: καὶ τοῖς παισὶ τῶν ἐν τῷ πολέμῳ τελευτώντων ἐκ δημοσίου γίνεσθαι τὴν τροφήν, ὡς οὔπω τοῦτο παρ' ἄλλοις νενομοθετημένον. If there was no care of war orphans, as distinct from other orphans, in Athens before about 445 B.C.,[43] then we may safely assume that little concern was felt during the epic period for a war orphan such as Astyanax.

Aristotle continues: ἔστι δὲ καὶ ἐν 'Αθήναις οὗτος ὁ νόμος νῦν καὶ ἐν ἑτέραις τῶν πόλεων (1268 A 8 ff). Newman insisted that the words beginning ὡς οὔπω expressed Hippodamus' opinion and that νῦν in this passage means 'in reality', but this strikes me as rather forced, as indeed does Newman's entire argument.[44] My explanation of this text agrees with the information we have concerning the separate duties assigned to magistrates in respect of orphans.

Hippodamus' aim here was to adopt a new stance. Newman was right to call it 'unusual' and, in my opinion, this special care of war orphans was quite new. It was a means by which the fourth class of the population, the *thetes*, could achieve a higher status. Their children could at least become *hoplites*. We have records of provision for war orphans from fifth century Athens, but not as a continuous occupation of magistrates performing a regular duty. The measures seem to be occasional, sometimes even a product of opportunism,

---

[43] Here uncertainty prevails. Stroud, *op. cit.*, p. 288 is more positive about IG I². 6 + 9 (see p. 54 below). Bolkestein, whom I am inclined to endorse, is negative about SIG³ 42 (*op. cit.*, p. 281).

[44] ὡς οὔπω τοῦτο παρ' ἄλλοις νενομοθετημένον refers, in my opinion, to one of Hippodamus' ideas. The following words: ἔστι δὲ καὶ ἐν 'Αθήναις οὗτος ὁ νόμος νῦν καὶ ἐν ἑτέραις τῶν πόλεων are supplementary information provided by Aristotle.

for instance after the Persian invasions, during the Peloponnesian War, or after civil strife between oligarchs and democrats. The following more or less continuous account must be read with this restriction in mind. The well known words from Pericles' Funeral Speech will offer a good starting point.

War Orphans

In Athens, the child of a father who had fallen in war was educated until he was an adult. Financial support ended then and the young man was given the panoply. This is related in Thucydides II. 46: τὰ δὲ αὐτῶν τοὺς παῖδας τὸ ἀπὸ τοῦδε δημοσίᾳ ἡ πόλις μέχρι ἥβης (18 years) θρέψει. This measure, mentioned by Pericles, does not give the impression of having been in force very long. The words τὸ ἀπὸ τοῦδε constitute a difficulty which even Gomme did not discuss. Does it mean that the children received the allowance from the time that the speech was made or from the time that their fathers died? I think that the first is more likely,[45] since, if the measure had been in existence for long, there would have been no need to mention it. Moreover retrospective legislation was virtually unknown in Greek society.[46]

In the Menexenus 248 E ff., Plato has this to say. First, the state should contribute to the education of orphans, so that they are as little aware of their orphaned status as possible. The state should take over the function of the father for as long as they are still children. Secondly, as soon as they are of age, the state should allow them to go to their own estates (to improve them). Before this, however, they will have been given the panoply. Thirdly, the state should show them the bearing of their fathers, which should always be in their minds, by giving them the instruments of their fathers' courage (the weapons). The state also allows them, on the basis of a happy augury, to go for the first time to the 'hearth', that is their father's house (οἶκος), so that they can assert themselves with their new weapons.[47] I should like to make a few comments on this statement by Plato.

---

[45] Cf. R. Warner's translation: 'for the future their children will be supported at the public expense by the city'.

[46] The fact that αὐτῶν is placed before τοὺς παῖδας,—according to one commentator 'effectively placed before' (Classen, cf. 1. 30. 3)—, stresses, I believe, the exceptional nature of this measure.

[47] The children and parents of the fallen were cared for by the state, but not the widows; see above, p. 34.

(1) The verb συνεκτρέφει (249 A) shows that there were two authorities: the original guardians or protectors from the family and (presumably at a later period) the guardians appointed by the state.

(2) The state concerned itself with the care of orphans, but this apparently no longer functioned very well in the fourth century. An appeal was therefore made (as in the earliest society) to private persons. The participles γηροτροφησόντων and ἐπιμελησομένων refer to something that has still to come (or will come again), but which does not exist at present (or does not at least enjoy official recognition). For what concerns the state, the speaker appeals to a law that was once upon a time in force.

(3) Reference is made only to boys who are orphaned. Girls are not mentioned in this patriotic piece of prose, which is after all a parody. In reality, girls would also have enjoyed legal protection. The fact that girl orphans are not named is in itself remarkable. It probably points to something that is relevant to the position of women in Greek society. The law is mentioned by Demosthenes (43. 75) and a scholion on this passage says that widows were to receive care on the basis of the same measure. But this only applied to the pregnant widow of a husband who had died on military service. It is therefore clear that the authorities were primarily concerned with the child.

(4) The panoply was regarded as a gift which would strengthen morale and increase solidarity with the fathers who had died. There is also a social aspect. The children were made members of the third class of citizens. The 'hearth' that is mentioned was probably also the state hearth. If we may assume that the father had already been dead for some time, then it is probable that his house would have been disposed of and the flame of the state would symbolize the house and the security of the individual, including his financial security (in the οἶκος).

It has been suggested that this law went back to Solon. This idea is based on a very late and not very reliable source (Diogenes Laertius I. 2, 9). Sometimes an appeal is made to Thucydides 2.46 in an attempt to prove that the law was authentic. Thucydides does not, however, refer to this law. Solon's law is quoted by Diogenes Laertius in the place quoted, referring to orphans. A guardian was not allowed, according to this law, to cohabit with the widowed mother and anyone who might become an heir after the possible death of the children was also not allowed to be a guardian. What is in doubt, of course, is whether this law really goes back to Solon. The arguments in favour have been set out by Linforth.[48] Another source that has sometimes been quoted in support of the greater antiquity of this law is Aristophanes (Aves 1660 ff). But Solon's law on inheritance, which is the one actually referred to in this passage, has nothing to do with our problem.

The Presentation of War Orphans to the People

Two passages in the literature of ancient Greece deal with the presentation of war orphans to the people. These are Aeschines, Against Ctes. 3. 154 and Isocrates, De Pace 8. 82. At the Great Dionysia, before the tragic competitions, the sons of citizens who had died in war were presented to the people in their new armour. A herald announced that their fathers had died as brave men and that the state had therefore brought the boys up and was now about to let them manage their own affairs, since they had become adults.

Isocrates criticizes the way in which this practice was carried out in his own day, that is, in the middle of the fourth century B.C. It would seem that by that time this presentation of the young orphans was a perfunctory business. Attitudes had become milder and feelings of hatred against the enemies of the past were no longer aroused. Isocrates thought differently. He looked back to a time when the balance of the tax was originally shared out at the Great Dionysia in the presence of the people assembled in the theatre—this must have reminded the Allies of the time when they had been exploited by the treasury of Athens and its officials (this at least is Isocrates' implication)—and the sons of the fallen were then brought on to the stage.

There is a disputed reading here of the word for tax—it could be either φόρων or πόρων. In the first case, there is a clear allusion to the allies and their contribution to the Delian League.[49] In the second, general revenue is meant, or, as the French commentator Mathieu has it, 'L'argent restant des revenus publics'. In this case the text is more neutral and less offensive to the allies.

---

[48] I. M. Linforth, *Solon the Athenian* (1919), p. 281. See also E. Ruschenbusch, *Solonos Nomoi, die Fragmente des solonischen Gesetzeswerkes mit einer Text- und Überlieferungsgeschichte, Historia, Einzelschriften*, Heft 9, Wiesbaden, 1966.

[49] In accordance with Αθπ. 24. 3 (in fine), the reading would be φόρων.

There is still the problem, however, of knowing exactly where the money came from. It seems likely that the custom in abeyance according to Isocrates, that is, the public presentation of the war orphans was not an old one hallowed by tradition, but rather a late introduction associated with the sensitive national feelings persisting since Athens' defeat by Sparta in 404 B.C. The passage referred to occurs in Isocrates' *De Pace*, but it is unlikely that those hearing the speech remembered very much about the actual events of that unhappy date fifty years before.

It seems to me that the date of the so-called law about the orphans is not so well established as many modern authors assume. Some do remain vague and say only that the law was instituted 'after the Persian wars'. If this is to be understood as directly after the Persian wars, then the original reading of φόρων could hardly be the correct one, since there was at that time hardly a question of the allies paying tribute.

In the Aeschines reference the important theme is patriotism. He thought that it was 'a pity that it' (the custom) 'had been abolished'. The orphaned sons were educated because their fathers had been brave. He does not refer to any moral right. This is, moreover, the most frequently quoted source on the question: 'the orphaned children of those who had fallen in battle for Athens, such as had reached a suitable age, were caused to parade in the theatre in full armour and receive the blessing of the People'.

Clearly, then, this custom and the feelings it represented fell into abeyance. As the same author has correctly pointed out: 'This practice appears no longer to have been followed in the time of Aeschines and Demosthenes'.[50] The whole institution has, moreover, been disputed but more often by modern than by ancient writers.[51] For it is not the case that Aθπ 24, 3 throws doubt on it or views it with reserve. That is pure fantasy. Nor is there any evidence that the number of persons deriving benefit was reduced after 403 and that fewer and fewer benefits were given as time went by until the practice was finally abolished, although it was still continued in Aristotle's time.[52]

---

[50] Both quotations are derived from A. Pickard Cambridge, *The Dramatic Festivals of Athens*, Oxford (1953), p. 57.

[51] See Mathieu's edition of Isocrates, *Belles Lettres*, Vol. III, p. 33.

[52] *Politica* 1268A 8.

The Task of the Archons

We have a certain amount of information about the various tasks attributed to the archons from a scholium on Demosthenes (Schol. Dem. 24. 20). It mentions the *polemarchos* as having charge of the education of war orphans. The *archon eniausios* (= *archon epony-mos*) was responsible for widows and orphans and certain other categories. The latter may have included war disabled, but this is not certain. The text of the scholium is as follows: εἶτα ὁ πολέμαρχος, ὅστις ἐπεμελεῖτο τοῦ τρέφεσθαι ἐκ τοῦ δημοσίου τοὺς παῖδας τῶν ἀπο-θανόντων γενναίως ἐν τῷ πολέμῳ, εἶτα ὁ ἄρχων ὁ ἐνιαύσιος, ὅστις ἐπε-μελεῖτο τῶν χηρῶν καὶ τῶν ὀρφανῶν καὶ ἄλλων τινῶν.

Several conclusions can be drawn from this. First, war orphans were cared for by the 'Ministry of War'. Secondly, only war orphans were supported from the 'city treasury', but this also implies that guardians or *epitropoi* were responsible for the care of other orphans (see above). Thirdly, in this passage, widows are also mentioned, so that we may conclude that they were not entirely unprotected (at least in the fourth century B.C.). It should be noted, however, that war widows are not mentioned separately as receiving support.

The Burial of those killed in Battle

The following text is among the inscriptions of Thasos: 'The *ago-ranomos* must neglect nothing . . . on the day when the obsequies take place, before the obsequies take place. No one may wear a sign of mourning, whatever it may be, in honour of the brave for more than five days. Such a one would be in a state of religious impurity. The *gynaikonomoi*, the *archontes*, and the *polemarchoi* should not neglect this, but should possess the authority to impose punishments as provided by the law.

What is more, the *polemarchoi* and the secretary of the Council should have the names and patronymics of those killed in battle engraved on the list of the brave and their fathers and children should be invited to offer sacrifice to the heroes in honour of the brave. The recipient should pay each of them compensation and should also pay the same to those received in the exercise of offices. Their fathers and sons should also be invited to sit in places of honour at the games. A place should be reserved for them and the organizer should make a platform for them.

For as many of those (who have been killed in battle) who have left children behind, to their children the *polemarchoi* are to give to the boys greaves, a breastplate, a dagger, a helmet, a shield and a spear, all together being worth no less than three *mnai*, at Heraclea during the contests, and their names are to be made public. If they are girls, for their dowry . . . if they are fourteen years old'.[53]

Further information can be gained from Pouilloux' very full commentary, from which it is quite clear that the measures taken in Thasos were more or less the same as those known elsewhere and discussed above in connection with Athens. Pouilloux does not indicate this, but it is also clear that in this case too the widows are not included.

Dating

We have already seen that it was said in antiquity, and also by modern authors following ancient sources, that Solon was responsible for measures in support of widows. The basis for this view is a text in Diogenes Laertius (i. 2, 9), which is full of anecdotes but has no historical foundation. All the anecdotes refer to Solon. The words that are important for us here are: 'the *epitropos* may not marry the mother of his ward. No one who may inherit the fortune on the death of the children may become an *epitropos*'.

In this context Dem. 43. 75 has also been cited and K. Hönn clearly regarded this text as of decisive importance in his book on Solon,[54] but it is questionable how far it really does refer to Solon.

We have also seen that importance was attached to the words 'after the Persian wars', apparently on the basis of AΘπ 24. 3, in which the financing of the measure by the allied is discussed in connection with state expenditure. This was moreover promoted by the Athenian who had formulated the rule concerning the contribution to be made by the allies, namely Aristides. There is no mention, however, of the dating in this passage or of the question as to whether the item was granted in 478, when Aristides formulated his plan. Such an early date seems very unlikely, since the φόρος had at that time not been imposed consistently, or as a general tribute.

If all these data are taken into account, we are bound to conclude that at Athens there were rules governing the care of war orphans, but that there is no trace of any 'laws' before the fourth century, which saw the publication of so much legal literature. Before that

---

[53] Pouilloux, *Thasos* I, No. 141, p. 371; Inscr. Inv. 1032.
[54] K. Hönn, *Solon: Staatsmann und Weiser*, Vienna (1948), p. 80.

time, obligatory state rules, binding on guardians, did not exist.

According to Thucydides, the care of war orphans was a new institution. According to Aeschines and Isocrates, moreover, it was an institution of radical democracy, with the aim of raising the status of the Thetes. The panoply made all children members of the third class of citizens, the Zeugitai. There is no question here of moral obligations or sentiment. It was above all a financial matter and the accompanying ceremony acted as a stimulus to national feelings. The care of war orphans could take place on a large scale; in Isocr. 8. 82, we read, for example, of a 'multitude of orphans'. There is no edifying commentary on measures of a high moral character. The orphans were well cared for, but the interest of the state was the main motive and personal feelings played little or no part.

It is clear from Ps.-Xenophon 3. 4 that this was a financial question; among the many obligations laid upon Greek magistrates [55] was that known as ὀρφανοὺς δοκιμάσαι. This was not just an ordinary investigation as to whether the orphans were able to assume control of their estates, but was concerned with the question whether they had a right to their fathers' property. It is not said in Bekker (An. Gr. 235. 11: δοκιμάζονται δὲ καὶ οἱ ἐφ' ἡλικίας ὀρφανοὶ εἰ δύνανται τὰ πατρῷα παρὰ τῶν ἐπιτρόπων ἀπολαμβάνειν), that these are specifically war orphans. This passage in my opinion applies to all orphans. I am also inclined to agree with Kalinka, who assumes that 3. 4 refers to a physical examination, not, as has often been assumed, to an examination of property. I shall be returning to this question of physical examination later, but in the meantime there is another possibility: that it was an investigation into the legitimacy of the orphans. If this is the case, it is not so much a question as to whether the father had fallen in battle (this would be important for the purpose of obtaining maintenance). There is, however, in the passage in Bekker reference to those who had come of age (οἱ ἐφ' ἡλικίας). It becomes obvious, however, that there must have been an examination on coming of age when we remember that war invalids also had to submit to one (not a medical examination, but an investigation into their status as citizens).

Quite apart from this passage in Bekker, however, we are justified

[55] Kalinka: the people's courts; see also the Budé edition of Aristophanes Vesp. 578. Gelzer maintains that the βουλή was in charge; this is also Frisch's opinion (p. 315).

in thinking that the guardians also had to submit to an examination, to establish whether they had administered the property in their care correctly. If they had carried out their task badly, a complaint of κάκωσις was served against them. (See above, p. 40).

I shall not discuss here the difficult question as to whether there may not have been a case of unfairness towards a young orphan who had come of age, had lost his father and was in general not in a position to administer his own estate, but who no longer had a guardian and therefore did not need to take over the administration of the property from the guardians (παρὰ τῶν ἐπιτρόπων ἀπολαμβάνειν). Law cannot provide solutions for *all* situations.

As far as the physical examination is concerned, a passage in Aristophanes' *Vesp*. 578, παίδων τοίνυν δοκιμαζομένων αἰδοῖα πάρεστι θεᾶσθαι, is sometimes quoted as a possible explanation for the passage in Bekker. This passage refers to a physical examination, but there is nothing to say that it only applies to orphans. It cannot therefore be cited as proof that an examination of orphans took place *every year* in the case of every orphan. Kalinka did this, on the basis of the conviction that one examination, before the orphans came of age and were given the panoply, could not have been so much work that it could have been regarded as a hard task for the people's court. The objection can, however, be made that at the time Pseudo-Xenophon had in mind, there was probably a war on and that there were for this reason many orphans. As so often the difficult question of the date of this text is important. If there is a question of it being wartime, Kalinka's argument cannot be maintained. Παίδων cannot be used in favour of his view, because the *epheboi* could be called *paides* just before they came of age.

In my opinion, then, since this verse of Aristophanes cannot be connected with orphans as such, it cannot be used as proof that the examination of orphans took place before the people's court. My opinion therefore goes counter to the traditional view, including that of the excellent commentator on Aristophanes, van Leeuwen: 'pueros dicit *orbos*', and: 'sistebantur iudicibus ut ab his efficeretur maturine essent et apti qui sui iuris fierent'. It is clear that this explanation has to do with discrimination. The examination of orphans, then, would have taken place before the people's court, whereas the other young men, the non-orphans, came before the Council (Aθπ 42. 2). This seems to be a strange distinction.

What, then, does *Vesp*. 578 really mean? I believe that it refers to a physical or medical examination of all young men before they came of age, probably for military service. It has, in my view, nothing to do with an examination for possible deformity, based on superstition. One consequence of this idea about a general examination would be that Aristophanes and Aθπ 42. 2 were both alluding to the same event, but that in the earlier period the examination was carried out by the people's court and in the later by the Council.

It is finally important to point out that there may have been a physical examination to find out whether the orphans had been brought up properly by their guardians and not badly treated. If this is the case, this examination may have taken place every year (as Kalinka believed), but it would then have been something very different from what is described in the scholion (Bekker), that is, an examination on reaching adulthood (ἐφ' ἡλικίας).

An inscription (I.G. I². 6) has been quoted in connection with the text. Meritt and Robert have also engaged in controversy about the correct form of the text.

It is not possible to go into this question here because of the uncertainty of the text, which makes it impossible to draw any conclusion from it. There has been no progress in this matter since Bolkestein pointed this out.[56]

My conclusions are the following:

1. All the measures known to us are for orphans with property;
2. The only exceptions are war orphans maintained by the state (even if there was no property);
3. There is no reference anywhere—with the possible exception of Aristides' daughter (Plutarch, *Arist.* 6)—that the state supported any others but those mentioned under (2).

Bolkestein was right in his contention that these measures had nothing to do with care of the poor. I disagree with him, however, in not believing that there is any reference to a moral right, or even a hint of it.

The war orphans were given a complete panoply—armour and

---

[56] Meritt in *Hesperia* 15 (1946), pp. 249-253, and J. and L. Robert in *REG* 59-60 (1946-7), pp. 314-315. See also M. P. Nilsson, GGR², I (1955), p. 656, note 2, 663, note 2. Stroud (*supra*, n. 28) is more positive concerning I.G. I². 6, following F. Sokolowski, *Les Lois sacrées des cités grecques*, Paris (1962), p. 13, but has to admit that 'no defining phrase is added' (*op. cit.*, p. 288).

equipment—although many of their dead fathers were Thetes, that is, members of the lowest class of citizen, whereas soldiers in the infantry belonged to the class just above this. Because of this, the support given to these war orphans was, in my opinion, a social measure taken to prevent social unrest. This would also explain the very sober way in which Pericles informed his listeners in his speech about the fallen warriors (a manner which strikes us nowadays as harsh) and his encouragement to the war widows (a way of speaking that we now find repugnant). There were no demonstrations of care for orphans in the fifth century B.C.; only war orphans were cared for and, in times of peace, more spectacular demonstrations like the parade were not held.

Although the few legal proceedings we know of took place in the fourth century, I would not go so far as to maintain that guardians, ὀρφανοφύλακες, and archons did not function in this way in the fifth century. The law concerning the celebration of the Eleusinia in 406 B.C. may have acted as a norm with regard to the care of orphans. This, however, is pure speculation. The state care of war orphans is not in any sense a general care of orphans. All that is certain is that a child of the fourth class of citizen who lost his father because of sickness or old age did not receive a suit of armour.

The older 'laws' for care of war orphans had their corollary in the precarious situation after the Peloponnesian war. A new decree was formulated by Theozotides, providing for the sons of those Athenians who had suffered violent death during the oligarchy (the Thirty in 404/3). As R. S. Stroud, the editor of the recently found inscription, puts it: 'In return for the εὐεργεσία and ἀνδραγαθία of their fathers, it was decided to extend to the sons the privileges enjoyed by the sons of those who fell in war'.[57] Illegitimate children and foreigners, νόθοι and ποιητοί, however, were excluded. This discrimination is remarkable. Four years earlier party politics did not dominate Athenian legislation: Slaves, metics, and foreigners who fought at Arginousai in 407/6 were rewarded with Athenian citizenship.[58] Here if anywhere the public maintenance of the orphans was a question of politics, not of moral right.

---

[57] Stroud, *op. cit.*, p. 300. For Theozotides see also J. K. Davies, *Athenian Propertied Families 600-300 B.C.*, Oxford (1971), p. 222 f.

[58] Stroud, *op. cit.*, p. 299. See Aristoph. *Frogs* 190-191, 693-694; Hellanicus fr. 25 (Jacoby); Diodorus 13. 97. 1. On the rights of νόθοι see A. R. W. Harrison, *The Law of Athens*, (1968), p. 63-5, rightly opposed by P. J. Rhodes, 'Bastards as Athenian Citizens', *CQ*, N.S. 28 (1978), p. 89-92.

Emotion

Warmth or tenderness are noticeably absent from the sources of
the classical period that deal with the fate of orphans. They are
not to be found in the Iliad either. It is possible to suppose that
this was because they were traditionally provided for. This is, however, very doubtful, as is clear from what I have already said. Another important factor is that the references only concern war orphans and the rich. But undoubtedly there must have been others.
We may even assume that these other orphans, from different social
environments, were in a majority. If they were not to starve, they
must clearly have had to beg for their food or depend on individual
charity. For themselves they had little claim to civil rights. Hesiod's
complaint still applied.

Plato has given us an indication, in his description of Socrates'
disciples after the death of their beloved master (Phaedo 116A),
of how orphans felt: ἀτεχνῶς ἡγούμενοι ὥσπερ πατρὸς στερηθέντες διά-
ξειν ὀρφανοὶ τὸν ἔπειτα βίον.[59] The reference to widows and orphans
in the same sentence is also found in a scholion (Dem. 24. 20) and
at a later period in Libanius, *Or.* 62, p. 379, 2 F.

In a recent work dealing in detail with charities and social aid
in Greece and Rome, A. R. Hands has correctly concluded that
the most important aim in the care of orphans in the Greek and
Roman worlds was to safeguard their property rights. In his view
measures of protection mainly concerned the propertied class. The
state was able to take such measures, but did not always do so.
He has also pointed to the absence of orphanages maintained by
the state and of institutions for foundlings as something that marks
an important difference between the ancient world and all modern
social theory and practice in this sphere.[60]

Orphans in Jewish Society

Two passages in the Pentateuch can be taken as a basis for our
understanding of the care of orphans in Israel. These are Exod.
22. 21 and Deut. 24. 17. There is also a valuable reference in

---

[59] Other data can also be quoted—for example, Lucian, *De Morte Per.* 6
and other passages, for which see W. Bauer⁴ under ὀρφανός; Epictetus, *Diss.*
3. 24. 15: ἤδει γὰρ, ὅτι οὐδείς ἐστιν ἄνθρωπος ὀρφανός, ἀλλὰ πάντων ἀεὶ καὶ
διηνεκῶς ὁ πατήρ ἐστιν ὁ κηδόμενος. See also John 14. 18. Other modern
works are mentioned on p. 37, note 28 (above).

[60] A. R. Hands, *Charities and Social Aid in Greece and Rome*, London
(1968), pp. 73-74.

ThWNT, V, under ὀρφανός. In the first text, we read: 'You shall not pervert the right of the stranger and the orphan'.[61] This was not only a norm of justice for the Israelites; it was also a universal precept. In Deut. 27. 19, the man who tramples this precept underfoot is cursed. The orphan was clearly regarded as helpless; according to Ps. 82. 3, justice had to be done to the poor and to orphans. This is clearly very similar to Hesiod's complaint and there is, in this case, very little difference between the Greek attitude and that of the Jews.

Unlike the Greeks, however, the Jews regarded God as the father of orphans (see Ps. 68. 5). Orphans were under God's protection (Mal. 3. 5). Passages may be found in the Pentateuch, the prophetic books, and the psalms referring to this question. The orphan's sense of self-respect had to be safeguarded (Exod. 22. 21). If the orphan had no redeemer in human society, God himself would redeem him (Exod. 22. 22-23).

The Talmud accorded certain legal facilities to orphans. They were, for instance, either exempt from paying taxes or enjoyed tax relief. They did not have to provide completely new goods to replace damaged property, but were only obliged to effect repairs. (Others had to compensate fully for damaged goods). They also had a certain status in the law of property and estate, which in their case was not tied to the statutes governing tithes offered to the Lord.

Widows and orphans also enjoyed the right of being able to place their money in the Temple, with the result that they were supported by the Temple. This situation once led to great disturbances (2 Macc. 3. 12). The property of orphans was regarded as no less holy than that of the Temple. It should, moreover, be noted that there was no question of alms or benefits. It was, in fact, a practical solution and was often more effective than the function of the guardian in Greek society.

Legislation and Care in Judaism

The data of this legislation had a certain importance which Bolkestein, for example, did not value sufficiently. He insisted that the Torah was not law. This may be so, but they were closely related to each other, especially in their religious basis, as F. Heichelheim has pointed out in his criticism of Bolkestein.[62] Heichelheim is cor-

---

[61] See below, p. 59.
[62] F. Heichelheim, *Erasmus* II (1949), pp. 471-473.

rect in his claim that the data taken from the early books of the Bible have considerable historical value in comparison with what took place in Greece during the fifth and fourth centuries B.C. precisely because of their early date. He is also correct in his reference to the great gap in Bolkestein's work due to the latter's failure to assimilate the Talmud.

Having said this, I should like to point to Deut. 14. 28-29; 26. 12-13, according to which the Levites and the poor were to be fed from the tithes paid by the Israelites. This was in no sense almsgiving. Every third and sixth year, this ten percent of the harvest was given to the poor. It is clear from Tob. 1. 6 that this gift of the tithe was regarded as a religious duty. Because he gave his tithe, Tobit was called a god-fearing man. We must also bear in mind that what we might now regard as alms was then a law, so that all the gleanings of the fields, not only of the corn, but also of the olive and the vine, must be left for the poor (see Deut. 24. 19; Lev. 19. 9-10).

These gifts were not alms that the poor and the orphans must ask to receive. This is clear since the text does not read: 'You must give (the gleanings) to the sojourner, the fatherless, and the widow', but 'It shall be for them' (Deut. 24. 19). In other words, the owner of the fields, the orchard or the vineyard had no right to this part of the harvest nor any right to dispose of it himself; it belonged to this category of needy people. This was, therefore, a legal provision and not in any sense condescension or charity.

According to Deut. 16. 11, human dignity was safeguarded, since it was necessary to take widows and orphans on pilgrimages to religious feasts. The words 'you must rejoice . . .' in this text show that the widows and orphans were not given humiliating alms, but had to be taken as guests whose presence would increase and indeed determine the joy of the festival. All this may sound very exalted and it could be said sceptically that it has little relevance to practice, but I do not doubt that these exalted legal forms and practices existed and were current in the world of the Jews, who did not enjoy a very peaceful existence and whose land was often a battlefield during the time of expansion of the Greeks. This was a reason for mutual solidarity and for rules and laws which bore witness to this. We may also note that, according to 2 Macc. 8. 28, 30, part of the booty of war was distributed to the widows and orphans.

Guardians for the Care of Jewish Orphans [63]

There was a clear duty in the Jewish world to care for blood relations and this duty was carried out in practice. According to Cohn and others, one result of this was the absence of adoption. This view has been disputed by certain scholars, who rightly claim that adoption existed in Jewish society.[64]

As family links became weaker, guardianship became an institution, but it is not until the Mishnah that the Hebrew equivalent of the *epitropos* is found. It is possible that this development took place in stages. The foster-father may have come from the family if the family as a whole did not accept the duties. The only foster-father named in the Old Testament is Mordecai (Esther 2. 7). This word is translated in the Vulgate as *nutritius*. (See Gen. 12. 5).

This guardianship goes back to Deut. 24. 17 in the Talmud.[65] This text was discussed in detail by the commentators, but it need not detain us here since it is a late development that has nothing to do with the matter with which we are concerned in this study. Taking orphans into one's home and bringing them up was always highly regarded in Jewish society. This is clear, for example, from Job 31. 18 and from the Midrash.

Many modern scholars specializing in classical antiquity clearly neglect the Old Testament completely. Even if the law dates back to the post-exilic period, this does not make any real difference to the relationship with Greece of the fifth and fourth centuries, which is the period with which we are principally concerned here. The Old Testament law in question was not simply a result of social demands —it was also regarded as a divine commandment. The Jew served God by behaving according to the law.

It was also in this way that liability for debt was regulated in the Jewish world. The Jew was liable with his property and with his body. Slavery based on debt was known in ancient Israel, just as in pre-Solonic Athens. When the Jews came into contact, during their exile, with other systems, their own laws concerning debt underwent certain changes.[66] R. K. Sikkema's dissertation correctly

---

[63] The relevant passages in the Old Testament are Lev. 25. 25, 47-49.

[64] See M. David, *Med. Kon. Ned. Akad. van Wet., afd. Letterkunde,* N.R. 4 (1955), pp. 85-103.

[65] M. Cohn, 'Jüdisches Waisenrecht', *Zeitschr. für vergleichende Rechtswissenschaft* 37 (1920), p. 417-445.

[66] R. K. Sikkema, *De lening in het Oude Testament (Bijdrage tot de kennis van het vraagstuk van schuld en aansprakelijkheid),* Dissertation, University of Leiden, 1957.

did not make a distinction between debt and liability. This is quite clear from the passages which the author discussed. The Israelite could not act as surety for another's debt. If he stood as surety for another person, he took on that person's debt and all its consequences. In addition to this, liability was also established in Israel by lien and suretyship. Here too, the whole person was involved, but later lien and suretyship became questions of property law. We cannot unfortunately go into this matter in detail here, but must stress the importance of the example as showing that Israel's law developed in certain ways and that what took place in the case of loans in the Old Testament also applied to family law. We may in any case say that the law governing strangers, widows, and orphans was inviolable (Deut. 24. 17: 'You shall not pervert the justice due to the sojourner or the fatherless or take the widow's garment in pledge'). Lien or taking in pledge was, according to this text, regarded as inflicting an injustice; it was not always a written law, but it had to be kept as a law. In this way, the widow and the orphan were protected in Jewish society. There was no question of condescension. It was above all a law that had to be applied in the case of these groups of people whose lives were threatened.[67]

In Jewish and Greek society, state and religion were intimately interconnected. This is clear in many ways, including the relationships between the citizens themselves. Duty towards one's fellow-citizen was a religious duty. In the written and unwritten laws of the Greeks, this whole system of obligations was known as *eusebeia*.[68] This was not a purely human virtue that was rewarded. It was rather a demand, even a commandment and, according to this 'piety' as we would call it, the Greek would act as he had to. *Eusebeia* did not enable a man to prepare a way towards a good place in the world after death (Elysium); on the contrary, those who had precedence were, because of their understanding, the philosophers. Priests, those who believed, occupied the lowest place (the fifth), according to Plato. We can, I think, regard Plato as representative of the Greeks in general. They thought that it was impious to violate the sacred and unwritten laws, but did not think that the man who kept them acquired a merit that he could take with him to the grave and profit from it in the hereafter.

---

[67] R. K. Sikkema, *op. cit.*, p. 65.

[68] See D. Loenen, *Eusebeia en de kardinale deugden, Med. van de Kon. Ned. Akad. van Wet.*, N.R. 23, 4 (1960).

Is this absence of *eusebeia* among the high human virtues in any way connected with the idea that it was good enough for the mass of the people? (This suggestion was made by Loenen). I doubt this, since, if it were true, *eusebeia* would have acquired an unpleasant connotation among the Greeks and there is hardly any evidence of this in the sources. I believe that it was more a question of its having been an aspect of pious human behaviour that was taken for granted than of its having to be included in a system of virtues, which recalls a society of privileged people who were familiar with the virtues. *Eusebeia* (which we translate as 'piety') was, in my opinion, rooted in the very essence of the Greeks' relationships with each other. It is striking that there is no description of it to be found, with the result that it was more a question of matter of course acceptance than of a legal formulation.[69] In classical antiquity, there are many undefined or scarcely defined concepts of this kind; these were accepted more or less unquestioningly because they formed part—and indeed were the foundation—of society, to such an extent that the people were unable to distinguish between a defined formula on the one hand and undefined experience on the other. An example of this type of experienced but not strictly formulated concept was known to the Romans as *auctoritas*.[70]

---

[69] This gap in our bibliography cannot be filled by the often meritorious lexicographical studies of the school of H. Bolkestein, although the latter certainly provide material for an exhaustive study. See J. C. Bolkestein, "Οσιος *en* εὐσεβής, Dissertation, Utrecht, 1936; W. J. Terstegen, Εὐσεβής *en* "Οσιος *in het Griekse taalgebruik na de IVe eeuw*, Dissertation, Utrecht, 1941; a critical discussion of the first of these works has been written by M. van der Valk, *Zum Worte* ὅσιος, *Mnem.*, T.S., 10 (1942), pp. 113-140.

[70] H. Wagenvoort, *Auctoritas*, *RAC* I (1950), p. 902 ff.

CHAPTER FIVE

NEIGHBOUR AND LOVE OF NEIGHBOUR[1]

In this sphere there is a contrast between Judaism and the society of ancient Greece. According to *ThWNT* 6, 312, the Hebrew words used in this context express the idea of 'companions in the covenant' and the rights and duties attached to it. The commandment to love one's neighbour (Lev. 19. 18), which would not seem open to more than one interpretation, is applied to Israel's companions in the covenant with Yahweh and not simply to all men.

In Lev. 19. 34, this commandment to love one's neighbour is extended to the strangers living in the land (see also Deut. 10. 19). This is, however, a confirmation of the first and limited significance of the commandment. It is in any case certain that the concept is given a wider meaning in Lev. 19. 34.

There is a further extension of the meaning in the Septuagint. The Hebrew words are translated—and not fortuitously—by πλησίοι. This word should, but cannot, be limited to the idea of 'companions' or 'partners' in the covenant. There was considerable controversy among the rabbis as to whether the concept should be interpreted in its wide or in its narrower sense. This is borne out by the parable of the good Samaritan.

Turning from Jewish to Greek society of the same period,[2] we find fewer data. From the time of Theognis onwards, the word πέλας (see, for example, Eur. Med. 86: ὡς πᾶς τις αὐτὸν τοῦ πέλας μᾶλλον φιλεῖ) and its noun ὁ πλησίον, the person who is next to you in space, the man near you with whom you can speak and do the same work, are found (e.g. Plato, Charm. 155 C). The same word occurs in the army (see Josephus, Bell. Jud. 5. 295). The word πλησίον also has an ethical and secondary meaning (which is also spatial) in Aeschines, Contra Ctes. 174. (See also Plato, Apology 25 D).

The word πλησίον has an important ethical function in the doc-

---

[1] An almost complete summary of the books and articles published on this subject can be found in *ThWNT* 6, 309 (1959), under πλησίον (Fichtner and Greeven).

[2] These data are taken from Greeven in *ThWNT*, 6, 309. For the Jewish ideas, see A. Bertholet, *Die Stellung der Israeliten und der Juden zu den Fremden* (1896).

trine of concentric circles with man occupying the central place. This is the teaching proposed by Hierocles, the Stoic philosopher.[3]

The modern attitude towards the concept of neighbour in the ancient Greek world has been determined by the conviction that, in the 'lived morality' of the Greeks, the neighbour was a fellow-Greek and certainly not a barbarian or a man living in another country that was not Greek. In the chorus on τὰ δεινά in Sophocles, Antigone (332), the man mentioned is not a stranger or a neighbour, but Greek man in general. It would therefore be wrong to think that the Greek word πλησίον was the same as the Latin *quivis alius,* 'any other' and that it could therefore be equated with, for example, the French word *autrui.*[4]

On the basis of Pittacus' text, in Stob. 3. 120 H, Bolkestein has assumed that there was, in lived morality, an indefinite sense of the equality of all men with regard to certain moral obligations. In what followed in his work, however, he partially withdrew this, with the result that his argument is ultimately rather unsatisfactory.[5] This becomes even more apparent when, thirty pages further on (p. 122), we read that, according to the moralists, these obligations applied to all the Greek's neighbours or fellow-men, 'as in the valid morality'. He goes on later to restrict even this interpretation by claiming, on the basis of Epicurus' teaching, that the latter was thinking of his friends when he spoke of 'neighbours'.

One has the impression that, according to Bolkestein, general love of all mankind must have acted as a norm for the Greeks' attitude towards their neighbours. There is certainly a concession (which is not discussed any further) that the modern author tends to speak about the 'Greeks or at least their leading spirits'. These leaders would then have extended their love of their own community, the polis, to love of their guests, thus preparing the way for a humane attitude towards all men.

The argument used in support of this claim is, however, very unsound:

1. There was certainly solidarity among the Greeks, but this does not mean that they loved the whole of mankind. On the contrary,

---

[3] See *Ethische Elementarlehre,* ed. H. von Arnim (1906), pp. 61, 10 ff; Musonius, 65. 6. See also Greeven, *op. cit.,* 6, p. 310, lines 7-11.

[4] Bolkestein, *op. cit.,* p. 88 ff; Bolkestein is here following Wilamowitz.

[5] See Bolkestein, *op. cit.,* p. 89. The passage in question is ascribed to Pittacus: ὅσα νεμεσᾷς τῷ πλησίον, αὐτὸς μὴ ποίει.

they were extremely reserved with regard to the barbarians. When Plato declared that the Greek ought not to have another Greek as his slave (*Resp.* 469 C), he was not speaking about a love of all mankind. The same applies to his statement in Protagoras (337 C), which Bolkestein interpreted correctly in its context.[6] It would also be wrong to refer here to the mild treatment of Athens by Sparta after the Peloponnesian War (see Xenophon, Hell. 2. 2. 20).[7]

2. Data relating to the community of all mankind have been produced from time to time, but they deal with the cosmos and have nothing to do with the equality of man. The source for these data is Antiphon (see Diels, II[6], pp. 352-353):[8]

ἐν τούτῳ δὲ πρὸς ἀλλήλους βεβαρβαρώμεθα, ἐπεὶ φύσει πάντα πάντες ὁμοίως πεφύκαμεν καὶ βάρβαροι καὶ Ἕλληνες εἶναι, σκοπεῖν δὲ παρέχει τὰ τῶν φύσει ὄντων ἀναγκαίων πᾶσιν ἀνθρώποις· πορίσαι τε κατὰ ταὐτὰ δυνατὰ πᾶσι. καὶ ἐν πᾶσι τούτοις οὔτε βάρβαρος ἀφώρισται ἡμῶν οὐδεὶς οὔτε Ἕλλην· ἀναπνέομέν τε γὰρ εἰς τὸν ἀέρα ἅπαντες κατὰ τὸ στόμα καὶ κατὰ τὰς ῥῖνας καὶ ἐσθίομεν χερσὶν ἅπαντες.

If these lines are to be properly understood, it is important to bear in mind that they are preceded by the statement that 'we respect and venerate those who are descended from distinguished fathers, but we do not respect and venerate those who are not'.[9]

Here is a translation of the first line, in four different versions:

1. 'In this we behave like barbarians towards each other'
   or
2. 'In this we are barbarized towards each other' (Waszink);
   or
3. 'It is the sign of ignorance or a dullard' (Merlan);
   or

---

[6] Bolkestein, *op. cit.*, p. 123, note 2.

[7] In this context, H. R. Breitenbach, *Historiographische Anschauungsformen Xenophons*, Fribourg (1950), p. 105 ff, 107, 110), has good things to say about Xenophon.

[8] Recent research has shown that Antiphon the Sophist and Antiphon of Rhamnus were the same man; there were strong arguments for this view in the past. See R. Kent Sprague (ed.), *The Older Sophists* (University of South Carolina Press, 1972). See also the discussion by G. B. Kerferd in *CR* 25 (1975), pp. 231 ff. For a translation of the passage, see below, p. 68 (Waszink).

[9] The Greek text is heavily restored: τοὺς ἐκ καλῶν πατέρων ἐπαιδούμεθα καὶ σεβόμεθα, τοὺς δὲ ἐκ μὴ καλοῦ οἴκου ὄντας οὔτε ἐπαιδούμεθα οὔτε σεβόμεθα.

4. 'In that way we are like citizens of different nations'

(W. Jaeger, *Paideia*, English edn., 1. 327)

Waszink's translation is generally speaking preferred and it is also in accordance with Diels' German translation. It is quite clear from this that the attitude of the barbarians (the passive of βαρβαρόω is used here, meaning to act as barbarians) is not in any sense approved of.

In the same context, a passage is often quoted from Plato's *Gorgias* (507 E): 'According to the wise, the sky, the earth, the gods and men are bound together and have friendship, a sense of order, moderation and justice; the universe is therefore called a cosmos'. Who these 'wise' men are is not certain. They may have been the Pythagoreans or the philosopher Empedocles, but the identity of the 'wise' is not very important.

This quotation does not, moreover, tell us much about the human community or about attitudes towards one's neighbour. The same applies to a passage from Theophrastus (On Piety, 97. 14; Bernays) and to Xenophanes' conviction (fr. 7 D): In this text Pythagoras expresses sympathy for a badly treated dog, because he believes that he can hear the voice of a friend's soul in the dog's yelping.

Heraclitus' *logos* is also of little use to us in this context. All men possessed this logos (fr. 2 D), especially the philosopher himself, who distinguished himself scornfully as an aristocrat from the mass of men: 'One is for me worth ten thousand!'

We are bound to proceed carefully with the few data at our disposal. There is, in connection with the question of the love of all mankind, a frequently quoted statement attributed to Socrates: 'Men are by nature well disposed towards each other' (Xenophon, *Mem.* 2. 6. 21). This statement may reflect either a universal and optimistic view of reciprocal human relationships or a momentary and impulsive thought. Whichever it may be, it is certainly not an expression of a conscious love of one's fellow-man, although this suggestion has been made. The same applies to Aristotle's statement in *Eth. Nic.* 1155 A 22. I am not alone in doubting from time to time whether mankind as a whole is meant in such statements attributed to Socrates. It may simply be Greeks. In the case of Aristotle, however, many scholars who are quite sure of their interpretation insist that it is a reference to man's relationship with his neighbour. I am not so sure that this conclusion is justified. In the passage from Aristotle, the words that I have spaced out give rise to doubts in my mind: ἴδοι δ' ἄν τις καὶ ἐν ταῖς πλάναις ὡς οἰκεῖον ἅπας ἄνθρωπος ἀνθρώπῳ καὶ φίλον.[10]

What Antiphon in fact says is that all men are equal in all necessary things: 'They all breathe through their mouths and noses and they all eat with the help of their hands.'[11] Sinclair has dealt very well with this quotation, although he claimed that the words bear witness to a love of barbarians and to an aversion to social contrasts.[12] This, however, is precisely, what is doubtful; there is too much emphasis on *love* of barbarians in this interpretation. Generally speaking, however, Sinclair deals very well with Antiphon the philosopher and he is also careful to take reservations into consideration.

This type of idea is found again and again in the literature of a later period. It is possible to trace it back to Antiphon, but since we have so few data from this earlier period, it would be very risky to attribute too much to this one author, in whose work the idea of universal love has been found.

The same idea of universal love of mankind has been made the basis of many scholars' treatment of Alexander the Great, in connection with *homonoia*. The best known publication on this subject was written by W. W. Tarn. Since Badian's convincing refutation of this idea in *Historia* 7 (1958), however, fewer scholars have supported it. It is perhaps valuable to consider it briefly as it attracted a great deal of attention in the past.

P. Merlan's study [13] was written with the purpose of disputing Tarn's hypothesis that Alexander the Great was the first Greek to propose this *homonoia*. His principal argument was based on the passage from Antiphon quoted above. The text in question was translated rather tendentiously by Merlan as 'It is a sign of ignorance or a dullard to base social distinction on high or low birth. For we all—Greeks and barbarians alike—have the same nature in every respect'.

---

[10] 'Even on our travels we can see how near and dear every man is to every other'. This is the experience of 'sight-seeing'. 'The bond of affection exists, as Aristotle says, also among animals: mankind as a single species distinguished from all others'; so rightly, H. C. Baldry, *The Unity of Mankind in Greek Thought* (1965), p. 90.

[11] See Diels, II, pp. 352-353, col. 2.

[12] *Greek Political Thought* (1951), p. 70.

[13] P. Merlan, *Alexander the Great or Antiphon the Sophist?*, CP (1950), p. 161 ff.

Here, the word βεβαρβαρώμεθα has been given a very special meaning that is not, in my view, covered by the fragment of Antiphon. A passage from Aristophanes' *Clouds* is often quoted in this context (*Nub.* 492) to show that this may be a case of a negative judgement on the foolishness of those who take the challenged view. There is, however, no basis for this in my opinion. The word βάρβαρος occurs in the passage in Aristophanes' *Clouds* with the meaning 'brutal' or 'rude'. It is possible that the word βάρβαρος, which originally only had a linguistic connotation (meaning, in other words, non Greek-speaking or only speaking Greek badly), was used by some Athenians, with their experiences in the war against Persia, in the sense of 'uncivilized' or 'violent'. This does not mean, however, that it ever had the significance of 'ignorant' or 'foolish'.

The rest of the passage from Antiphon is translated by Merlan as follows: 'This can be seen from the fact that the natural necessities (breathing, eating) are the same for all men and can be provided for by all men in the same way (we all breathe through the mouth and nose and eat with our hands) and in none of these respects (i.e., neither as to our needs nor as to our ways of satisfying them) is there a difference between Greek and barbarian'.

This paraphrase of course points in the direction of 'the ignorance or the dullard'. It is a free rendering to which little objection can be raised if it is borne in mind that there is no reference in these physical similarities to men being equal in all respects, with the result that it is possible to speak of one identical species of men. The text does not give us any reason to think this.

The text of Heraclitus (107 D) discussed by Merlan and Nenci [14] does not mean what Merlan thought it meant. I follow Diels, who translated the fragment as: 'Schlimme Zeugen sind den Menschen Augen und Ohren, sofern sie Barbarenseelen haben'. The important words in this statement that human eyes and ears are bad witnesses are the last ones: 'insofar as they have the souls of barbarians'. Diels' explanation of this is that they are souls which, like the barbarians, cannot properly understand the evidence of the senses. This is, in my view, the right translation and explanation and other scholars, who are mentioned by Diels, have also suggested the same.

It is also possible to raise objections to the translation 'for we all—Greeks and barbarians alike—have the same nature in every

---

[14] 'La filobarbaria di Ecateo nel giudizio di Eraclito', *Riv. Filol. Class.* 77 (1949), pp. 107-117, especially pp. 112-114.

respect'. In the first place, the Greek perfect is incorrectly translated and, in the second, there is no place for 'for' here. Two dis-
similar factors are joined together here by Antiphon. Tarn was right
in claiming that the author was alluding to 'physical similarity' in
this case. It is not proved that Merlan was right in what he adds to
this: 'While actually Antiphon does it only to prove by it the all-
inclusive human quality'. If this 'all-inclusiveness' implied a spiritual similarity in every respect, then we are bound to object to it.
Merlan went so far, however, as to regard the fragment as anti-
cipating 'fraternity and equality' and he pointed out that this did
not originate in religion: 'The idea of brotherhood of men originated
without the idea of the fatherhood of God as its counterpart. It
originated as a non-religious idea, as a protest against prejudice in
the name of nature—this nature being conceived, as far as we can
see, without any divine quality. The equality of biological functions
is the all-important factor in interhuman relations. It is obvious
that the correct interpretation of the Antiphon fragment is of great
interest'.[15] It is possible to agree with the last part of this statement,
without necessarily agreeing with the explanation given by Merlan.
There is a great deal of uncertainty as to whether his claim is justified. I doubt very much whether it is.[16]

In his inaugural address, entitled *Humanitas* (1946), J. H. Waszink correctly referred to a 'universal nature'. We have already
quoted the first line of his translation of the passage: 'In this we
are barbarized towards each other. By nature we are, after all, all
equipped in every respect and in the same way to be barbarians
and Greeks. We can perceive this in the needs that all men experience by nature. These can be satisfied in the same way by all
men and in this none of us occupies a separate place as a barbarian
or a Greek, for we all breathe the air through our mouths and noses
and we all eat with the help of our hands'. Waszink has added to
this: 'His contemporary Alcidamas (Aristotle, Rhet. Schol. 1. 13;
1373 B 18) said: "The Deity has left all men free; nature has made
no one a slave" '.

Waszink points out that the power of the polis was still too strong,

---

[15] Merlan, *op. cit.*, p. 164.
[16] M. Scheler, *Vom Umsturz der Werte* (2 vols., 1919), see especially I,
pp. 43-236, above all pp. 161-165; see also J. Mehwaldt, *Das Weltbürgertum
in der Antike, Die Antike* II (1926), pp. 177-189; W. Jaeger, *Paideia*, I (1939),
p. 323 ff. (Eng. ed. I³ (1946), p. 327).

but he also suggests that the concept of 'universal human nature' was also strong enough to emphasize ethical and social obligations with regard to one's fellow-men. *'Within the frontiers of the polis,* there was an increasing sense of solidarity towards man as a whole, in other words, with the weaknesses that are inherent to mankind'. In my view, the stress should fall on the words italicized in this quotation.

Not only Waszink referred to Alcidamas. Merlan also made the same quotation: 'All men have been placed in the world by God as free men and no one was by nature a slave'. Various commentators, including Sauppe (Or. Att. 2. 154), have, however, pointed out correctly that Alcidamas probably only meant the Greeks and not other people in this text.[17]

There would seem to be an irresistible tendency to see more in Antiphon and Alcidamas than their texts in fact contain. This is abundantly clear from E. R. Dodds,[18] who claims that Antiphon even went so far as to reject as superficial the distinction between Greeks and barbarians (p. 101). It is difficult to see how he could substantiate this claim that Alcidamas rejected this as *superficial.* Also Dodds claims to have discovered the first explicit condemnation of slavery in the ancient world; this, he says, is expressed in Alcidamas' words: 'The Deity has left all men free; nature has made no one a slave'.

Sauppe's question, however, is still relevant: did Alcidamas cross the frontier of what was human insofar as it was Greek? This can certainly be doubted very much. We may want the fifth-century Greeks to have rejected slavery as something that went against human nature and we may want very much to find only one representative of this attitude, but it has to be admitted that it is

---

[17] Even Aristotle's *Politics* (*Pol.* 3, 4 and 5) can be seen in a different light if Merlan's interpretation is considered—with certain necessary reservations. The passages in question are 1253 B 21-22 and 1255 B 4-5. (See E. Barker, *The Politics of Aristotle,* index under Slavery). According to Merlan, Antiphon was one of the participants in the debate on law versus nature. This can be compared with what Herodotus (3. 38) said about burial, although he took part in the controversy in a different way. In any case, it is true to say that he was originally a friend of the barbarians and had a deep conviction that the Greeks and the barbarians were equal. It is, however, difficult to say with certainty whether he believed in anything more than a physical equality. See Schmid and Stählin, *Geschichte der griechischen Literatur,* I, 2 (1934), p. 566, note 1; see also p. 579 ff.

[18] *The Ancient Concept of Progress and Other Essays on Greek Literature and Belief* (1973), p. 101.

very uncertain as to whether this mark of honour can really be attributed to them. Dodds is right to insist that none of the more important Greek philosophers ever dared to recognize this idea, but when he uses the word 'dared' here, we suspect that it has a modern nuance.

Euripides made several allusions to this question, as Guthrie has pointed out,[19] but he never made an explicit statement about it. I would not wish to conceal the fact that Guthrie did not ascribe a universal significance to Antiphon's text and that he correctly observed that he never made an explicit statement of the kind made by so many scholars (including, as we have seen, Dodds). On the other hand, however, it cannot be denied that Guthrie believed that Alcidamas' words could only have had a general meaning. Guthrie was well aware that these words occurred in a speech to the Spartans, urging them to set Messene free. The Messenians had for centuries been serfs of the Spartans. This might bear out what Sauppe claimed, namely that this is a statement that must be read in its historical context. Guthrie rejects this idea (p. 159), claiming that the words 'God', 'all' men' and 'nature' ensure the principle of universality. A choice clearly can and must be made here. I am bound to say that I am not convinced by Guthrie's argument. I am more convinced by his careful explanation of Antiphon's statement and his extremely clear exposition of the passages in Euripides. These are very damaging to the arguments of those who see the poet as one of the few who criticized slavery. These passages in Euripides do not, moreover, explicitly delineate the universally human characteristics that are undoubtedly present in Euripides' tragedies.

I do not wish to say that there could have been no antitheses in the views held by the sophists, since some of these thought that men were equal and others that men were not equal. Both Callicles and Hippias attacked the idea of equality. The first thought that men were by nature unequal. The second believed, unlike Callicles, who regarded the idea of equality as too wide, that it was too narrow (and possibly applied only to citizens). He wanted to extend the idea of equality and affinity to all men.

According to Jaeger,[20] the same ideas can be found in Antiphon. He wrote: 'With relentless logic Antiphon abolishes not only national

---

[19] W. K. Guthrie, *History of Greek Philosophy* III, pp. 157-159.
[20] W. Jaeger, *Paideia* I (1946), p. 326 ff.

differences, but social differences too'. As far as the second is concerned, it is quite clear that Antiphon rejected class distinctions
when he said: 'We have respect and veneration for men of high
birth and only for them: in that matter we behave like barbarians
towards our own people'.[21]

In my opinion, we have to be aware of the discriminating word
'barbarians', especially when something that is disapproved of is
termed 'behaving like barbarians'. It is difficult to maintain that
such a disapproving attitude should not be in our minds when we
read these words. This is one of my most important reasons for
doubting the validity of what I call the optimistic modern interpretation of the data of classical antiquity. We cannot discern with
certainty what the ancient author meant if all that we possess is a
small number of fragments. Let me, as an example, quote a text
from Hippias that is found in Plato's Protagoras (337 C):

Ὦ ἄνδρες, ἔφη, οἱ παρόντες, ἡγοῦμαι ἐγὼ ὑμᾶς συγγενεῖς τε καὶ
οἰκείους καὶ πολίτας ἅπαντας εἶναι—φύσει, οὐ νόμῳ· τὸ γὰρ ὅμοιον
τῷ ὁμοίῳ φύσει συγγενές ἐστιν, ὁ δὲ νόμος, τυραννος ὢν τῶν ἀνθρώπων,
πολλὰ παρὰ τὴν φύσιν βιάζεται.

('Gentlemen, he said, who are here present, I regard you all as
kinsmen and intimates and fellow-citizens by nature, not by law,
for like is akin to like by nature, whereas law, despot of mankind,
often constrains us against nature').[22]

Hippias' thoughts here probably went no further than the Greeks
themselves. It is also doubtful whether Hippias himself was really
the author of these words in the Protagoras. Diels doubted this,
since he included this fragment in the section entitled 'Imitation'.[23]

Some scholars have claimed that there is a development to be
found in Aristotle's attitude towards slavery. In my opinion, his
ideas about this phenomenon always remained the same. Who is
right here? On the one hand, Aristotle's work contains passages in
which kind things are said about barbarians and slaves. On the
other hand, there are also passages in which he clearly regards the
slave as a piece of furniture or a tool—the traditional image, in other
words.

---

[21] See above, p. 64 and note 9.
[22] This translation is taken from L.C.L.
[23] *Op. cit.*, p. 333.

How can this be explained? In the following way, I think. Aristotle upholds the traditional image of the barbarian as a slave by nature without any difficulty, but is able to defend a different view of barbarian states. In the first case, barbarians form the social infrastructure, in the second they form the social suprastructure. In the second case, it is of no importance at all if the people are Greeks or barbarians, that is, people who do not know Greek. It is possible to deal with the government of a non-Greek state, but when the Greek comes to the slave market to buy slaves, he is not dealing with the state to which the unfortunate slaves belong. He is acting as an individual, dealing with individuals. We should not forget that international law, which hardly exists even nowadays, did not exist at all in classical antiquity.[24]

I am bound to conclude from these passages that love of one's fellow-men in the form of a universal love of mankind cannot be found in any of the texts. If the whole problem of slavery is taken into account in the philosophical question of the antithesis between nature (*phusis*) and law (*nomos*), it has to be recognized that the affective element, in which two kinds of men, the free man and the slave, are regarded as equal, is not discussed at all. The only equality that was thought to exist was a natural or physical equality, not based on any law. This accounts therefore for the words: 'All men have been placed in the world by God as free men and no one was by nature a slave'. It would be very wrong to think that questions of law or fairness were in any way involved here. Alcidamas comes close here to what we would now call a universal love of mankind, but in my opinion he is simply pleading for a recognition of the fact that all men look the same by nature and share the same fate and that slavery did not come about by nature, but by *nomos*. He is not trying to disqualify slavery. This is something that even those who are inclined to derive everything from the Greeks must not claim.

Digression

Very many mistakes are made in our attempts to understand the ethics of the ancient world. As we have already seen, it is common to assume, on the basis of a few fragmentary texts, an attitude of disapproval towards slavery among the Greeks. It is wrong to read

---

[24] For Aristotle, see E. Badian, *Historia* VII (1958), p. 440; the author criticizes Tarn in a separate section entitled 'Aristotle and the Barbarians'.

a modern attitude into the ethics of the Greeks. This results in a distortion of the image of antiquity. Arguments based on human emotions, so easily accepted by modern man, made little or no appeal in the ancient world. The greatest similarity can be found in time and space between the various populations of our planet in the almost biological contact between man and woman, and parents and children. With this, however, all similarity often ceases.

The same applies, in the question of ethics, to a value-judgement that is often made with regard to the popular ethical concept that is usually expressed in the 'golden rule': 'treat others as you would like them to treat you'. This is not a very high-minded statement that is always made in the conviction that mankind must form a unity. It is none the less a decent principle ('take care not to harm your neighbour so that your neighbour will not harm you') and it can form an excellent basis for human relationships.

My slight objection to Dihle's introduction to the history of moral thought in classical antiquity and the early Christian period,[25] which is in many ways so admirable, is that the author makes a distinction between philosophical ethics and what he calls *Vulgär-ethik*. This latter concept can easily lead to an understanding of ethics as a development from the past to the present. In other words, it encourages the idea that ethics were in the earlier period influenced by selfish and irritating ideas of retribution, but that they developed later into a philosophy, according to which man was to love his enemies and those who expressed their hatred of him. To insist on this development and to apply this value-judgement and regard it as historically correct is to distort the ancient concept of ethics. It is, moreover, clear that Dihle did not attribute a high ethical value to this golden rule of retribution.

The art historian H. van de Waal argued in favour of a different understanding of the ethical concept of mutual retribution. In one of his essays,[26] he told the story of the Rabbi Hillel. This story from the Talmud was quoted with evident approval by Van de Waal, who stressed that Hillel was anxious to find out what was the essence of moral responsibility. It was, the Rabbi thought, the same golden rule passed on by Tobit to his son Tobias: 'treat others as you would like them to treat you'. To this, Hillel added: 'This is the

---

[25] A. Dihle, *Die Goldene Regel*, Göttingen (1962).
[26] *De Gids* 119 (1956), pp. 40-44; included in *Steps towards Rembrandt*, Amsterdam (1974), p. 9.

whole teaching. All the rest is commentary. Go and teach!'

What is remarkable is that Van de Waal wrote this in 1956 and that Dihle's book was published in 1962. It is clear, however, that the latter had not read Van de Waal's essay. Yet he began his book with the same story and commented that this golden rule was clearly held in great esteem in the later Jewish world. Dihle went on to point out that the commandment in Lev. 19. 18, that man should love his neighbour as himself, occurred again in the gospel (Matt. 5. 43) and a hundred years later in the teaching of Rabbi Akiba—and that both marked a great advance in human ethics. It was clear, Dihle insisted, that the leaders of society regarded this golden rule as one of the corner-stones of a really good human society. They could, after all, hardly be blamed for that.

What is really remarkable, however, is Dihle's repeated insistence in his book on the symbiosis formed by philosophical ethics and *Vulgär-ethik*. Both forms of morality, in other words, belonged to lived and to preached morality. The golden rule was the corner-stone of society. It was also imparted to young children. There is an opposition between the views of Van de Waal and Dihle, but it is not important for our argument. The interesting point for us is that both belong to lived and to preached morality. They show that a division cannot be made, either in literature or in history, between lived and preached morality. This opposition was one of the corner-stones of Bolkestein's edifice, but in practice there is little that the historian can do with it.[27] Let us look once again at Bolkestein's antithesis in connection with our present question, the love of one's neighbour in classical antiquity.

Preached morality is taught in the so-called Aristotelian and Peripatetic excerpts in Stobaeus. We have no data concerning the universal love of mankind in the early period of the city-state. According to preached morality, all men had the same origin. This thesis stands apart from such ideas as φιλία (which is to some extent a cosmological concept) and *caritas generis humani*. In much modern research they are connected and interpreted as referring to a consciousness of community. This is an excellent idea so long as it is borne in mind that no deep moral conviction is necessarily reflected in this consciousness. Indeed, it is usually absent from it. All that may be present are the feelings that we all have in common of

---

[27] This has been pointed out previously in this book, p. 2 ff.

belonging together, and of being dependent on one another through our own behaviour.

Theophrastus' περὶ εὐσεβείας (Bernays 81. 294 and 97. 9) yields the following: 'With regard to men, we have a relationship; that is, the Greek with the Greek and the barbarian with the barbarian, and we say that all men are related or of the same race for one of two reasons—either because they have the same ancestors or because they are alike in nourishment and habits and are of the same blood'. What we have in this quotation is clearly a cool statement. There is no word of love of the whole of mankind. Eratosthenes and Plutarch both provide a similar view of human unity. It could be called a policy of merger.[28]

As far as Aristotle and the barbarians are concerned, following Badian's example in the article mentioned above, this can be added to what we have already stated: Although part of the *Politics* was written after Alexander's accession, we can find no influence of the King's own ideas (whatever they may have been) on Aristotle's philosophy.[29] The development of Aristotle's view is, as we have already pointed out, very difficult to verify. I believe that his view was the traditional one, with very little change. Our empirical understanding of Aristotle's work is often such as to make it a grandiose accumulation of the achievements of his Greek ancestors which he systematized. His genius was expressed in the structure that he created out of this mass of material. Plutarch was clearly much more moderate in his judgement of Alexander's past than many of his contemporaries, but even he did not regard the policy of merger practised by the king of the Macedonians as a moral task, but purely as a practical one.

A fragment preserved in the work of Porphyry (3. 220. 16-18) was taken over from Theophrastus by Stoic philosophers. This has been demonstrated by Bernays.[30] Text and translation follow here.

---

[28] See Plut. Mor. 329C.

[29] Cf. Badian, *op. cit.*, p. 303. See p. 66 above.

[30] J. Bernays, *Theophrasts Schrift über Frömmigkeit*, Berlin (1866), p. 96. This is one of the masterpieces of a great scholar who receives at last the attention he deserves in many ways. See A. D. Momigliano, *Jacob Bernays, Mededelingen der Kon. Nederlandse Akademie van Wetenschappen, Afd. Letterkunde*, Nieuwe Reeks, Deel 32, Nº. 5 (1969) pp. 151-178 (= *Quinto Contributo alla storia degli studi classici e del mondo antico*, Roma (1975), p. 127-158, with extended bibliography).

τοὺς ἐκ τῶν αὐτῶν γεννηθέντας, λέγω δὲ πατρὸς καὶ μητρός, οἰκείους
εἶναι φύσει φαμὲν ἀλλήλων καὶ τοίνυν καὶ τοὺς ἀπὸ τῶν αὐτῶν προ-
πατόρων σπαρέντας οἰκείους ἀλλήλων εἶναι νομίζομεν, καὶ μέντοι καὶ
τοὺς ἑαυτῶν πολίτας τῷ τῆς τε γῆς καὶ τῆς πρὸς ἀλλήλους ὁμιλίας
κοινωνεῖν. Οὐ γὰρ ἐκ τῶν αὐτῶν ἔτι ποτε ἢ ἀπὸ τῶν αὐτῶν τοιούτους
ἀλλήλοις φύντας οἰκείους αὐτοῖς εἶναι κρίνομεν, εἰ μὴ ἄρα τινὲς τῶν
πρώτων αὐτοῖς προγόνων οἱ αὐτοὶ τοῦ γένους ἀρχηγοὶ πεφύκασιν. . . .
οὕτως δὲ καὶ τοὺς πάντας ἀνθρώπους ἀλλήλοις τίθεμεν συγγενεῖς καὶ
μὴν καὶ πᾶσι τοῖς ζῴοις· αἱ γὰρ τῶν σωμάτων ἀρχαὶ πεφύκασιν αἱ
αὐταί. λέγω δὲ οὐκ ἐπὶ τὰ στοιχεῖα ἀναφέρων τὰ πρῶτα ἐκ τούτων μὲν
γὰρ καὶ τὰ φυτά. ἀλλ᾽ οἷον δέρμα, σάρκας καὶ τὸ τῶν ὑγρῶν τοῖς ζῴοις
σύμφυτον γένος· πολὺ δὲ μᾶλλον τῷ τὰς ἐν αὐτοῖς ψυχὰς ἀδιαφόρους
πεφυκέναι, λέγω δὴ ταῖς ἐπιθυμίαις καὶ ταῖς ὀργαῖς, ἔτι δὲ τοῖς λογισ-
μοῖς καὶ μάλιστα πάντων ταῖς αἰσθήσεσιν. ἀλλ᾽ ὥσπερ τὰ σώματα,
οὕτω καὶ τὰς ψυχὰς τὰ μὲν ἀπηκριβωμένας ἔχει τῶν ζῴων, τὰ δὲ
ἧττον τοιαύτας, πᾶσί γε μὴν αὐτοῖς αἱ αὐταὶ πεφύκασιν ἀρχαί. δηλοῖ
δὲ ἡ τῶν παθῶν οἰκειότης.

'We call related to each other by nature first, those who have the same progenitors, that is the same father and mother. We also regard those who are descended from the same ancestors as related to each other. We also think of our own fellow-citizens as related, because they inhabit the same country and form a society with each other. In the case of the latter, we do not apply any criterion as (we do for those) who are related, because they are descended from the same, apart from the fact that their very first ancestors were the same (people) as the ancestors of the race or that they were descended from the same.

'We are therefore, I believe, speaking now of a mutual relationship of Greeks with Greeks and barbarians with barbarians and of all men, for one of the following two reasons: either because they have the same ancestors or because they share the same food, disposition, and race.

'We would therefore suggest that all people are related both with each other and with all living beings (= animals). For the fundamental parts of the body are the same.

'(I maintain, however, that this cannot apply to the first elements, since the plants also consist of these). But (I am referring to) skin, flesh and the fluids that are peculiar to all living beings.

'Even more striking, however, are the similarities present in the souls that live in them: similarities in desires and impulses to anger, also in rational reactions and above all in perceptions.

'As matters stand with regard to bodies, however, some living beings have perfect souls, whereas others have souls that are less perfect' (literally, 'less of the same nature'), 'but all have the same fundamental parts. The relationship' (Nauck's 'homogeneity' is, in my opinion, better) 'of the emotions proves (this)'.[31]

Dirlmeier has examined Theophrastus' teaching in depth.[32] He believed that there was a development in the idea of community and love of all mankind from the time of the sophists, in other words, from Antiphon onwards. In a note, however, he contradicted what he was claiming in the text: 'All the elements of the natural foundation of morality are peripatetic or rather Theophrastic'. This does not apply to the element of solidarity with one's neighbour or the sense of community. For these two essential ideas it is necessary to go further back into the past, as Dirlmeier himself asserts. His conclusion—'that Theophrastus was the creator of the first Oikeiosis doctrine'—can be accepted (p. 75). He also insisted that the doctrine of morality had a natural or biological basis in Theophrastus (pp. 90-91). In my opinion, however, this is turning things on their head. The biological foundation had always been present in the Greek mind from the very beginning in its attitude both to slavery and to barbarians. Antiphon and others believed that, from the biological point of view, all men were by nature equal, but they never had a doctrine of *morality* and such a doctrine could hardly have existed without a basis of biological observation. For centuries, it was only this biological foundation that claimed all attention. In this situation, however, Theophrastus' statement is so important that I have given it in full with a translation. The whole passage in which this text occurs is one in which Theophrastus is expressing his disapproval of blood sacrifices. He was opposed to the sacrifice of animals, but not to the killing of harmful beasts, which he compared to the putting to death of criminals. The latter action he accepted as a matter of course, even though these were, for the

---

[31] Since the appearance of Bernays' incomparably good edition, this fragment (Porphyry 3; Nauck, pp. 220-221) has been republished and translated by W. Pötscher: *Theophrastos*' Περὶ εὐσεβείας (Greek text with translation and commentary, but no commentary on this passage), *Philosophia Antiqua* XI (1964), Fr 20, pp. 182-184.

[32] F. Dirlmeier, *Die Oikeiosis-Lehre Theophrasts*, Philol., Suppl. III, 1, p. 73, note 1.

reasons given, our fellow-men. Theophrastus probably went so far that the dividing line between men and animals ceased to exist. It was not until Antiochus' system (Antiochus of Ascalon was Cicero's teacher) that the sharpness of the οἰκειότης became blunter and both Antiochus and the Stoics made a clear dividing line between men and animals. The idea of οἰκειότης (= *caritas generis humani*) then became a firm basis for ethical teaching.[33]

Wider Concentric Circles

It is possible to show that a Greek concept such as φιλία developed in its meaning. In Aristotle, it still had a very limited meaning. It was not until the time of the Peripatetic School, after Aristotle himself, that the idea of *philia* included the whole of mankind. The spread of this concept to cover a wider field was due to Theophrastus. We can leave aside here the question as to whether he linked his ideas to those of Aristotle or whether he was solely responsible for the extension in meaning of the concept of *philia*. All that we can say with certainty is that there was a link later between Theophrastus and the Stoics.[34]

It is important to bear Theophrastus in mind when considering Cicero, since the latter, who exerted a greater influence in this question on Roman thought than in a later period, when Rome's mood was largely anti-Ciceronian, was always the source of knowledge about Theophrastus. The most important passage in Cicero that we have to consider here is in his treatise *De finibus bonorum et malorum* (III. 62, 63), in which he argues that the love of children and parents exists by nature, in other words, φύσει. This idea is essential to any *communis humani generis societas* in Cicero's view.

Wider concentric circles are also discussed by Cicero in *De Fin.* V. 23, 65,[35] in which he speaks about *philanthropia*. Bolkestein, who partly quoted this text, added the following statement by Cicero. I cite it here: 'Nihil est tam illustre nec quod latius pateat quam coniunctio inter homines hominum et quasi quaedam societas et communicatio utilitatem et ipsa caritas generis humani (i.e. φιλαν-

---

[33] Bernays, *op. cit.*, p. 102.

[34] See M. Pohlenz, *Die Stoa* II, p. 65. See also Zeno, *SVF* III. 340-348, also III. 314; Stob. II. 75, 8. 109, 17 W: universal mankind. For the Stoics, the result of this was that moral demands were made; these were expressed by Seneca, Epictetus, Dio of Prusa and Philo.

[35] See Bolkestein, *op. cit.*, pp. 125-126, where this text is quoted in part. See p. 79 note 36 (below).

θρωπία)'. The following is particularly important in our context: 'Quae nata a primo satu quod a procreatoribus nati diliguntur et tota domus coniugio et stirpe coniungitur, serpit sensim foras, cognationibus primum, tum affinitatibus, deinde amicitiis, post vicinitatibus, tum civibus et iis, qui publice socii et amici sunt, *deinde totius complexu gentis humanae*'.[36]

This text has given rise to a certain amount of controversy among scholars about the origin of the idea of the *universal* human community;[37] it has been argued that this community did not originate with Christianity, but had been suggested long before, in pagan antiquity. It is, however, important to comment on this. This *societas generis humani* or unity of the human race, was a community of interests which, at least *initially*, had little or nothing of idealism in it. It did not contain any suggestion of an inner unity of the human race, if, by inner unity, a universal love of all mankind and a true brotherhood of man is meant. The word *phratria* is found in many ancient civilizations (in the language of the people concerned). It is clear that *phratria* is connected with 'brother', but the underlying thought in this case was certainly not the state of being brothers or sisters in a family, but rather the same state in a broader context, which may originally have been based on the family, but eventually acquired a much more universal significance.

The same undoubtedly happened in the case of the idea of *societas* in the ancient world. We need not discuss here whether there was initially ever a deeper foundation to this idea, but what is, in my opinion, certain is that there never was any question of an inner unity or emotional solidarity. Although it has frequently been forgotten, what Gordon Childe said about people in community should, in fact, never be forgotten. What he said was that if people speak about the baker, what they mean is the man who is responsible for

---

[36] Cicero, *De Fin.* V. 23, 65: '(In the whole moral sphere) there is nothing more glorious nor of wider range than the solidarity of mankind, that species of alliance and partnership of interests and that actual affection which exists between man and man, which, coming into existence immediately upon our birth, owing to the fact that children are loved by their parents and the family as a whole is bound together by the ties of marriage and parenthood, gradually spreads its influence beyond the home, first by blood relationships, then by connections through marriage, later by friendships, afterwards by bonds of neighbourhood; then to fellow-citizens and political allies and friends and lastly by embracing the whole of the human race' (translated by H. Rackham, LCL). See also *De Fin.* III. 19, 63.

[37] Bolkestein, *op. cit.*, p. 126, note 1.

providing bread in the neighbourhood. This is the primary meaning. If he is also a member of the same local church or other ideal community is secondary. The baker is there to provide bread.

Even if one is not a historical materialist, as Childe was, it is possible to agree with this idea. It is sober and is based on life together in society, including society in the ancient world. There is, then, no question of a universal love of all mankind in the writings of Cicero, who, as an ex-consul and senator would not have known what this concept meant. In *De Fin.* V. 66, he wrote about what we would now call an inherent 'public spirit' and what the Greeks called 'politics'.

I do not think that φιλία had very much to do with an inner bond of community or neighbourliness. The latter was far too ideal and too firmly based on an obvious tendency to trace all kinds of ideas which arose at a later period and were stimulated by Christianity in pagan antiquity. Although I agree that the division between the pagan world and Christianity should not be exaggerated, I recognize that there are certain fundamental differences between them. It is ultimately not to the advantage of classical antiquity in comparison with the rest of the ancient world if everything that emerged later is claimed for Greece and Rome. This attitude is summed up in the striking, but romantic and unhistorical statement of Sir Henry Sumner Maine, who said: 'Except the brute forces of nature nothing moves in the world which is not Greek in its origin'.

What, then, is Cicero's original contribution? I believe that Cicero was, in his *De finibus bonorum et malorum*, looking for a connection with the primary need of human beings to procreate and their natural instinct to protect their young and that he was demonstrating that the natural love that man felt for his descendants was transformed into a natural love for his fellow-men. The theory that the affection that man feels for all members of the human race is an extension of the love that he feels for his family cannot be found in the writings of the earlier philosophers that have come down to us, with the possible exception of Theophrastus.[38] It is, however,

---

[38] See M. E. Reesor, *The Political Theory of the Old and Middle Stoa*, New York (1951), p. 51, whose conclusion is summarized above. See also H. F. Reijnders, *Societas Generis Humani bij Cicero*, Dissertation at Utrecht University (1954), discussed by G. J. D. Aalders, *Mnem.* IV (1956), pp. 81-82. See also Appendix below, pp. 89-92.

possible that Theophrastus had already prompted Cicero's idea here by comparing the bond of affection existing among all the members of the human race with the love felt by man for his family.[39]

As we have already seen, this idea of human solidarity and the extent to which it may have existed in the classical Greek period (the fifth and fourth centuries B.C.) has been frequently debated in recent years, but I believe that the results of this discussion should be viewed with scepticism. This scepticism is also necessary with regard to the existence of this idea in later centuries. Mühl, for instance, has spoken of a product of abstraction and of Stoic intellectualism,[40] even though, in later practice, the influence was immense. I also doubt very much whether it is true that the theory of a universal love of humanity resulted in practice in an improvement of the position of slaves. It was precisely in the heyday of the Polis and during the early Hellenistic period that, in certain places at least, slaves enjoyed a better position than ever before. The Roman conquests gave rise to a much worse situation for slaves, dominated by attitudes like those of the Carthaginian planters in Sicily. It may be true that the distinctions between Greeks and the barbarians were gradually reduced by this theory, but I cannot accept that it removed one of the bases of Greek contempt for slaves or that it resulted in slaves being better treated. It is indeed true to say that slaves were treated in a way that we would regard as much more shocking during the Roman period than they had been before.[41]

---

[39] Stobaeus, *Eclogae* II (pp. 118. 5 to 147. 25 W) forms the basis of our knowledge of Theophrastus. See H. von Arnim, *Arius Didymus' Abriss der peripatetischen Ethik*, *Sitz.-Ber. Akad. Wiss.*, Vienna 204 (1926), p. 1 ff; M. Schäfer, *Ein frühmittelstoisches System der Ethik bei Cicero*, Munich (1934). The important passages in Stobaeus' Eclogues are 120. 1 ff; 121. 22; 125. 21 ff; 127. 3 ff; 143. 11-6; 147. 7; see also 118. 2.

[40] M. Mühl, *Die antike Menschheitsidee*, Leipzig (1928), see quotation on p. 51: der Stoiker predigt die allgemeine Menschenliebe, aber sie vermag im Frost des Intellektualismus nicht Blüt' und Frucht zu tragen; Bolkestein, *op. cit.*, p. 126, note 2, for a different view.

[41] For this treatment, see especially Vogt, *Ancient Slavery and the Ideal of Man*, Oxford (1975); this book is a translation of the author's *Sklaverei und Humanität* (1960; 2nd edn. 1972). It is also advisable to consult the discussion of this book by M. I. Finley in the *Times Literary Supplement*, 14 November 1975. See also Westermann, *RE*, Suppl. 6. Finally, M. I. Finley has also written well on this question and has provided a summary of his earlier admirable and excellent works in this sphere in his book *The Ancient Economy* (1973). See also below, p. 205 ff. 'Views and Controversies' have been edited by Finley in *Slavery in Classical Antiquity*, Cambridge 1960. See notes on p. 239 f. (below), addendum.

Anything that can be said about the treatment of slaves has always to be linked with the time and place—there was no universal attitude towards this question in ancient Greece. It is, of course, always possible to quote Pseudo-Xenophon Aθπ 1. 10 and Dem. 9. 3, but these refer to Athens at a particular period. The first text, moreover, reflects the attitude of an author who chose to emphasize equality in order to show how badly the Athenians behaved towards their citizens, with the result that even slaves enjoyed certain rights. He also stressed the point that the slaves in Athens had a very good life. This suited his case quite well and he therefore exaggerated to make his point. The contrast between this and the arbitrary and completely lawless treatment of the helots in Sparta has also to be borne in mind if we are to draw attention to a totally different attitude that existed at the same time in the Greek world. All that can be said, then, is that our knowledge is local and confined to a limited period. We know practically nothing about this question in the other city-states.[42]

We may conclude this section by saying that the dependence of the slave can be contrasted more effectively with the situation of the rich non-worker than with that of the greater group of small independent people. It should not be forgotten, however, that it was members of the first of these two groups of people who wrote about this question, they were the profiteers. This is important to remember in any evaluation of Ps.-Xenophon and others.

Greece as opposed to Rome

As long as it remained a farming community, Rome's attitude towards slaves continued to be rather better than that of Greece. In Roman society, in which work on the land was carried out by the owners of small plots together with their slaves, there was a basically patriarchal relationship between masters and slaves. There were also relatively few Roman slaves. The care of slaves was determined by laws and, as they were a capital investment, they were used sparingly. Generally speaking, they were regarded as cattle and most farmers treat their cows, sheep, and goats well because they are his capital. It can be said therefore without sentimentality

---

[42] I agree here with what Westermann said in the above-mentioned article: 'The explanation for this is that slaves were more often seen as a capital investment in Athens—they lived in a relationship of semi-dependence as the μισθοφοροῦντα σώματα—than as living in a situation of greater philanthropy attributed to the Athenians (see Daremb. Saglio, IV 1261)'.

that the situation was apparently favourable to slavery in the agrarian society of Italy where farming was operated on relatively small plots of land. On the other hand, however, it cannot be denied that the situation became much worse for subordinates in general and slaves in particular, although it would be wrong to attribute this deterioration entirely to Roman imperialism. It should be borne in mind that slaves were sometimes trained in trades which were not commonly practised, such as the working of jewels or precious stones and even teaching. It is not difficult to imagine that slaves with special skills were better off than those slaves who are often called 'chattel slaves'. It is true to say that the unskilled slaves were in general used for the lowest forms of work, both in Greece and in Rome. Despite its high level of civilization, Athens was no exception. The slaves employed in the silver mines at Laurium are a good example of this exploitation of slaves. Generally speaking, the heavy and painful work of excavating or mining for mineral wealth or precious metals was almost always carried out by those at the lowest level of society. In this respect, Greece and Rome were no different from most other societies.[43]

A Fundamental Principle

What is the explanation of these strict relationships in ancient society and these rigid differences between higher and lower levels? Even though it is always possible to find exceptions in men of a higher status who could get on well with those of lower status and vice versa, these differences undoubtedly existed to a marked extent. I think that the basis for this situation is to be found in the administration of justice. Both in Greek and in Roman legal procedure, there is a conscious division between classes, the lower classes being punished more severely than the upper.[44]

---

[43] The reader should consult recent bibliographies for books and articles on this question. M. I. Finley, op. cit., has provided a very good bibliography. This author is, of course, one of the leading experts in this field.

[44] For Rome, see P. Garnsey, Social Status and Legal Privilege in the Roman Empire, Oxford (1974). In this book, the author shows the influence that accompanied membership of a higher social group in the period in question. It has to be remembered, however, that what Garnsey discusses in this book applies not only to the Roman Empire, but also to the republic and the Greek city-states (although to a lesser degree). Recent studies on social mobility, such as that by M. K. Hopkins, have indicated that, although it was not extensive, it cannot be entirely ignored. A good article on this question has been published by H. W. Pleket in TvG 84 (1971), pp. 215-251.

The most important basis for the differences in social attitudes, in my opinion, is to be found in what was thought and expected of the gods in antiquity. The gods acted according to their sovereign will and men had little to say about it. This teaching is found in many of the Greek tragedies and is especially noticeable in Sophocles' *Ajax* and *Oedipus*. At the beginning of the *Ajax*, the goddess Athena declares that she is far superior to the mortal Ajax in power and intends to play a game with him. This is a variety of religious experience that strikes us as cruel and that we cannot accept. The Greeks accepted it, however, and Sophocles was more popular than any other Greek tragedian. In the case of Oedipus, we can, of course, always argue that he did not know that it had been predicted before he was born that he would kill his father and marry his mother.

This is, of course, one of the most atrocious dilemmas in which a man can be placed. Many scholars have tried to gloss over this and give it an acceptable appearance by calling it a case of 'tragic guilt'. By this, they mean that a man who is placed in a given situation will behave like a machine and not be able to exercise his will. In this way, they have made Oedipus' existential problem into a philosophical discussion about the determination of human fate and free will.

This is clearly a regrettable narrowing down of what the author intended to say. He was presenting the sovereign action of the gods which was for him supra-ethical and which man, as a believer, had to obey without being able to hold the gods to account. Man had to bow and obey. This was Oedipus' attitude and, although he could do nothing to change the course of his life and did not know what was in store for him, he none the less felt guilty.

The best modern parallel with the case of Oedipus is, I think, that of a driver who is driving carefully, but runs over and kills a child who suddenly crosses the road in front of his car. No one would accuse him and everyone would, on the contrary, acquit him of any guilt, because 'he could do nothing about it'. Despite this, however, the driver in question may well have the feeling that he was guilty until the day he dies. Of course, it is possible that it may be thought that guilt has been overcome in such a case because there is no legal guilt, but the driver who has killed the child— although he was not guilty from the legal point of view—may still continue to feel guilty or uneasy because of the tragedy that he has caused.

This case can be applied to Greek antiquity, although I am bound to point out at once that many modern people cannot accept it. Let me quote the opinion of an Englishman concerning the fate of Oedipus.[45] 'The rigid and gloomy determinism of the Greeks destroys, for me at least, the tragic values of the Oedipus saga. When the broken, blinded old man cries "I had no choice" he speaks full truth and so betrays the weakness of the whole conception . . . The doomed slaves of destiny in the Greek legends are helpless puppets of gods who are no better than sadistic torturers. Their inescapable sufferings can yield plenty of misery, but no tragic conflict can emerge from their impotence. Yet, because Greek tragedy was part of a religious ritual and far closer to a church service than to our box-office theatre, the well behaved dramatists had to maintain that these gross injustices were all divinely right and proper. Says the chorus: "Phoebus our Lord, be this according to thy will". Sophocles was no probing philosopher and certainly no rebel. He did a conservative's noble best for the repulsive, and even absurd, myth. (Was Oedipus, Voltaire asked, a lunatic that he had made no searching inquiries before marrying his mother?) It remained for the much more sensitive and intelligent Euripides to ask a few questions of this outrageous theology and to do that so cunningly that he could fit his implicit rationalism into the framework of the religious festivals that brought the drama into being. But that sort of mind pleases only the few. It was Sophocles who had honour and prizes showered on him'.

The discussion about these basic questions of human existence can, of course, go on for ever. Certain individual faults in the anonymous argument can be indicated without difficulty, but the central thesis is clear. It is that the writer is sincere and cannot accept the supra-ethical aspect of Greek religion.[46] Man's understanding of the gods as a creature enabled him in ancient Greece to accept everything from the deity, even if he did not comprehend it. He did not speak of the arbitrariness of the deity, but only of the fact that the god was superior to him and, because he was immortal, knew better than he did what was good for him. It has to be admitted, however, that J. C. Opstelten was right when he

---

[45] The passage is taken from a newspaper which I cannot trace because the clipping was undated.

[46] W. B. Kristensen, *Het boven-ethische in de godsdienst,* in the collection *Symbool en werkelijkheid,* Arnhem 1954, pp. 36-48.

6

maintained that the dramatist did not offer any comfort to man in his suffering.[47] At the same time, it is clear that, although suffering is presented in a very impressive way in Greek drama, it does not contain any moral teaching. It is this that strikes modern man as unacceptable. Many religious groups test the authenticity of faith against the moral consequences of religious action in everyday life and it is therefore very difficult for modern man to grasp the Greek concept. That was that all men were subject to a divine plan—the man who was guided by the deity, the man who lived apart from his fellow-men, the contemplative, the rascal, the privileged and the underprivileged, the one who prospered and the one who always failed. The Greek had no knowledge at all of social justice as a guide-line for the action of the gods.

It is clear from a recent study by J. P. Poe that modern philological research cannot dissociate itself from Sophocles' background.[48] It is also clear that a new way of thinking is introduced by describing Sophocles' attitude towards the gods and their relationship with men as 'grotesque'. I think that the author is following the wrong course here and also in his description of Sophocles' background—in other words, his 'philosophy'—as not monolithic, but as revealing different tendencies. I believe that he was certainly not monolithic, but that he presented one fundamental idea in the whole of his work, which was, moreover, not a popular idea. His attitude towards life, which emerges from all his dramas, can be summarized in the words 'immortal' and 'mortal', by which he meant that the immortal gods were completely sovereign and mortal man was completely unimportant. This conviction also emerges from the Philoctetes, which Poe obviously finds difficult. Poe takes about fifty pages of his book to provide us with the most modern theories about this matter. It is disconcerting to note how many scholars believe that their own problem can be found in Sophocles, but it is equally disturbing to observe how blind they are to the primary religious experience which made the Greek author write as he in fact wrote.

In observing that Philoctetes is treated in the play as a victim, Poe is clearly introducing an idea that is not in accord with the

[47] J. C. Opstelten, *Sophocles en het Grieksche pessimisme*, Leiden (1945), p. 189.
[48] J. P. Poe, *Heroism and Divine Justice in Sophocles' Philoctetes*, Leiden (1974).

religious attitude of the author. This is a conclusion drawn by a modern scholar. It may be interesting, but it has little to do with the real interpretation of the fate that befalls this sympathetic hero, a man whose moral behaviour leaves little or nothing to be desired and who, at the end of the drama, experiences a divine dénouement which must surely be regarded as satisfactory, even by the most strict moralist, who would call the gods to order if their behaviour was not in accordance with human morality.

Everyone tends to speak in accordance with the extent of his own knowledge and everyone is similarly influenced by the ideas of the period in which he is living. Poe is conscious of the meaninglessness of the events and the unimportance of the human behaviour in Sophocles' drama. He is, of course, correct in this. But when he goes on to make a comparison between the Philoctetes and the novels of Kafka and the comedy of the absurd, which are rooted in twentieth century existentialism, he is, I believe, on the wrong track.[49] This kind of comparison is dangerous. The gods are not central either in the novels of Kafka or in the comedy of the absurd. In Sophocles, however, the gods are most emphatically central. We must therefore take Sophocles at his word. We do not have to try to find a way out of his difficulties by speaking about universally human behaviour, the meaningless of man's existence, the inexplicable quality of man's activities and above all the unaccountability of human suffering. Philoctetes' acquiescence was not philosophically based. It was an acceptance of what was bound to happen to him because he knew that he was mortal. Sophocles found that many Greeks were ready to follow him in this and he was popular in the Greek world because of this attitude towards the gods and men. His fellow Greeks were moved by his presentation of the problem and they responded positively and with full consent, in striking contrast to many modern commentators, who seldom do this. Philoctetes' complaint that the gods apparently care for the wicked and neglect the just is in accordance with the experience of believers throughout the ages, who are 'envious of the arrogant', seeing 'the prosperity of the wicked' (Ps 73. 3).

I know, of course, that, in quoting from the Old Testament, I shall be accused of confusing two different spheres of culture and two different religions. I shall, however, have to ignore this objec-

---

[49] J. P. Poe, *op. cit.*, p. 39.

tion, because I believe, with William James and others that, although religious experiences may show a remarkable multiplicity among different peoples, they may also be very much in accord with each other. It would, of course, be far too rough and ready to assume a complete identity, but there are certainly similarities in human religious experiences and the variants that occur in them and this is, I think, an example of such a similarity. Both the Jew and the Greek thought of themselves as creatures and therefore as nothing in the presence of God or the gods and this is an essential experience that occurs in many religions. It forms part both of the Jewish and of the Greek religion.

We may go further and say that it would be good if the deplorable division that has been made in the name of science between the two religions were seen in a different light. It would also be good to find what unites rather than what divides them. That this has not been done is the fault of two hundred years of philological and historical research into Greek culture and literature. The division between the Jews and the Greeks has been emphasized in an artificial way again and again. In this context, it is remarkable that a completely secularized world of scholarship has been guided by Tertullian! Very little attention has been paid to other voices in the ancient world, beginning with Paul himself in the first chapter of his letter to the Romans. Paul speaks there of a common grace uniting the Jews on the one hand and the gentiles on the other in the same Christian faith in accordance with their shared understanding of God.

What we have here, then, is a case of one believer meeting a colleague who believes in another religion and agreeing with him in certain essential points, since, however different the formulations may be, there is a similarity in experience and this is recognized. Philoctetes' objections to the treatment that he receives are moral objections. The change that he suddenly proposes is not explained, but it certainly comes from him. All scholars have experienced difficulties with this text. This is, unfortunately, the fault of the scholars themselves, since they are troubled by a way of life that is not their own and for that reason unacceptable to them. Is it really possible for what is unacceptable to the person himself to be given a place in historical research? Surely it is not very important whether modern man can accept certain ancient attitudes or not. This is all the more relevant when the texts themselves are quite clear. What is important in this context is that the scholar should be honest in his attitude towards the ancient source and towards the man who is expressing himself in that source and that an attempt should be made not to block his way, so that his message will be heard as clearly as possible. Poe's book is in itself not so very important, but it does reveal the spirit of modern research and that is important. Poe is certainly one of those modern commentators. We may say, in a nutshell, that the misunderstanding of ancient religion is based on modern morality.

It is true that I have said too much here about the Greeks and too little about the Romans, but this can be justified when it is remembered that Rome was, in the later period, so influenced by Greek attitudes that what I have said so far about the Greeks can to a great extent also be applied to the Romans.

Appendix

It is worth while at this point to reconsider the *societas generis humani* in the work of Cicero. The general vagueness of his presentation of ideas only gives emphasis to the fact that two basic concepts occur in his work. In the first place, he stresses that the equality of all men would seem to be demonstrated by the harmony that prevails in the cosmos. Everything takes place in the macrocosm according to certain laws. A similar harmony based on laws is also discernible in the lives of all men. It has been widely assumed that this concept was taken from Posidonius. In the second place, the harmony and unity of the individual is also extended into a wider involvement, moving, as it were, in concentric circles that become constantly larger. This concept, it has been claimed, comes from Panaetius, although many scholars believe that Theophrastus was originally the source of Cicero's teaching about the concentric circles.

We need say no more here about the sources, which are not elucidated in the general vagueness of Cicero's work. What is important to note in this context, however, is that Cicero believed that men had obligations towards each other because of their common humanity. This humanity was not, however, based on his biological nature (and now also on his spirit); it was rather based on the fact that men associated with each other as citizens in the state. It has therefore been concluded—in my opinion, correctly—that the *societas generis humani* has no basis of reality in Cicero, but that men behaved unselfishly towards each other according to a completely different pattern, that of the family and the fatherland. We have already seen how the idea of a universal humanity was very rare in the Greek world and how humanity was usually linked with citizenship. In the Roman state and especially at the higher social level of Roman society to which Cicero belonged, there was similarly no question of a universal love of all mankind; there was rather a loyal association of citizens in the one *res publica*, which was a 'commonwealth' and the best for all men, although 'all men' here meant the citizens.

Slavery should also be seen in the same light. It is clear, for example, that some place should be given to Aristotle and his influence. Let me quote here a passage found in H. F. Reijnders' work [50] which has been given too little attention: ἧ μὲν οὖν δοῦλος, οὐκ ἔστι φιλία πρὸς αὐτόν, ἧ δ᾽ ἄνθρωπος, 'insofar as he is a slave, there is no friendship with him, but only insofar as he is a man' (Eth. Nic. VIII 11. 7). This passage points clearly to a recognition of slavery as such, but it has also been claimed that it also draws attention to the human rights of the slave. This is not the case. The slave may be called a man in this text, but it is not said that he has any rights. He was distinguished from all other living beings only because he had the same image and form as the true man, the free citizen. The words of Aristotle cannot therefore be interpreted 'humanly'.

Returning to Cicero, we can see that he was quite traditional in his attitude towards slavery. He spoke about *humanitas*, but it is doubtful whether this refers to a universal love of all mankind. During his lifetime, there were certainly no laws or social rights that applied to slaves, so that Cicero undoubtedly meant no more, when he used the term *humanitas*, than the position that every man occupied by nature and not the rights that he possessed. This does not necessarily mean that the slave had any further security in the community. The vagueness displayed by Cicero in this question was a characteristic of the Roman world both before and after his time. His ideas cannot be fitted into any development towards more cosmopolitan concepts and ideals—he was altogether Roman.[51]

---

[50] H. F. Reijnders, *op. cit.*, p. 73. Cf. p. 78 above.

[51] See H. F. Reijnders, *op. cit.*, p. 69 ff. My main objection to this otherwise good dissertation is that the author places too much emphasis on right and not enough on biological similarities. My criticism only applies to his treatment of slavery. His outline of the two bases of Cicero's ideas concerning the *societas generis humani* is excellent.

The fact that slaves did not share in any particular appellation may also prove that they were not regarded as human beings. Generally speaking, the word *socius* (and its derivative *societas*) was used in Latin to describe the relationship between men, but it was never used to point to the relationship between slaves and free men, only to indicate the relationship between free men themselves. Of course, this use of words may be due to chance and it is not possible to investigate the use of this particular word in Latin literature.[52] All the same, although we are unable to view the situation as a whole, we can draw a number of conclusions.

In the first place, there is the etymology of the word itself. It is connected, according to some scholars, with the root of a word meaning 'hero' or 'man'. A more common view is that it derived from the verb *sequor*, to follow. If this is so, it can be translated as companion, friend, the man who helps and so on. What, then, is the use to which this word and its derivatives is put in Latin? What conclusions can we draw from this use?

The person designated by this word shares in the activities and experiences of the person with whom he is associated. This can take many forms. Two persons who are independent of each other or two groups of persons can, for instance, come into contact with each other. In that case, there is a principle of voluntary co-operation and of communal tension in order to gain a mutual advantage. This principle can be extended to states, especially in the question of defence. Within the state itself, there can also be a *societas*, the members of which are united in order to achieve an aim that is determined by the whole economic structure of the community. People associated with each other, for example, for the purpose of farming out Roman taxes, because a very great amount had often to be brought together in such cases, too much for a single individual to find. Co-operation of this kind in the sphere of economics played a considerable part in the politics of the state. In connection with our particular theme, what is important is that the men who associated with each other in this way were not slaves. They were free men who had a certain amount of capital and who trusted each other and acted according to certain mutually understood rules.

Military partners were also often chosen in the same way and there were various possible relationships with such allies (*foederati*).

---

[52] The TLL containing the letter S has not yet been published.

The most important were collective relationships between free states (*civitates liberae*) and what were usually personal and individual rather than communal relationships, such as that of the mercenaries (*stipendiarii*). All states or individuals who were linked with Rome in this way entered into a voluntary agreement. This was, however, something that a slave could not do. He could therefore not be called a *socius*. It is therefore important to recognize that an etymological derivation of this word based on pure imagination has to be firmly rejected. This is especially important in view of the fact that the word *socius* was, as we have seen, traced back to the verb *sequor*, meaning 'to follow'. This theory led to the completely unfounded explanation that the verb was originally a hunting term and used to describe the hound's function to follow the huntsman in tracking down the game. I am convinced that there is no reason for this theory and it is quite wrong to change the word 'hound' into 'slave' in order to include the slave in the concept of *socius*. It has to be stressed that the word *socius* cannot mean either 'hound' or 'slave'.[53]

---

[53] A detailed discussion of this question will be found in M. Wegner, *Untersuchungen zu den lateinischen Begriffen Socius und Societas, Hypomnemata, Untersuchungen zur Antike und ihrem Nachleben*, Heft 21, Göttingen (1969).

CHAPTER SIX

PRODIGIUM AND MORALITY

The Incomprehensible

In Roman society, the limits of human understanding were very much a community affair. As we have already seen, however, the Greeks were conscious of divine intervention more on the personal than on the communal level, so that a link with morals is easier to establish. In a strictly regulated state like that of Rome, however, though morality and a sense of guilt were undoubtedly present, morality was above all a phenomenon experienced publicly as a threat to the existence of the community, and therefore a matter of state. This distinction between personal and collective morality was not fundamental. Nonetheless, as we have seen, Oedipus became the king of Thebes, inheriting the kingship of the man who was his father (although he did not know this) and whom he killed, with strange and terrible results which drew the community's attention to past events. There was a difference between the way in which the Greeks experienced the incomprehensible personally and the way in which the Romans explained and disposed of it collectively, but this difference was barely felt in practice, a matter of degree rather than principle.

Terrifying events that were also inexplicable were recorded in the literature of classical antiquity. We have a traditional *Liber Prodigiorum*, compiled by Julius Obsequens, who recorded a large number of incomprehensible events thought to have taken place between 190 and 11 B.C. Historians had no hesitation in recording such uncomprehended phenomena. Livy, Tacitus and Suetonius all included them. They continued to be regarded as important until the writing of Roman history came to an end. They were placed on record sometimes in fairly complete form, at other times selectively, with mention only of the most striking aspects, but always as events important for the community.

The etymology of the word *prodigium* is itself revealing. It is probably derived from the verb *agere* and explained as 'emerging from the hidden into the public sphere'.[1]

---

[1] The data concerning the *prodigium* are assembled in a very convenient

Was there a sense of guilt when a *prodigium* occurred? Was guilt involved when Siamese twins were born or when domestic animals gave birth to a sheep with five legs or other monstrous young? We today should not feel that guilt had anything to do with it, but the situation at that time was very different.

A *piaculum* or expiation was thought necessary. This was a sacrifice in which the individual or the community attempted to restore harmony to the relationship between the divine and human worlds disturbed by a terrible *prodigium*. In other words, the original *pax deorum*, the situation of peace between gods and men, was broken and must be mended.

There is, in my view, a parallel here with the Roman understanding of cosmic harmony. It would be futile, on the other hand, to try to establish whether this conviction regarding harmony and disturbance was inherited from the Etruscans or whether it was originally Roman. Generally speaking, the real understanding of a phenomenon is not much advanced by trying to trace it back to a particular source and this is also true here. What is important for our purpose is that many scholars feel the idea of guilt to be present, but are excused in modern terms from worrying too much about it. It is claimed that the sense of guilt regarding the *prodigium* was secondary and that it was of primary importance to carry out a certain rite. This was a political action which put the community back on the right track but had nothing to do with personal guilt.

I find this very doubtful. There is a popular story that has been handed down to us by Phlegon which points in an entirely different direction.[2] According to this Polycrites, an Aetolian who was a benefactor of his city, died and after his death his wife, who was from Locris, gave birth to a hermaphrodite. Her relatives took it to the market place and engaged in discussion with a number of experts, including miracle-workers. Some of them explained the mon-

---

form in *RE* XXIII 2 (1959), pp. 2283-2295, by P. Händel. See also E. Riess, *RE* I, I ('Aberglaube'), 18, I (Omen) and 18, I ('Ostentum'). Händel also refers to early works. Two of these are clearly indispensable to anyone wishing to go more deeply into this question. The first is L. Wülker, *Die geschichtliche Entwicklung des Prodigienwesens bei den Römern*, Leipzig (1903). The second is F. Luterbacher, *Der Prodigienglaube und Prodigienstil der Römer*, Burgdorf (1904, reprinted). A useful modern work is R. Bloch, *Les prodiges dans l'Antiquité classique*, Paris (1963), in which both Greece and Rome are dealt with.

[2] This story can be found in Jacoby's fragments; see Jacoby, *F. Gr. Hist.*, 257, 36. The commentary is on pp. 345-346 and in the text pp. 1171 f.

ster as a portent of war between Aetolia and Locris. Others said the mother and child should be taken over the frontier and burnt. The dead father then appeared and asked for mercy on his child who should not fall victim to priestly foolishness. The people refused. The father again returned, tore the child to pieces while those present stoned it, devoured it all except the head, and disappeared. The head prophesied from the ground, advising the people not to go to the oracle at Delphi, and predicting war between Aetolia and Locris. (This war did in fact take place). The head then asked the people to place it on the east side of the city and not to bury it.

Leaving aside the gruesome details of this story, it is clear that personal and communal or political elements are closely interwoven in it. The whole community is involved, the priests of the community give judgement, the people think about it, the father too is deeply concerned, calling for magnanimity and pardon. His opposition to the decision to put the child to death is given a rational colour by denunciation of priestly foolishness. But it is all in vain. There is also a personal element in the conclusion, when the head asks to be put on the east side of the city and not to be buried. Similar phenomena occur in other sources. Obsequens, for example, mentions, for 136 B.C., the burning of Siamese twins, and there are examples also from the later Roman and Byzantine periods. It is obvious that *this* particular example has nothing to do with the Romans. This is clear from the facts that it concerns Aetolia and Locris and that Phlegon himself refers to a Greek rite (᾽Αχαϊστί). All the same, portents of the kind mentioned in this story can be found in a Roman setting and we should not therefore dismiss this example. Händel's summary of the *prodigia* [3] shows how often Roman society was thrown into disorder by phenomena of this kind.

Phlegon's text makes it possible for me to make free use of the *prodigia* in my discussion.[4]

In Rome from the earliest times a great deal of attention was given to abnormal births. Wülker summarized instances from Livy

---

[3] See above, note 1.

[4] There is also a medical link between mythology and religion. See, for example, L. Bolk, *Mythologie en Teratologie*, in the yearbook of the Kon. Ned. Akad. van Wetenschappen (1928-1929) and J. F. A. Beins' medical dissertation, *Misvorming en verbeelding* (1948). The title of Bolk's contribution draws our attention to the Greek concept τέρας. This has been dealt with outstandingly well, as a word and a concept in Greek and oriental civilizations, by Rengstorf, *ThWNT*, 8, p. 113 ff.

and Obsequens in a relatively short section of his book. There are about ten instances between 209 and 117 B.C. and another eight from Obsequens. They are concerned mostly with hermaphrodites among animals, rather than with human beings. The change of sex from female to male is also recorded (Liv. 24. 10. 10 and Plin. *Nat. Hist.* 7. 36) for the years 214 and 171 B.C. respectively. From the world of human beings we have the stories of women giving birth to animals, such as snakes. The snake birth indeed is found repeatedly, and at an early date in the Alexander cycle.[5]

Human monsters and deformities are bound to claim most of our attention in this context, because babies so born were done away with, killed or abandoned from popular superstition and at times also for economic reasons. They were in any case always placed outside the community. There were, for example, children who were *trunci corporis* at birth. The cases recorded by Livy have been summarized by Wülker. In the same way, there are references in Livy and elsewhere to children born with more than two arms or legs or with too many toes (see, for example, Festus (P. Diac. p. 157); Cicero, *De Div.* I. 121). In addition, there are portents such as the birth of a girl with teeth in 174 B.C. (Liv. 41. 21. 12) and other strange births (Obs. 26, 40, 53). It is reported that a woman had horns in 206 B.C. (Cass. Dio 17, fr. 37. 60) and that a human monster had its left hand on its head (Cass. Dio 42, 26. 5). There are several mentions of twins, triplets, and multiple births of even higher degree. These are, of course, exceptions. Among the *prodigia* are also included animals born with a human head, face, or limbs (see, for example, Liv. 27. 4. 14; 31. 12. 7; 31. 9. 3; Val. Max. I. 6. 5; Obs. 14).

One interesting aspect of this question is that these disturbing examples are also reported in the course of classical history as having played a part in sexual pleasure. In imperial Rome, for instance, it is said of hermaphrodites: 'Olim in prodigiis habiti, nunc in deliciis'. It would, however, be a vain hope to imagine that a 'history of attitudes' (*histoire des mentalités*) could ever be built up on a basis of these data and their occurrence in ancient Rome, since it would be impossible to find a series of such phenomena at such an early period of the kind that is so popular in more recent history.[6]

---

[5] In the world of ancient Rome, there are examples in Plin. *Nat. Hist.* 7. 34; Obs. 57 and App. b.c. I. 83.

[6] See, for this modern development in historiography, the school of the Annales, Economies, Sociétés, Civilisations, in Paris, and one of its present leaders, P. Chaunu for 'histoire sérielle'.

Without drawing any conclusions from this fact, it is nonetheless interesting to note that these phenomena seem to have been reported in greater numbers at the time of the Gracchi (133-121 B.C.) and in the nineties B.C. It is, of course, tempting to associate this particular sensitivity to abnormal phenomena with the social upheavals and political turbulence of the period. It is, however, wise to be cautious here, since we have too little material at our disposal and cannot make a comparison with other, possibly quieter periods of Roman history.

Sources

There are differences of opinion regarding the frequency of these phenomena. We have no comparative material relating to the ancient world. Nor do we know how much or how little of this material has survived. Yet we do know that the greatest historians, Livy and Tacitus, were sufficiently concerned with the matter to have reported such phenomena again and again. We cannot discuss here whether they themselves attached any great religious importance to them although I may mention my belief that Livy took them more seriously than Tacitus. It is remarkable, however, that there is an almost continuous thread running through Roman literature on this topic and that even so great and central a figure in Roman thought as Cicero mentions it again and again. Livy provides instances between 218 and 167 B.C., the period covered by his surviving works.[7]

It also struck the Greeks who wrote about Rome that the subject provided an important source of historical data about the everyday life of the Roman citizen and his relationship with what was strange or with the stranger. Dionysius of Halicarnassus made great use of the younger annalists but it is only in 12. fr. 9 that Piso is named as the source. Dionysius was a rhetor, so that his original reports are highly coloured (see, for example, 7. 68; 8. 89. 3).

Although his work contains some examples (32. 12. 2; 38. 5), Diodorus of Sicily was less influenced by these phenomena.

Pliny the Elder is not a reliable source, because he was more

---

[7] It is clear too from the epitome of Livy, Granius Licinianus, the Periochae, Valerius Maximus, Augustine, Orosius and Obsequens. The following passages in Cicero refer to the subject: *Div.* 2. 45 ff; *Cat.* 3. 18 ff; *De nat. deor.* 2. 14; *De Rep.* 1. 15; *Ad Quintum fratrem* 3. 5. 1 and perhaps also *In Verr.* 4. 108. We may also include *De Rep.* 1. 25 and *De Div.* 1. 78, 98-99 in this list. See Wissowa on *De har. resp.* in *Religion und Kultus der Römer*[2] (1912), p. 543 ff.

interested in natural science than in history. He usually refers to
the expiation of guilt, but not to the *prodigium* as such (7. 20;
18. 2. 86; 28. 12). There are, however, exceptions to this (7. 36;
10. 35, 36). Münzer has pointed out that Pliny's chief source was
Varro.[8]

There is no need for us to discuss the many data concerning this
subject in the work of Tacitus, as they are well summarized in *RE*,
under 'Prodigium'.[9]

What was done with deformed Children?

Our point of departure here is Dionysius of Halicarnassus (2. 15):[10]
'Romulus ordered all the inhabitants of the city to bring up all
their male descendants and the first-born of the girls and not to
kill (that is, allow to die) any child before the age of three, unless
the child was deformed, in which case it was to be put to death
immediately after birth. He did not stand in the way of such children being exposed on condition that the parents had first shown
them to five neighbours'.

Nothing certain can be said about the historicity of this statement. Weiss (*RE*) doubted the correctness of the last condition on
the ground that neighbours were never called in as judges in ancient
Rome, but I do not agree with this. It must have been a matter of
great concern above all to the neighbours if a deformed child was
in the neighbourhood. Its presence might, according to popular
superstition, cause such disasters as infertility. Mme Delcourt has
also correctly pointed out that the case is psychologically revealing
with its insistence on the lapse of a three year period to ensure that
the parents did not get rid of a normal child.[11] Deformed children,
however, were got rid of at once, without even waiting to see
whether the defect could be remedied. Dionysius uses the verb
ἐκτιθέναι (expose, put out). Some scholars have suggested that a
different verb would have been used in Greek in comparable situations, namely ἀποτιθέναι (reject, put away). The difference in my

---

[8] For the seventh book of Pliny's *Naturalis Historia*, in which most of the
oracles that concern us and the *prodigia* occur, see R. Schilling's edition,
Pline l'Ancien, Histoire naturelle, livre 7, Paris (1942).

[9] See above, note 1; see also below, p. 112 f. For Tacitus' scepticism, see
R. Syme, *Tacitus*, Oxford (1958) pp. 522 f.

[10] See *RE* under 'Kinderaussetzung' (XI, 1, 464-471).

[11] Marie Delcourt, *Stérilités mystérieuses et naissances maléfiques dans
l'Antiquité classique*, Bibl. de la Faculté de Philosophie et Lettres de l'Université de Liège, Fasc. 83 (1938).

view is minimal.[12] In any case, it was the parents who got rid of the deformed child and were responsible for banishing the τέρατα.

The law of the twelve tables also refers to the power of the tribune in this respect, making the elimination of deformed children a public act. But there is no reference to the punishment of parents who allowed such children to live. The reference, however, is to cases of abnormal births during the wars of the Republic, in other words in circumstances of general distress. I should imagine that parents were more likely to get rid of deformed children in times of trouble than in prosperous times. Sometimes parents are particularly attached to a deformed child, and such a child often brings happiness to a family. The fact that the parents were apparently not required to get rid of the deformed child suggests a continued preference for the earlier law, ascribed to Romulus, which, as we have seen, was merely permissive. The particular law contained in the twelve tables, by which parents were commanded to expose such children, has not been handed down to us directly. It can, however, be found in Cicero (*De Leg.* 3. 19). In this passage, Cicero's brother Quintus speaks about the power accorded by law to the people's tribune:

'For it seems to me a mischievous thing, born in civil strife. For if we take the trouble to recall its origin, we shall see that it was begotten in the midst of dissension among our citizens, after part of the city had been occupied and besieged by armed forces. Then, after it had been quickly killed,[13] as the twelve tables direct terribly deformed infants shall be killed, it was soon revived again, somehow or other, and at its second birth was even more hideous and abominable than before'.[14]

It is worth looking a little more closely at certain passages in Livy, which are sometimes supported by passages in Obsequens, in order to observe the suspicion with which strangeness and the stranger were regarded in Roman society, especially in cases of deformity and what was thought contrary to nature. I am not concerned here with attitudes to strangers who came from outside the community and were accepted by it, but with strangeness of people

---

[12] ἐκτιθέναι is the normal word for 'expose' (an infant); ἀποτιθέναι is perhaps somewhat 'stronger'.

[13] The reading *legatus* is wrong. Marie Delcourt preferred *delatus*, which corresponds with ἀποτιθέναι and ἀποπέμπειν. But *necatus* corresponds with Dionysius' ἀποκτιννύναι. Marie Delcourt herself observed this was possibly a brachylogy; *op. cit.*, p. 50, note 1.

[14] The translation is C. W. Keyes' (LCL, p. 481).

or things occurring inside the civic life of Greece or Rome. In that context, Livy's examples are undoubtedly to be taken seriously.

Between 215 and 186 B.C., so we are told, a series of abnormal events took place, particularly cases of children who were able to speak before the age of speech and others who could only utter animal cries. Among these abnormal creatures were also hermaphrodites. They were all regarded as of evil omen. What is particularly striking in this context is that there was no longer any belief in such *prodigia* at the time when Livy himself was writing, that is, in the first century B.C.: 'Non sum nescius ab eadem neglegentia qua nihil deos portendere vulgo nunc credunt, neque nuntiari admodum nulla prodigia in publicum, neque in annales referri'. (43. 13).

Livy mentions infants speaking *in utero matris* and at six months old.[15] Cicero (*De Div.* I, 121) also points out that, according to Herodotus, one of Croesus' sons was able to speak as an infant and that this was an evil omen for his father's reign and his whole kingdom. The same is said by Pliny in his *Naturalis Historia* (9. 112. 4).[16]

Not only infants who could speak, but also hermaphrodites made a great impression on the popular mind and Etrurian *haruspices* for this reason concerned themselves with them.[17] According to Livy (39. 22. 5), 'a twelve-year old child that was a hermaphrodite was discovered in Umbria and had to be put to death'. What is interesting here is that it was not a new-born child. It should also be noted that the event took place in 186 B.C., a time of war when old buried fears come to the surface and make themselves felt. (See also Obs. 3; also other data relating to 122 B.C. in Obs. 32 and to 117 B.C. in Obs. 36).[18]

---

[15] Liv. 24. 10 (214 B.C.); 21. 62 (218 B.C.).

[16] A. S. Pease believed that Pliny did not understand the word *mutus* and therefore used the word *infans* instead (C.Ph. 15, 1920, p. 201). Marie Delcourt, to whom I owe a great deal in the preceding section, believed that the substitution of *infans* for *mutus* may have been a consciously affected use of language by Cicero. This would be hard to prove, but I do not myself think it need have been so. We may compare Horace, *Sat.* 2. 5. 40: *Puer infans natus* ff. According to Marie Delcourt, *semestris* was borrowed by Pliny from Livy 21. 62. We cannot, however, be sure of this. *Infans* in the sense of 'not speaking' might be a technical term in this specific context; the same might be the case with *semestris*.

[17] See Livy 27. 37; for 207 B.C., see Livy 27. 11. 4 and for 208 B.C., see Livy 28. 11. 3. The first are mentioned by Plutarch (*Marc.* 28. 2). Livy (31. 12. 8) also speaks of 'deporting' (*deportare*).

[18] There is, in Obs. 3, a crux in connection with the word *natus*, that was changed, in my view correctly, to *inventus* by Barth. This mistake can be

Livy also has a case of 193 B.C. (35. 21), but the reader should consult Wülker for this and the other passages related to this subject. From 167 B.C. onwards, Livy tells us nothing, but Julius Obsequens, who covers the period from 190 to 11 B.C., with a few gaps, is of great importance for this later epoch. His *Liber Prodigiorum* contains data for 166 B.C. (Obs. 12), 163 B.C. (14), 147 B.C. (20); 143 B.C. (21) and 108 B.C. (40).[19] He mentions, for example, a slave child with no natural orifices which must have died and Siamese twins born in 136 B.C. (Obs. 25). Such *prodigia* had to be got rid of as quickly as possible. Siamese twins, for example, were burnt by order of the *haruspices* and their ashes were thrown into the sea. It is surely understandable that people were disconcerted when they saw this *prodigium* to which a slave had given birth, with four feet, hands, eyes and ears and two sets of genital organs. No more was needed at a time of great superstition. The same treatment was meted out, probably also by order of the *haruspices*, to animals when they were found in a place to which they did not belong, for example, cows on a roof or wasps in the forum (Livy 35. 9. 4; 36. 37. 4). The standard way of disposing of hermaphrodites was to drown them in the sea. Examples of this treatment are found in Obs. 22 (141 B.C.), 27a (133 B.C.), 32 (122 B.C.), 47 (98 B.C.), 50 (95 B.C.), 53 (92 B.C.).

I have just used the word 'superstition' and it is no doubt understandable that this word should come to mind more readily than 'belief' or 'faith'. It is very difficult for us to imagine that these forms of religion were authentic expressions of a feeling of incomprehensible and passive dependence on spirits and powers which determined the lives of men. What Kristensen has said in this context is very important.[20] I would like to quote one passage in

---

explained by the fact that new-born children were generally put to death if they were abnormal, but we are told that the hermaphrodite here is twelve years old. This passage has been dealt with very well by Marie Delcourt, *op. cit.*, p. 58, note 1.

[19] See Jahn's edition of Obsequens (1853), but the same book is provided in the last instalment of H. A. Müller's edition of Livy (Weissenborn and Müller). Haupt's *Animadversiones criticae in Iuli Obsequentis prodigiorum librum* (Progr. Bantzen 1881) is also very important indeed in this context, as is Rossbach, *RM* 52 (1898), pp. 1-12. An important recent work is P. L. Schmidt, *Julius Obsequens und das Problem der Livius-Epitome. Ein Beitrag zur Geschichte der Prodigienliteratur*, Akad. der Wiss. u. Lit., Abh. der Geistes- u. Sozialwiss. Klasse, Mainz (1968), 5.

[20] W. B. Kristensen, *The Meaning of Religion. Lectures in the Phenomenology of Religion*, The Hague (1960), p. 182.

particular: 'We are speaking in particular of that sense of fear which according to the reports of missionaries and other observers dominates the life of the primitives—certainly not the only feeling, but indeed a very real and concrete one. The Roman concept *religio* is close to it and can help us to gain some understanding of this sense of fear. Cicero derives *religio* from *re-lego*, meaning "to keep together", "to ponder", "to be attentive and cautious"; thus *religio* is awe and fear. But it also indicates the object of this awe: the supernatural, the mystical, magical nature of something, the "mana" (*fani religio*, the sacred nature of the temple, the awe which the temple arouses). The *fascinus*, a phallic symbol, protects the child *religione*, by its "sacredness", its mystical, magical effect. The *prodigia*, the portents, are *religiones*, supernatural revelations'.[21] This is all summarized by Kristensen in a well chosen quotation from Aulus Gellius' *Noctes Atticae* (4, 9, 8): 'Religiosum est, quod propter sanctitatem aliquam remotum ac sepositum a nobis est', in other words, *religiosum* is 'what is removed and separated from us by some kind of holiness'. Holiness fills us with fear, it deters us, but it also has a positive aspect in that it can become the source of supreme power. This supreme power was not wanted in the form of the supernatural, which was, or seemed to be, in the particular case of deformed children, unnatural, so that the children in question were drowned, burnt to ashes, or cast out. The attitude to what was strange was thus expressed in a manner of great importance to the community.

The strange and the alarming are closely connected in ancient religions. It may seem arbitrary to combine them, but the two aspects are in fact very closely related. We should not try to separate them today because they were not separated in the ancient world. The attempt to separate them amounts to a critique of Greek and Roman antiquity which is anachronistic. It is historically conditioned by our own way of thinking today. Modern, purely rational views about attitudes towards the strange thing or person scarcely apply here. In ancient Greece and Rome the two aspects were merged, though even there not for everybody. In antiquity too there were those more disposed to think rationally who found the merger difficult to accept. We have already seen Livy's comment on the *prodigia*. All the same, we must take serious account of the evidence

---

[21] Kristensen is referring here to Pliny (28. 39) and Livy (37. 3).

of life in the lower social levels of Greek or Roman society. To my knowledge, this has not yet been done in the case of the *portenta* (Greek *terata*). Scholars seem to be reluctant to make a connection that certainly existed in antiquity, but which they nowadays cannot accept.

The result is that the arrangement of the facts is often determined by the attitude of the scholar. The sources themselves provide no justification for this arbitrary and high-handed attitude. These concepts do not appear in Bolkestein's great work and this is not surprising. He may well have experienced a certain 'social' emotion with regard to the civil states of the ancient world, but this was no reason for him to devote attention to hermaphrodites, Siamese twins, deformed infants and individuals whose sex changed in the course of their lives. Reactions towards this type of phenomenon have not varied very much throughout the centuries. It is possible that it was not until fairly recently that men's attitudes have in fact changed at all.

Attempts were always made to explain and interpret signs in the ancient world and these interpretations were usually religious. Sometimes these signs were formed by the stars, at others they were the result of casting lots, the position in which the entrails of a sacrificial animal were found, or the abnormal life of a deformed infant. All these supranatural and suprarational elements determined men's fate, which in turn was conditioned by the gods. It is therefore understandable that men's faith—we would call it superstition—led them to certain conclusions regarding the state of the universe. All this had a great deal to do, then, with men's service of the gods as those who regulated the universe.

An Androgynous Prediction (Phlegon, *Mirabilia*, 10)

At the beginning of this chapter, I quoted from Phlegon.[22] I should like to add to this discussion of the *prodigia* that of another passage by the same author, illustrating the importance attached to hermaphrodites in the community. We are fortunate in having this text handed down to us in an excellent form.[23] A translation of the two oracles contained in the text follows.

---

[22] See above, p. 94.
[23] H. Diels, *Sibyllinische Blätter* (1890); see also Jacoby, *Fr. Gr. Hist.* 2 1179 (257, fr. 36X).

Oracle 1

'The fate of mortals, who only learn later where they are destined to go—all the miracles and miseries which divine fate has
decided for them—will loosen' (= reveal) 'my loom, if you ponder
this in your spirit, believing in its power' (= of the loom).

'I tell you that a woman will give birth to a hermaphrodite with
5 all the male sexual parts and the sexual parts of young girls.

I shall not be silent about the sacrifices of Demeter and holy
Persephone; I will gladly proclaim these sacrifices to you. If you
believe this, the goddess' (= Moira), 'the ruler herself, will' (proclaim the sacrifices) 'for venerable Demeter and holy Persephone.

10   When you have brought a great sum of money together to one
place, everything that you want of strange towns and yourself,
have this brought as an offering to Demeter, the mother of Kore.

Furthermore, I command you to sacrifice, at the expense of the
state, three times nine bulls . . . , brilliant cows with good horns,
15 white cows that are, in your opinion, the most excellent.

Let an equal number of girls' (= 'as many as I said before';
that is, in verse 13, regarding the bulls) 'make this sacrifice solemnly
and purely, in the Greek manner, to the immortal queen with
prayerful singing at the sacrifices.

Then she must receive each year sacrifices from your women,
20 but during your own life they must, trusting in my loom' (= predictions), 'offer a brilliant' (torch) 'to the most venerable Demeter.
If something like this is repeated' (that is, the birth of a hermaphrodite), 'they must take three times as much, offer everything
without wine and throw it in the great fire, that is, all old women,
25 who understand the art' (the sacrifice), 'should be prepared.

And others must also gladly take just as much, that is, all girls
in the first bloom of their womanhood, virgins, and they must im-
plore the venerable wife of Pluto, her who is learned in everything,
to stay in the country despite the raging of war, so that the neglect
of the town and of' (the goddess) 'herself may cease. The boys and
girls must bring an offering of money.

Oracle 2

30   (If you believe in) 'the loom moved by God, the venerable
spouse of Pluto must be attired with many coloured garments, so
that the evil may cease. And they must gladly give' (the garment?)
'that is the most beautiful and most worthy of praise' (or of prayer)

'on earth for mortals to look at to the royal virgin as a gift. The loom (= the oracle) 'persuades you to make this gift.

35 But, if you have' (prayed) 'to Demeter and holy Persephone to keep the yoke away from your country', (you must offer) 'the blood of a black ox to Aidoneus Pluto' (in procession), 'attired in festival garments together with the herdsman, who, trusting in the will of

40 the oracle, will kill the ox here and all' (must also offer sacrifice) 'who, full of trust, are together in the fatherland.

For no man who does not have that trust' (faith) 'may share in the sacrifices, but' (he must stay) 'outside, where it is customary for an unbeliever to make these sacrifices without a meal. All those who, during the sacrificial feast, being acquainted with our oracles,

45 come to the feast, must approach the venerable ruler Apollo with the offerings, having gladly sacrificed the fat knuckles of white goats as the ultimate sacrifice' (that is, of the sacrifices of Hades, mentioned in verse 37).

'Know, all of you that the procession must pray to Apollo Paieon with covered heads' (or garlanded), 'so that there may be redemption from the approaching disaster. After returning from him', (the

50 procession must pray) 'to the queen, mighty Hera' (= Juno Regina), 'offering a white cow according to the customs of the fathers, as befitting. And they' (= the girls) 'must sing a song, they who are the most distinguished among the people'.

(Two lines are missing here).

'Just as the inhabitants of the islands' (have done the same as is now demanded of the Romans by the same oracle, that is, the dedication of a wooden image and the foundation of a temple), 'when they once again occupied the Cumaean land of their op-

55 ponents, so too must these, with due regard for the ancestral customs, dedicate a wooden image and found a temple for the vener-

57 able queen Hera. This' (disaster) 'will come not in your own lifetime, but much later (59), if you have obeyed my words in all these things, after having approached the most venerable queen in sacrificial procession and having made libations without wine' (read *te* instead of *ke*) 'every day of the year.[24]

61 The man who does this' (= offers sacrifices), 'his strength will last for ever. Gradually making these sacrifices of drink and rams to chthonic gods, you must do this.

---

[24] The lines have been transposed at this point for the sake of the acrostic that is discussed below, p. 110.

If, from now on, you keep a temple of Hera that is in every
65 respect great and if the wooden images are carved well, know, then,
on the basis of my leaves' (= predictions)—'through the medium
of fate I covered my spell-binding eyes with a veil after I had taken
the glittering leaves of the fruit-bearing olive—redemption from
disaster.

If indeed the time comes for you when all monstra' (portents)
'take place suddenly, a' (or: the) 'Trojan will redeem you from all
disasters and at the same time from Greece' (help will come).
70 'But where shall I dwell and where will you spur' (me) 'on to
speak?' [25]

Our first comment on this remarkable poem is that the Trojan
towards the end is the Emperor Hadrian, who was Phlegon's contemporary. Greek civilization and the Roman experience of leadership and government were united in him. There could indeed have
been no better symbol of the unity of outlook between the Greeks
and the Romans on such *prodigia*. The hermaphrodite can be shown
to be an example of this, since it appeared in the year 125 B.C.,
just before the party struggles round C. Gracchus. What is more,
the oracle speaks in this passage of the Greek rite. This rite was
already well-known and connected with the introduction of Greek
practices at a time when Rome was experiencing great distress after
Hannibal's great victory at Cannae in 216 B.C. In 125 B.C., Rome
was again going through turbulent times. Although the oracle was
not preserved in sources before the forties of the second century
A.D., when Phlegon published it in his *Mirabilia*, even the most
severe critics believe that the material itself is much older. The
importance of this text is not in any way diminished by the author's
predilection for the most abstruse details, as recorded in his *Mirabilia*.

The text does not tell us what happened to the child (and this is
of course our chief interest here), but the measures taken by the
Senate show us clearly that it took the matter very seriously. The
decemviri sacris faciundis, who were responsible for cultic affairs,
had to consult the Sibylline books in their possession [26] and the

---

[25] This restored line gives Hera's words and should be combined with line
57, see Diels, *op. cit.*, 124.

[26] For a concise history of these Sibylline books, see M. P. Nilsson, *GGR*
II, p. 103.

Carmina Marciana, which were predictions given to the Senate by the prophet Marcius in 212 B.C. One of these *decemviri* was Fabius Pictor. Although it is possible, it is, in my opinion, too modern a thought that Fabius and the other *decemviri* made additions of Greek type to the Roman cult. Diels has made the attractive suggestion that Phlegon found the text in the works of Posidonius who may have collected these pious stories in his Περὶ μαντικῆς in order to confuse (or convert) cynical unbelievers, thus using the same method that Cicero employed later in *De Divinatione*.

The *procuratio*, prescribed in the first oracle, is as follows:

Oracle 1

1. The collection of an offering in money for Demeter;
2. The sacrifice of three times nine bulls;
3. An offering of white cows by three times nine young girls and prayer by the same girls according to the Greek rite in honour of the queen (of the underworld) or Juno Regina. The latter is more probable, however, since the white colour mentioned here in connection with the cows is not directly associated with chthonic gods, even though, as Radke has shown,[27] white-coloured gifts were made to them;
4. A sacrifice from the older women or matrons, a daily libation;
5. Torches for Demeter.

If the same frightening *prodigium* occurred again:

1. The libation to Demeter by the matrons must be made three times;
2. The same libation must be offered to Persephone, accompanied by supplications by the young girls;
3. The collection of an offering of money.

This, then, was a *procuratio* or provision for which the women of the community were particularly responsible. The sacred number three times nine clearly played an important part and this detail was also connected with the chthonic cult. The dead were capable of influencing and mitigating the effects of frightening and atrocious *prodigia*.

The torch, which also played a part in this ceremony, was, of

---

[27] G. Radke, *Die Bedeutung der weissen und der schwarzen Farbe in Kult und Brauch der Griechen und Römer*, thesis Berlin (1936), Jena (1936).

course, the usual attribute employed in nocturnal and subterranean feasts of the dead.[28] No expiatory sacrifice could take place without this attribute, the use of which found wider application, e.g. as birthday candles and nuptial torches. This is in fact a very elemental aspect of Greek and Roman religion in general, the torch being connected with the idea that life and death are an extension of each other, since both share in a higher form of life. Kristensen has given the name 'absolute life' to this.

Oracle 2

The offerings made in this case are:

1. Garments for Persephone;
2. A gift for Persephone (the most beautiful and best in the world);
3. The sacrifice of a black ox for Hades-Pluto. The sacrificial procession was made in festive garments;
4. The sacrifice of white goats for Apollo;
5. Prayer to Apollo with garlanded heads;
6. The offering of a white cow for Hera Basileia;
7. The singing of young girls;
8. The dedication of smooth wooden images to Hera;
9. A daily libation and other offerings made to Hera;
10. The sacrifice of a lamb to the chthonic gods.[29]

Events such as the birth of Siamese twins and other *prodigia* can also be found reported in the Roman *fasti*. A birth of this kind was mentioned in 200 B.C. (Liv. 31. 12. 6). The same offerings were made as those discussed earlier in this chapter and three times nine virgins sang and took a gift to the queen of heaven, as existing already and reported in 217 B.C. (Liv. 22. 1. 13). In the year that Tiberius Gracchus died, the birth of a hermaphrodite was regarded as an evil omen (Obs. 27). In this passage only the singing of the young girls is reported. Obsequens is also very brief about the *prodigia* and the *procuratio* in the year 125, to which the Sibylline oracle in Phlegon refers. In the later case of the hermaphrodites of 119 B.C., Obsequens only mentions that the virgins sang (Obs. 34, cf. 36). In 104 B.C., during the disasters caused by the Cimbri, reconciliation was made for the many strange and fearful births

---

[28] Diels, *op. cit.*, p. 47.
[29] Diels, *op. cit.*, p. 49.

by the twenty-seven virgins bringing gifts to Ceres and Proserpina and singing.[30]

The only possible conclusion that can be drawn from all these events is that they were intimately related to the life of the state and that they could only be overlooked on pain of death. The repeated equation or juxtaposition of joyful and sad events to do with birth, marriage, and death is certainly connected with religion and is not simply a poetic fabrication. We have to recognize that such events were taken very seriously in the ancient world. The attribute of the supplicant is the garland and this is what he wore when he approached the god or goddess from whom he sought a favour.

We should not be surprised by the part ascribed to Apollo, in this poem and elsewhere, if we remember that this god continued to play an important role in the practice of the decemviri. What is more, this factor is connected with the origin of the Sibylline books and the poems from Cumae. The foundation of this city is reported in verses 53-56. Obviously, Diels' solution to this problem is the correct one.[31] The islands that are mentioned are the two islands of Ischia and Pithecusae, now known as Procida, which was first occupied by the Greek seafarers who had come from Chalcis. The same colonists later went to the mainland opposite the islands and then Cumae was founded there. This, of course, explains the term 'the inhabitants of the islands'.

The oracle therefore says that the Sibyl prophesied to the people of Cumae long before the foundation of their city. The report of the founding of a temple and the dedication of wooden images also comes from the early period, that of the origin of the saga. This is probably the model for the dedicated gift that was required later. As was so often the case in Greek and Roman ritual, this is basically a repetition of what took place in the distant past. This type of evidence can be found everywhere in the Greek world. The deity appeared, for example, in Tanagra in order to avert an epidemic of the plague. He had a lamb on his shoulders. This ritual was later repeated to commemorate what the deity himself had done. Again, in Sparta, young men had to steal cheeses from the altar of Artemis Orthia as a sign of their maturity. This action was in fact a repetition of what Hermes had once done, taking the cheeses that the

---

[30] This case as well as other and later cases are all summarized in Diels, *op. cit.*, p. 45 ff.

[31] Diels, *op. cit.*, p. 98 ff.

goddess herself had made, not from cow's, goat's or sheep's milk, but from that of lionesses.[32]

This idea of ritual, which went back to a very early event that was thought to have taken place in the world of the gods, is found again and again as an explanation of certain practices. What is more, the Romans, who had hardly any personal gods at all in their original religion, took over Greek practices to such an extent that we can legitimately speak of a later amalgamation. In many other respects it is not possible to speak of a true historical development, but we are bound to assume that, although there was no question of borrowing, the Roman and Greek worlds certainly shared a common religious heritage.

This is certainly what happened in the case of the Greek *terata* and the Roman *prodigia*. The ritual reported in the oracles was stated formally as in Greece, but it has rightly been assumed that the practice was closely connected with an Italian custom.

The artificial structure of both these oracles is very striking, especially when the first letters of the lines are examined. The earlier editors believed that they formed two acrostics. The following acrostic is contained in the first oracle: <M>οῖραν ὀπισθομα-<θῶν, τίν' ἔ>φυ πᾶς εἰς τόπον ἐλθ<εῖν> which means: 'the fate of the mortals who do not experience until later where they are destined to go'.[33] The second acrostic is found in the second oracle:

Ἵππῳ ἀγαλλόμενος, πάλιν αὖ κακὸν εἰς νέον ἥξει·
Αὐτὰ <ρ καὶ τότε οἱ λύσις ἔσσεται αἴ κε πίθηται>

to which Diels added a first line:

<Οἷα πάθη Μοίρας, τὰ μὲν αἴ κε τις ἔλθη ἀλύξας>

His translation is as follows: 'the disaster threatens in many ways; whoever may have escaped one misfortune and has returned on his proud steed will soon find himself involved in a new misfortune. But even then the Sibyl knows what to do'.[34]

---

[32] See my *Laconian Studies*, p. 264 ff.

[33] Diels, *op. cit.*, p. 31: 'Das Geschick der Sterblichen, die erst hinterher erfahren, wohin zu gelangen ihnen beschieden ist'. To this, Diels adds: Ὅσσα τέρα καὶ ὅσσα παθήματα δαίμονος Αἴσης, Ἱστὸς ἐμὸς λύσει. Which he translates as: 'Alle Wunderzeichen und Plagen, die das göttliche Schicksal über sie verhängt, wird mein Webstuhl lösen'.

[34] Diels, *op. cit.*, p. 28: 'Mannigfach droht das Unheil: wer dem einen entronnen, auf stolzem Rosse heimgekehrt ist, wird bald wieder in neues Unglück geraten. Aber auch dann weiß die Sibylle rat'.

Altogether, we must conclude that there is a great deal of uncertainty here. In his commentary, Jacoby [35] doubted—indeed, he
even denied—that Hadrian was the man alluded to in verse 69.
Mommsen suggested that it was Sulla, but Jacoby questioned this.
I have not been able to establish—and I am not prepared to follow
Jacoby in this—why it should not be Hadrian to whom this verse
refers. Everything fits quite clearly into the contemporary pattern.

We must also take into consideration the fact that there is a
terminus ante quem in the year 149. The objection that Hadrian was
not a Trojan but a Spaniard seems insufficient to me. The emperor
was included in the succession of the Julian-Claudian house as a
monarch of divine descent. It is wrong to refer here to his romantic
philhellenism or to *Epit. De Caes.* 14.[36]

It is possible to single out many other particulars. The olive, for
example, was the tree of the chthonic gods, whereas the laurel was
the tree of the celestial gods. Here too death and life were united.
The loom refers to the fate woven on the loom of human destiny.
The garland also has a chthonic significance. It was used when there
was a question of purification and expiation. The Greek rite used is
a sure indication of east Mediterranean influence.

In view of the extensive measures taken in the case of a phenomenon such as that mentioned in Phlegon's text as calling for an oracle, we are bound to conclude that these irrational factors continued
to play an important part in the lives of the Romans (and, when
we recall Cumae, in those of the Greeks as well). The significance
of this for the Greeks is emphasized by the word Ἀχαϊστί. What
is important is that there is no question of killing the hermaphrodite,
but the offerings themselves show how very disturbed the community was by the birth. For purely linguistic details we can refer
to Diels' study.

Suetonius (Cal. 5) describes a situation which must have been
typical of the popular belief in supernatural things, especially those
phenomena that were observed during disasters. In this case, we
have an event that took place when Germanicus died: 'Quo defunc-
tus est die, lapidata sunt templa, subversae deum arae, Lares a
quibusdam familiares in publicum abiecti, partus coniugum expo-
siti' ('On the day when he passed away the temples were stoned
and the altars of the gods thrown down, while some flung their

---

[35] *Op. cit.*, p. 846.
[36] In this I cannot agree with Diels, *op. cit.*, p. 24.

household gods into the street and cast out their newly born children').[37]

This took place on the day when Germanicus' death was announced.[38] It is clear that temples were not destroyed and children were not abandoned every day. It is noticeable that there is no mention here of deformed children. This is, moreover, not the only example of an expression of popular mourning. How should such phenomena be interpreted? Temples and altars were, I think, destroyed, because the people were enraged against the gods for their failure to have protected such a popular ruler as Germanicus. I am reminded here of a devout Catholic woman who had brought her gift to the statue of Mary, but whose prayer had not been answered. In her anger, she declared: 'Now Mary won't get her flowers!' She did not, however, go beyond this and break the statue.

The abandonment of children can be explained by the fact that a child born on such an unlucky day was believed to be a bearer of misfortune. Suetonius has been shown to be an unreliable historian and it is possible that these events did not take place as he described them. This is not very important, however. What is more important is that the account points to a certain state of mind. At that particular moment, these children were as dangerous as abnormal children always were, at least according to the Romans.

We can also draw a conclusion of more general significance. There are many ideas and elements in Greek or Roman literature that agree with this passage from Suetonius and they are all aspects of a history of attitudes which dates from the beginning of the imperial period in Rome. The historical truth of these facts has often been questioned by modern scholars. They have frequently concluded that they are not historically authentic and have then ceased to be interested in the early source itself.

This strikes me as regrettable. If a second-century writer like Suetonius found it worth while to report such facts, we ought to accept what he says as something that was important to his readers. Suetonius was, after all, a popular author and wrote for a wider public than, for example, Tacitus. That is one reason why he is so important in modern research, which is to a great extent concerned with the reactions of ordinary people. Such people in the second century B.C. were interested in Suetonius' stories and read them

---

[37] The translation from Suetonius Lives in L.C.L.
[38] M. Delcourt, *op. cit.*, p. 63.

gladly, because Suetonius appealed to their sentiments and skilfully exploited their attitudes. It is, of course, not the first time that valuable data have been provided by historians of a lower category. Such historians often report, in passing, impressions made by catastrophes on the population and this information may be very important in the history of attitudes. It is clear that the Romans were always emotionally involved in what happened in politics whether on a small or a large scale (as the Italians still are). Tacitus was concerned with this aspect of history; an unforgettable example of this is his description of Agrippina coming ashore after returning from the east with the urn containing her dead husband's (Germanicus') ashes in her hand. He also describes in his Annals the great clamour made by the population of Brindisi and the great display of public mourning that accompanied the princess and her procession through Italy from the town in the south to Rome. Even Emperor Tiberius found it too much and probably interpreted it as a threat to his own position that so much attention was given to his dead stepson, his wife and children, who were naturally included in the imperial, and more especially the political, deliberations concerning the succession.[39]

It has often been pointed out that there is very seldom reference to the killing of abnormal infants. This is indisputable, but when it is claimed that it is never mentioned, I can point to one exception at least (Dion. I. 84), in which ἀποκτίννυναι should probably not be regarded as meaning 'to kill', but rather as 'to let die'. What is more, it must be assumed in the case of certain legal enactments that the older generation took an active hand. Whether they were the parents or not need not trouble us here. According to a law of the twelve tables there was, as we have seen, a regulation that a deformed child was to be killed (necatus). This should surely be taken literally as an article of the law and not simply as meaning 'to let die' in order to soften the impact of what seems quite atrocious.

I am convinced that Marie Delcourt went much too far in her attempt to stylize this type of practice, in other words, to suggest that there were certain rules of behaviour for parents and older persons.[40] It is obvious that the natural parents of an abnormal child would hesitate to kill it or get rid of it. It is therefore not

---

[39] Tacitus, Annals 3, 1-2.
[40] Delcourt, op. cit., pp. 63-64.

surprising that some parents did not get rid of their abnormal offspring at once or that they did this by placing it in a chest or coffin
and setting it afloat to see what would happen. This method of
dealing with a deformed child is reported by Livy (26. 37). There
is also, of course, the very well known story of Moses in the book
of Exodus, but this has to do with a law of the pharaoh of Egypt
and not with an abnormal child.

The hesitation of the parents because of their natural affection
for their child caused them to look for a way of delaying the death
of the infant or of providing for the possibility that it might survive.
It would be meaningless to go further into this natural desire to
preserve the child's life. Human beings can be very ingenious in
finding ways and means, especially when they are motivated by
parental love. It is therefore understandable that, after the twelve
tables, there are references in Greek and Latin texts to a vague
'taking to the sea'. This does not always mean 'to drown' and the
observation that these children were drowned when they were older
is ridiculous.

It sometimes causes surprise that such cruel acts were often
associated with religious conviction. We have already encountered
the superstition that such children could have an evil effect on the
whole community. But there was a religious inhibition against the
killing of young children, and this was in no sense an extension of
the commandment against murder. There are frequent references
in classical literature to the fact that children were killed pre-
maturely, sometimes violently (the Greek words are βιαιοθάνατοι
and ἄωροι). As Waszink has pointed out,[41] people believed that these
children were a danger to the community.

The 'taking away' of children was a placing of them in the hands
of the gods, a way of expressing trust in the gods to protect the
child. This was not a sentimental attitude. It may be assumed that
many parents prayed in this way when their children were taken
from their care or when they were obliged to give up caring for
them. This idea must have played a part in the case of particularly
alarming separations, but attitudes must have been determined by
the idea that the community took precedence.

It would be futile to try to indicate the origin of this Roman
practice. Etruria has been suggested, as it often is in cases where

---

[41] See *RAC*, under Biaiothanati and the bibliography in that section.

the origin of Roman practices is sought. Liv. 27. 37 may be quoted in support of the theory that the elimination of unwanted children was of Etruscan origin. On the other hand, Cicero is silent in his *De Divinatione* about abnormal children, just as he is silent about the influence of Chaldaean astrology and Etruscan knowledge of meteors. This has been taken as evidence against the view that these peoples influenced Roman practice.

In any case, I think there is not much point in labouring the matter. The phenomenon was widely known among the primitive communities of the ancient world, it was part of the general pattern of life. There are also many parallels in modern times, especially among the underprivileged. The terrible economic consequences of poverty, epidemics, and bad harvests, have made men hard, and with their threat to the survival of communities influence attitudes to individual death. Parents of the kind described in Roman literature, who entrusted their children to others—or to the mercy of the wind and the waves—did this frequently with a certain resignation to the inevitable and also—why deny it?—in the conviction that the healthy child needed the scarce products of the earth more than the abnormal child. With too many mouths to feed, those of less use go to the wall first. This may be hard, but the Romans saw it as inevitable.

In certain communities, including Rome, abnormal children were not buried after death. The material remains were allowed to waste away in a remote spot, but they were not placed in the ground. The origin of this practice is nowhere explicitly stated. It may be guessed that it was thought wrong to give the earth, as the mother of all life, abnormal food and thus cause it to reproduce the evil.[42]

In contrast to this, there was also a practice [43] according to which normal children were buried, not cremated, when they died young. Dieterich has pointed out that the earth had a different significance here. The children were too young to be burnt and were buried because of a close kinship with the earth. The soil's blessing could bring the child's soul to rebirth. The normal child could benefit from the powers of the earth and must therefore be buried, not burnt, when it died, so that it had a chance of new life. Seen in the light of this belief, the abnormal child could not be treated in this way, because

---

[42] Marie Delcourt was correct here; she was enlarging on what A. Dieterich said in *Mutter Erde*, Leipzig (1906), p. 21 ff.

[43] Juvenal 15. 140; Pliny 7. 72.

it could not be allowed to return to life with the same abnormality. Religion and social history are clearly interconnected in the explanation of this burial practice. Many scholars have found it impossible to explain why such a sharp distinction was felt between the death of normal and abnormal children. The distinction ceases to be strange in the light of the community's deepest religious feelings rooted in earth's blessing on young children. What is remarkable in this context is that the opposite is also true, although there is no example available from ancient Greece or Rome. The example that Dieterich gives us of the effect of a blessing operating in the opposite direction, that is, of a blessing not on the children, but on the environment from the children, is taken from North America. The Huron Indians were in the habit of burying children who had died before they were two months old not in the communal burial-place, but along the trait, so that they could enter women who passed by and in this way be born again, thus making these women fertile. This may seem strange to us today, but it may also help us to understand how deeply men have always been concerned, in all parts of the world, with death, burial, and the stimulation of new life.

It is clear that the formidable and incomprehensible aspects of the actions of the gods determined human actions in this type of practice. The *prodigia* proclaimed the anger of the gods and propitiation was therefore necessary. This act of propitiation had to be preceded by the removal of all traces of the portent that had caused terror. It is interesting to note in passing that even lightning, which is harmful, was solemnly buried in a ceremonial act.[44]

No clear single line can be found in any of these remarkable practices, but two general factors can be stressed. Deformed infants were killed and hermaphrodites were disposed of in a special way, in other words, by drowning.[45] Persons who had changed their sex were sent to a lonely island (Plin. 7. 36) and deformed infants were almost always burnt (Obs. 25). Even animals that appeared in an unusual place were burnt (Liv 35. 9. 4; 36. 37. 1; Obs. 26).[46]

---

[44] Varro (*De ling. lat.* V. 150); although it would take us too far from our subject if we were to discuss it here, this statement is often linked with the etymological explanation and part of a story, which need not occupy us here.

[45] Liv. 27. 37. 6; 31. 12. 9; Obs. 22, 27b, 32, 34, 36, 48, 50; Phlegon fr. 54.

[46] For further details, see L. Wülker, *Die geschichtliche Entwicklung des Prodigienwesens bei den Römern*, Leipzig (1903). Wülker relies heavily here on Wissowa. For *prodigia*, see also the article in *RE*.

Conflicting Judgements

In verse 41 of Phlegon's oracle, there is a reference to those who did not believe in what the oracle was suggesting. This is clear evidence of the fact that, at least in the second century A.D., there were many conflicting views about these strange phenomena. Indeed, how could it have been otherwise? A few examples of these conflicting judgements may be given.[47]

A line of Tibullus: 'Prodigia indomitis merge sub aequoribus' (2. 5, 80), implies that *prodigia* are made harmless by drowning. Seneca says very much the same in his *De Ira* I. 15: 'Portentosos foetus extinguimus, liberos quoque, si debiles monstruosique sunt, mergimus. Non ira, sed ratio est, a sanis inutilia secernere'. In this passage, however, weak children are treated the same as abnormal ones. In Livy we read (207 B.C.) that a large strong child which looked at birth as though it was four was 'removed' (which is a euphemism for 'killed'), because it was as dangerous as a hermaphrodite. Seneca lumped together weakness and abnormality; this reflects a basically utilitarian attitude, but it contains an originally religious element.

Pliny the Elder, however, makes a statement which does not bear out Seneca's opinion, but is quite different. In his *Naturalis Historia* (7. 3), he says that *prodigia* are a pleasant freak of nature. He is referring in this case to hermaphrodites. They should not be put to death. The whole evolution is seen by Pliny to be good: 'Hermaphroditi olim in prodigiis habiti, nunc in deliciis'.[48] The same applies to a monstrum in Egypt with two faces and four eyes (11. 113). On the other hand, superstition also played a part. Agrippa was born feet foremost and therefore belonged to the *aegre partos*, who later bore his name. Even though he was not himself an unlucky portent the two Agrippinas who became the mothers of Caligula and Nero were. This and his personal misfortunes led to the commentary: 'luisse augurium praeposteri natalis existimatur'—"He was deemed to have paid the penalty which his irregular birth foretold".[49]

At the higher levels of Roman society, families apparently gave up the practice of making away with abnormal children. The ordinary people continued, however, to regard it as uncanny and I

---

[47] M. Delcourt, *op. cit.*, p. 59 ff.
[48] See also Fr. Gr. Hist. II BD (commentary, p. 846).
[49] Plin. 7. 46. Cf. pp. 124, 126 below.

am personally not sure of the attitude of the upper classes, since
Augustus himself declared, according to Suetonius (Aug. 83), that
he had thought these phenomena dangerous. All the same, he had
a dwarf, Lucius, among his retainers (Aug. 43).

It should be pointed out that another Sibylline prophecy, also
preserved by Phlegon (Μακροβίων 5), and in Zosimus II. 6, occurs
in connection with a celebration of Ludi Saeculares. Diels was right
to assume a connection of Horace's Carmen Saeculare (17 B.C.) with
Phlegon's text (Fr. Gr. Hist. fr. 37, 5).

He was also quite right to call Phlegon's version of the oracle
pedantic in that it contains a number of obvious explanations, but
leaves the more difficult questions unexplained. Examples of such
obvious statements are lines 13 and 16.[50]

In any case, in our digression, we would prefer to stress the practical consequences of a rite for the whole community. We are much
less interested in the origin.[51] Zosimus' account is the nearest of all
to a popular approach to the celebration of the feast.[52]

What, then, does Zosimus tell us? His digression on the origin of
these feasts is contained within a historical account of the Secular
Games of 297-8 or 304 A.D. given by Maximian, so that we may
presume there is a link between the two. Be this as it may, we can
certainly say that the text deserved closer inspection, and here
Paschoud's treatment can help us.

In the first place, Zosimus discusses the name of the games and
suggests that *saeculum* represented the greatest length of a man's
life, a hundred years, which was the total of a generation if this
included the whole human life.[53] In classical antiquity, there were

---

[50] See Diels, *op. cit.*, p. 15.

[51] For this question, the reader should consult J. Gagé, *Recherches sur les
Jeux Séculaires*, Paris (1934) and H. Wagenvoort, *Studies in Roman Literature, Culture and Religion*, Leiden (1956), pp. 193-232: 'The Origin of the
Ludi Saeculares', which also contains bibliographical data. See also K. Latte,
Römische Religionsgeschichte, Munich (1960), pp. 245-248, 298-300. All these
works contain extensive bibliographies. Recent studies are also mentioned
in the French edition of Zosimus: *Zosime, Histoires Nouvelles*, Vol. I
(Livre I et II), which forms part of the series 'Les Belles Lettres', Paris
(1971), edited by F. Paschoud. Zosimus' account is more useful to us in the
present context than the account of Valerius Maximus (2. 4. 5).

[52] Paschoud's notes are particularly illuminating here.

[53] There has been a good deal of controversy about the meaning of the
words γενεά and *saeculum*. I have myself ventured to connect the *saeculum*
of human life with the *saeculum naturale*, which indicated a generation of the
human race.

two current etymological explanations of the word *saeculum*, both of them wrong. It was derived either from the word *senex* or from the verb *serere*, to sow, beget. The latter derivation thus referred to the *saeculum naturale*, indicating the time that elapsed between the birth of the father and the birth of the son, or originally perhaps between the conception of the father and the conception of the son. Clearly this time could vary. In one community the interval between the father's birth and the son's might be twenty-five years, in another thirty years, the generation changing accordingly. In another there could be three generations in a century, in another again a generation of thirty-five or even forty years.

Forty years was the case in Sparta because legal marriage there was contracted later in life, with the result that, in practice, there was a fairly long gap between the father's birth and that of his first legitimate son. Until he was thirty-five, the Spartan citizen lived in a male community in barracks. This did not mean that they had no intercourse with women before they were married. It was a question of the legitimate child, the only one who counted in the tally of generations. Some years ago, I suggested that a corrupt text in Herodotus (3. 48) should be interpreted as though a generation was a hundred years.[54] This interpretation did not, however, arouse much response among the critics.[55] Yet the usage is in any case well attested, as early as in Varro (L.L. 6): 'Saeculum spatium annorum centum vocarunt dictum a sene, quod longissimum spatium senescendorum hominum id putarunt'.[56]

One could venture a suggestion that at least 'one hundred' years had to elapse before a feast of this kind could be repeated and all μακρόβιοι had passed away, sometimes after some less than 100 years, sometimes some more. Perhaps also, as I think, Zosimus' *Historia nova* Book 2 shows that there was, in linguistic usage and in practice, a period of 'one hundred' years [57] in addition to a natural saeculum in the cycle of birth. It is obvious too that a certain confusion existed among authors, and values of 100, 96, or 110 years are found. How a community counted depended on the actual situation among the very old, or on what people wished to believe.

---

[54] See my *Laconian Studies*, Amsterdam (1954), p. 64.
[55] See, for example, K. von Fritz, *Die griechische Geschichtsschreibung*, I: *Von den Anfängen bis Thukydides*, vol. II, p. 208.
[56] For further data, see Paschoud, p. 181.
[57] See p. 123 below.

Having said this as an introduction to our discussion of Zosimus, we can now look more closely at his text. He says that the family of the Valeriani was descended from the Valesius with whom he deals in this passage. This, however, concerns us less than the fact that Valesius himself was, according to Zosimus, a respectable man among the Sabines and that there was a sacred wood full of enormous trees in front of his house. This wood was struck by lightning and all the trees were destroyed by fire. In addition to this, there was also a calamity in Valesius' family life—his children all became ill. He called on the doctors and the soothsayers to help him and to provide an explanation for his children's sickness. This, in brief, is the content of the first chapter. The second chapter tells how Valesius and his wife were so anxious about their children that they offered expiatory sacrifices to the gods, prostrated themselves before Vesta and promised her that they would offer two adults in the place of their children, in other words, themselves, the father and mother of the children.[58]

Later, Valesius looked at the trees and thought that he heard a voice telling him to take his children to Tarentum, to heat water from the Tiber there on the altar of Dis and Proserpina and then to give the water to the children to drink. The distance between Tarentum and Rome and the danger of the journey with his children made Valesius despair. How could he obtain water from the Tiber in Tarentum? How could he take this water with him if he intended to make the journey there? How could he heat it on the altar of the gods of the underworld? He was in despair.

The priests whom he consulted told him, however, that he should not disregard the warning that he had received, since they had also received a similar instruction. Valesius therefore decided to obey the deity, took his children on board a boat and sailed along the river, presumably towards the sea. He spent the night in a shepherd's hut, however, while he was still in Roman territory, and there he heard that he could go to Tarentum by land. What is more, this Tarentum was not the city in the south of Italy, but another place quite near. Valesius fell on his knees and thanked the deity for this

---

[58] For human sacrifice in the ancient world, see F. Schwenn, 'Die Menschenopfer bei den Griechen und Römern', *RGVV*, XV, 3 (1915); see also M. P. Nilsson, *Gesch. griech. Rel.*, I² (1955), especially p. 396 ff. I would not be surprised if this is an early aspect of the story, an example of *devotio*. It disappears from the narrator's perspective because of the (happy) ending.

good encounter and told the steersman to sail to this Tarentum. On disembarking, he took water from the Tiber, heated it and gave it to his children. They were at once cured.

The children then fell asleep and dreamed that black animals had been sacrificed to Proserpina and Dis and that nocturnal feasts were celebrated every three years with singing and dancing. They told this dream to their father, saying that a great male figure had admonished them to celebrate these feasts on the Campus Martius and more precisely on that part of the Campus known as Tarentum, where cavalry exercises were held. Valesius had an altar made and discovered, while it was being built, that an altar already existed on the spot, with the inscription 'for Dis and Proserpina'. This made the instructions quite clear. When the altar had been built, black sacrificial animals were slaughtered there and nocturnal feasts were celebrated.

What we have here is a very well known legend explaining the origin of a feast. It contains early elements, not because the feast itself was very old, but because early details handed down from generation to generation were connected in the oral tradition with it. Dis and Proserpina had ordered the feasts that were later to be so celebrated in the same place. The feast was thus to some extent consecrated and thereby gained a certain religious distinction. Political considerations also played a part. The inhabitants of Rome were, we are told later, at war with the people of Alba. But when the two armies confronted one another, a monstrous creature in a black animal skin appeared and admonished them to celebrate the feast together in honour of both deities. This apparition is another element that is found again and again in the foundation of religious feasts. It is part of the model of the foundation of new feasts that a divine figure should appear and then disappear. The Greeks used the word epiphany and the Romans the word *adventus* for this (meaning appearance and arrival respectively). Zosimus goes on to tell us that the altar was set up and the sacrificial feast was celebrated. After this, the altar was concealed twenty feet below the surface of the earth, so that it would remain a secret from everyone except the Romans. After the altar had been covered and the sacrifice had been offered in nocturnal feasts, Valesius was given a new name: Manius Valerius Tarentinus. The name Manius may be related to that of the gods of the underworld, the *manes*, Valerius to the good health that was obligatory on those who made the sacrifice (the word may be derived from *valere*) and the third name, Tarentinus, was of course given to him because the sacrifice was made at 'Tarentum'.

We are also told that a plague was raging in Rome in 509, the first year after the kings, and Publius Valerius Poplicola offered a sacrifice at the altar of Dis and Proserpina. This offering of a black bull and a black heifer cleansed the city of the epidemic and an inscription was made on the altar: 'I, Publius Valerius Poplicola, have consecrated this field that belched forth flames to Dis and Proserpina and I have organized processions in honour of Dis and Proserpina for the liberation of the Romans'.

Paschoud has commented correctly [59] that, since the whole context of this story is legendary, it contains no accurate information about the war between Rome and Alba discussed at the beginning of this chapter. All that we can learn from what follows is that tradition established the history chronologically before 509 B.C., during the period when Rome was ruled by kings, and that the war discussed was a fairly long time ago (in the period of Valesius), since the existence of the buried altar had become entirely forgotten in the mean time. It will be noticed how typically chthonic elements of a very early date are combined here with all kinds of other elements. Black is the original colour for the animals of the underworld. Another very early element is the burial and digging up of the altar at a subsequent celebration of the feast. (The aim here is, I believe, not simply caution, but magic; the power of the altar and that of the sacrifice was reserved for Rome). Later, Zosimus, as a historian, provides a number of dates when the same great lustration feast was celebrated at the same altar. Opinions differ about this as there is no strong tradition. These opinions have little bearing on our case, so I shall simply follow the information given by Zosimus himself. [60] A similar calamity occurred 502 years after the foundation of Rome. This year, in which there were wars and epidemics, would therefore have to be equated with 252 B.C. It is generally supposed, however, that the year in question must actually have been 249 B.C., that the lapse of years from the foundation of Rome would have to be changed from 502 to 505. Other feasts are also mentioned in this context by Zosimus.

---

[59] *Op. cit.*, p. 73.

[60] For the chronological problems that are connected with this, see Paschoud, *op. cit.*, p. 184 ff.

There are also considerable difficulties in connection with the name of the consul in his fourth consulate, Marcus Popilius. It is clear that the year intended by Zosimus must be 348 B.C. Popilius was consul with Valerius Corvus in 348 and it was this tradition that Zosimus had in mind, although almost certainly he did not know the right year, when he spoke about him. The third celebration of the Secular Games took place in 249 during the consulate of Claudius Pulcher and Junius Pullus. The well-known celebration was during the reign of the Emperor Augustus. Zosimus' reference (4. 1) to the *decemviri*, whose task was to direct the feast, is an echo of the later *Quindecimviri Sacris Faciundis*.[61]

It is clear, then, that Zosimus linked the consul of 348 with the feast that probably took place in 249, but which he dated 252. It is not rare to find mistakes of this kind in the dating of consuls and references to them, both in late authors such as Zosimus and also earlier.

Zosimus moreover seems to have had no idea of the date of Augustus' restoration of the Secular Games. He names Ateius Capito, who explained the rite, and mentions the games during the consulate of Lucius Censorinus and Manius Manilius (149). It is here too—not earlier—that he mentions the fifteen men who had the task of preserving the Sibylline oracles. In this context it is worth noting the oracle to which we have already referred—we shall not discuss it here, but it is included in Diels' edition of Phlegon's text.

Zosimus goes on to say that Claudius celebrated the feast after Augustus but does not specify the number of years. He then goes on to Domitian's celebration of it, with no further mention of Claudius, but he does point out that 110 years elapsed between Augustus' and Domitian's celebrations—according to the rule he established to start with. After these two emperors, according to Zosimus, it was Severus who next followed the 110-year rule and organized the feast with his sons Antoninus and Geta, during the consulate of Chilon and Libo. His fifth and last chapter contains a description of the feast itself. We need not linger over this, since it is not related to the problem of religion, which is what concerns us here, and refer the reader to F. Paschoud, the most recent editor of the text. Various contradictory judgements are reconciled thus

---

[61] See I. B. Pighi, *De Ludis Saecularibus Populi Romani*, Milan (1941), 2nd edn. with addenda, Amsterdam (1965); see also J. Gagé, *Recherches sur les Jeux Séculaires*, Paris (1934).

forming a kind of Vulgate. The supranatural is thus incorporated into 'normal' life.

Private Omens

It is hardly possible to make a distinction between the various Latin terms for supernatural phenomena, such as *prodigia, portenta, ostenta, omina*. Wülker and Wissowa were surely wrong [62] in believing that signs and portents were always a symptom of divine anger. There was also the question of predicting the future without any direct reference to divine intervention. 'Signs' could occur in many different ways. A baby, for instance, could be born with a full mouth of teeth. This extraordinary phenomenon could be interpreted by the parents as a sign from the gods, but it was less likely to be one for the whole community. A child could be born with a caul and this could be important for the family, but not directly important for the community. Again, in the case of a breech birth, this might be significant in the delivery, but such a birth is usually successful and all that remains is a collection of family stories.

I give below a number of places in which the word *ostentum*, or *omen*, is used, or rather examples of what a modern author would group together under the heading of *ostentum*. [63]

For a normal child to have been delivered by breech birth meant bad luck. Such a child was, as we have seen (p. 117 above), an 'Agrippa' and it was said explicitly that M. Vipsanius Agrippa was the only exception to a generally tragic future—he had a successful life. His descendants, on the other hand, had misfortune (*Naturalis Historia*, 7. 46). If a girl was born with closed genitals (*concreto genitali*), this was also regarded as an *omen infaustum* (*Naturalis Historia*, 7. 69). There is, then, clearly an element of predicting the future in this and similar cases.

Encounters by the wayside could also have unfortunate results and the list of such meetings is endless. Many Romans were nervous, too, at meetings with madmen, old crones or dwarfs. [64]

[62] See *Religion und Kultus der Römer*, p. 538 ff.

[63] E. Riess, under *ostentum* in RE 18, Vol. I. The texts are Cicero, *De Div.* I. 121 (with Pease's note); Lucretius, *De Rerum Natura* 2. 700-706; 4. 508-594; 5. 837-845; Virgil, *Aen.* 9. 128; Horace, *Epist.* ii. 3, 187; Pliny, *Naturalis Historia*, 7. 33, 36, 68, 69; 8. 173; 11. 272; Tacitus, *Ann.* 15. 47; *Hist.* I. 86; Suetonius, *Jul.* 61; *Galba*, 4. 2. See also another article by Riess, 'Aberglaube', *RE* I, col. 92 and his article on 'Omen', *RE* XVIII, I (1939).

[64] These phenomena will be found in Frontinus, 2. 4, 18 and Pliny's *Naturalis Historia*, 7. 28, 48 and 84, 50 respectively. See also Daremberg and

An immediate and obligatory interruption of public life was occasioned by an attack of epilepsy. The falling sickness was famous, or rather infamous. It was called the 'sacred' sickness among the Greeks and by a very special name, *morbus comitialis*, among the Romans, because any assembly or meeting was adjourned if an epileptic present had an attack. The illness was therefore a remarkable form of '*assembly sickness*', which is, of course, the literal meaning of the words.[65] People protected themselves against it by spitting (*Naturalis Historia*, 7. 38, 35). If a person in the vicinity of someone who was about to make a journey had a fainting fit or became unconscious, the journey was called off, not only for reasons of personal health, but also because of the evil omen (see Suetonius, *Nero*, 19).

The birth of more than one child was also regarded as an *ostentum*. According to a passage in Pliny's *Naturalis Historia* (7. 33), it was only in Egypt that this was not so. For the Egyptians, it was a good omen and above all an omen of fertility. For the Romans, however, it was quite different. Indeed, the feeling of apprehension increased with the number of children at a birth. We are bound to feel that this was not concern over too many mouths to feed so much as fear of the unusual. It emerges clearly from a reference to quintuplets in the *Digesta* (46. 336). In a case of triplets in 163 B.C. (Obs. 14) the need for an expiatory sacrifice is recorded.[66] Many cases of twins are mentioned—Neleus and Pelias, Zethus and Amphion and, the most famous of all, Romulus and Remus.[67]

From all these phenomena, many of which are found arbitrarily juxtaposed in modern summaries, we gain the impression that there would be no point in looking for any form of systematization in the ancient world and that it would be misleading to attempt a classi-

---

Saglio, Dictionnaire des antiquités, under 'devotio', in which a rich collection of sources will be found, providing the basis for all later research, although this is not always acknowledged. Modern authors often borrow their material from a predecessor who, without mentioning his source, has drawn on this incomparable lexicon; the lemmata 'devotio' and 'divinatio' date back to 1892, and were written by A. Bouché-Leclerq.

[65] Fest. 268, 13 L. A modern classic is O. Temkin, *The falling sickness. A history of Epilepsy from the Greeks to the beginnings of modern neurology*, Baltimore (1945).

[66] For the books and articles dealing with multiple births, see Van der Kolf, *RE*, XVI, 2274.

[67] A summary of this material will be found in McCartney's *Papers of the Michigan Academy*, 4, 1924. This phenomenon also occurred elsewhere, e.g. in Madagascar, where parents got rid of twins; see Van Gennep, *Tabou et Totémisme à Madagascar*, Paris (1904), p. 176.

fication of the phenomena under the different Latin words mentioned above, such as *prodigia, portenta, ostenta* etc. From studying the terms in a dictionary, we might well conclude that they were distinct from one another. But it was not so. There were many reputable persons in classical antiquity of whom it was widely known that miraculous events had occurred in their lives or at their birth. Agrippa was, as we have seen, a good example of this—he came into the world 'in the wrong way'. It must be assumed, however, that cases of the kinds I have mentioned here were relatively infrequent among them. The birth of the mother of the Gracchi, Cornelia, with a closed vagina, is no more than a popular tale which remained current because the child of whom it was said did in fact become a mother—Cornelia, mother of the two famous tribunes and a family of twelve. Pliny frequently mentions celebrated people who were distinguished in some special way at an early age. Manius Curius Dentatus was born with teeth, for example, and a son of Prusias, the king of Bithynia, was said to have been born with a solid ridge of bone instead of teeth.

The author who noted all this quite indiscriminately was Pliny the Elder. We should not, of course, follow his bad example, but it is very remarkable to observe how many have tried, or have at least felt the need, to reduce all that Pliny said in this context to a clear, well-ordered whole. It would be equally difficult to do the same with the many phenomena of popular superstition, most of which, like those recorded by Pliny and others, do not even have a fixed nomenclature.

One event which was perhaps the most prominent of all in classical antiquity was the suckling of the famous twins, Romulus and Remus, by a she-wolf. McCartney has discussed practically all these cases of animals—tigresses, goats, she-wolves and cows—suckling children.[68] The phenomenon has generally been regarded as miraculous, but several non-miraculous cases have been recorded and discussed in modern times.

I conclude my survey of these phenomena by briefly considering McCartney's most striking example.[69] It comes from Procopius' history of the invasion of Italy by the Goths (*De Bello Gothico*, 2. 17). When John's army entered Picenum, the population was extremely

---

[68] E. S. McCartney, *Greek and Roman Lore of Animal-nursed Infants*, see note 67 above.

[69] *Op. cit.*, p. 30.

disturbed. Some of the women managed to make their escape before it was too late while others were taken captive. One of the former, from 'Urbs Salvia', left behind her a baby to which she had just given birth, wrapped in swaddling clothes. When the baby began to cry, a she-goat that had also just given birth came and suckled the human child and protected it against dogs and other animals. For some time there was a confused situation in Picenum as the war raged around it and the baby remained in the care of its 'foster mother'. When finally the women did return to their homes, they were astonished to find the baby alive and well looked after. They were at a loss to explain it, particularly as some of them tried to feed it, only to find it refused human milk. The goat stood nearby bleating. It seemed distressed at the women fussing about the baby and exciting it. Eventually they all stood aside, whereupon the goat came over and suckled it with great care. It was therefore called 'goat-child' (Aegisthus).

Procopius concludes his story thus: 'When I happened to be staying there, the people, wishing to show a thing that taxed belief, took me to the child and annoyed it on purpose, that it might cry, but the goat, which was only a stone's throw away, on hearing it, came running to it, bleating loudly and, reaching it, stood over it that no one might disturb it further. Such is the story of this Aegisthus'. McCartney has correctly pointed out here that he finds no reason to doubt this story. He finds that it contains a circumstance of hard fact absent from all the other stories, namely that the child was used to goat's milk. It is well known that children who are fed on the milk of animals persist in preferring the taste, and this, he thinks, gives some historical authenticity to the occurrence. The second point he makes is that the baby was not thereupon built up into a future prodigy or person of importance. It was simply one child among many. There was therefore no reason for any such story to be fabricated. Finally, Procopius was a historian who was serious about his facts.—I have thought it reasonable to conclude with this example my survey of material, derived from the fringes of history. It clearly demonstrates that it was *possible* for what in the ancient world was regarded as a miraculous event also to be true. We are bound to be gratified at being able sometimes to come to such a conclusion.[70]

---

[70] For the Near East in antiquity, see H. M. W. de Jong's dissertation, *Demonische ziekten in Babylon en Bijbel*, Amsterdam (1959). For the super-

stitious treatment of sicknesses in the works of early Christian authors, see H. J. Frings, *Medizin und Arzt bei den griechischen Kirchenvätern bis Chryso- stomos*, Bonn (1959). This book is discussed by H. Chadwick in *CR* (1962), p. 170. For the sympathy for those who were sick and deformed in the ancient world, see W. Burkert, *Zum alt-griechischen Mitleidsbegriff*, Erlangen (1955); discussed in *Gnomon* (1959), p. 389. H. Dörrie, *Leid und Erfahrung, die Wort- und Sinnverbindung im griechischen Denken;* discussed in *Gnomon* (1959), p. 469, by F. Solmsen. Burkert shows clearly that there is hardly any sign of sympathy for the oppressed and deformed in the literature discussed by him (mainly archaic Greek).

CHAPTER SEVEN

THE DEFORMED

In the previous chapter, we discussed those *prodigia* which were connected with abnormal cases or wonders of nature and which often had the effect of horrifying or deterring. But it is also important to discuss cases of deformed children in the community itself and their treatment by the community.[1] We have a good deal of information about this because of a religious ceremony in certain Greek cities. It is clear from this that the question was not simply one of how to deal with deformed children. It also concerned the treatment of individuals either deformed or coming to public notice in one way or another as somehow troublesome to the community.

Thargēlia

In various Ionian cities there took place every year, as we know, the festival of the Thargelia.[2] This was held on the sixth day of the month Thargelion and is defined as a feast of purification, sometimes combined with a fertility rite. In its oldest and crudest form the sacrifice made on that day was a human one, meant to reconcile the city with the gods. The results to be expected from the sacrifice depended to a great extent upon the willingness with which the expiatory victim met his death. As a rule, therefore, only those for whom life had become a burden, men who were starving or hopeless invalids, were willing to be sacrificed. The prospect of a year's provision of good food (white bread, figs and cheese) amply compensated for the death that was to follow. (We need not ask what famine conditions must have existed to persuade a poor man to exchange his life for one year's provision of food). The victims in no sense enjoyed the respect of their fellow citizens. They were referred to in terms of vulgar abuse, in words which expressed the most profound con-

---

[1] The paragraphs that follow appeared originally in Volume 24 of a series *Leidse Voordrachten* (1957), entitled *Grieken en de Grieken*. This article was also published in an English version, 'Greeks and the Greeks', in the *International Review of Social History* IV (1959), pp. 91-110.

[2] See Nilsson, *Griechische Feste* (1906), p. 106 et seq.; Deubner, *Attische Feste* (1932), p. 179 et seq.

tempt.[3] The best known example, although of a much later period, is the word 'offscouring' in St. Paul's first epistle to the Corinthians: 'being reviled, we bless; being persecuted, we suffer it: Being defamed, we intreat: we are made as the filth of the world, and are the offscouring of all things unto this day'.[4]

There is no need to follow up the question of whether human sacrifices were made in democratic Athens. The scanty data indicate, in my opinion, that this was not so. One may likewise pass over the question as to whether the scapegoats, or *pharmakoi,* did no more than purify the city or whether they were also believed to promote fertility. For social history it is of importance that people who were looked upon as inferior (but who were not slaves) were elected to be sent out from the city during the festival. They had no hope of being granted permission to return later.[5] Who were these people? One of the sources mentions 'people against whom nature had conspired' (i.e. defectives), and in Athens we hear of 'the unemployable, and people without *genos',*[6] this last word being explained by modern scholars as 'a bastard','son of an alien mother and an Athenian'; as such the child could not be a member of a family, he was an *agennos.*[7] The term 'unemployable' probably referred to invalids (not war-invalids; these received a pension from the State and were held in respect).

Whilst data from elsewhere indicate that the best were chosen for this substitution-offering—as in the saga of Codrus and in the biblical story of Jephtha's daughter [8]—the persons selected as *pharmakoi* were inferior. In this connection, but not in Athens, mention is made of criminals who had already been sentenced, of starving wretches who were glad to end their lives with a good meal, and also of deformed persons.

One can well appreciate that a ritual of this kind hardly squares with the ideal picture of *the* Greeks. Gilbert Murray, the embodiment of the tendency to idealise and to generalise about the classical

---

[3] Such invectives are thus used by Eupolis Fr. 117 (K).

[4] I Cor. 4. 13. Compare the comments of H. Lietzmann in the *Handbuch zum N.T.,* ad loc.; and Stählin in *Theol. Wörterb. zum N.T.,* s.v. peripsēma (vol. VI, 2, 1955, pp. 89-91).

[5] That return was impossible is proved by [Lys.] 6, 53.

[6] Passages in Gilbert Murray, *The Rise of the Greek Epic*[2] (1911), p. 327.

[7] This explanation in V. Ehrenberg, *The People of Aristophanes*[2] (1951), p. 161.

[8] Lycurg. *Leoc.* 84-87 (Codrus); Judges 11. 34-40 (Jephtha's daughter).

period, has attempted to free the Athenians at least from the blemish of this custom. He compares the Thargelia with Guy Fawkes Day and the banishment of the pharmakoi with the burning of the 'Guy', the effigy representing the incendiary.[9] Murray's comparison is not a happy one—an effigy is not a human being—; and his argumentation is unsound, even though he presents all the data with a disarming honesty. He cannot escape the facts. In democratic Athens in the time of Aristophanes a pharmakos was banished for ever at the feast of the Thargelia in fulfilment of a religious duty which the city could not escape.[10] On the other hand, it is to the credit of the Athenians of the golden age that there are no indications of a similar banishment taking place on any other occasion (in times of emergency or misfortune).[11]

In studying the religion of the Greeks one is frequently faced with the problem of guilt and purification from guilt. One of the greatest political controversies in democratic Athens cannot be properly understood without an appreciation of the deep-seated fear of a blood-guilt which must be expiated. The family of the Alcmeonids, pioneers of radical democratic ideas, is always described as the 'polluted' because of a real or presumed guilt incurred at a time long past. Ancient historians devote much time and patience to demonstrating *not* that the belief in blood-guilt was superstition (as might perhaps have been expected in the rational fifth century), but that the Alcmeonids were innocent and that the most famous scion of their house, Pericles, was therefore not a 'polluted' man.[12] At Athens, furthermore, the influence of religious ideas also served to determine political and military action. The mutilation of the Hermae, when the disastrous expedition to Sicily had been decided on, is well enough known; but some years previously the entire foreign policy of the city had depended, at one moment, on the interpretation given to an earthquake.[13]

Thucydides provides the clearest proof of the great influence of

---

[9] *Op. cit.*, pp. 326, 329.

[10] Gebhard in Pauly-Wissowa under *Pharmakoi* (2. Reihe, V, Kol. 1291) rightly against Murray. See also Nilsson, *GGR*, I² (1955), p. 107.

[11] This is rightly indicated both by Deubner, *op. cit.*, p. 185, and by Nilsson, *loc. cit.*

[12] Hdt. V, 70 et seq. and Thuc. I, 126 are main sources; see F. Jacoby, *Atthis* (1949), in particular p. 186 et seq. for the traditions among the Atthidographers.

[13] In 420; see Thuc. V, 44-46.

omens and oracles during the Great Peloponnesian War.[14] It is one-sided to consider the historian's contempt of this superstition as 'typically Greek'. And to believe that his 'characteristic reliance on the intellect' is also 'characteristically Greek' [15] is equally unhistorical. One may find examples enough in Thucydides' historical writings to give the lie to this sort of idea: the invocation to the gods made by the Plataeans, by the Melians, by Nicias on the occasion of the retreat from Syracuse,[16] vain though they were, were uttered by people of whom the majority were 'ordinary' people, men and women in distress. If Demosthenes really used the words which Plutarch puts into his mouth,[17] namely that Pericles and Epaminondas did not believe in oracles, but considered a belief in them to be an excuse for cowardice, then the statesmen he named are not truly representative of *the* Greeks; they were Greeks, indeed, but so were their fellow citizens and contemporaries, who for the most part attached sincere credence to the oracles.[18] And these, too, it was who knew within them the fear of religious impurity, who celebrated the Thargelia, who banished the *pharmakoi*.

We have seen above that the *pharmakoi* could be people 'against whom nature had conspired'. It is generally accepted that these words refer to the deformed. In Greece the state took upon itself the care of those members of the community who had been maimed in battle. It is to its everlasting honour that the Greek state did not allow those who had served their country with life and limb to waste away in misery. This rule, as I see it, deserves all the more praise, when we consider that other maimed or otherwise deformed persons were more likely to be treated with hostility by the community. In dealing with this group in greater detail it is not my intention to censure the Greeks, but rather to emphasize that it was by no means self-evident that war invalids should be well cared for. Here again, it shows how dangerously thin is the dividing line between humanity and cruelty.

Hesiod [19] describes the fortune of a city whose citizens are honest men. One of the good things which falls to their lot is that the women

---

[14] Thuc. II, 8. 2; 17. 2; 54; V, 26; VI, 70, 1; VII, 50. 4; 79. 3.

[15] J. H. Finley, *Thucydides* (1942), p. 310.

[16] Thuc. III, 58; V, 104-105; VII, 77. 3-4.

[17] Plut. *Dem.* 20.

[18] Compare M. P. Nilsson's summing-up, for the 5th and 4th centuries, in *Cults, Myths, Oracles, and Politics in Ancient Greece* (1951), p. 133 et seq.

[19] *Erga* 225 et seq.

bear children who resemble their parents,[20] in other words: healthy children, not *terata* or *portenta*. The significance of this line is entirely misunderstood if it is translated as: 'children who resemble their fathers', i.e. children who, because of their resemblance to their legitimate fathers, furnish proof that their mothers have not committed adultery![21] On the contrary, it is here a question of malformed children who are seen as a curse on the community. Aeschines [22] has preserved an ancient curse said to date from the First Sacred War in the time of Solon. At that time the men of Cirrhae had profaned the temple at Delphi, and an oracle had ordered that, in punishment, their country was to be laid waste. The Amphictyons promised to do this, and with a solemn undertaking laid a curse, in the names of Apollo, Artemis, Leto and Athena, on all who might fail to carry out their religious duty. In this curse occur the words: 'That the women may bear no children who resemble their parents'. An interesting parallel, expressed in the same words, occurs in the oath which the Athenians are supposed to have sworn when they were on the point of joining battle with the Persians at Plataea. Although it is practically certain that the oath itself is unhistorical, this is irrelevant for the present investigation. Here we are concerned with the mentality of the Athenians who formulated this oath and who preserved it on a column in the deme Acharnae.[23] Basing his arguments on a number of inscriptions from many places in the Greek world, Louis Robert [24] has demonstrated the general existence of these same imprecations, even though the formulation of them sometimes differs from that at Acharnae.

To have given birth to deformed children was generally looked upon as a punishment, and it is understandable that the community took measures against these unfortunates whenever possible. The individual is a member of the community: what injures him, injures it. In Sparta, where the individual had less freedom than elsewhere,

---

[20] Line 235. These and other literary texts, though unfortunately not the inscriptions, have been treated by Mlle Marie Delcourt, *Stérilités mystérieuses et naissances maléfiques dans l'antiquité classique*, Bibl. de la faculté de Philos. et Lettres de l'Université de Liège, fasc. LXXXIII, 1938.

[21] E.g. Mazon, and also Gow ad Theocr. XVII, 43, et seq., where he quotes Hes. (Theocritus ed. with translation and commentary II², 1951, p. 334).

[22] c. Ctes. III.

[23] D. W. Prakken, 'Note on the Apocryphal Oath of the Athenians at Plataea', *AJP*, LXI, 1940, pp. 62-65.

[24] *Études épigraphiques*, 1938, pp. 307-308.

the decision as to whether a new-born child should be permitted to
live was a right reserved to the oldest members of the father's *phyle*.
If the child was well-formed and strong it was allowed to live. But
if it was deformed or weak, it had to be sent to the *Apothetae*, a
precipice near the Taygetus.[25] Those born deformed in Athens likewise faced an unpleasant fate. Even if no positive data about this
were available there exists an *argumentum e silentio*, which in this
particular case is of considerable significance, although as a rule this
type of argument may be thought dangerous. In his *Respublica
Lacedaemoniorum* Xenophon wrote about those customs in Sparta
which would strike other Greeks as being different from their own;
in this monograph he makes no mention whatever of the attitude
towards the deformed. Apparently what happened in Sparta was
commonplace. But there are also positive indications that, in this
connection, the same sort of thing in fact occurred in Athens.
Theaetetus maintains, in Plato's dialogue of the same name,[26] that
knowledge is nothing more than perception. This thesis is, says
Socrates, Theaetetus' new-born infant and he, Socrates, is the midwife. Pursuing the comparison, he believes that an Amphidromia
(i.e. the feast at which the child was carried around) should be held
in order to see whether this new-born child was worthy of being
nourished or whether it was nothing more than wind and lies. If the
latter, it must be exposed. And Socrates concludes with the query:
'Will you endure his being criticized before your eyes and not become angry in case your first-born be taken away from you?' The
whole comparison makes nonsense unless the custom of abandoning
deformed children really existed. Even a first-born child did not
escape it. A father parted reluctantly with his first-born: but he
had to, and he did, but with reluctance since it was his first-born.
A Scottish scholar has said of the concluding words of this passage:
'It suggests the reluctant exposure of the first-born, because he is a
weakling, a defective'.[27] But this explanation shifts the emphasis to
the first-born; it lies, however, on the defective. The writer should
have said: 'It suggests the exposure of a weakling, a defective,
reluctantly because he is the first-born'.

Other passages in Plato, the interpretation of which, for that
matter, is uncertain, are deliberately not taken into consideration

---

[25] Plut. *Lyc.* XVI. Compare P. Roussel in *REA*, 45, 1943, pp. 5-17.

[26] 160c-171a.

[27] Gomme, *Population* etc., p. 82.

here.[28] For we do not know to what extent the Platonic concepts of the ideal state ever mirror what was the reality at Athens. The passage from the Theaetetus, however, clearly shows that it was a common practice to abandon defective children. This is indirectly confirmed by Aristotle,[29] who demands that an abnormal child be repudiated and 'made away with' after its birth. Aristotle gives further information about another custom, the exposure of (healthy) children in order to remedy too great an increase in population; on this point he says that there are states where the 'moral standards' object to such a practice. Apparently in his time it was generally considered both necessary and natural that newly-born defective children should be abandoned, for in this provision he does not mention a 'standard' that was contrary to custom.

A voluminous amount of literature on the exposure of children in Greek antiquity has gradually been built up.[30] Evidence from the classical period in no way allows us to suppose that the custom was general as far as healthy children were concerned. On this point Isocrates speaks in unequivocal terms. In his *Panathenaeicus* [31] he sums up offences that did not occur in Athens; included among these is the abandonment of new-born children. No matter how rhetorical this passage is thought to be, it must be taken seriously. What is more, it is confirmed by Aristotle: in Athens (even though he does not mention the city by name) the 'moral standard' (*taxis tōn ethōn*) was opposed to the exposure of children purely and simply on grounds of over-population. This is in striking contrast with the attitude towards children cast out by reason of deformity. It is indeed but a thin partition that separates humanity from cruelty. If it is the regular thing to reject defective children, one is standing on a slippery slope; other reasons beside deformity may then be found for not accepting children into the community, economic reasons for example. Thus Aristotle finds himself able to mention as a noteworthy fact that the Egyptians reared all their children;[32] Strabo was to repeat this in the first century.[33] And in the same way, in the

---

[28] Tim. 19a; *Resp.* 460c.
[29] Aristotle, *Pol.* 1335b.
[30] Specially H. Bolkestein in *Class. Philol.*, XVII, 1922, p. 222-239; A. Cameron in *Cl. Rev.*, XLVI, 1932, pp. 105-114.
[31] 121.
[32] Fr. 283 (R).
[33] 824.

second century of our era it can be accounted worthy of special
record that the exposure of children was forbidden in Thebes;[34] and
in the fifth century that this was permitted in Ephesus only if the
father was a pauper.[35]

Let us however return to the Golden Age of Athens. There are no
grounds for suggesting that the practice of exposing children was
generally prevalent at this time. If, however, a child was defective,
then other sentiments, such as, for instance, a superstitious fear of
the 'abnormal', probably entered into the picture. In such cases
parental love no longer counted; all that was considered was the
interest of the community, which might be threatened by the
'abnormal' child.

The history of humanity does not reveal a uniform evolution from
a lower to a higher level. The zigzag line, which we can sometimes
distinguish only vaguely, weaves its way through the history of
man, and in the process through Greek history as well. That the
Greeks could be humane, that they were able both to establish and
to uphold the dignity of man, that they could serve and honour their
fellowmen, that they could respect the convictions of others—all
this can be proved from their literature from Homer onwards. On
the other hand, that they could be cruel and that they could trample
human dignity underfoot can also be demonstrated by examples
drawn from their literature. Both of these opposing forces reveal
themselves in all that concerns man. The observation of this truth
is a fascinating privilege which the historian owes not least to his
studies. However, to postulate a uniform evolution in the ancient
history of the Near East and Greece, with the Greeks at the summit
of it, born out of nothingness, but suddenly in being as complete
creatures of lofty moral standards resembling the Athena of mythology, the goddess born fully armed out of her father's head, is to fill
the stage of classical Greece with a mythological tale of one's own
making, and to tread the facts of history underfoot. And, what is
the worst point about this way of thinking, the Greeks are denied
the honour which is their due. A difficult struggle to attain something which has to be wrested from one's own egoism is more
honourable than an exalted superiority that has always been one's
possession.

---

[34] Ael., VH II, 17.
[35] Proclus in Poet. min. gr. II, 305.

Dignitas humana

This part of my argument can be illustrated by an anecdote. In 1953, one of the oldest high schools in the Netherlands celebrated its seven hundredth anniversary. A special display was arranged to mark this anniversary and among the exhibits were examples of penmanship. One of these showed examples of handwriting by children in the Middle Ages, including sentences from the Vulgate such as *simplex velut columba* ('simple as the dove'). There were also examples of handwriting by pupils in the seventeenth century— translations into Latin of the Heidelberg catechism. The oldest French version was: 'Incapable par nous-mêmes de faire le bien' ('incapable by ourselves of doing good'). Thus the visitors to the exhibition were able to see, within the framework of the history of a well-known Dutch school in a small provincial town, examples not simply of school exercises but of widely differing views of man.

The question often asked in this context is, where does the *dignitas humana* that makes man as innocent as a dove come from? Various answers have been suggested. One of the most frequent is that the origin of human dignity is to be found, as the story of creation in Genesis tells us, in man's having been created in God's image and likeness. Many later commentators have taken this view. Others have pointed to classical antiquity as the source of the concept of human dignity, although this is not found until quite late in the tradition. Although the concept was already known, an essential assumption was that a terminology pointing in the direction of personal dignity was first found in the writings of the Cappadocian bishops of the fifth century A.D. There is, however, a tendency in modern scholarship to assume that these authors borrowed this terminology from the pagan world. It has also been suggested that the term 'human dignity' was laicized or secularized at a much later period, for example, in the veneration attributed to the Kremlin and the constitution formulated by Stalin, who, it has been suggested, raised the human dignity of the Soviet citizen from its previous low standing.

I have the greatest respect for the scholar who outlined this scheme,[36] but I am bound to say that his proposals are open to serious doubt. The central text is taken from the writings of Basil

---

[36] J. Kamerbeek Jr., 'La dignité humaine', *Neophilologus* (1957), pp. 241-251. The passage of Basil is from his *Commentarius in Esaiam prophetam*, II 9, *Opera* II, Parisiis, 1637, p. 81 B. For Gregory of Nyssa, see De hominis opificio c. viii, Patrologia Graeca, t. 44, col. 144.

the Great: τοῦ ἰδίου ἀξιώματος ἐπιλανθάνεσθαι ('forgetting his own dignity' or 'not taking into account his own dignity'). What Basil is considering in this context is humility, a virtue in which the feeling of merit or selfrespect is overcome. I feel bound to question the idea of an interpretation linking it with the 'know yourself' tradition, and thus giving it a pre-Christian, Hellenistic origin. The interpretation is even more open to doubt when it is connected with a statement by Gregory of Nyssa: 'Man's form is upright and he looks up to heaven. These things are also imperial and they point to royal dignity'. This text is clearly concerned with man as the crown of creation, which is a biblical concept (see, for example, Ps. 8). The observation that man was distinguished from the animals by the fact that he walked upright was certainly not confined to the Greeks. If the author of Ecclesiastes was not greatly impressed by man's upright posture and did not think it raised him above the animals, his opposition to the argument at least shows that he and his readers were familiar with it. We might reply that Ecclesiastes contains many Hellenistic elements, whereas the 8th Psalm is our guarantee of a surviving Jewish tradition. I am also of the opinion that Kamerbeek's interpretation is not borne out by Gregory of Nyssa's text. We may therefore conclude that the concept of human dignity cannot be found in the pagan Greek and Roman authors.

A related subject, *humanitas* (ἀνθρωπισμός) has been dealt with by another scholar, J. D. Meerwaldt.[37] Two opposing tendencies can be found in Greek thought and these are later reflected in Roman thinking. According to the first of these tendencies, man and human civilization were held in high esteem. Some scholars have tried to trace this movement back to Democritus and other fifth-century thinkers. Man is presented as a being who creates a certain culture, educates his fellows to that level, and so brings true humanity to man. This idea is illustrated with lines of development starting from the works of Democritus, and then by way of Aristippus down to Panaetius. It is a possible theory but the links are somewhat tenuous. In actual practice Aristippus himself was a successful educator. There is the story of his shipwreck when finding himself with his stranded companions on a deserted beach, he saw two prints and exclaimed 'Courage! I have seen human tracks!' They followed them to a city where Aristippus was so much admired

---

[37] J. D. Meerwaldt, *Vormaspecten*, The Hague (1958), pp. 7-28. I have taken a number of Meerwaldt's points in this section.

for his philosophical dissertations that he was able to earn enough in gifts to equip himself and his friends for the return journey.

The question we are bound to ask here is whether it is really a question of human dignity or more simply that of the feelings of a shipwrecked man on an (apparently) desert island. Whatever the answer, I am sure it is wrong to attach so much importance to this type of tradition. We can only conclude that there is so far no evidence of human dignity in the writings of pagan and christian authors, even when they speak of humanity.

What is more important is that many Greeks and Romans were far from venerating man as a culture-bearer. On the contrary, though he was regarded by one school as much higher than the animals, there was another where he was viewed as a dog, thought to possess all the bad qualities of that animal and even called after the dog in some cases (κυνικοί or Cynics).

The cynic school did not take *humanitas* as their point of departure, but rather the uncivilized character of natural man. They were also firmly opposed to the idea of the unspoilt man satisfied with the barest necessities of life, and thus rejected any fundamental optimism about culture and human development. They did not venerate man as the bringer of culture but regarded him, like the Titan Prometheus, as rash and liable to punishment by the gods. The hero who did his duty and worked hard to achieve results was, they believed, the one on whom the advancement of civilization depended.

I do not accept the witty description by E. Schwartz who took sides with the Cynics against 'the philistines of civilization',[38] but I do think that this popular school had too little regard for the *dignitas humana*. But what is more important, Cynicism was a particularly attractive way of life, in a period when little of 'the earlier urbanity' of civilization was left in general human behaviour. In the opinion of many of those who belonged to the first group, civilization was limited to those who used language correctly or, as Cicero put it in his *De Oratore*, spoke purely (*latine loqui*). Civilization was therefore defined by the technical terms for correct and incorrect linguistic usage and these have nothing to do with *dignitas humana*. It is, moreover, irritating to be told that human dignity depends on the mastery of a certain way of speaking or behaving.

---

[38] E. Schwartz, *Charakterköpfe aus der antiken Literatur* II³, Berlin 1919, 16 f.

Also in classical antiquity, it was known that a man's value was measured by his response to the demands made by the community. *Dignitas humana*, however, is something universal and cannot simply be dismissed as the property of a philosophical school with a monopoly of wisdom. It is fascinating to see how scholars confine their research to a small superstructure with its norms and practices, and make hardly any contribution to our understanding of historical situations in the larger community. What they give us are concepts rather than everyday behaviour in the community as a whole. This is a fundamental question of historiography. Bolkestein was right in his article on this subject [39] to dismiss such concepts as having nothing in common with the ideas that were really alive and influential in the community.

It is in fact extremely difficult to determine how far certain concepts which have been current in history were characteristic of the whole community. This is not the case here, however, for the view of man which plays a part in so many communities is also relevant here. In our own times, collective phenomena attract more interest than the speculations of a small social superstructure. It is none the less remarkable how lovingly such speculations are investigated, because of their high prestige. It must always be borne in mind, however, that they are confined to a very small section of a given civilization (*humanitas*) or else are entirely lacking (*dignitas*). The reactions of such people to the whole of a society is limited and it would be misleading to allow our historical perspective to be determined by their ideas alone.

A useful parallel is the information that is available in many European countries—certainly in the Netherlands—about the U.S.A. We obtain this information from correspondents who for the most part live in New York or Washington. Occasionally these east coast journalists visit the west coast and gain some insight into what is happening in intellectual circles in San Francisco, Berkeley, or Stanford. But the great America of fifty states and infinite shades of experience and everyday life remains unknown to us in Europe. What we in fact hear is geographically limited and above all intellectually limited to an intellectually highly qualified group of people. The European may feel drawn to this representation of American life, because he belongs to a similar circle in his own country. It is,

[39] H. Bolkestein, 'Iets over de begrippen menschheid, menschenliefde en menschelijkheid bij de Grieken', *Hermeneus*, 2 (1929), p. 67 ff.

however, a false picture, which Beichman did well to correct in his *Nine Lies about America*.[40]

This comparison may be thought too modern and at the same time a dangerous use of a modern example to judge the distant past. This may be so, but it is also true that historical research has often suffered from the failure to connect the past with our own times. I simply wanted a striking parallel to an idea of humanity that has been canvassed with a great display of learning though in fact it had few roots in the ancient civilization under discussion.

If *humanitas* was a cultural ideal confined to a small group of people in the upper levels of society, then we are bound to affirm with regret—or with other feelings, depending on our attitude—that this cultural ideal had little influence and that the word *humanitas* has changed considerably in the course of time. When we use the word, we think at once of moral values. We think in fact of human dignity and of what is and what is not permitted by the laws of human conscience. But there is no trace of such feelings about the use of the concept *humanitas* in classical antiquity.[41] The ideal that prevailed in society at that time is perhaps best expressed in a fragment (264 D.K.) from Democritus: 'One must above all have selfrespect and this must be written on the soul as a law: do nothing that is in conflict with this'.

It is worth reflecting on these words for a moment. The author speaks of 'doing' and of a law that is 'written on the soul'. I think this goes no further than what is said by the same author in another fragment (185): 'The expectations of those who have been formed in mind and spirit are more valuable than the wealth of those who have never learned' or in another (180): 'Formation of mind and spirit is an ornament in days of prosperity; in days of adversity it is a refuge'.

I think that many of those who favour intellectual isolationism can take warning from this. When there has been fundamental change in human relationships during times of trouble, culture has indeed often been a refuge for many people, who believed that their

---

[40] A. Beichman, *Nine Lies about America*, Pocket Books, New York (1973). See also Chomsky's Huizinga Lecture at Leiden (1977), for the traditional opposite view.

[41] The term φιλανθρωπία has also, originally, no general ethical connotation but is restricted to 'community of interests', see p. 72 f, above; S. Tromp de Ruiter, 'De vocis quae est φιλανθρωπία significatione atque usu', *Mnem.* 59 (1932), 271-306. *ThWNT* 9 (1973), 107 ff.

ideal of culture had deeper roots in society than we believe today. This sense of refuge can, of course, lead to isolationism, a sulky attitude, a sense of being betrayed, of frustration. There were many frustrated people in classical antiquity as there are now, who accepted as their highest ideal: 'The first and most important aspect in man is, I believe, his formation'. This ,in the words of the ancient saw, is an ideal of school rather than of life, whereas: *non scholae sed vitae discimus*, 'we do not learn for school, but for life' is the opposite view.[42] One may be quite ready to go far to meet the ideal of culture in education, but refuse to regard it as the only way to salvation and to say, as so many sophists said, that the formation of people, by which they meant their own education, was the highest aim.

Although many intellectuals are quite convinced of the value of a more all-embracing education than the one usually given today, they feel bound to protest against a cultural ideal that is *only* concerned with the formation of people in the intellectual sense and not with the whole of life, of which that formation is only one aspect and not an all-embracing ideal. It has to be stressed once again that the idea of *humanitas* would seem to have been taken from a school and an intellectual activity. One of the most remarkable developments of human optimism is to be found in the fact that this idea of *humanitas* came to mean something more exalted in course of time, with a different view of man, in other words, that it came to express the bond between men. It is a surprising achievement of human optimism that, undeterred by past adversity, it has been able to associate humanity with high ethical ideals and impose a view of man himself as a creature of dignity, of responsible ethical behaviour based on norms set by society. Those who favour a different view of man cannot pass by this moving cultural optimism with a shrug of the shoulders. However illusory they may think it, they must realize that it does contain a heroic attempt to raise man above the 'ordinary' level. Those who oppose it may convince themselves that its would-be exaltation of man is a failure but they can hardly withhold admiration, however, embarrassed of those who do make the attempt while they themselves stand aside. The divided view of man has this tragic result that the pessimistically minded cannot and will not plumb the needs of human society to its depths.

---

[42] Seneca, *Epist.* 106.

In the history of classical studies we find many scholars who believe that Greek morality was purely intellectual, the Orphics being the exception that proves the rule. From Socrates they quote the tag 'Virtue is knowledge'. With an intellectual explanation of the concept 'virtue', Greek morality can easily be contrasted with that other form of morality which is bound up with religion, something the Greek ethos apparently is not.

A very good example of this attitude can be found in the work of the American scholar, H. Baker.[43] It is worth spending a little time on this author's book on human dignity in classical antiquity. His argument can be summarized in one sentence: The Greeks believed in the primacy of reason, and that is their 'humanism'. Baker therefore speaks of "the ethics of 'humanism' ", basing it on Socrates' saying that 'virtue is knowledge'.

It is, of course, possible to argue about the content of rationality or irrationality in the concept of virtue. From the derivation of the word itself we may infer a suggestion that I for one find it hard to reject—that the concept of virtue here is an adaptation to particular circumstances. Such adaptation, moreover, is not always an intellectual process and sometimes has no intellectual side to it at all. Whatever the truth in this case, explanations of Socrates' use of the word have made a separation between morality and religion. Morality has been derived from the rational and moral insight of man not from a revelation from above. Moreover, an Old Testament saying that is really meaningless in the context is often quoted here, 'The fear of the Lord is the beginning of wisdom'. Or sometimes quite the contrary is asserted that virtue is wisdom and thus innate in every individual.

Confusion is thus complete. Yet in the Old Testament case there is no question of the fear of the Lord determining *all* wisdom. The fear of the Lord, we are told, is the *beginning* of wisdom and room is undoubtedly left for rational human knowledge. Similarly with the Greeks, the beginning of wisdom is sometimes present for them in the revelation of a god through an oracle. This does not mean that human wisdom plays no part in the development of legal principles and practice. It cannot be denied that divine right or *themis* was at the beginning of human wisdom in the Greek world. It was determined by the gods and in its turn determined man's ethical

---

[43] H. Baker, *The Dignity of Man*, Harvard University Press (1947).

relationships. If man did not conform, his attitude was regarded as wrong and his *dignitas humana*—our point of departure—was affected. This last, however, was a secondary development, which found expression in a later interpretation by Pico della Mirandola in his *Oratio de hominis dignitate* of 1486. For two hundred years the topic was under continued debate, so much so that Francis Bacon spoke mockingly about the 'discours délicieux et élégants sur la dignité de l'homme, sur ses misères, sa condition et sa vie'.[44]

In Baker's exposition it is clear in what follows where the joy of life is associated with the expression of joy in beauty, that we have a serious misunderstanding of, and indeed an aversion to, what is usually known as the divine origin of law. He clearly believes that the Jews had no respect for man and his actions and consequently did not share the joy of life and beauty, or allow man a position of central importance.

I find Baker's reconstruction quite mistaken. I do not think him right in attributing to the Greeks a belief that man was his own master. This was certainly not the case, at least in the completely laicized sense in which Baker presents it. It leads to the further misunderstanding of the Orphics. It is true that the Orphics were different from most of the Greeks e.g. by teaching original sin, but for all Greeks, also those who did not belong to the Orphic sect, morality was based on the idea that the gods ruled men and punished wickedness. This idea, of course, prompted those hostile to a religious sanction, like Critias, to argue that man's fear of the gods was an invention to induce him to follow the gods. Critias would never have thought of this if the divine sanction for wrongful acts had not been inculcated by community leaders, heads of families, parents, and others in those subject to them, family members and the young. This inculcation was simply the handing on of a tradition of divine providence. Though eternal salvation in the Christian sense was not yet an aim of man, his salvation after this life was. Some of the greatest thinkers in Greece propounded it. The idea of an Elysium in which there was no evil originated in Greece and has nothing to do with Christian deviation or backsliding or whatever words are used to reveal one's own modern prejudice. At a time when Christianity did not even exist, there were in the Greek world such concepts as guilt, expiation, and retribution. Various other

---

[44] I have taken this quotation from Kamerbeek, *op. cit.*, pp. 242, 248.

religious forms from the east, including Christian forms, later became connected with these. It should not be forgotten that the strict division we make between Jew and non-Jew is a modern construction. The great missionary successes of Christianity would be hard to explain if the contrasts had originally been as great as the laicized philologists seek to demonstrate in their patterns of historical development.

The following quotation from Baker's book on the Greek and his religious attitude is characteristic of the whole work: 'His goal was not "salvation"—the concept of being saved from innate sin was foreign to the Greeks, save the Orphics—and for sin they had no word.[45] Man could live brutishly, enslaved by animal passions and bound to matter. Or he could live divinely, and satisfying the natural demands of his sensitive soul under the guidance of reason. The chariot of his soul was drawn by all the forces of his integrate nature, but reason, proudly triumphant, was the driver who held in check the plunging beasts'.[46]

Baker's final words in this quotation are clearly an allusion to the image used by Plato in his Phaedrus. The American scholar has clearly not understood it, however, because, according to Plato, the charioteer was dependent on both horses, one of which was rational and the other sensual. It often happened that the first—the 'good' horse of the soul—came off worse and the other, bad horse got the upper hand. In his image of the charioteer in the Phaedrus, Plato left both possibilities open and in this way, by using the image of the two horses, combined the rational and the irrational elements in man. It is very significant that Baker misunderstood and therefore misinterpreted Plato's text here. Clearly, it was not only Plato, but Greek language and thought which eluded him. Apart from their wrong interpretations of various texts, speculations of the kind indulged in by Baker are often full of anachronisms. He is not alone in that.

Reflections on human dignity are often combined with discussions of the 'human condition'. The combination, after all, is a fairly natural one. When we see human dignity trodden underfoot, we can

---

[45] What about *hamartia* in this case? See J. M. Bremer's study for this question: *Hamartia*, thesis Amsterdam (1969). Bremer deals with 'sin' in this book, but at the same time points clearly to a development in the use of the word ἁμαρτία.

[46] *Op. cit.*, p. 105.

be very understanding and say that it is 'only human' to make mistakes: 'Human nature being what it is . . .', and we apologize. It seems trivial but need not be so. It may in fact be a question of a deep appreciation of man and an awareness of his tragic situation in which he again and again wants the good, but does the bad. The text is St Paul's (Rom. 7. 15-20), and has had enormous influence precisely because it states so succinctly the universal human experience of 'falling short'. This idea can, of course, be combined with that of 'sinning', and the Greek *hamartia* does indeed combine them both. Human shortcoming and human error are connected.

In this context, it is interesting to note that the expression 'the human condition' or 'the human predicament' (both terms can be used to translate the original French 'la condition humaine') only entered western thought quite late. Kamerbeek has written a short but valuable study of the term.[47] His attention, like that of all western European intellectuals of his generation, was drawn to it by the title of André Malraux' book of 1933. It is not pure chance that it became current just at a moment when the philosophy of progress had become discredited and the movement of human history was no longer believed to be upward, but more generally downward. Human shortcomings had become so painfully obvious that scholars began to look for evidence in the past of a consciousness of such shortcomings or of the inadequacy of the situation in which man was placed.

The term was discovered in Cicero's *Tusculanae Disputationes* 3. 34. Kamerbeek, who is sometimes inclined to situate the origin of such terms further back in the past than his material would suggest, believes that this one had a Greek model, perhaps going back to the pre-Socratic philosophers. This can only remain speculative. As there is no evidence either for or against, we cannot say whether there was one or not. We are, however, on firm ground with Cicero. This need not surprise us, since Cicero lived at a time when there were great divisions in society, especially in the political sphere. He bore witness to these divisions by presenting the human condition clearly in his own person. There was nothing particularly admirable in his acts with the result that he was despised by many as a man without 'higher principles'.

---

[47] J. Kamerbeek Jr., 'Le titre de "La Condition humaine" dans sa perspective historique', *Le Français moderne, Revue de Linguistique française*, 38 (1970), pp. 440-446.

The context in which Cicero used the term *conditio humana* was that of human illness. We need not discuss it here. Christian authors discovered the term in pagan literature and took it over. The term is to be found, for instance, in the Roman Missal, in the prayer to God to take the fragility of man's condition into account. After having been given a place in the Church's liturgical texts, the term was given a new lease of life in the seventeenth and eighteenth centuries by Montaigne and later by Pascal. This later development does not, however, concern us here. I have mentioned Kamerbeek's valuable study to show that the weakness of the human condition, which is closely connected with human dignity, is a topic with a relatively recent literary tradition which has moreover come to the fore again in our own times as the result of the emergence of Nazism in Germany.

Stoicism

No one who specializes in this aspect of Greek philosophy would deny that the philosophy which played a part in the lives of ordinary people in Greece and Rome was Stoicism, either in a more primitive and crude form or in the more civilized teachings of the philosophers themselves. Wagenvoort has also shown very clearly [48] how practically the Stoic ethos adapted itself to Christian morality. The Stoics sometimes had an exalted view of man's value and at others were more pessimistic. Both views were united in a synthesis, which gives a somewhat wavering impression, but which was apparently sufficient, during the period in which this philosophy was developing, to express what men thought and experienced.

In Stoic philosophy, the difference of man from the animals was almost proverbial. He could fall into animal situations, but by nature he was distinguished from animals because he was gifted with reason. It is noticeable, however, that the Stoics never spoke, in this context, of *dignitas humana*. On the other hand, they did stress that man had a special place in what was known as the world, which was a cosmos or an ornament. To speak of anthropocentrism here is, I think, wrong, since the Stoics never forgot that the divine element was always above the human, in daily life, religion and ethics. Man was, in their view, dependent on the deity for his actions and this, of course, meant that man could no longer be com-

---

[48] H. Wagenvoort, *Varia Vita*. A sketch of philosophical and moral ideas in Rome and Italy between 200 B.C. and A.D. 200, 1952[5] (in Dutch).

pletely central. He was governed in every respect by the deity. The Stoics thus proposed a natural theology or Providence watching over the lives of men and nature. Man lived, as it were, on the borderline between nature and the divine life and was closely related to the divine, because he was gifted with reason. This dependence on divine providence did not save him from the need to be active in achieving his aims. There was no practical difficulty for the Stoics to recognize the existence of a divine power transcending human activity and it is easy to understand how such a loose ethos of human action, in which man's responsibility was combined with divine predestination, lent itself naturally to the practice of Christian life. There are many passages in the works of Christian authors that derive from Stoic ethics. As in the theology of the Jews, so too in the works of leading Stoics such as Posidonius a distinction was made between higher and lower forms of life. Plant and animal life belonged to the lower forms and above them—indeed, exalted far above them—was the deity. There was, however, an intermediate being connecting the lower forms of life with the divine life—man. In this theological ethos of man's responsibility towards everything that is beneath him in the world, there is also a responsibility that operates from below to above. In other words, man is not only responsible towards what is below him in the world—he is also responsible to the gods who have given him that responsibility. This is a typical example of the seriousness with which the Stoics viewed man's existence in the whole of the cosmos. What is most striking, however, is that there is no mention in all that the Stoics said on this subject of *dignitas humana*. Man's place in the cosmos was seen by them to be rather one of duty and subjection than that of a dignified ruler above his subjects.

Eusebius inserted into his 'Theophany' a song of praise to man and, apparently without any difficulty, followed passages which were traditionally associated with this question in the popular mind of the ancient world. Cicero's *Off.* 2. 12-15 and *De Nat. Deor.* 2. 147-153 were particularly drawn on.

This list of a few of the more striking characteristics that form a link between Christian ethics and the pre-Christian morality does not exhaust the subject of Stoicism in the present context.[49]

---

[49] The best summary of the teachings of the Stoics and their enormous influence on the ancient world, both pagan and Christian, is to be found in Max Pohlenz, *Die Stoa. Geschichte einer geistigen Bewegung*, 2 vols., Göttingen (1948). A reprint of this work appeared recently.

The basic principles of Stoic ethics do not provide us with any opportunity to stress human dignity. The Stoics had an enormous influence and it was, I believe, because of *their* reticence on this subject that thinkers in the later ancient world so rarely emphasized human dignity. There can be no doubt too that the more pessimistic view of man played a part here, an attitude according to which there was little good in the development of life on earth.

The Stoics believed that history was moving in a downward direction. They were not materialists, like many of the Epicureans, who tried to make progress in the material sense attractive. No trace of this is to be found in Stoicism. The Stoic teaching was in this respect more of a 'people's philosophy'. With regard to world order, the situation in which man finds himself, pessimism was commoner than optimism and this has always been so. It is really only since the development of modern technology, medicine and biological knowledge that man has been heartened about the future and has therefore become much more optimistic.

Optimists must be on their guard, however, because every time things go badly those who are more conscious of the downward movement in history raise their heads again. What is important in this context is this: neither of these two movements has anything to do with the increase or decrease of *dignitas humana*. We can hardly imagine how inevitably the difficulty of man's daily circumstances must have affected his thinking so that pessimism was the norm. It is remarkable that it has never occurred to us that the development of ideas, which are often thought out and perfected by men over several generations, is to a very great extent determined by human weakness and man's inability to escape from economic and social misery. In the past, contagious and infectious diseases, epidemics and death, affecting men, animals, and plants, were of central importance. This is an indication of the part played by difficult, precarious, or dangerous circumstances in human life. It is also evidence of the influence of such circumstances on man's thought. It is not surprising that men whose lives were led in the conviction that every day brought death closer were more attracted to a pessimistic view of man. This means, of course, that we can hardly expect great stress to be placed on human dignity.

It should, however, not be imagined that such a pessimistic view of man excluded all idea of the greatness of certain men. There are many examples of admiration on the part of contemporaries and later generations for men who endured sickness, adversity, and death with greatness of soul. It is not this worship of great-hearted men that we are considering here, however, because that was for individual men and their achievements, not for a collective reality such as a whole generation of men or the whole human race. For there, after all, was nothing much to be seen either good or admirable.

CHAPTER EIGHT

RICH AND POOR

The Rich and Wealth

We begin with a point of terminology. In Athens, the *penētes*
were not the poor in the strict sense of the word. They were those
who earned a living by their hands. The word *penētes* is connected
with *ponos*, labour or toil. The *penētes* included not only artisans,
but also small farmers. The majority of the citizens of Athens belonged to this group.[1] This does not mean that they were legally
inferior to the rich (the *plousioi*). Their place in society as full
citizens was guaranteed by the Athenian *isonomia*, or equality before the law. In Greek literature there are more examples of the
penētes putting down the rich than of the rich suppressing the
penētes. But these literary examples are not correct historically and
show how careful we have to be in our use of the sources, most of
which originated within the propertied classes.[2]

The term *penētes*, then, does not refer to those who were as poor
as beggars and it is advisable to treat it with care in our investigation, since it refers to a group of citizens who within the democratic
structure of Athens were in many respects consciously in control.
This does not, however, mean that the adjective cannot be applied
to people who had nothing. This use does in fact occur. *Plousios*
(rich) is contrasted with *penēs* (poor). As both Bolkestein and Hauck
have pointed out, however, it is important in such cases to notice
the period, the social status, and the person in question.[3] What is
more, the word *penēs* must be distinguished from poor as a beggar
or mendicant (πτωχός).[4]

---

[1] Because there are so few data, we have to limit ourselves here to Athens.

[2] Bolkestein, *RAC* I, p. 699; the same can be said of Pseudo-Xenophon,
the 'Old Oligarch', a conservative citizen, presumably of Athens, who made
colourful comments on events in the city. A. W. Gomme has written an
excellent commentary on this author's text, published in a supplementary
volume of the *Harvard Studies in Classical Philology* (1940). See also G. W.
Bowersock in *Xenophon, VII: Scripta Minora, L.C.L.* (1968). See also
below, p. 179 ff.

[3] *ThWNT* VI, 38, 4.

[4] *ThWNT* VI (1966), p. 885 ff (Hauck). A recent summary has been
provided by M. I. Finley, *The Ancient Economy* (1973), p. 41 ff.

The word *penētes* is often used in the political sense and is then found contrasted with the *oligoi*, the small ruling class in power. These *penētes* were the *dēmos*, the 'people' and the modern word 'democracy' is derived from them. The term can always be interpreted in the writings of conservative Greek authors as contemptuous or disapproving from the author's point of view.

In Greek life, the Old Oligarch was not an individual exception. He referred to people as 'the lesser', 'the lower', 'the working' (folk), and so on, in distinction from 'the best' and 'the most useful'. It is obvious that the last two terms indicated his own rank and the conservative oligarchy. In the context of the history of morality, we do not have to ask whether many of the *penētes* may have been well off, although this does seem to have been the case. Bolkestein was triumphant about this, because it enabled him to affirm that there was only a slight difference between poverty and wealth. I do not dispute this, but it must at the same time be pointed out that there was in operation a social prejudice which found expression in contempt for the working class among the oligarchy. We should not, of course, generalize too much from the attitude of such figures as the Old Oligarch, but it must be emphasized that people thought as he wrote and that there was a strong social division, to the extent that the rich—and this is the other side of the coin—were called the παχεῖς, 'the fat folk'.[5]

The Oligarch was, however, not alone. 'Poverty', moreover, was sometimes regarded as a stimulus to work and the creative function, mostly it is true, by philosophers who had enough to eat. More often indeed, it was looked on as a cause of crime,[6] but its supposed creative function was by no means in Greek society rejected by the philosophers. It was not a matter of wealth or poverty, they claimed, but of the inner life. This seems to me to be a very dangerous theory, an obstacle to social and material improvement. Yet it must be confessed that the Greek writers who are our sources seem very little concerned about this objection. The point of view taken by the Cynics was best expressed by Antisthenes (see Xenophon, *Symposium* 4. 34 ff). We must also remember that the view of poverty

---

[5] Herodotus 5. 30 and 77; 6. 91, 2; 7. 156. See also Bolkestein, *Armenpflege*, p. 184, note 1.

[6] Bolkestein, *op. cit.*, p. 186 ff; Ehrenberg, *People*[2], p. 248. Aristotle was not alone in claiming that 'poverty causes rebellion and crime' (*Pol.* 1265 B 12). See Bolkestein, *RAC* I, p. 699. In his inaugural address in Amsterdam (1953), D. Loenen, *Stasis*, pointed to the political aspect of rebellion (στάσις).

as performing a social function has its good points. The example that has often been quoted in this context is that of piracy, which was a great nuisance to trade in Greek and Roman history, but which was attacked at its roots in the later Roman Republic by helping the pirates to embark on a new way of life. Bolkestein, full of his modern views, quotes this episode with great satisfaction, declaring that 'this attempt was only possible in a world in which the distress of poverty had been recognized as the social cause of criminality'.[7]

It is, however, possible to ask whether the Romans themselves saw it in this light. His source is not a good one—Plutarch, writing in the second century A.D., in his life of Pompey (28. 2). I am reminded in this context of the French historian Carcopino, certainly not a friend of Pompey, who eventually broke the power of the pirates. The French scholar gives him the credit for this—correctly, in my opinion. The aim was to liberate trade, not to help the pirates embrace a more honest way of life. This was at the most simply a means used to free the seas from piracy.[8]

The *penētes* and the *plousioi* were not extreme groups at each end of the prosperity scale, Bolkestein has correctly claimed,[9] but were rather two groups which bordered on each other and even overlapped. Greek society consisted of these two groups at the beginning of a period of general impoverishment. This was the period of the expansion, when, it has been said, Greece was bled white. It was, in other words, the time of Alexander the Great and his conquests in the East. It has been observed that instead of calling this historical process the westernization of the Near East we should speak rather of the easternization of the Greeks. I think there is something to be said for both points of view and that there was give and take on both sides. The Greeks learned from the East and the East learned from the Greeks. This question is, however, not central

---

[7] *Armenpflege*, p. 332; see also *RAC* I, p. 701.

[8] See Carcopino, *Histoire Romaine* II, pp. 565-566; see also Ormerod, *CAH* IX, pp. 374-375. It is clear from the criticism evoked by these measures that others were not always in agreement with Pompey. It is also clear from this criticism that Bolkestein's triumphant claim must be taken with a grain of salt. See for a balanced judgment M. Gelzer, *Pompeius*, München (1959²), 76 f, and above all E. Badian, *Roman Imperialism in the late Republic*, Oxford (1968²), 76 ff.

[9] Bolkestein, *op. cit.*, p. 456.

to our main theme.[10] To return to it, I should like to make four comments on Bolkestein's statement:

1. It is very difficult to make out what is really meant by the beginning of a period of general impoverishment. As we have seen, it has been suggested that this was the period of Alexander's journeys. There are, however, other possibilities: the end of the Peloponnesian War in 404, the battle of Chaeronea in 336, when Greece lost her freedom, and Alexander's death (not his travels), which put an end to the unity and thrust of the Hellenization of the East.

2. The suggestion that only the two groups mentioned here, the rich and the poor, were involved is too simplistic in its approach. Both groups belonged to the ordinary privileged citizens. In addition, however, there were also the mendicant poor (πτωχοί), although these were not numerous in prosperous times. We do know, however—and there is no difference of opinion here—that there was a serious threat to welfare in the fourth century, although we do not know all the causes.

3. We can only accept the fact that the two groups overlapped with reservations, since the Old Oligarch (1. 4) regarded the opposition between the two groups of 'rich' and 'poor' as irreconcilable. He included the *penētes* among those who prospered (εὖ πράττοντες). For him, the structure of society was aristocratic. The social aspect must, however, be separated from the political and, from the political point of view, the two groups, the *penētes* and the *plousioi*, formed a unity. It was also possible to move into a higher social group, although it was difficult to become one of the upper ten. It was certainly possible to move from the fourth class of citizens (the *thētes*) into the third class (the *zeugitai*), because various state duties or trades offered promotion to the third class for those who belonged to the lowest class and practised those trades. It should be borne in mind that the higher circles in Greek society, the highest we might say, were very exclusive.

4. To speak about Greek society as a whole, as Bolkestein has done, runs the risk of generalizing too freely. We have to remember Sparta and the helots,[11] Thessaly, Euboea and probably also the

---

[10] The reader should consult the recent studies of Alexander the Great, collected in Vol. XXI of the *Entretiens sur l'Antiquité Classique* (Vandœuvres, Geneva 1976).

[11] One of the most recent studies of the whole question of the helots has been written by J. Ducat, 'Le mépris des hilotes', *Annales*, 29 (1974), pp. 1451-1464; there is also a revival of Jeanmaire, *REG*, 26 (1913), pp. 121-150.

islands, where there was a sharper division between rich and poor, not only in the social, but also in the political sense.

Our conclusion, then, is that the poor who lacked property were related to the propertied precisely by that, but that the division between *plousioi* and *penētes* was small and must be separately defined for any given situation. Within the group of full citizens, however, there were certainly social distinctions and we shall deal with these first, before discussing the 'poor'.

There are signs that social distinctions existed up to the highest level in Athens. It was usually men of older families who were chosen for office and the *homines novi* are attacked in court and in the theatre for their origin. In a modern democracy this would be considered bad taste, but it was not so in democratic Athens. A person could deride his political opponents for their lowly origin even in the people's assembly and it is most striking that the laugh was on his side. All the priestly functions remained in the hands of the most distinguished families. When Athens had experienced radical democracy for a whole century, the priesthood was still reserved for them. We have only to recall the *exēgētai* an office instituted, I believe, at a late stage [12] and filled from among the Eumolpidai. Those girls who had certain duties to perform at religious feasts, such as carrying baskets full of sacrificial gifts, had to come from good families.

We must try to understand exactly what this means. It seems to us absurd that these offices and functions should have continued in a democracy and that they should have been promoted and in certain cases even created by that democracy. We find it perplexing that functions unimportant in themselves but greatly desired because they were striking and spectacular were entrusted to the young and in certain cases also to the elders of aristocratic families only.

What we have here is a form of snobbery among the lower classes who in Holland, for instance, like the village burgomaster to be the local squire or biggest farmer. The Athenians too liked to be governed by 'gentlemen'. This cannot be explained so easily from the psychological point of view alone. It is true that people like to be ruled or represented by men of good family—the Russians, for in-

---

[12] The controversy about the position of the *exēgētai* culminated in the studies by J. H. Oliver, *The Athenian Expounders of the Sacred and Ancestral Law* (1950) and F. Jacoby, *Atthis* (1949). I do not wish to continue it here.

stance, like to receive ambassadors from western countries who belong to the nobility. Clearly, Athenian democracy was strong enough to support this snobbery of the democrats. No judgement is expressed here about the composition of the priestly families or the special position of girls of noble families in processions. It does, however, tell us something about the fairly informal way in which Athenians of high or low rank were able to co-operate with one another. It was also an important advantage and indeed greatly to the credit of the Athenian state in its democratic growth that no change was made in the legal equality of all the citizens when something of this kind was, as it were, slipped into the hands of the aristocracy.

The Holding of Office

To begin with, I should like to consider a few facts about political offices in Athens. (I shall confine myself mainly to Athens because of the lack of data about other places). It is well known that, even in the heyday of radical democracy, not all offices were open to everyone. Pericles himself pointed this out.[13] Direct election (not drawing of lots) was used fairly often and, in the case of important offices, always. Moreover, the Athenian people was 'snobbish' in the choice of its leaders, choosing for the most part aristocrats.[14]

In what follows, I shall try to show how the legal position of the citizen was often defended not by reference to a moral right, but rather by recognizing certain positions of power and giving the citizen rights in this way. Legal equality had a moral content for the philosophers, but in practice morality was always pushed into the background by political considerations. In his *Memorabilia* (3. 4. 1) Xenophon describes how Nicomachides, an experienced soldier, was beaten in the elections of the *stratēgoi* by a rich man who knew nothing about military matters. Such situations undoubtedly occurred quite frequently. The Old Oligarch's testimony in this particular respect is above suspicion (1. 3). He speaks in this context of offices in the radical democracy which called for responsibility and which could only be carried out by experts or δυνατώτατοι and of certain jobs which were paid. I would emphasize

---

[13] Thucydides 2. 37. 1.

[14] Aristotle, *Pol.* 2. 12. 2. 1273 B. For the fourth century, see J. Sundwall, 'Epigraphische Beiträge', *Klio*, Beiheft IV (1906), par. 2, 5, 8. See also J. K. Davies, *Athenian Propertied Families, 600-300 B.C.* (1971).

especially the first part of the Old Oligarch's argument, in which he speaks of the self-discipline of the people. The responsibility for really important matters, calling for technical knowledge, must be put into the hands of men who were capable of carrying it out.

Finally, there are other questions that astonish modern readers and confirm their opinion that morality was not and could not always be placed in the foreground in politics. The law was of paramount importance. Although many attempts have been made throughout history to reconcile them, the law and morality are two quite different things. Demosthenes, who was a very keen democrat, made play with the lowly origin of Aeschines in a fashion that we should consider in bad taste. It did not apparently so strike the Athenian jury.[15] In the same speech Demosthenes mentioned what were for him the qualifications for high office—the trierarchy, the liturgy, and so on. In the same context we may place the popular gibes at Cleon and other politicians by Aristophanes because of their 'low' connections with manufacture or trade.[16]

In political power the rich did not come off too badly. The criticism found so often in the literature, principally by philosophers, that democracy was government of the rich minority by the poor majority, is simply not true. As we have seen, the higher offices were for the most part in the hands of the rich.[17] The orators of the fourth century, who were often politically influential, came for the most part from good families. It was rare for self-made men such as Phrynichus or Aeschines to have political influence. A rich man or an aristocrat found few obstacles in his way to political success, whereas a poor man or a man of lowly birth was often subject to ridicule in his career by orators or the authors of comedies. Because of the democratic principle of equality before the law, this ridicule never engendered political inferiority, but it is certain that social inferiority existed in ancient Greece.[18]

It is this social inferiority with which we are concerned here. It is possible to ask why the *penētes*, who formed the majority in the

---

[15] Dem. 19. 237; see 282 for what follows. See also A. H. M. Jones, *Athenian Democracy* (1957), p. 49.

[16] M. I. Finley, *The Ancient Economy* (1973); see index under 'trade', 'manufacture', 'craftsmen'.

[17] M. I. Finley, *Athenian Demagogues* (1962), reprinted in *Studies in Ancient Society* (1974), especially p. 24 ff; Ps-Xenophon, 1. 3; Dem. 24. 112; Aristotle, Aθπ. 21. 1; Eupolis, Frag. 117; Sundwall, *op. cit.*

[18] A. H. M. Jones, *Athenian Democracy* (1957), pp. 45-50. This author has dealt very well with political equality.

dēmos, behaved in such a snobbish way, laughing whenever the orators or writers of comedies drew attention to the lowly origin of their leaders. We may also ask why the members of the jury were not offended by this kind of argument.

The answer to these questions can, I believe, be found in the fact that Athenian democracy was quite different from our own, because it had a census. This enabled the social divisions which were in normal times not politically dangerous to continue to exist and even emphasized them. It is possible to say without exaggeration that the *thētes* made the Athenian empire great. These people, however, had no higher ideal than to cease to be *thētes* and to become *zeugitai*. The Athenian settlements in allied states were manned by *zeugitai*, the *thētes* being promoted to this class on being sent there. More than ten thousand Athenian citizens were able to climb the social ladder in this way. This resulted not only in a reinforcement of the hoplite army, but also in raising the standard of living in a social sense.[19]

All this can, of course, be found in any modern democracy. In a working-class quarter of any town, it is well known that a higher rent has to be paid for a better house. The person who lives in one of these better houses or on the more expensive side of the street is a 'better' person. Such social distinctions especially those between 'classes' very close to one another, are anxiously preserved by those higher up. The situation can be compared with the social results of the differences in modern society between skilled and unskilled workers; the former always place great emphasis on their particular trade status.

Why were the *thētes* never able to become archons? It is not so much that they were in practice unable to become archons. It is rather that they were more interested in losing their status as *thētes* and becoming *zeugitai* than in acquiring the rights of *zeugitai* while remaining in the class of the *thētes*. The social significance of possessions or property here is not so very different from that in the Homeric epics—the loss of wealth was at the same time a loss of the status of noblemen.[20]

---

[19] See especially A. H. M. Jones, *The Economic Basis of Athenian Democracy, Past and Present* I (1952), pp. 13-31, from which I have taken certain data. Jones later included this essay in his monograph, *Athenian Democracy*, which is a collection of essays on the same theme; see note 18, p. 157 and p. 179 (below).

[20] Iliad 24. 525-533; see above, p. 30 f.

Ploutos or wealth was a situation in life in which one did not work. This attitude was somewhat modified in favour of work for the rich, after the epic period, by Hesiod.[21] The attitude was already present indeed in the condemnation of dishonesty among the rich and exploitation of the poor. This is clear from the story of the hawk and the nightingale.[22] But this condemnation which was later to result in the political and juridical protection of the 'poor' and their equality as citizens, did not remove the aspiration to reach a higher situation in life and the property class. The aspiration proved to be stronger than the internal solidarity of the (lower) census class.

In Sparta, the status conferred by wealth continued unchanged. There was no means of achieving wealth by manual labour. There was no possibility of reaching a higher census class—a man already belonged to the class of the 'rich' in virtue of his property or was excluded by poverty.

One possible view of the situation is this.[23] In the very early period, the ethical attitude towards wealth was individual, whereas in the later period of the city state it was social, because an important part was played in the second case by the community of the polis and a person's place in it. But the distinction thus drawn needs modification since in the aristocratic morality of the Iliad no less than in Sparta wealth also had a social function. The place of the individual in society was determined by it. The difference was that this place in the early period was determined both socially and politically, whereas in a more advanced democracy it was determined only socially.

Hauck, who has suggested that the moral attitude toward wealth was individual, was at the same time aware of a flaw in his argument, because he admitted a connection between the earlier and the later period. He saw it in the fact that 'wealth was the obvious and all-embracing expression of a social order that was felt as an 'order of being' ("Seinsordnung")'.

Hauck also postulated a difference between 'Homer' and later authors (after Hesiod). He declared that in later times there was no 'indubitable social order or fixed norms governing such an order', but this is also wrong. The Athenian census classes continued to

---

[21] Hesiod, *Op*. 308: 'through their *work* men become rich'; see also 311 ff.
[22] *Op*. 202-212.
[23] Hauck, *ThWNT* VI, p. 318, lines 38 ff.

exist and a firm social distinction was defined by them. It is something quite different—and it is clear from what follows that this is probably what Hauck meant (although he has an unfortunate way of expressing himself)—that economic pressure and periods of uncertainty made men realize the impermanence of wealth, a point to which the philosophers and upholders of preached morality return again and again.

The heroes of the Iliad had a good deal to say about the impermanence of wealth—the bitter fate of Astyanax is a good example. The idea that 'wealth does not bring happiness and is fleeting' is met with again and again and is, of course, equivalent to the biblical statement 'wisdom is better than jewels' (Prov. 8. 11).[24] Experience had taught the Greeks too that a poor man was often more civilized than a rich one and that wealth did not always go together with moral goodness.[25] Yet though moralists might preach this truth, lived morality remained firmly attached to the census classes and repeated attempts were made to rise from the lowest of them.

It is to be regretted that the sources, in the *Theologisches Wörterbuch zum Neuen Testament* especially those relating to classical antiquity, have been used in a very unfortunate way. Above all, nothing is said about the Athenian census-classes, or the Spartan institutions, in this dictionary.The argument moves from the 'early period' (*Frühzeit*) to the pre-Socratics and then in a short survey takes Greek philosophy on to Aristotle. This is followed by the 'Cynics' and the 'Stoa'. No distinction is made between these great movements. The whole of preached morality is thus dealt with very superficially and, because no shades of meaning are brought out, it is not possible to learn very much of the true relationships. This is a serious error of judgement, especially if what follows is taken into account. What, then, is really the case?

Our sources are misleading. What the propertied classes—and our sources are from authors who belonged to these classes—thought about wealth as opposed to poverty should not form our point of departure in a historical examination of the subject. Our point of departure should certainly be an existing social structure in the community, in other words, the census-classes.

---

[24] Democr., Frag. 302; see also Theognis, 659-666. See also Democr., Frag. 77, 185.
[25] Solon, 4. 9.

It is also incomprehensible that so much importance should be accorded, especially in everyday matters, to philosophers and preached morality. The resulting contradictions are inevitable (cf. Hauck in *ThWNT*, *loc. cit.*). The old aristocracy saw in landed wealth (πλοῦτος) the basis of happiness. Would their view then not have asserted itself at least in practice everywhere? What was the alternative? That of a Dutch hymn, 'Take my silver and my gold, so that nothing remains to me'. Even in the singing of Christian communities this seems like hypocrisy. Yet some of the noblest spirits in Greece, as elsewhere, have in poverty practised what they preached, that 'wealth does not bring happiness'.[26]

An equally unfair tendency among aristocracies is to identify nobility of birth with nobility of soul. In ancient Greece, this led to the belief that evil and crime were always the work of the poor, while the rich lived always in moral purity. Studies of the Greek words πλούσιος and πένης show this very clearly. Naturally enough the belief was on the whole confined to the nobility. There is a complementary view about the effects of wealth, that it 'makes a man not a criminal but a decent citizen', which has also often had a surprising though restricted continuity in the upper levels of different communities. I readily admit that there were also other views, some of which may even have been very different from the aristocratic morality to which I have just referred. But I object to the label 'morality among the aristocracy' being applied to a phenomenon generalized later by the same modern scholar as universally Greek. This confuses the issue and distorts our view of social relationship.[27]

καλοὶ κἀγαθοί [28]

For generations, we have been told that this term should be translated as 'gentlemen', but there are certain objections to this.

---

[26] The most important study in this field is by J. Hemelrijk, *Penia en Ploutos*, Utrecht (1925), especially pp. 111-121.

[27] Hauck himself has said in this context (p. 38, line 35): 'In the Greek world, there was a general tendency to regard πενία as the cause of evil actions'. This statement itself is so generalized that it is unhistorical. It is indisputable that such statements have existed. Bolkestein has provided a summary of the most striking texts, mainly following his pupil Hemelrijk.

[28] See Gomme, *CQ* (1953), p. 65; *Commentary* III, pp. 480-481, 731-732. See also G. E. M. de Ste. Croix, *The Origins of the Peloponnesian War*, London (1972), pp. 371-376, with a recent bibliography on this subject. The striking contrast he observes between the orators and earlier authors may be

The word had a social significance and this is reflected in the usual English translation.[29] There are, however, texts in which it has a political meaning and might therefore also include other classes of people apart from the nobility, the *eupatridai* or the *eugeneis*. Used with this social significance, it was a title employed by the aristocrats or the rich themselves,[30] often to distinguish themselves from the people. It then acquired a political significance.[31]

Let me give an example, that of Hipparchus in the Pseudo-Platonic dialogue of that name. He is called 'beautiful and good' because he undertook the education of his fellow-citizens (228c). We can therefore say that every man who had certain qualities and made use of them was 'beautiful and good'. It was also a title of the upper class in Greece for virtues which the members of that class wanted to reserve for themselves. It was also often used for a 'man of honour' or an *honnête homme*.

We may therefore conclude that everyone had an opportunity to be 'beautiful and brave' in the army, but it should not be forgotten that the *thētes* did not fight in the army. I know of no example of 'brave and beautiful' applied to the oarsmen of the fleet. Generally speaking, the terms could not be separated in the language of the code of honour of 'decent' men. It was not a question of either one or the other; it was rather both one and the other. Each word had a moral significance, but at the same time, the quality of the words was also determined by a primary or secondary social significance.

πένης *and* πτωχός

In pagan terminology *penētes* was used to describe a social group that was not poor in our sense of the word, that is, mendicant. This does not mean, however, that it was not possible for the word to signify 'poor enough to be a beggar'. This is clearly the case when the word is found reinforced by 'rogues' (πονηροί). Even without

somewhat too subtle. I agree with K. J. Dover, *Greek Popular Morality* (1975), pp. 41-45 (quotation on p. 45): 'Until persuaded otherwise by arguments which I have not yet encountered, I make the assumption that the poor Athenian was normally willing to apply the expression Kalos Kāgathos to any man who had what he himself would have liked to have . . . and was what he himself would like to be'.

[29] See Gomme's very good examples from Jane Austen's *Persuasion* and Trollope's novels.

[30] Thucydides 8. 48. 6.

[31] In the sense of the Old Oligarch; this meaning is also found in the lexicon of L.S.J.[9].

this more precise definition, *penēs* could also mean 'poor' in a very striking sense. It is therefore possible to understand that scholars, such as the Septuagint translators, did not always make a distinction between the two words for poor—mendicant and without a fortune (πτωχός and πένης)—.In the translation of Ps. 107. 41, for example, 'he raises up the needy out of affliction', one word is used to translate the two words for poverty found in the Greek Septuagint version: ἐβοήθησε πένητι ἐκ πτωχείας, and in addition to this: ὑπερεπαρεῖ πτωχὸν ἐκ πενίας. A very striking example can be found in Prov. 22. 2: 'The rich and the poor (πτωχός) meet together; the Lord is the maker of them all'. It is clear that it is God's will and plan that the rich and the poor should be on earth, but it is not his will that they should be separate from each other and despise or abuse each other.[32] I am therefore of the opinion that those texts in which both (or one of the two) translations occur should be considered in any question regarding the place of poverty in the Old Testament. Because the pagan Greeks gave a special significance to the word *penēs*, which was different from that of mendicant poverty, however, we have to examine the meaning of the word πτωχός also in pagan literature.[33]

We have seen that the *penētes* were not the poor in the sense in which we should speak of the poor. For many pagan Greeks, the *penētes* were the lower middle class; in political language this was often a term of abuse, but the *penētes* also often possessed slaves.[34] Solon's legislation made the *penētes* the bearers of democracy.[35] The word *penētes* must therefore be excluded from any examination of the 'attitude to the poor'. In this case an examination of the word πτωχοί, the mendicant poor, yields a better result.

It is quite wrong to contrast the Greek attitude to the *penētes* with that found, for example, in the Old Testament towards the mendicant poor, since there is no word in the Old Testament for the group known in Greece as the *penētes*. What, after all, is remarkable here? Not, surely, that a poor man could also be a citizen, but that in both cases (for citizen and non-citizen) the pagan Greek

---

[32] *ThWNT* VI, p. 39, note 13. See also B. Gemser's Commentary on Prov. 14. 20 and the text mentioned here (Prov. 22. 2).

[33] *ThWNT* VI, p. 885 ff, under πτωχός; for πένης, see *ThWNT* VI, p. 39.

[34] *Penia* (poverty) is also, of course, a term for 'bitter poverty', especially when combined with an adjective such as 'difficult' (χαλεπή); see Theognis 182.

[35] See Hauck, *ThWNT* VI, p. 38, line 15 ff.

word for mendicant poor occurs in Septuagint terminology. The pagans themselves found an equivalent of πτωχός in the word *tapeinos*, low or lowly. In Plutarch's Life of Theseus (c. 36), we read that the runaway slaves and 'all men of low estate' found shelter in the temple of Theseus, the hero who founded Athens. Apparently the mendicant poor also (not alone slaves but others, perhaps even citizens) occurred in the pagan Greek world. This is not surprising to those who do not idealize the Greeks, but it does surprise those who believe that Greek democracy resulted in social equality—an equal society that never existed in fact. In ancient Greece, the *penētes* were regarded as politically important. In the theocratic East, this 'middle class'—which certainly existed—was not in the forefront politically. From the social point of view they were just as free, or rather just as little free, in their own desire to make progress and in public opinion about it, as in society today. That is why I object strongly to Hauck's observation: 'Since the *penētes* were so active in the state, they were not regarded politically as oppressed or at a disadvantage in a court of law (as they were in the Old Testament). The idea that the *penētes* had a special helper and protector in the deity was therefore alien to the Greeks' (p. 38).

This is a highly prejudiced account, due to faulty thinking. We have already seen that poverty existed in pagan Greek society and theocratic Jewish society. In neither society was it banned. The word that the Greeks used for the mendicant poor was πτωχός. It can be compared with the term the Jews used for the mendicant poor, which must be rendered in Greek as ταπεινός meaning lowly and destitute. In both societies these mendicant poor had certain protectors, mostly deities. What, then, is special about the Greek case? It is that they had the word *penētes* as well, which in the course of time acquired a political connotation and lost the significance of destitution. It came in this way to be applied to citizens of the lower classes. It was used to mark a distinction from the upper classes, the members of which often used the term contemptuously of the democratically minded lower classes. This phenomenon, of a word acquiring a special political sense and colour, is not infrequent in history. In Dutch, the word *geus* originated with the liberation of Holland from the Spanish yoke in the sixteenth century. Before this, *geus* meant beggar (French *gueux*), but came to be used of a particular subordinate group among the population, the members of which resisted the Spaniards. Centuries later, the

Dutch students who resisted the Germans during their occupation of the Netherlands in the Second World War called their underground newsletter *De Geus* and their movement came to be known by the same name. No one would ever think of making a study of the Dutch word *geus* on the basis of an examination of poverty in the history of the northern Netherlands, but this has happened in the case of the word *penēs* in the study of Greek social history, thus greatly hindering a true understanding of the situation. It has also helped to manufacture a distinction between Mediterranean society on the one hand and oriental society on the other. We can only conclude that there was no such distinction between the Greek and Jewish societies which was, after all, the main point of comparison.

God as the Helper of the Poor

God's 'help' of the poor has often been regarded as the great difference between the Greeks and the 'Orientals', but it is very clear from Homer's Od. 6. 207 that this is a harmful generalization. In this passage, Nausicaa says: 'All strangers and poor are from Zeus'.[36] The same words are also spoken by Eumaeus.[37] Pope's translation is very much to the point here:

'By Jove the stranger and the poor are sent
And what to those we give, to Jove we lent'.

The presence of human selfishness in generosity is apparent in the second line. Alms are 'lent to God' by man to be received back with interest in the hereafter or later in life, since it is God who gives prosperity. The idea of reward and loan is absent from Nausicaa's words, but such a secondary meaning is not necessarily absent from human transactions. Philemon and Baucis were, for example, also given a reward, although these two old people were not selfish. When our attention is drawn to the reward of the benefactor, we should not, however, think at once of pure selfishness, as for instance in Hesiod, *Op*. 343 ff, in which the help that neighbours give each other is discussed and from which we may conclude that a good neighbour was better than a distant friend.

The second line of Pope's translation can be disputed as purely anachronistic. Bolkestein's explanation of Homer's words strikes

---

[36] πρὸς γὰρ Διός εἰσιν ἅπαντες ξεῖνοί τε πτωχοί τε.
[37] Od. 14. 57.

me as far fetched.[38] He has tried to eliminate from them the idea
that the poor had anything to do with the gods, because to accept
that they did would have brought the Greeks too closely in line
with the Jews and the Orientals in general, whose morality was,
in his opinion, very distinct from that of the Greeks.

Two Dutchmen who rated his book very highly have nevertheless
offered serious and well-founded objections to this aspect of his
theories.[39] One of them, Thiel, believed that his sharp distinction
between East and West must be accepted, but argued that Bolkestein need have had no objection to reading the text of the Odyssey
just as it was, because the poor were protected by god during the
period of 'Homeric' aristocratic ascendancy, but had rights as citizens during the period of the democratic state, so that god was no
longer required. This distinction between aristocratic and democratic society cannot be maintained, however, when we recall that
the right of asylum in the temple of Theseus was still in force in
the later period, according to Plutarch, who noted it there in the
second century A.D.[40] There is nothing to prevent us from supposing that it had so continued without interruption. There have
always been poor people and if no one offered them help they called
on the gods.

We are therefore bound to assume that the poor also enjoyed
divine protection during periods later than the aristocratic state
and that the impression they sometimes made on other Greeks was
often that described by the word (θάμβος) 'amazed awe'. Priam, for
example, was filled with this awe when he saw a poor supplicant.
It can only be explained by his belief that the poor man was under
divine protection.[41]

Dodds was also guilty of the same generalization.[42] Whereas Thiel
thought that Nausicaa's words fitted well into the Homeric period,
Dodds was of the opinion that they were more characteristic of that
of Hesiod, declaring that 'in fact, the Hesiodic avenger of the poor
and the oppressed begins to come in sight'. I do not deny that the
deity was the protector of the poor during the Hesiodic period, but
I believe that the deity had the same function during the Homeric

---

[38] *Op. cit.*, p. 177.
[39] J. H. Thiel, *TvG* 55 (1940), pp. 300-302; A. G. Roos, *Mus.* 48 (1941),
pp. 182-185.
[40] See p. 164 above.
[41] A. J. Festugière was right in this; see *Hist. Gén. des Rel.*, p. 41.
[42] E. R. Dodds, *The Greeks and the Irrational* (1951), p. 32.

period as well. There is a striking text in Hesiod that is relevant to this question: 'The watchmen of men who come from Zeus and see injustice' (Op. 253). Hesiod, it should be noted, called Zeus an avenger of the oppressed, not simply an avenger of the poor.

In the Homeric epic, Zeus is angry about the wrongful administration of justice (Il. 16. 384 ff) and this, of course, also includes the protection of the oppressed. But even if we confine ourselves to the poor, the Homeric testimony cannot be disputed, that is, that the poor come from Zeus. In the earlier society, there was no solidarity among the mendicant poor. Hesiod said of his own time: 'The poor man is jealous of the poor man (πτωχὸς πτωχῷ φθονέει)' (Op. 26). We are bound to ask here whether Hesiod was thinking of a lack of political solidarity. I believe that it was rather a lack of solidarity in the social sense, but there is a measure of uncertainty. There is even more uncertainty with regard to the word *penētes* in Athens, where the social aspect was often more prominent than the political.[43]

The real division between social groups in the East and in the West was between the propertied classes, which included both the *plousioi* and the *penētes*, on the one hand and the *ptōchoi* or mendicant poor, who were the outcasts of society,[44] on the other.

Some Old Testament scholars believe that poverty was the hallmark of piety. The man who devoted himself to the study of Scripture and spent day and night pondering the law had no time to earn money. Others are aware of the position of the scribes in Jewish society, but provide a false interpretation of the situation, by claiming that the typically Jewish phenomenon of scribes and schools where the scribes were educated was general throughout the Near East. This has resulted in a distortion of various relationships.[45] I think the idea 'the pious are poor' can be placed alongside

---

[43] See the following dissertations: J. Hemelrijk, *Penia en Ploutos*, Utrecht (1925); J. J. van Manen, *Penia en Ploutos in de periode na Alexander*, Utrecht (1931).

[44] The most detailed treatment of the mendicant poor and beggars is in Bolkestein, *op. cit.*, p. 202 and W. Bauer, *GGA* (1940), p. 360. See also above, p. 151. Another Greek text that should be mentioned is Plato's *Politeia* 555e, where the lazy vagabond (κηφήν) and the beggar are mentioned in the same breath. See recently A. Fuks, 'Plato and the social question. The Problem of Poverty and Riches in the Republic', *Ancient Society*, 8 (1977), 49-84.

[45] Bauer, *op. cit.*, p. 366, is opposed to Bolkestein, *op. cit.*, pp. 413, 460, here.

the idea 'the poor are pious'. Our point of departure, I think, should be the evidence that poverty and holiness go together. This idea is generally reserved for the later period of Roman antiquity, that of mendicant monks, holy men and saints who lived at the top of pillars or in other ways renounced the world. It does seem to me, however, that something can be said here about an earlier period in history. In Paul's letter to the Romans, for example (15. 26), there is reference to 'the poor among the saints at Jerusalem'; there was clearly a group here. Paul does not speak of all the saints being poor, but of men who lived in poverty among the pious or the saints.[46]

In his commentary on Rom. 15. 25, H. Lietzmann has pointed out that from the religious point of view the poor and the saints may well have been the same, but I would insist that they did not always have to be identical and that it is doubtful whether this is the case in this particular text from the letter to the Romans. Lietzmann has referred to R. Otto's book *Das Heilige*, which is certainly concerned with saints, in other words, men who were involved in the mystery of the end of time, but has nothing to say about the poor.[47]

There was certainly a phase in the development of social awareness in which the poor had a definite task, one that can be called 'divine'. I am thinking here of such feasts as the Saturnalia, when slaves were permitted a degree of freedom for a certain time, giving them, as it were, a foretaste of later freedom, which seemed possible. In our investigation, however, what we have are free, individual, poor members of the community who were sometimes citizens of the same city or state. The members of this social group may certainly have hoped for a reward in the hereafter and believed that they would be cared for later by the gods. In other words, they may well have thought that they would receive a recompense in the hereafter for what they had suffered here on earth. The evil that the rich had done on earth also found its recompense in the hereafter. A New Testament example of this idea can be found in the story of the rich man and Lazarus the poor man (Luke 16. 19-31).

What we observe here, then, is that there was no such explicit idea in pagan Greek or Roman society of the poor enjoying the protection of the gods, although the slaves (not the poor citizens)

---

[46] See K. Holl, *SAB* (1921), pp. 937-939.
[47] See E. Williger, 'Hagios', *RVV* 19, Heft 1.

were given a definite part to play in the Saturnalia.[48] In future, much more attention than has been given in the past will have to be given to a development 'in each early civilization' with regard to the attitude towards the mendicant poor and the destitute in society. The differences that existed in the civilizations around the Mediterranean as far as the Jews, Greeks, and Romans are concerned were not very great.

Theoretical Statements about Help Given to the 'Poor'

The generally accepted view today is that the needy were supported in ancient Greece, but that this relief was not explicitly recommended by the moralists as a virtuous act. It was apparently regarded as universally human, self-evident and without any special significance.

'Without any special significance', however, is rather severe. Bolkestein uses it [49] after having indicated the political meaning that was certainly intended by a number of statements by the Greeks themselves, on the theme that the poor were not members of the non-propertied class, but were impoverished. Bolkestein attempts to relate this to the support they received for political reasons.[50]

It is moreover not true that a positive attitude to relief was simply self-evident. The poor were not given relief as a matter of course and without anyone noticing.[51] That would imply that the desire to help others was universally human. History, however, teaches us differently. It has often happened that it was not the hungry man who deserved his neighbours' sympathy—it is often said to be a man's own fault if he is poor—but the respectable man hit by misfortune, whose poverty was in no sense his own fault. Unfortunately, poor people of that type, who might well appeal to the rich to part with their money, rarely enter the minds of the rich themselves. Men who have had serious set-backs and then lost their

---

[48] For Israel, see C. van Leeuwen's dissertation, *Le développement du sens social en Israël avant l'ère chrétien. Studia Semitica Neerlandica*, Utrecht (1955). For a later period, see J. R. Smeets, *La chevalerie de Judas Macabé*, Dissertation Groningen, Assen (1955), especially the continued influence of social themes up to the thirteenth century. For the Saturnalia and the slaves, see K. Latte, *Römische Religionsgeschichte* (1960), p. 254, note 3; W. B. Kristensen, in his essay, mentioned on p. 208, n. 11 below.

[49] *Op. cit.*, pp. 130-133.

[50] *Op. cit.*, pp. 132, 171, 460.

[51] The studies of P. Veyne and others concerning 'évergétisme' illustrate quite different motives. See his recent book *Le pain et le cirque*, Paris 1976.

property may arouse some compassion among those who are of the
same class. This does not apply, however, to a man who has been
mendicant poor from birth. Such a person is often regarded as a
parasite. The idea that 'there are no poor in a good political situation' is based on an attitude that attaches too much importance to
spontaneous charity as a motive for politics. Bolkestein's chapter
on the judgement of poverty [52] gives examples enough, proving
hard-heartednes of the rich. But they are in conflict with the passage
on p. 133 of his book. This passage appears in italics—this was done
quite deliberately by the author—and is given below.[53]

Anyone who preaches that a person in danger of perishing from
want can find charity everywhere makes a rhetorical statement
without historical foundation—either in the past or the present,
either in Greece or anywhere else including the ancient Near East.
This is because covetousness and prejudice (it's all his own fault!)
are greater than our willingness to help.[54]

On the Borderline between Theory and Practice

Hesiod's experience taught him about poverty which, he believed,
deprived man of his sense of human dignity: 'An evil stigma at-

---

[52] *Op. cit.*, p. 185 ff.

[53] Bolkestein's text, which is freely translated in the first paragraph of
this section reads as follows: '*Unterstützung wurde aber nicht etwa von den
Moralisten als hohe Tugend mit Nachdruck geboten, sondern galt offensichtlich
als bedeutungslose, selbstverständliche und ganz allgemein menschliche Hand-
lung*'. The author's quotation (p. 131) from Isocrates 7. 32 ff is in conflict
with the general argument above: 'The less well-to-do among the citizens
were so far from envying those of greater means that they were as solicitous
for the great estates as for their own, considering that the prosperity of the
rich was a guarantee of their own well-being. Those who possessed wealth,
on the other hand, did not look down upon those in humbler cicumstances,
but, regarding poverty among their fellow-citizens as their own disgrace,
came to the rescue of the distresses of the poor ...'. In this quotation the
poor are not the mendicant poor, not the πτωχός who is the object of this
part of the author's *Armenpflege*. Bolkestein assumed that Isocrates' statements in the passage quoted reflected the usual Utopian ideals of the fourth
century B.C. I agree with him, and I doubt whether an optimistic idea of
that kind, according to which the poor man was not at all jealous of the
propertied man, could come about if there had not been great bitterness in
fact between the rich and the poor. As far as Isocrates is concerned, this is
apparently what Bolkestein believed. Once again, I agree. This, however,
makes the words quoted above from the German text of his book (p. 133)
incomprehensible. There was tension and it continued to exist.

[54] The rhetorical question that ought to prove the opposite can be found
in Stobaeus, Ecl. II, p. 121: τίνα δ' οὐκ ἂν ἐπαρκέσειν ὑπ' ἐνδείας ἀπολλυμένῳ;
(Who will not offer help to someone perishing of poverty?).

taches to a destitute man' (Op. 317). The author of the Odyssey also knew this (Od. 17. 322) 'because far-seeing Zeus deprives a man of half his worth on the day when slavery overtakes him' The aristocratic Theognis also knew it as well as Hesiod: 'The man who is bound by poverty can say nothing and do nothing, but his tongue is fastened in his mouth' (177-178).

The last statement is typical of one who has known better times and is now cast down. Again and again men had to cope with the outside world. The Delphic oracle, which warned the rich against pride and the poor against servility, emphasized this fact of life (Stobaeus, III, p. 115).[55] These and similar quotations show how the ancient world was characterized by the same kind of hazards as those we know today. Poverty brought frustation in its wake. This caused discontent which in turn may sometimes have given rise to political rebellion, although this happened very rarely in the ancient Greek world, since there was so little chance of its succeeding.

A faulty notion of historical development has led some scholars to assume that there were no such feelings in the later period of Greek civilization. To judge by human attitudes at other periods of history, this is very doubtful, although we are bound to admit that there is no textual evidence to the contrary. But there is an explanation for this. The higher and more untroubled the development of the settled 'middle class' in any society, the less room there is for the underprivileged. I therefore think it incautious at the least to use the argument from silence to prove that there was no distinction between poverty and destitution. What we often find is that it is said to be the poor man's own fault if he is poor and that poverty is equated with wickedness. Yet we are aware also of the deeper note in the complaints of the poor in the work of Hesiod, Homer, and Theognis. Hesiod and Theognis were above all men who lived practical lives. Although he was describing a different society, Homer was one of the most outstanding figures in world literature for knowledge of the human heart. The lessons of practical living will teach us that complaints about the loss of human possibilities and abilities (ἀρετή) are real, even though few statements by the poor themselves have been preserved.

---

[55] Bolkestein, op. cit., p. 185 ff, deals excellently with these texts and I have nothing to add. The whole framework within which his argument is set, however, in other words his fundamental distinction between East and West, is questionable.

Finally, I must mention once more the remarkable practice at
the feast of the Thargēlia in Athens, to which I have already referred,[56] when a poor beggar was cast out of the community with the
guilt of that community on his shoulders. There is nothing to indicate that this practice was abolished in a later, supposedly more
civilized period.[57]

The Community, the Plousioi, and the Penētes

It was possible for the community, as opposed to the state, to be
generous towards the poor. There were private initiatives in the
way of loans and welfare to fellow citizens. They occurred especially
at the community level because the state had its own means of
evening out differences between poor and rich, here described as
penētes and plousioi. There were the heavy charges imposed on the
rich by the Greek system of taxation. I have not yet considered
these political measures taken by the democratic state in my examination of the whole question and will confine myself to saying that
those who were less well off for worldly possessions got exceptionally
favourable treatment in regard to taxes. I shall also have to leave
out of consideration what 'benefactors' did for the state in the form
of taxes which they voluntarily undertook to pay. This sense of
community was extremely important in the relationship between
the rich and the poor, but it must be distinguished from personal
help given to those who were less well off.

What should always be borne in mind is the difference already
noted between the two words penētes and ptōchoi. We are bound to
say that the last category did not figure in this form of assistance.
This is the very question we have to consider in any detailed discussion of the differences between rich and poor in ancient Greece
on the one hand and the Ancient Near East on the other.[58] If we
also consider the question of private charity to the ptōchoi in the
Greek community, we find that this hardly existed. The reason is
quite clear. In oriental society, the mendicant poor formed part of
the community and had a function in it. As we have seen, they had
a similar function in the western community. In both it was believed that the poor had been given to the community so that they

---

[56] See above, p. 129 ff.

[57] I have dealt with this question in my article 'Greeks and the Greeks',
International Review of Social History IV (1959), p. 91 ff.

[58] See Bolkestein, *op. cit.*, p. 431 ff.

might receive private charity and be given asylum. In this the God of the Jews and the founder hero of Athens took identical lines.

What is remarkable is that the main sources we have for private charity are the lessons in the works of some philosophers.[59] Private charity can be found in Democritus, the Anonymus Iamblichi, and the *Memorabilia* of Xenophon.[60] There is not very much material and the interpretation of the texts is, in my opinion, quite clear.

Democritus says: 'The laws make no objection to everyone living as he thinks fit, so long as no one harms another, for jealousy is the beginning of strife' (Frag. 245 DK). Jealousy of the man of property is clearly indicated in this text and strife (stasis) was a source of possible danger in any community in which men lived together. What is implied too is that men could not really live just as they pleased and that they had to think of their fellow men. It is also clear that this took place within the framework of the community in which the rich and the poor lived together as fellow-citizens.

Another fragment of Democritus tells us: 'If those with property will take the risk of giving loans to those without, of helping them and doing good to them, this action contains all the mercy, common feeling, brotherliness, mutual aid, harmony between citizens and all other good—so much that no one could add it all up' (Frag. 255). According to Democritus, then, harmony between citizens was guaranteed by people helping one another. Will was right to speak of an *éthique civile* here. What is emphasized above all is the preservation of harmony in the community.[61] This is far removed from an obligation of private aid imposed by law. This text above all concerns a society that was only possible when the citizens helped one another. The emphasis, I am bound to point out again, is on 'citizens'.

The texts from the Anonymus Iamblichi (successively 7. 1-2; 7. 8; 3. 4-6) [62] are far less convincing. The Anonymus taught that observance of the law created an atmosphere of trust which was of

---

[59] For the passage from Pericles' *Funeral Speech*, Thucydides 2. 40, in this context, see p. 176 below.

[60] E. Will, *Numismatique antique. Problèmes et Méthodes. Annales de l'Est*, publiées par l'Université de Nancy, II, Mémoires No. 44 (1975), pp. 233-246. The title is: *Fonction de la monnaie dans les cités grecques de l'époque classique.*

[61] *Op. cit.*, p. 236.

[62] *DK* II⁶ (1952), p. 401 ff. Modern bibliography in C. J. Classen (ed.) 'Sophistik', *Wege der Forschung* 187, Darmstadt 1976, p. 676 f.

benefit to all men. He included this trust among man's greatest
possessions, since money was, in his opinion, a consequence of the
trust that men placed in each other and, even though there was
at times not much of it, it was enough so long as it circulated.
Without mutual trust, however, it would not have been enough
even if a great deal had been available. He goes on to say that the
conditions in which they were living were very good for all men,
as the result of good laws, that there was prosperity and that it was
clear from men's attitudes to life that they got on well together.
All those who lived in these happy conditions enjoyed prosperity
and security and were not attacked. What is more, those who were
prosperous and richly blessed with this world's goods also helped
others. This resulted in a situation in which men trusted each other.

Will has spoken here of a *solidarité*, but there is little sign of this
as far as I can see. This is his translation of the Greek word *epimeixia*.
The term relates to economic transactions that bring money into
circulation so long as there is mutual trust among those taking part.
It has nothing at all to do with solidarity among citizens. As a
commercial term ('dealings', 'transactions') it throws the whole
question of mutual relations in a community such as the Greek *polis*
into an entirely different light. It fits much better into the sort of
community development envisaged by Anonymus.[63] What, then,
is the case?

The Anonymus regarded the rich man as someone who had to
be prepared to lose his property. Property was valuable as an insurance so that the owner could support himself in bad times, sickness, and old age. His fellow-citizens had therefore to be given
moderate relief for their needs, since the rich man's property was
not inexhaustible. It is obvious that this concept of mutual help
could not have been based on solidarity in the community and on a
sharing of poverty and a fair distribution of wealth to all members
of the society concerned, so that everyone benefited. The Anonymus
lived in a society with a very precarious state of economic equilibrium. He had therefore to subject the aid given to his fellow-citizens to certain conditions, such as the return of money given or the
payment of interest as well as other safeguards. This is clearly a
long way from granting the citizen a specific right to be supported

---

[63] The translation of M .E. Reesor, in *The Older Sophists*, ed. by R. Kent
Sprague (Columbia, South Carolina, 1972, p. 276) is correct: *Epimeixia* =
'their common dealings'.

by his fellows. On the contrary, it is clear that there were well defined limits to such support. We may go further and say there is evidence that a person did not cease to have the status of a poor man because of the gifts made by others to relieve his poverty. On the contrary, he had to live contentedly. He had, in other words, to be 'satisfied with his lot', to use a saying that was common at a different period of history and in a different civilization.

Let us now look at the Anonymus' text to see whether this view is borne out by what the author says:

3. 4 'If, by giving financial support (to others), a man becomes a benefactor of his region, he will necessarily become "bad" (kakos) when he gathers wealth again. What is more, he could not accumulate the money, the capital, in such a great amount that his resources would not fail while he makes his gifts and presentations. This second evil (kakia) will also appear if the benefactor, after he has collected the money having been a rich man, becomes a poor man and from having been a member of the propertied class, sinks down into the non-propertied class'.

3. 5 'How, then, could a man be a benefactor, if he does not distribute money, but uses some other means and that without an evil (kakia) resulting from this, but rather so that "virtue" (aretē) will reign? And how, if a man gives, can he arrange it so that his giving is inexhaustible?'

3. 6 'It will only be possible in this way—if he commits himself to right and to the laws—for it is this which unites cities and men and binds them together'.

Various aspects of the above text have to be explained. An exaggerated generosity clearly led, according to the Anonymus, to ruin (kakia) and the ruined man was—or became—a kakos. I would agree with Will—these terms are almost untranslatable. Poverty, a low social status, and moral inferiority are all rendered by kakos. I do not, however, agree with him in his translation of the word for 'community' or 'living together' (synoikizon) by 'solidarity'. There is no question of its being 'solidarity'. It points to men's communal life, their living with each other in a geographically defined territory. There is no secondary ethical significance.

The beginning of the passage is perhaps the most interesting. If a man is too generous in distributing his wealth, the author is saying, he will not only fall a victim to the *kakia* that is inherent in poverty—he will also encounter another *kakia*. This is because everyone who is not rich or no longer rich and who tries to become rich or to become rich once again can only do this by becoming a *kakos*. The Anonymus used the word *kakos*; others spoke of an *adikos* or an 'unjust man'.

How, then, should we understand this? Why should the desire to be rich or to become rich imply an evil or an unjust action? Will asked this question very pertinently and it is possible to agree with his answer. It may in this case be a question of wealth that has been gained in a dishonest manner or by means of violence towards others. There is, however, more to the question. According to this view, the whole concept of social order implied that that order was based on irrational 'justice', according to which society included both rich and poor. The gods had given wealth to one man and poverty to another. It was therefore right for the rich to help the poor, but a desire to cease to be poor and to become rich was contrary to justice and the will of the gods.

It is clear, then, that these reflections of fifth-century philosophers have brought us to the same point that we reached in an earlier part of our discussion. There was no intention of causing a change in the circumstances of society. The *ptōchoi* were to stay as they were, retaining their status, and if a citizen belonging to the middle class *penētes*, fell into grinding poverty he too had to remain in that condition. Indeed, if a rich man was guilty of exaggerated generosity and became poor, he pronounced a judgement on himself. With all his liberal aspirations, he found himself in a lower social class and had to stay there. This, then, is the Anonymus' concept of the practice of generosity.

The Anonymus had a great deal in common with the Old Oligarch I would also like to add to this brief survey that a frequently quoted text in Thucydides has nothing to do with the problem that concerns us. This passage comes from Pericles' funeral oration (2. 40):[64] 'Again, in questions of general good feeling there is a great contrast between us and most other people. We make friends by doing good to others, not by receiving good from them. This makes our friendship all the more reliable, since we want to keep alive the gratitude of those who are in our debt by showing continued goodwill to them:

---

[64] The translation is Rex Warner's, *Thucydides, The Peloponnesian War* (Introduction and appendices by M. I. Finley) Harmondsworth 1972.

whereas the feelings of one who owes us something lack the same enthusiasm since he knows that, when he repays our kindness, it will be more like paying back a debt than giving something spontaneously. We are unique in this. When we do kindnesses to others, we do not do them out of any calculations of profit or loss: we do them without afterthought, relying on our free liberality'.

It is clear that Pericles was speaking here of the relationship between the Athenians and their allies, not of the duty that the citizen of Athens had towards his neighbours or the generosity of the citizens with regard to each other. Unlike Will, I prefer to keep this text out of the present discussion.

We must, however, consider the concept of *koinōnia* or 'community' in this context. This term has been discussed at some length in a dissertation by Endenburg and the author's results were later assimilated by his teacher Bolkestein, in the latter's *Armenpflege*.[65]

There is a great deal that we can take over from these studies. If we are to understand this concept, we must take the idea of being a participant or partner in something as our fundamental point of departure. The social aspect is apparent in the first part of the word, *koinos*. The basic word and the various combinations point to friendliness in associating with others, someone who is *koinōnikos*, 'clubbable' and so on. A similar meaning can also be associated with the word *philanthrōpos*. The latter has nothing to do with charity or well-doing ('philanthropy'). It indicates love of mankind in the strict sense of the word and friendly and polite ways of associating with our fellow-men, who would in this case, of course, be Greeks and free men.[66] It does not mean, then, fellow-men in the later [67] and modern sense of the word, fellow humanity or human fellowship, with all the political overtones of these words. It is obvious, so it is alleged, that this is distinct from the 'East', where a man's attitude to the poor, in the sense of mendicant poor, was given more prominence. Rom 15. 26 can be quoted to illustrate this distinction. 'For Macedonia and Achaia have been pleased to make some contribution for the poor among the saints at Jerusalem'. Heb. 13. 16 is also relevant: 'Do not neglect to do good and to share

---

[65] The dissertation is by P. J. T. Endenburg, *Koinoonia en Gemeenschap van Zaken bij Grieken in den Klassieken Tijd* (1937); see also Bolkestein, *op. cit.*, p. 431 ff.

[66] Cf. p. 141, note 41 above.

[67] See p. 143 ff. above.

what you have (*koinōnia*), for such sacrifices are pleasing to God'.

Bolkestein drew the conclusion from this: '*Koinonia*, which, in Greek society, was a readiness to share with one's fellow-men, became relief of the poor in oriental society'.[68] This is a complete misunderstanding of the whole question. Bolkestein clearly did not take the *ptōchoi*, who were dependent on alms and acts of benevolence in the ancient pagan world, both classical and post-classical, and in the Jewish world, into account at all. For the Athenian citizen, only his neighbour, or rather the man situated nearest to him, was his fellow-citizen, the man who belonged to a smaller or slightly lower social class and to whom he could lend or give money, but not too much, so that he could recover from the loss again. If the Athenian sank to the lowest class, however, this meant in practice, as in the Homeric epic and in later literature, that he had stepped outside his class and had therefore become rejected.

The only conclusion that can be drawn from all this, then, (and this is no more than a repetition of what I have already said) is that some present-day specialists in the social history of classical antiquity have tended to compare only one of the two Greek words for poor, *penētes* with the Jewish conceptual system. But the two were used in completely different ways, and as a result they have come to a conclusion which they certainly would not have reached if they had taken the other Greek word (*ptōchoi*) into consideration in their studies.[69]

---

[68] 'Die Koinonia, in der griechischen Gesellschaft, die Bereitschaft, den Mitmenschen einen Anteil zu bewähren, ist in der orientalischen zur Unterstützung von Armen geworden', *op. cit.*, p. 432. But 'Mitmenschen' (fellowmen) are restricted to members of their own community, neighbours, *some* 'subsidized poor'—this is what Bolkestein forgets.

[69] Many of the passages discussed in this chapter and a great deal of the material involved were included in the article κοινός and under the words derived from κοινός in *ThWNT* III, p. 789 ff (F. Hauck).

CHAPTER NINE

THE OPPOSITE SIDE OF THE COIN

Man and Citizen

From what I have said so far the reader might have got the impression that I was making a complete separation between social and political history in ancient Greece. This has certainly not been my intention. It may therefore be useful to recapitulate briefly and see what others have said about the political rights of the *penētes*. The classical authors were generally unfavourable in their judgement of the democratic city state. This is hardly surprising, as most of these authors came from the upper class and could not reconcile themselves to the extension of political and civil rights to the lower class citizen majority. One of the first advocates of the latter was the 'Old Oligarch', author of a treatise on the Constitution of Athens mistakingly attributed to Xenophon, whom we have already encountered. It has been rightly said that this man regarded it as his special task to make small what was great.[1] Lucian was another who knew how to make what was great at least ridiculous. Statements that are similar to those made by the Old Oligarch can be found in Lucian's *Cock* (21-23).

Coming closer to the time when the Old Oligarch himself was writing, we can also mention Plato among those who were hostile to many aspects of Athenian democracy. At the same time, however, he apparently did not realize that he was only able to write as he did because of the democratic government of the city. The attitude characteristic of the oligarchs was that the majority of the people were 'slaves' of the few which they regarded as an ideal situation (Old Oligarch 1. 5).[2] The term often used for this 'ideal' situation of the lower class was actually *douleia*, literally 'slavery', but having somewhat changed this meaning. Whereas Aristotle, for

---

[1] A. W. Gomme has dealt brilliantly with the Old Oligarch in the Supplement to the *Harvard Studies in Classical Philology* (1940). For the negative judgement of the Athenian democracy in Greek literature, see A. H. M. Jones, *Athenian Democracy*. (1957). Cf. p. 151 above. One of the best modern surveys: W. G. Forrest, *The Emergence of Greek Democracy*, London (1966) (first edition).

[2] See F. Jacoby, *FGrHist IIIb*, Suppl. II, p. 93, note 83.

example, used the word in its literal sense, where entire families were reduced to 'slavery' because of debt, the Old Oligarch used it to indicate the absence of political rights. The terminology of the right wing of the oligarchy was not changed. The viewpoint was invested with its own logic Aristotle provided an outline of the radical democracy of Athens, followed by a recognition of the aims, logical structure, and consistent nature of what was for him a detestable system. (*Athenaiōn Politeia* 2 and 5).

It has often been claimed that the economic character of the party divisions in Athens was clear at the time of Aristotle, but not in the fifth century. This is simply not true, as more and more scholars are coming to recognize.[3] Xenophon, an aristocrat, distinguished the *dēmos* from the 'richer people' (πλουσιώτεροι),[4] defining it as the *penētes* among the citizens (*dēmokratia* being the rule of the *dēmos*). In his pamphlet containing a dialogue between Alcibiades and Pericles and included in the *Memorabilia* (I. 2, 40-46), Xenophon contrasted the mass of the people with the propertied class, which he claimed that they even tyrannized. The opposition between the two is formulated quite drastically in such terms as to provoke a strong reaction. The good and the bad, the employable and the unemployable were opposed to one another.

The same situation prevailed in the Roman republic: the *boni* were opposed to the *improbi*. The ordinary people were explicitly equated in various places with the *penētes*. In every state the 'best' were the opposite of the democrats. It is of course possible that most Athenians of the upper class rejected many of the Old Oligarch's propositions or at least watered down his stark presentation of them, but this is not really relevant. The Old Oligarch was undoubtedly writing for a non-Athenian public and his pamphlet is particularly valuable because of the light that it throws on the views of the upper classes in other states. But many of the well-to-do citizens of Athens thought like him. The Old Oligarch's picture is in black and white and over-simplified, but it cannot be denied that the citizens of the Greek states were divided into two great economic and social categories and that there were serious tensions

---

[3] G. E. M. de Ste. Croix, *The Character of the Athenian Empire, Historia* III, pp. 1-41, especially p. 24 ff. In much of what I say here this author's works have been my guide. I also record my debt to M. I. Finley's *Athenian Demagogues* (see p. 157 above).

[4] *Hellenica* 4. 8, 20.

between them. This is confirmed in the work of other authors.[5]

If we look at the great political and military leaders of ancient Greece, we have a different picture. The demagogues of the fifth century were automatically condemned by the aristocratic writers, appreciation being reserved for such aristocratic leaders as Cimon. The latter actually was not a demagogue, but a general who also served increasingly radical democracy.[6]

Pericles' political life was overshadowed by his dispute with Thucydides, son of Melesias. According to Plutarch (Pericles, 11. 3), this Thucydides appeared as a politician in opposition to Pericles. He was also the first professional politician. He was not a soldier and he held no office of responsibility. After Thucydides had been ostracized, Pericles must have had only personal attacks to endure, not as party politician so much, but as leader of the government.

Cleon and Nicias were rivals, but the latter was a loyal servant of the Athenian democracy after Pericles' death. Each of these leaders did his best, in his own way, to win the Peloponnesian War. Other eminent aristocrats such as Laches, Eurycrates, and Nicostratus were also active and loyal, as were the members of the mainly aristocratic cavalry. There was no party that was opposed to the Athenian empire and none that was in favour of a cowardly peace with Sparta.

This has above all been stressed by Gomme. He may perhaps have concentrated too much on Athens in a state of war thus under-emphasizing party differences. It should be borne in mind that the Old Oligarch too was aware of collaboration between the parties. In 1. 3, he mentions the fact that the highest offices, even in a democratic state, were occupied by aristocrats.

The much dispute figure of Cleon always comes to mind whenever political equality is emphasized in the context of social inequality. I do not propose to go over the ground of the controversy that has engaged modern historians in connection with this political leader.[7] What is important is that this man, whose origin cannot

---

[5] De Ste. Croix cites the speech of Athenagoras of Syracuse (Thucydides, 8. 39. 1 ff); see also *Eur. Suppl.*, lines 238-245.

[6] Jacoby, *FGrHist.* IIIb, II Suppl., p. 92.

[7] See Gomme, *op. cit.* (1940). This author has presented the situation in too rosy a light, although his article is otherwise admirable. See also Jacoby, *op. cit.*, p. 94, note 99, who does not conceal his admiration for Gomme's article, but adds: 'though perhaps he paints too bright a picture'. For Cleon, see also de Ste. Croix, *op. cit.*, pp. 34-35, and A. G. Woodhead, in *Mnem.* 13

be traced back to the aristocracy,[8] had the greatest possible in-fluence after the death of Pericles. The demos, gathered in the People's Assembly, were able to elect their own members. We should not think here of such modern phenomena as 'action groups', since the People's Assembly did not consist of groups of that kind, but was far more of an official body in the eyes of the Greeks, at least when they had engendered a sense of responsibility in them-selves by their membership of the council and their participation in discussions and offices. It was in fact the sovereign body of the Athenian state and this is, of course, not something that can be said of an 'action group'. That is why it was such a great achieve-ment on the part of Pericles to have been able to exert such a deep influence on the Athenian state for thirty years almost without interruption, while holding one of the few offices that was not filled by drawing lots, but by direct election. (His office was that of military commander). Pericles was, however, an aristocrat by birth, even though in his politics he was a democrat and, what is more, by intention a radical democrat.

In the Greek city state, then—and Athens is the most familiar example—there was a predominance of democracy which lasted for a long period, despite the continuance of social prejudices in op-position to 'left-wing' leaders and their supporters. This indicates a certain maturity among the members of Athenian society—their great social differences did not result in political cleavage. As Gomme has pointed out: "To write as though the hoplites and the rich (or the farmers and the rich) formed one class opposed to the *thētes*, the demos, or even that the rich, or the aristocrats, were consistently the enemies of the demos in every way, the constitution, foreign policy, and the empire, is to falsify history on the evidence that we have, including that of Pseudo-Xenophon".[9]

We may go even further and say that Gomme was right in his

(1960), pp. 289-317. This view was for a long time regarded as *communis opinio* and was included in the volume on Thucydides in *Wege der Forschung*, 98 (1968), pp. 557-593. Some years ago, however, this opinion was rejected by Pritchett in 'The Woodheadean Interpretation of Kleon's Amphipolitan Campaign', *Mnem.* 26 (1973), pp. 376-386. (I regard Pritchett's article as more of an attempt to reject Woodhead's view rather than as a successful reversal of the theory).

[8] See J. K. Davies, *Athenian Propertied Families* (1971), under the name Kleon.

[9] *Op. cit.*, pp. 242-243.

dispute with de Sanctis.[10] These two scholars were in disagreement over the population of Athens in 431 B.C., Gomme claiming that there were 18 000 *thetes* and 25 000 other citizens, whereas de Sanctis believed that there were 23 000 *thetes* and 18 000 others. According to the latter, it must have been a majority which had the ruling power. Gomme thought it was equally difficult to understand how an unarmed and unorganized majority of 23 000 could dominate an armed and organized minority of 18 000. De Sanctis' reply was that this was the case in the British parliament: the half plus one ruled. Gomme insisted that this was precisely what it was all about. The situation in England was not that an unarmed majority opposed an armed minority. The 'poor' could dominate all the 'propertied' people, but they did not, and the propertied class also wanted to serve their country loyally. That, Gomme contended, was also the case in Athens.[11]

What are we to say? Gomme was clearly concerned with the political aspect. However, there have been divisions enough in the social and economic sphere and these have to a great extent determined the political structure.[12] Gomme's argument therefore does not invalidate de Ste Croix' exposition. Gomme was concerned with the leaders and, even if they belonged to the upper class in society, their position remained unchanged. The people simply relied on their loyalty. This is borne out by Pseudo-Xenophon (1. 3).

One factor that has not yet been discussed is the fear among the socially inferior of an oligarchic conspiracy. The Pseudo-Xenophon does not tell us that the oligarchs met together in clubs and were sometimes, in comedy often, characterized as conspirators (Aristophanes, *Knights* 257).[13] This is no doubt exaggerated for comic effect, but there was certainly widespread fear that democracy would be overthrown with the help of oligarchs from elsewhere. Because of this fear the Oligarch speculated, 'If Athens were an island . . .' (2. 15). The democrats regarded the policy of the oligarch clubs (*hetaireiai*) as nothing but tyranny and thought anyone who

---

[10] *Riv. di Filol.* XV, (1937), pp. 288-290; XVI, pp. 169-172.
[11] Gomme's article, *The Old Oligarch* (1940), was republished in *More Essays in Greek History and Literature* (1962). See especially p. 66 ff.
[12] See Pseudo-Xenophon 1. 6.
[13] See Calhoun, *Athenian Clubs in Politics and Litigation* (1913); V. Ehrenberg, *The People of Aristophanes* (1951²), p. 110.

rode (a horse) had tyranny in mind, of the kind that had existed in the reign of the tyrant Hippias.[14]

It is said that *ostraca* with the name of Themistocles were widespread before the vote which condemned him and his policy. This was a fraud which undoubtedly occurred, but it cannot be said to have been general. According to Plutarch (*Pericles* 11), political organizations existed under the leadership of Thucydides the son of Melesias.[15] It is clear from the Old Oligarch that there were social conflicts. In this context, I prefer the term 'social' to 'class' conflicts or differences because 'class' has a fixed meaning and invites comparison with modern class conflict. The comparison is not valid, but we must give some thought to the whole question for a moment.[16]

Class conflict is a term that has a special meaning deriving from the industrial revolution in western Europe in the nineteenth century. There have always been different levels of the population at all periods of history, but the word class implies a group solidarity that did not exist in Greece during the period that we are discussing here, namely the fifth and fourth centuries B.C. It is also difficult to recognize organized 'classes' in other periods of Greek history. We have a decided impression that there were differences between groups in the population, but these differences are at the same time counterbalanced by the possibility of movement from one group to another. There was, in other words, far greater political mobility in ancient Greece than has frequently been suggested.

Even though these differences are exaggerated in the bitter writing of the Old Oligarch, we should not try to obscure or deny them.[17] There is a distinction here between ancient and modern literature, but it is quantitative rather than qualitative. There is general agreement that these differences existed, but less agreement about how far they were developed. It is clear, for instance, that there was a strong consensus in politics not over-weighed by social antitheses. This situation is frequently found in mature societies—greatly to the discomfort of those who like polarities.

---

[14] For the existence of parties, not in our sense of the word, but as groups of like-minded people, see Ehrenberg, *op. cit.*, p. 340, note 4.

[15] See H. T. Wade-Gery in *JHS* 52 (1932), pp. 205-227 and especially p. 208; this article was included in the author's collection, *Essays in Greek History* (1958), pp. 239-270, especially p. 243.

[16] G. E. M. de Ste. Croix's book *The Class Struggle in the Ancient Greek World* had not yet appeared when this book was sent to the printer.

[17] D. Loenen has pointed to this in his inaugural lecture in Amsterdam, *Stasis* (1953).

To what extent, then, did this opposition between the classes —if we are to use the word class—operate in ancient Greece? I would like to say once again that the answer given to this question depends above all on the attitude of the scholar himself. Is there any way of checking on the subjectivity of the ancient or modern historian? I think that this check can be found in comedy. It is, however, a precarious way of checking, because very wild ideas exist concerning 'historical exactitude' and 'comic exaggeration'.[18] If we are to be cautious, we can summarize the whole question in the following way. The writing of history, which was a task that was in the main carried out by those who belonged to the upper social class, must be able to stand up to the reality of history. We may therefore reject a claim that everything said by the writers of history was untrue. We may conclude that what the historians opposed in ancient Greece certainly existed. Even if we reject eighty percent of what the Pseudo-Xenophon said, the fact remains that there were social and economic differences in Greek society which were at least partially kept in balance or rather prevented from leading to social upheaval, by the fact of political equality. It cannot be denied, however, that these social differences had an effect on political life and gave rise to political differences and oppositions.[19]

To summarize my argument I quote from Ehrenberg: 'In the pamphlet of the Pseudo-Xenophon the two social strata are contrasted with each other under various names and from every point of view—their political, their social and economic outlook as well as their military importance and their education. We cannot deal with all the various epithets which simply indicate the writer's wish to emphasize, indeed to over-emphasize, the difference between the two social classes'.[20]

What is of importance for us is that political life can have a conciliatory effect on social conflicts. This is a human phenomenon that occurs again and again. Anyone who reads the autobiographies of English parliamentarians will constantly be surprised by the manner in which members of parliament who were socially and politically far removed from one another have associated with one

---

[18] As we shall see, comedy was used and appreciated in the same way when it dealt with the position of slaves.

[19] De Ste. Croix provides a correct assessment of the situation here.

[20] *Op. cit.*, pp. 97-98.

another, grown together, and worked in close co-operation for the common good. This mutual friendship and appreciation softens the social differences and makes political co-operation possible, not only in times of crisis, but also in ordinary parliamentary matters.

This comparison can be applied to the Athenian council, the members of which came from the various districts of Athens that were united in the ten *phylai*. One year's co-operation as a member of the Council and a year co-operating in the Council's working commission of the *prytaneis* promoted a conciliatory and moderate attitude which was reflected in the whole life of the community. This balancing factor must be considered in our investigation, in which social differences have played the dominant part. Without it, the picture I have tried to give would have been distorted. It was a political attitude also with a strongly moral flavour. The Athenian was committed to the common good. At a later period, he swore an oath as an ephebe, an oath of a patriotic nature with binding force.

The society of Athens, and the Greek city state in general, managed to survive for several centuries, and the Dutch, for instance, whose constitution is not yet a hundred and fifty years old, should hesitate before passing judgement on what happened in those small societies. There were always opposing forces at work, able to maintain equilibrium between the various groups. This was a practical reality which had something to do with the citizen's sense of responsibility. This, of course, brings us back again to the moral sphere.

Does it at the same time bring us back to religion? It may be so, since the Greeks always tried to support morality, including political morality, by appeals to the gods. It may also be dismissed rather contemptuously as too difficult a question, but in the ancient world it was taken for granted, even for instance in the oath sworn by the young Athenian when about to take up military service. It is impossible to escape the impression that moral behaviour was backed by religious authority, even though this may have been vague. This is, moreover, not surprising. The Athenian was scarcely aware of any separation between *Athenai* and Athena, the city and its protecting goddess. Anyone who guarded the temple of Athena also guarded the Acropolis of *Athenai*.

In a recent book on the social situation in Athens in the fifth century B.C., the American scholar W. R. Connor has correctly argued that Cleon's father was, for example, a well-to-do man who possessed a prosperous business.[21] This was in striking contrast with the fact that Cleon was in debt when he entered public life and that he left great debts behind him when he died. As Connor has correctly assumed, this had no bearing on his character and his personal morality was not involved. It simply indicated the circumstances from which he came. If we take these stories of Cleon's debts seriously, we are bound to conclude that he was a man who was going down in the world. Connor does not dispute this. It was of no significance then, that he belonged by virtue of his origins to a superior class. Social mobility was upward or downward.

At the other end of the social scale, Connor, it seems to me, rather overemphasizes the withdrawal from politics of the best men in response to the intrusion of demagogues of Cleon's type. He observes justly, that fewer men were produced, during a certain period at the end of the fifth century, by the aristocracy or oligarchy for government posts in the city of Athens. There can be no doubt that the propertied class was, as he claims, discouraged from politics for very short periods there. These moods in democratic Athens may also be paralleled in modern democratic societies, and Connor's work merits attention both as a study of the distant past and as a clear insight into a contemporary tendency in certain western European states and the United States, as the following quotation shows.

At the end of his book, Connor has this to say: "Repelled, annoyed, disaffected, the *chrestoi* of Athens withdrew from politics and denied the city the wisdom and ability of which they had so often boasted. Their response was intelligible and natural, as were the attempts of the new politicians to win political power. Neither group can easily be condemned. But if we are reluctant to judge, we must not be reluctant to learn. The withdrawal from politics of intelligent, well educated and capable citizens was a symptom of a serious malaise in Athens and a prelude to revolution. Other ages, other continents, may recognize that the same symptoms betoken the same illness".[22]

---

[21] W. R. Connor, *The New Politicians of Fifth-Century Athens*, Princeton (1971), p. 151. I prefer Davies's series of historical facts referred to above (p. 182 note 8).

[22] *Op. cit.*, p. 198. I should like to emphasize that certain things that merit attention are pointed out in Connor's book. What he has to say, for instance, about the concept 'party', *op. cit.*, p. 8, is particularly interesting.

There is also a case for a connection between religion and the historical social and political situation. We remember that what mythology provides are often not mere isolated tales but justifications of definite social institutions. It was for good reasons that a myth was often attached to an existing historical situation, especially if it told about gods who had made an institution of something. The social relevance of the myth seems to mean that men needed a sanction in such cases, and even the '*chrestoi*' were kept in politics by such means.

An example that comes to mind is the story of Hermes the ram-bearer that is found in many Greek states.[23] According to this story, Hermes was the deity who purified the state or city by carrying a ram around it; the ram would take on the impurity of the city and thus purge it. One of Hermes' epithets was Kriophoros, the ram-bearer, and this name, even if used alone, made it clear to everyone that the god Hermes was meant. A ritual was also enacted every year, recalling what Hermes was supposed to have done in the distant past. A young citizen had to carry a ram, just as he had, round the city, which was thus quit of all its religious debts, that is, its guilt was purged.

It is clear then that religion played an indisputable part in social life and determined what was and what was not guilt. To begin with, this guilt was very irrational, but later it was rationalized and its legal aspects were discussed in detail. Communication between citizens was also very often determined by religious processions and duties. Definite families were entrusted with the performance of certain obligatory religious ceremonies. From a great number of facts like these we can infer that the historical situation at a given moment in time was partly determined by factors rooted in the deepest beliefs of the community. How far this went was not always directly detectable, for we must always take account of the

---

I agree, however, with A. H. M. Jones, *Athenian Democracy* (1957), pp. 130-131, and R. Sealey, 'The Entry of Pericles into History', *Hermes* 84 (1956), pp. 234-247, that it is not possible to speak of a conventional party system in Athens. This was, of course, not the discovery of Jones and Sealey; it was something that had previously been pointed out very eloquently by O. Reverdin, 'Remarques sur la vie politique d'Athènes au Ve siècle', *Museum Helveticum* II (1945), pp. 201-202. We must, however, be satisfied with these few references in this context, as we are not dealing here with political history in ancient Greece, but with morality.

[23] Cf. p. 109 above.

possibility, the obvious fact even, that the feeling for religious values is apt to become eroded by time.

From the religious point of view this will be judged as decay but that cannot be our last word on the question. We are bound to take as our point of departure the situation as it was at that point in history, even though a continuous process of secularization may have given a different form and content to the concepts. It should be noted also that secularization itself is a problematic notion. It may mean not only demolition, but also the building up of something new. This new thing is also very often historically relevant to the community thus founded, both from the religious and from the moral point of view. It may also often mean that the original promoters of a new order make use of religious and moral arguments. In the political growth of many communities both inside and outside Europe, these unreal factors in political life are often stressed.[24]

I must make one more observation in this context. For reasons of honesty it must be emphasized that the political system may have a mitigating effect on social differences. Towards the conclusion of my argument I managed to keep the political system and the glamour with which it was sometimes invested in certain societies clearly in view. It is, however, important here and now to clear up one possible misunderstanding. In what I have said so far, I never intended to assert the holiness or inviolable character of the state or political system. The modern world has discovered to its cost that the deification of the state can have disastrous moral consequences for mankind. It was not my intention to support such tendencies, especially as the historical evidence for the period concerned certainly does not point that way.

---

[24] An important contribution to the understanding of the problem discussed here was made in the report of a symposium entitled *The Myth of the State, Based on papers read at the Symposium on the Myth of the State*, held at Åbo on the 6th-8th September, Stockholm, 1972. This book contains many ideas and historical data that support my argument. These are taken from Mesopotamia, the Old and New Testaments, ancient Egypt, Islam, the Evocatio Deorum, which is connected with the Romanization of Etruria, phenomena in Bantu Africa and among the pre-Christian Germanic peoples, and finally ideas that have been regarded as myths in western Europe during the Middle Ages. It is extremely interesting to note how, for example, the Metropolitan of Helsinki dealt in this series with ideas about the state put forward by ecumenical synods in the Byzantine Church. This symposium has opened up new territory. The method used was one of trial and error. There was also a great deal of criticism (see BiOr 30, 1973, pp. 505-507). Despite that, it seems to me a path that should be further followed.

A Moral Question in Practice: Payment for Services rendered to the State

The facts here are well known. Public offices were honorary at a time when government by oligarchy was additional, part-time work for well-to-do, for men with time to spare. It was not until democracy had become more firmly established that those holding office were paid and rewarded. In Athens, 6000 men who had taken an oath before the court of law, 500 councillors, and about 350 magistrates were paid at varying rates. There were differences in the prestige of offices and differences in payment. Military leaders and envoys were better paid than those who held an office as the result of drawing lots. Payment (*misthophoria*) was introduced so that public office might no longer be confined to the well-to-do. As always, however, this resulted in some Greeks believing that the attendance fee or recompense was too high, while others thought it was too low. In the fourth century B.C., the question of the attendance fee was debated in the Assembly. It is not difficult to understand how serious this question of payment was. If a man holds office for payment, the interest of the state is not always his own major interest. Everything depends on the size of the remuneration.

This payment of 'wages' was rejected by many of the philosophers. Aristotle, for example, was strongly opposed to it.[25] The question is how far from ideal the situation was in his day. To judge from the way in which they were addressed by the orators, the People's Assembly and the courts of law seem to have consisted mainly of the middle class rather than of poor men. The Council members too apparently were prosperous on the whole—in striking contrast with the picture suggested by Connor.

It is clear that rising prices affected the value of the attendance fee and the modern world will have no difficulty in understanding the problem of 'inflation-proofing' the fees or salaries of office-holders. Employment was much more important for many members than attendance in the Assembly. It is hardly surprising that the aristocratic Plato was opposed to payment: 'Pericles, I am told, made the Athenians into worthless, idle, and grasping gossips by having them paid by the state' (Gorgias 515e).

This was an accusation frequently made, and we are bound to ask whether it was justified. In a population of at most 40 000 and

---

[25] Aristotle, *Athenaiōn Politeia* 62. 3.

at least 20 000 adult males, being a councillor or a magistrate was
not a permanent paid post, except in a few outstanding cases. A
man was not allowed to be a member of the Council more than
twice in his lifetime. There was a certain continuity in being a judge,
but the pay was so low that only elderly men past the peak of their
working lives held this office in the fifth century (if we are to believe what Aristophanes said in his *Wasps*). Later, in the early part
of the fourth century, when the economic situation had deteriorated
the office was reserved for the unemployed [26] and the Assembly did
not always meet—or according to Aristotle, four times in every
prytany.[27] We may therefore conclude that the members did not
do very well out of it.

It is in any case clear that, if payment for state service was disapproved, it was only because of abuses. The moral argument that
is so often used in this context obviously plays no—or hardly any—
part at all here.[28] Plato's implicit moral objection was that it was
wrong to stimulate greed and from this he argued against the payment of office-holders. It is, however, not possible to speak of a
moral right to remuneration on the one hand and a moral objection
on the other to receive that remuneration. They were interdependent extremes. The salient features of the system of honorary offices
were directly opposed to those of the system of paid offices and 'the
moral standard' [29] to use a term that can in fact be found in Aristotle, played no part.[30]

We should make no mistake, however, about the background to
the democratic consciousness of the Athenians. If, for example, we
look at the position occupied by the law in Athenian society, we
find the following. The sovereign people was the highest authority
in that society and was able to change the law. (Opponents spoke
about 'displacing' the law). This could not be done arbitrarily, since
a law had to be treated with care. The individual citizen who tried
to change the laws of Athens was liable to be called to order on

---

[26] See Isocrates, 7. 54; 8. 130.

[27] Aristotle, *Athenaion Politeia*, 43. 3. In the time of Clisthenes once in
every prytany (normally 10 times a year).

[28] See the severe accusation in Ps.-Xenophon I, 3 (without a moral
argument).

[29] Aristotle uses the term 'taxis tōn ethōn', in connection with the exposure of children, see p. 135 above, and Preface.

[30] For the payment of those holding special functions in other states (not
simply in Athens), see G. E. M. de Ste. Croix, *Political Pay outside Athens*,
CQ 25 (1975), pp. 48-52.

charges of 'acting against the law'. This certainly happened when the citizen in question was attempting to obstruct or actuated purely by individual feeling.

The existence of the constitutional state was guaranteed. One guard was that the promulgation of the law was prefaced with the words 'the gods'. But the erosive process of secularization may have been at work too—the lawgiver not always believing in the divinity of the law's pronouncement sanctioned and supported by the gods, who it was hoped would see that it was carried out. Divine or not, in course of time there was a shift of emphasis from the law itself to the citizens. It was they who made it, acting together collectively in the Assembly, and in that capacity above the law. But 'the gods' were mentioned too, even at a later date. Thus secularization in the full modern sense of the word had not occurred.

We must not make the mistake of supposing that the Greeks called every decision by the people a law. They had a different word for measures less heavily sanctioned and with less wide-ranging effects. The word was *psēphisma*, a decree to meet a specific case, a particular situation, which was itself subject to the law, and could quite easily be changed or revoked by a new vote. The law itself was different. It must be debated in full Assembly and a direct majority was needed before it could even be introduced. The Council had to be consulted and its report was treated with much greater respect and care than reports about day-to-day measures. The difference between *nomos* (law) and *psēphisma* can perhaps be illustrated by the difference between the organic laws of the modern Netherlands, forming part of the constitutional law, and specific occasional legislation, passed for a budget. It is obvious that the organic laws in this state system are regarded as more important, since a two-thirds majority must be obtained in the Netherlands parliament in order to change them. In the case of occasional laws, an ordinary majority is usually enough. We do not know whether it was necessary to have a qualified majority if specific laws were to be accepted into Greek constitutional law. What we do know is that there was a difference between the two kinds of law. Modern scholars may well be right in their contention, however, that the difference was not always respected and that it was not until quite late in Greek history that the distinctions were precisely formulated.[31]

---

[31] See, for example, M. Ostwald, *Nomos and the Beginnings of the Athenian Democracy*, Oxford (1969), p. 2 ff.

The fact that it existed at all, however, is noteworthy, as an interesting sign of maturity in a society that distinguished between the more important and the less. Quarrelsome people treat all things as equally important. The Greeks were clearly not like that. They were flexible and knew that there had to be a certain relativity in legislation and other matters if the state system was to be made to function and the community was to be allowed to live. As a community, the Greeks never had any difficulty with this scale of importance. They never defined it, but they lived in accordance with it.

The idea itself was of gradual development. It clearly indicates how strongly the individual felt himself involved with the interests of society as a whole. It was not for him to claim equal priority for all his affairs. An order of precedence was determined by the whole body of the Assembly. This, it is true, was always guided by a leader, whose character may often have been less than ideal. We are well acquainted with the demagogues who hoodwinked the people. Yet it would hardly be possible to imagine the thousands of Assembly members doing their business without leadership and consultation. Clearly they did not always like their leaders and politicians in Athens did not lead happy lives. But it is a fascinating aspect of Athenian life that the sovereign people were led and accepted leadership from men whom they trusted. The leaders inspired confidence but not all deserved it, with the result that the people often felt cheated. They reacted sometimes with harshness or recalcitrance, but this is the human predicament—no system of government can ever function perfectly well and smoothly. This is something we can learn from the Greeks.

The Law and Morality

We can cite as a second example of maturity and independence in the communities of ancient Greece the refusal to identify law with morality. This is clearly connected with the fact that they spoke also of 'unwritten laws'. So far as I know, modern scholars have never asked themselves why all the unwritten laws were not written down at a given moment, for example, in a codification of the laws. The reason, in my opinion, was to preserve a certain latitude between the law and morality. We can only guess what lay behind this flexible attitude to the law. According to our ideas about law in the abstract and the legal code, the code at the moment where it is drawn up is the culmination of the law, but later it can become a hindrance to law. The hindrance can be prevented if a degree of latitude is allowed between 'unwritten laws' and the legal code. The tendency not to legislate for everything that may happen in a community can be very dangerous. The existence of 'unwritten laws', however, largely reduces this danger, as does also, to an important degree, the moral attitude of individuals in the community.

There can be great divergences of opinion as to what is good and what is bad in the moral sense within the same community. So can there be about what constitutes the law. People may try to force their own moral view upon others. This is not only morally and legally reprehensible—it is also as disastrous to the legal system as a consistent separation of law and morality. We should never forget how absurd it is for our attitude towards what is permitted in human behaviour to be determined by two systems of norms that are independent of one another. For the most part, our moral judgement or the 'unwritten law' is an extension of the written law (or vice versa). Discrepancies between the moral and the legal order, however, have always been inevitable in any dynamic society. Sophocles' *Antigone* is a clear statement of this dilemma as far as Athenian society is concerned. It is clearly shown up also by all situations in which there is a conflict between 'two rights'.

Citizens and Parties

The word 'party', in the context of Greek society, is a social rather than a political term.[32] In England, for example, the social groups are certainly not tied to political parties. In Attica, on the contrary, the social group represented from the very beginning a certain political interest. The citizen formed part of a social community. His *deme* or neighbourhood association was political in the sense that membership of it was essential for his citizenship. In Attica there were coastal, plain, and highland districts and each had its own interests and its own contribution to make to social and political life. These interests were first and foremost of a social and economic kind. Politics sometimes played a part, as for instance at the beginning of the Peloponnesian War when cultivated fields had to be cleared, but this was basically a military question. The local character of deme membership did change later on, when many of the inhabitants left their demes for the town.

---

[32] See W. R. Connor, *op. cit.* (see above, p. 187).

Another social bond besides the deme was provided by the *hetaireia* or 'club'. According to Thucydides (3. 82, 6), kinship groupings were superseded by the *hetaireiai*. It is clear from Greek comedy that these fellowships, especially when their members were prominent young men, were a potential danger to the democratic state in times of war.[33] These clubs became very important. In general, we may say that they were above all characterized by the mutual solidarity of their members, but that the basis and effects of their solidarity were not constant. It was not always the same members who did certain things, nor did the members always represent the same interests.

The term 'party', then, must be used with care when applied to ancient Greece. What is more, the various factions were not always democratic action groups. The conservatives were also democratic in their attitude and often formed groups for the defence of their party interests. It has sometimes been suggested that these *hetaireiai* were closely akin to the action groups of contemporary political life, but the comparison is faulty. The Greek parties were not parties in the modern sense, adhering to a political principle—a 'party' might take one point of view on one day and on the next go over to that of a previous opponent. It should not be forgotten that these were communities with relatively slight differences between rich and poor. Even the social differences between freemen and slaves— at least certain groups of slaves—were in many respects very small. For the industrial slave, it is true, the situation was much less favourable.

This, then, is the most important aspect of the social structure of the Greek *polis*. The Greeks were not able to build an empire on such a piecemeal foundation. In no more than fifty years, Athens had scarcely a chance of doing so. If we compare Greece with Rome in this respect, we find, of course, that the Roman structure did certainly allow the building of an empire, but only when the framework of a *polis* had become too narrow and had practically disappeared. Rome became an empire, in other words, when the city of Rome was no longer Rome.

The Relationship between Citizens

It follows from what I have said that the cultural climate in which a fashionable distinction can be made between rich and poor

---

[33] See Ehrenberg, *op. cit.*, p. 110.

did not exist in the Greek world. This absence of fashion is an important fact, not only economically, but also socially. Thucydides for instance, mentioned an old style of 'luxurious' dress among the nobility (1. 6. 2).[34] There are references in Greek comedy to ornaments and luxurious clothing, but this is greatly exaggerated and not a universal custom. Thucydides gives the impression that the fashion he mentioned was more or less popular for several centuries, so that we can hardly speak of fashions changing at short intervals. Generally speaking, one garment a year was worn until it was completely soiled and fell in shreds from the body. Nobody had soap and it is not difficult to imagine that the standard of hygiene then was very much lower than it is today! [35]

All this being granted, we are bound to ask whether social distinctions had entirely disappeared, in view of the very slight difference between rich and poor in ancient Greece. It is clear to anyone who has studied the collection of state revenue that the Greek taxation system and the distribution of taxes over the community functioned in such a way that the differences between rich and poor were kept to a minimum. Yet we must recognize that not all social differences had disappeared from Greece. Let us examine this in a little more detail.

In the first place it would, be extremely unlikely from the psychological point of view that all social distinctions should disappear. We can, for instance, compare a Greek *deme* with a neighbourhood today—a distinction is sometimes made between the people who live on different sides of the same street, those on one side being regarded as better situated because their houses have one more room and the rent is therefore higher. This means that the occupants are in a higher social class. It is also clear from the Greek sources that such distinctions were indeed made. The Old Oligarch contrasted the *chrēstoi* and the *ponēroi*, the gentlemen and the paupers, the ideal designation of the former being *kalos kāgathos*.[36] The Old Oligarch was, it should be remembered, a pamphleteer, while Aristophanes, who also refers to this distinction, was a writer of musical comedies but it is surely significant that these authors were the very ones

---

[34] See Ehrenberg, *op. cit.*, p. 97.
[35] In this connection, A. E. Zimmern had many worthwhile things to say in his book *The Greek Commonwealth* (1931[4]), p. 214 ff. These things are too often forgotten, even in his own country.
[36] See above, p. 161 ff.

to emphasize the ideals of the aristocracy. These ideals were very powerful and were generally associated with the ideals of the nation at large. In Aristophanes' *Knights*, the sausage-seller is proud to be a man of humble origin. Gradually, however, what was really an expression of aristocratic prejudice gained acceptance with non-aristocrats.

The drinking songs were a very good example of this. That about Harmodius, the killer of tyrants, was originally aristocratic, but it acquired a certain popularity among the people at large. It was approved for instance by Cleon, a popular leader.

In other respects, too, political relationships were more complicated than many scholars have suggested. The politics of the Alcmaeonidae, for instance, had a dual tendency—they were connected with Hippias, the tyrant, on the one hand and, on the other, they glorified Harmodius. One of their most famous descendants, of course, was Pericles, who was a great man of the people. There is nothing surprising in this. It is quite common for a man who was born an aristocrat to become a man of the people as a result of his own experiences. In the Athenian democracy there was no clear prospect of advancement for the aristocracy as such. The opposite also undoubtedly happened—having achieved power, a democrat might behave as an aristocrat.[37]

There is one very important factor, not mentioned yet, which must have to be taken into account by everyone studying the changes in political allegiances. That is the factor of time. In the age of tyrants there was neither democracy nor unchallenged oligarchy but clan warfare. The dynastic marriage between a tyrant and a chieftain's daughter had no more significance than dynastic marriages usually have and did not prevent the succession of exiles and assassinations which followed. A later age saw it all through the eyes of its own preoccupations with democracy (= Athens) and oligarchy (= Sparta), In the Alcmaeonid past there were Medizers (=traitors), heroes, liberators etc., labelled according to the political needs of a later age.

---

[37] For this kind of contrast, see, for example, F. Jacoby, *Atthis*, Oxford (1949), p. 160; B. Meritt, *Hesperia* (1939), p. 59. A different presentation of this situation has been provided by V. Ehrenberg in *Historia* I (1950). Ehrenberg's view is, in my opinion, however, less correct and too static. Aristophanes' description of social differences in Greece has less of a political emphasis than that of other authors. As a general rule therefore it is only with the greatest caution that he can be used as a source of information about them.

The Political Structure

Our examination of the social structure of fifth century Athenian society has enabled us to see that there were social differences, but that they were not very great and that they did not give offence. They had little impact, not only because they were not great, but also because each citizen felt that he was an individual with a worth of his own. In the community, he was seldom affronted by differences of social standing. But the Peloponnesian War had a disastrous effect on the harmonious development of Greek society. The social differences became much greater after the war.

Aristophanes has described an individual living at the beginning of this period, but still bearing the stamp of the old attitudes. This is Dikaiopolis, the main character in his *Acharnians*.[38] At the beginning of this play the 'hero' complains about the poor attendance at the Assembly. He is a lover of peace and enjoys the company of his fellow-men. He has a great deal of practical common sense and a sense of humour, albeit a rough one. What he wants to do is to go back to his rural deme and enjoy the feasting there. As far as the state is concerned, he is not uncritical of the rhetorical bombast of the politicians who want to deceive the peasants. He is a conservative. He is loyal to the state and its institutions and faithful to the gods and his fellow-men. He scoffs as easily at the gods as he does at Pericles or Cleon. The gods are rulers, just as men are rulers, and they are therefore the target of his scorn. It is not treacherous to mock at political leaders and mockery of the gods is not blasphemy.[39] His favourite tragic dramatist is Aeschylus, not so much because of the profundity of his ideas, which undoubtedly escaped him, as because Aeschylus had fought at Marathon. How absurd it would be to exchange this life-like characterization for the state-

---

[38] In what follows, I am indebted to W. K. C. Guthrie, *The Greeks and their Gods* (1950), p. 259. Philologists and historians have been wrestling for more than a century with the great problem of the value of Aristophanes as a historical source. One of the most convincing publications in recent years, dealing with the development of Aristophanes' thought and ideals, is M. Landfester's 'Aristophanes und die politische Krise Athens', in *Krisen in der Antike. Bewußtsein und Bewältigung*, Vol. 13 (1975) of the *Bochumer historische Studien 'Geschichte und Gesellschaft'*, edited by G. Alföldy.

[39] See the very interesting observation on Greek 'atheism' in H. Lloyd-Jones, *The Justice of Zeus* (1971), p. 134: 'Until the rise of Christianity, atheism in the ancient world was to present no social problem'.

ment that the Greek was more devoted to his party than to the state.[40]

The State and the Citizen

There is ample evidence that the Greek citizen was dedicated to his state. The tragic poets testify to this: the state is exalted in the *Seven against Thebes*, *Oedipus at Colonus*, and the *Medea*. There can be no doubt that Athens was glorified. This is also shown in the serious effort to raise the city's status or at least to make it a well-considered member of a nationally minded Hellenic association of states. Aristophanes' Lysistrata illustrates this well.[41] After the battle of Plataea an attempt was made to do as Aristophanes later desired, but ended in failure. The citizens' ties with their own *polis* were too close. Pericles made three such attempts at inter-Hellenic co-operation, but they too failed. It is clear, then, that the citizen of an individual Greek state was not above all a Hellene, but that he remained closely tied to his state. His civic rights were strictly defined and, to judge from the results, very closely observed. They leave us in no doubt that the citizen belonged to that particular place and to no other.

Attempts have been made to throw doubt on this generally accepted image of the Greek *polis* patriot. Nathan Marsh Pusey has done this in a study of Alcibiades and *polis* patriotism.[42] It is, however, extremely dangerous to take this man, who betrayed his country twice and was responsible for one of its unhappiest undertakings, as a point of departure. However that may be, it would certainly be true to say that the 'state' was not the only unit to which the Greek owed loyalty. There was also a decided ethnic bond. There is an example of this in Thucydides (1. 95): many

---

[40] See Grundy, I, p. 171; the author uses Alcibiades' speech (Thucydides, 6. 92) as evidence for his argument.

[41] See W. den Boer, *Nationalisme in Griekenland in de 5e en 4e eeuw voor Christus* (inaugural address 1946), *passim*. I would not call this pan-Hellenism. This term emphasizes the distinction between Greeks and barbarians. Nationalism, in this context, is what creates Greek solidarity, a political unifying sentiment which could take on exceptional importance in practice and was more than local patriotism. To my satisfaction, what I said thirty years ago can be found in a very recent article by S. Perlman, 'Panhellenism, the Polis and Imperialism', *Historia* 25 (1976), pp. 1-30.

[42] N. M. Pusey, 'Alcibiades and τὸ φιλόπολι', *Harvard Studies in Cl. Philology*, 51 (1940), pp. 215-231. Τὸ φιλόπολι, 'the patriotic element', was one of Thucydides' themes (6. 92).

Ionians used the fact that Athens was also Ionian as an argument in favour of giving Athens protection.[43]

Thus the ethnic bond or association of companions or the club, the *hetaireia*, combined their effects with the factions in the state. All together made the citizens into their instruments, with the result that patriotism declined and party interests were predominant, as described by Thucydides 3. 82.[44] It would, however, be foolish to conclude that men were for that reason no longer motivated by love of their state and that that form of patriotism no longer existed. From a period of decline and bitter quarrels, when Greece was in a desperate situation, it should not be inferred that mutual hatred was general or typical of feelings about the state. The critical situation that followed the Sicilian expedition and preceded the Athenian complete surrender—the time of the Four Hundred and the Thirty, in the years 411 and 404—cannot be taken as the norm. The politicians could have learned a lesson in judicious serenity about their own country from their greatest dramatist. Sophocles wrote the Oedipus Coloneus at this time and the play was performed posthumously in 405 with great success. This dramatic work and the reaction of the public to it should be taken as the norm rather than the desperate reactions of politicians to catastrophe.

These are some conclusions in contradiction of Pusey's claim that the behaviour of certain interest groups was universal (he does not in fact quote any parallels). It is interesting to read what Pusey himself said: 'To the Greeks, cities were places of social and economic opportunity, in which to lead a civilized life, not "fatherlands" demanding patriotic allegiance. But political parties ... were held in different regard. The majority of the Greeks were normally committed to the view that their personal interests could be safely pursued only in common with others of similar economic conditions and political persuasion'.[45]

It is impossible to deny that this outline of the Athenian citizens' pattern of behaviour is basically correct. It holds good for many, if not for all, human communities at all times. Nonetheless, with the examples quoted above in mind, I would venture to suggest that other specific bonds—loyalties, solidarity with clubs, and even patriotism—should also be included in any historical assessment of

---

[43] Other examples will be found in Pusey's study, *op. cit.*

[44] See Calhoun, *op. cit.*, *passim.*

[45] N. M. Pusey, *op. cit.*, p. 230.

communal behaviour. It is certainly true that these bonds existed in the community of the *polis*.

The Intrinsic Value of Democracy

One of the most difficult questions that can be asked is whether, seen from the point of view of morality, the democratic attitude of a particular statesman in Greek society was the result of deep feeling or simply of the political game. On the one hand, we are bound to recognize that a definitive pronouncement on this question can hardly be made by the historian. On the other, if it cannot be proved that there is some content of truth in a political conviction, it is very difficult to defend any political institution to the younger and more idealistic generation. It is therefore well worth going a little further into this question.

It would be calumniating the Greek citizen to say that the oligarchs and the democrats each stood for their own interests. The very names are incorrect, since both groups were democrats, although their means were different. A better terminology would be conservatives and radicals. Both groups appealed to the authority of Solon and Cleisthenes and both accepted the democratic state.

To say, as Pusey did, that Thucydides the son of Melesias, an older namesake of the historian, believed that 'democracy was an unjust usurpation of authority' shows a misunderstanding of the idea of freedom which was established by Solon and Cleisthenes and to which all Athenians were committed. The rather grand term 'oligarchical' is therefore best avoided.[46] (It is, however, appropriate to use this term for an extremist such as the Old Oligarch, the author of the Pseudo-Xenophon's *Constitution of Athens*, a pamphlet expressing extreme views).[47] In the *Pentecontaetia*, the *polis* was the

---

[46] F. Jacoby, *Atthis*, p. 293, note 22. This is one of the most noteworthy observations made by this great scholar, who was certainly not a social historian.

[47] Jacoby, *op. cit.*, p. 292, note 13, was, in my opinion, wrong to agree with those who are not well disposed towards Greek democracy by saying that Thucydides the son of Melesias, might have spoken like the so-called Old Oligarch. We have no knowledge of this and cannot therefore place Thucydides in the same category as the extremely aggressive and unfair author of this pamphlet. I regard it as very important that Plato mentioned him in the same breath as Aristides, the universally highly regarded 'just man' (*Laches* 179 a) and that he also placed him alongside Themistocles, Aristides, and Pericles in the *Meno* (93 c ff, especially 94 c). For this, see H. T. Wade-Gery, *Essays in Greek History* (1958), p. 239 ff, which originally appeared in *JHS* 53 (1932), p. 205 ff.

most important means by which the Athenians were held together, irrespective of their party. Later on, there can be no doubt that party and personal interests predominated. Critias was the least loyal Athenian, even more treacherous than Alcibiades.[48] It is therefore ridiculous to say that he was 'not guilty of patriotism', since his crimes were many. Pusey was also wrong to say that Theramenes was 'so often disloyal to smaller associations, that it has finally been concluded he must have been loyal to the state'.

One possible objection to this is that these examples have all been taken from the period of the Peloponnesian War and that other figures ought to be mentioned before a balanced assessment can be made. It is, however, very unfortunate that for the most part we must fall back on professional politicians. Cleisthenes, who was allowed into the city only after he had brought a Spartan army against it and who wanted to subject the Athenians to Persia in order to maintain his own position, was not a patriot in the opinion of many Greeks. Isagoras, who sought help from Cleomenes of Sparta to nip the recently established Athenian democracy in the bud, was even less of a patriot, as was Hippias, who took service with the Persians. The history of the practice of ostracism speaks volumes. Miltiades, a member of the family of the Philaidae, and Megacles the Alcmaeonid, and Xanthippus were all party leaders and not patriotic servants of the state. (It should be noted that it is Pusey who has drawn up this indictment).

Themistocles, a *homo novus*, was also no patriot. His aim was to preserve the economic supremacy of one class. He was very similar to Alcibiades in character and it will be recalled that Pusey based his study of τὸ φιλόπολι on Alcibiades' words: 'I feel no patriotism at the moment, since a greater injustice is being done to me; (I did, however, feel it) when I was fulfilling a function in safety in the state' (6. 93, 4).[49] (Once again, it should be noted that this is Pusey's presentation of the case).

The assertions here outlined, however, are not sufficiently attested. They tell us more about the scholar who made them than of the truth about Greek democracy as it might have been understood by the Greeks themselves. I have mentioned Miltiades and

---

[48] See the conclusion of J. H. Thiel's article on 'Themistocles', *TvG* 64 (1951), pp. 1-39.

[49] What Thucydides said in 1. 138, 2 about Themistocles; he was a man μᾶλλον ἑτέρου ἄξιος θαυμάσαι, has to be accepted, however.

Themistocles. Collaboration with the Persians was clearly the ultimate expression of antipatriotism and treachery. It also shows that the *polis* was of primary importance and Greece as a whole was secondary. This may be called shortsighted, but it was prompted by a patriotism that was anti-Spartan. It was of course, as shortsighted politically then to use the slogan 'Sparta or Persia' as it is today to use the slogan 'America or Russia', but in both cases the men who do so may well be good patriots.

I conclude by saying that it seemed worth while to look at Athenian democracy from the moral point of view. It is a remarkable fact that ancient Greek democracy is still discussed throughout Europe—for better or worse. We even notice a widespread feeling that democratic Athens is now under attack by scholars and non-scholars alike, whereas militaristic Sparta is extolled. I cannot find any examples of this in the Netherlands, but there is a recent attempt to show that in England Athens has long been regarded as far inferior to Sparta.[50]

It has also been claimed from time to time that Athens attempted to force its own democracy on its allies. Various examples of this have been given, but it can be said with certainty that Athens was politically too mature to want to impose its own form of government on all its allies. As the leader of a federation of states, Athens was more concerned with the task of preserving peace in a state that was subject to its supervision or power than with imposing its own system of government.[51]

I am bound to say that with all their imperfections the democratic societies of Greece were sustained by a great deal of human knowledge and idealism. Some Greeks accepted unstable situations and gave priority to democracy and second place to all the other material interests of the state. This is the strength that we observe in 'the Greek example'. Without deifying the Athenians, we are bound to admit that they made the best of it. Themistocles and Demosthenes are exemplary in this respect. Any treatment of Greek

---

[50] See G. E. M. de Ste. Croix, *The Origins of the Peloponnesian War* (1972); see also my discussion of this important book in *Mnem.* 27 (1974), pp. 430-438. In Renaissance scholarship Sparta was undoubtedly the great example, not Athens, see E. Rawson, *The Spartan Tradition in European Thought*, Oxford (1969), especially p. 158 ff. See also p. 238 below.

[51] See H. Popp, 'Zum Verhältnis Athens zu seinen Bündern im attisch-delischen Seebund', *Historia* 17 (1968), p. 425. The author also provides a wealth of bibliographical detail on this frequently discussed theme.

history can be tested against discussion of these two great figures.

Suggestions for Further Research

In dealing with this subject, the State and the Citizen, two different aspects have to be taken into account. These still need thorough discussion before the subject of the state and morality can be fully treated. So far there has been no methodical or systematic account of the demagogues and popular leaders of the fifth and fourth centuries. M. I. Finley has prepared the ground in a well known article, but the subject has not yet been clearly covered. This may, of course, be impossible, but it cannot be denied that the lack of a comprehensive treatment makes it very difficult for us to form a correct judgement of the codes of behaviour of leaders towards their political supporters, a subject about which very little is known. Most of our information comes from later authors who drew on an oral tradition, derived both from the battle of words in the Assembly and also from gossip in the market place and at home.

Another obstacle to the treatment of this subject is the fact that the Athenian parties have never been properly brought into the light. This aspect of the subject requires a re-assessment of the *Constitution of Athens* (Pseudo-Xenophon).[52] In a democratic community, it always has been very important to protect democracy. There is always a great danger that democracy will become a form of totalitarian government.[53]

[52] These two desiderata have been formulated by Jacoby in *FGrHist*, Suppl. II, pp. 95-96 and 130, in his commentary on the Atthidographers. Jacoby's words have lost none of their contemporary relevance, even though there have been several publications in this sphere since, especially M. I. Finley's paper on the demagogues (1962), reprinted in *Studies in Ancient Society* (1974), pp. 1-25, and Connor, *op. cit.*, pp. 109 and 143. On Council and Assembly, R. A. Laix, *Probeuleusis at Athens, A Study of Political Decision-making* (Univ. of Calif. Publ. in History, 83, Berkeley 1973); review *i. a* by H. W. Pleket, *Mnem.* 31 (1978), 328 ff.

[53] For the dangers involved, see E. de Strijcker, *Vrees als principe van staatsburgerlijke tucht in de democratie volgens Thucydides en volgens Plato, Handelingen IX van de Zuid-Nederl. Maatschappij van T. en L. en Gesch.* (1955), pp. 51-64. See also K. von Fritz, *Totalitarianismus und Demokratie im alten Griechenland und Rom. Antike und Abendland* III, p. 47.

CHAPTER TEN

SLAVES

'Every decade or half decade sees a new book upon the
subject; the same authors are ransacked; the same
evidence is marshalled; the same references and footnotes
are transferred, like stale tea-leaves, from one learned
receptacle to another; but there is a most startling variety
about the resultant decoctions'.[1]

Zimmern's statement, quoted above, is still valid, at least as far
as the 'startling variety' of conclusions is concerned, but what has
changed is that there is much more material. Zimmern wrote this
long before the article was included in the collection of 1928. The
original date of the article is not given. Pritchett repeated the
quotation.[2]

In modern scholarship, there have for a long time been very contradictory tendencies. The discussion by De Ste. Croix of Westermann's article on slave systems in classical antiquity[3] is an example of this. De Ste. Croix clearly regarded slavery as much more
influential than did Westermann. He was also opposed to Jones'
much more moderate study.[4] Finley too won his spurs in this subject.[5] Much more recently—indeed, only a few years ago—the same
author outlined the position of research into slavery in the ancient
world in a chapter of his book on the ancient economy.[6]

If the studies made over the last twenty years or so are examined

---

[1] A. E. Zimmern, *Was Greek Civilization Based on Slave Labour?* in *Solon
and Croesus* (1928), p. 106.

[2] W. K. Pritchett, *The Attic Stelai*, Part II, *Hesperia* 25 (1956), pp. 178,
317, which refers (p. 276 ff) to the slaves; cf. W. L. Westermann, *HSCPh*,
Suppl. 1 (1940), p. 452. See also above, pp. 78-83, for this subject in the
context of human solidarity, and p. 90 ff., for philosophical statements.

[3] G. E. M. de Ste. Croix, *CR* (1957), pp. 54-59; W. L. Westermann, *The
Slave Systems of Greek and Roman Antiquity* (1955), a revised edition of the
article *Sklaverei*, *RE* Suppl. VI (1935). This English edition is published in
the *Memoirs of the American Philosophical Society* 40, Philadelphia (1955).

[4] A. H. M. Jones, *The Economic Basis of the Athenian Democracy*, *Past and
Present* I (1952), pp. 13-31, later republished in the author's collection,
Athenian Democracy (1957).

[5] M. I. Finley, 'Was Greek Civilization Based on Slave Labour?', *Historia*
8 (1959), pp. 145-164, and other writings.

[6] *Idem*, *The Ancient Economy*, London (1973), in the third chapter:
'Masters and Slaves', pp. 62-94.

—and that is what I do in this chapter—the following facts emerge:

1. There is far more interest now than there was in the past in the history of slaves in particular industries (slaves in the mines were, for instance, studied by Lauffer), in particular environments (prisoners of war, studied by P. Ducrey in 1968) or at special periods (the later imperial period was studied by A. H. M. Jones and temple domains in Asia Minor by Broughton).

2. There is a fashion at present of comparing slavery in Greece and Rome with the same phenomenon in the Ancient Near East, the European Middle Ages and the modern era. The results would seem to point, however, to differences rather than similarities.

3. There is interest too in how the living circumstances of slaves changed with the times. What for instance did those who had been born slaves do in wartime? Several illuminating studies have appeared on this and similar subjects. (See, for example, Garlan, 1970, published in 1972).

The remarks quoted from Zimmern at the beginning of this chapter are not entirely fair. We recognize the limitations of later research, but believe it has made progress at some points.[7]

We must now turn to a number of topics affecting both with slavery in general and private morality.

The Place of Slavery in Society

There is certainly no one single view or *communis opinio* among modern writers on slavery in ancient Greece and Rome. The situation is very similar to that regarding Greek democracy, where there is great divergence of views and judgements. It cannot be the pure chance that the view not only of the Greek *polis* but also of the Roman Republic and the Roman Empire, as 'communities of slave-holders' has in various versions increasingly held the field. Any historical judgement is, after all, ultimately determined by political tendencies and the view in question is a necessary part of a historical attitude in more than half the modern world. If I am not mistaken, the leading authority on the history of slavery in the Graeco-Roman world, M. I. Finley, came closer to these views in 1976 than he did in his studies of 1959 and 1973. In one of his most recent publications, he defended the opinion that 'although the existence of slaves is virtually ubiquitous throughout the ages in all parts of the globe,

---

[7] See Addendum 1, p. 239 below.

slavery as an institution essential to a society, to its production and to its life style, was to be found only in classical Greece and classical Rome, and in the modern era in Brazil, the Caribbean and the southern states of the United States'. As far as imperial Rome is concerned, he added: 'In view of the understandable domination of American slavery in current discussions, it is worth stressing that, on any calculation, there were more slaves in the Roman Empire at the beginning of the Christian era than there were in the United States at the moment of emancipation. The two territories, further-more, were sufficiently comparable in size to make that a statisti-cally meaningful statement. It is also worth stressing that slavery thus emerged as an essential institution under two different econo-mic systems, two different social relations of production'.[8]

After reading this, we are tempted to consider the ancient empires of Asia and Egypt. There is a relationship between what Finley says here with such emphasis and two tendencies among modern historians specializing in classical antiquity who regard slavery from another point of view than Finley's. The latter regarded the factor of individual alienation from the family or tribe as of primary im-portance and thought that the loss of freedom was associated with this. The other historians see this question differently.

The first of the two tendencies opposed to Finley is represented by those orientalists who speak of 'so-called eastern despotism',[9] by which they mean that the historians who followed Herodotus were mistaken. The Greek principle of freedom, they claim, can be compared with the rise and fall of the *polis* and was based on a 'world order' in which 'change' prevailed, with the result that those who supported it did not experience the 'peace' that the absolute, religious monarchy brought to the ancient eastern world. The oriental idea of state and society was determined by two factors— the ruler and the land. It was not determined by the people or the subjects collectively. The king possessed the land and those who worked on it owed their existence there to him. They were there, as it were, as his creatures. Like the gods whose incarnation he was he never abandoned them. The organization of home, city, and land

---

[8] This quotation is taken from Finley's important article in the *Times Literary Supplement* of 2 July 1976, pp. 819 ff: *A Peculiar Institution?* This title comes from K. M. Stampp's book of 1956: *The Peculiar Institution: Slavery in the Ante-Bellum South.*

[9] B. A. van Proosdij, *Der sogenannte orientalische Despotismus (Symbolae P. Koschaker)*, Leiden (1939), pp. 235-242.

served to suppress chaos and was directed towards the stabilization of all that was passing and perishable. Man was above all the image and the victim of this perishable aspect of life. The king provided man with the necessary structures of a society in which he could find peace.

This peace, however, was clearly the peace of the graveyard and men paid a great price to obtain it. Because of the supreme power and arbitrary nature of the ruling despots, it undoubtedly cannot be compared with what the leading protagonist of this view called 'stability'. We can hardly suspect Finley of favouring a view [10] which would acquit the Assyrians of despotism, for all the sympathy and distress felt for the victims of their well-known form of government, by means of the magic word 'peace' and the ideal of 'world order'. If, however, the states that achieved political freedom for their citizens—as happened in the case of many of the Greek *poleis*— were at the same time the greatest slave-holders in the history of the world, it might imply—as it would do for me if I agreed with it —that men had paid too great a price for this democracy.

The second view mentioned above which I do not suspect Finley of sharing placed great emphasis on phenomena interpreted as 'primordial' and taken therefore from the distant past. They are derived from religious rituals of very uncertain interpretation. In certain festivals the king was called slave and the slave was treated as free. An example was the Roman Saturnalia. Such occasions are interpreted as a memory of a primeval equality enjoyed by all men. Both the king and his subjects are servants of one another and in the distant past, this equality was actually experienced by primitive man, in his daily life. With the advance of civilization, however, it was gradually lost and became quite unknown in the 'civil democracy' (this being a term of abuse). This view of mutual 'service' may have existed at some time in the history of mankind,[11] but disappeared from practical social life in historical times. Or at any

---

[10] S. N. Kramer has gone so far as to claim that Sumer had all the achievements that are traditionally attributed to the Greeks; see his book *History Begins at Sumer*, Anchor Books (1959) and my objections to it in *Hermeneus* 39 (1967-1968), p. 98 ff.

[11] For this idea of service, see an illuminating article by W. B. Kristensen, *De antieke opvattingen van dienstbaarheid, Mededelingen van de Kon. Nederl. Akademie van Wetenschappen, Afdeling Letterkunde*, 78, Series B (1934) (= *Verzamelde Bijdragen tot de Kennis der antieke Godsdiensten*, 1947, pp. 201-229).

rate, as the proponents of this theory maintain, there is no sign of its influence in later human conduct and legislation.

This discussion was needed to clear Finley and ensure that his position could not possibly be misunderstood. What then is the background to his bold assertion that slavery played such an important part in Greek and Roman society? As he says himself in the article quoted above, 'The slave (in Greek and Roman Antiquity) was always an outsider in the fullest sense of the term and that distinguished slaves as a class from all other forms of involuntary labour'. As for the Roman emperors, Finley compares them with 'the Ottoman rulers and their armies' and asks: 'What were the advantages of this particular system'?

The answer that he gives is 'that no other system offers such undivided loyalty as well as such absolute rights of control and discipline. These recruits came from outside the society. All other possible recruits retained traditional ties of kinship and community to balance against the claims of the emperor, and they had rights of one sort or another which could be troublesome psychologically even if no more than that. The slave-recruits in contrast were torn away, uprooted, from family, tribe, community, even from their religion in its communal aspects, and the only alternative focus of attachment allowed to them, so long as they remained slaves, was their master'.

When the situation is presented in this way, the Assyrians can be seen in a relatively favourable light, despite their mass deportations, compared with the Greeks and Romans, even though they did not lack massive forms of subjection that also undoubtedly kept individuals together because of the purchase of entire groups. One is bound to agree with Finley that mass enslavement and individual sale and purchase made a great difference to the life-style of slaves. I doubt, however, whether this distinction made a difference to the question whether, as Finley suggests, slavery was essential to a society and its production. I am inclined to answer this question in the negative. In ancient Egypt and the Assyrian and Persian empires, power was based on blind obedience and exploitation. These two factors dominated these societies and their production as well.

From the historical point of view, this exploitation was more important than the 'life-style' of native or foreign subjects. What is certain is that it would be a mistake to underestimate the influence of this exploitation in any discussion of morality, both on

the subjects and on the rulers. It had a deep influence on the life-
style as well. In my view, Sir John Beazley was right in the comparison that he made between the frieze on the Parthenon and the
reliefs on oriental palaces. On the one hand, the envoys of subject
peoples are shown in Persepolis as bringing tribute to the king of
kings; on the other, young men and girls are seen on the frieze of
the Parthenon as born free, and not as humble, cringing subjects.[12]

In the following sections, only Greek problems are dealt with,
since one particular aspect, that of private morality, cannot be
discussed in this way for Roman society. This is, of course, connected with the political organization of Rome, which has too often
—and wrongly—been called a *polis*, in imitation of the Greek historians.

Hoplites and Slaves

Even in recent publications, it has been commonly argued that
the hoplites, that is, all citizens with the status of hoplites, were
slave-holders. According to De Ste. Croix, 'the vast majority of the
hoplites must have owned at least a slave or two, who were used
on the land as well as in domestic and personal service'.[13] Thucydides mentioned servants (ὑπηρέται) of the Athenian hoplites and
said that each hoplite and his servant were paid two drachmae
(3. 17, 4). Elsewhere, he spoke of servants who were ordered to set
fire to defences in Sicily (6. 102, 2). Nicias also referred to the desertion of servants (θεράποντες) in Syracuse (7. 13, 2), but it is not said
that these were necessarily servants of hoplites or that each hoplite
had such a servant. There were, of course, many 'servants' taking
part in this great expedition.[14] In 7. 75, 5, we read that, at the time
of the collapse of Sicily, the hoplites and the *hippeis* not only wore
their armour, but also carried their provisions and that this was not
their custom. This does not, however, imply that each of them had a
servant in normal cases.

---

[12] *CAH* V (1927, reprinted 1953), pp. 440-441. Whether the nations
brought 'gifts' or 'tribute' is irrelevant here. The difference between the
two does not deminish the burden laid on these nations. Cf. the sensible
remarks of C. G. Starr, *The Economic and Social Growth of Early Greece 800-
500 B.C.*, New York (1977), 58-59.
[13] *CR* (1957), p. 58. His evidence is based on Thucydides 7. 75, 5 and
3. 17, 4; Dem. 54. 4 and Isaeus 5. 11; Theophrastus, Characters 25. 4. These
texts are investigated in the above.
[14] Gomme, Commentary II, p. 275.

In Thucydides, all that is left is 3. 17, 4 and Gomme has concluded from this that 'one would naturally suppose from this passage
that, like the Spartans (6. 16, 1), every Athenian hoplite had his
servant'. Over and against this, he maintains that

1. Such servants are seldom mentioned. In my view, this is not a
valid argument.

2. They would not fit into every description, for example, the one
in which soldiers are building the wall of Pylos (4. 4). The presence
of the ταξίαρχοι there shows that both hoplites and seamen were
included, but why was this menial task not left to the servants?
In Delium, there would also have been little need for the troops of
lightly armed men that are specially mentioned in this context if
each hoplite had had his servant with him (4. 90).[15]

The possession of a slave as 'batman' does not necessarily mean
that every officer had a 'butler'. We are bound to make this comparison if we want to conclude from the fact that a hoplite and his
servant were mentioned only at Potidaea (and there alone) that
only the hoplites had a personal servant and that this was their
own slave. The first conclusion is contradicted by the military
operations summarized by Gomme and mentioned above (under 2).
The second is rendered doubtful by the fact that nothing is said
about the social status of these servants.

In Theophrastus' Characters 25. 4, the coward in the war has a
παῖς, to whom he gives his shirt and whom he sends out of the tent
to find out where the enemy is. It would be dangerous to draw any
conclusion from this little vignette that could be applied to a historical situation. It is different in the case of the speeches in which
Isaeus said that a man had a 'follower' or ἀκόλουθος which the French
editor, P. Roussel, has rightly called a 'valet d'armée qui était
d'ordinaire un esclave'. Demosthenes said (54. 4): τοὺς παῖδας ἡμῶν
τοὺς ἀκολούθους.[16]

After having pointed out that it was the hoplites and other higher
classes who determined the character of military service, apart perhaps from some period during the second half of the fifth century,
de Ste. Croix went on to say that, if they had been deprived of the

---

[15] As for the latter, I cannot help saying that it is in conflict with Gomme's
case against Grundy—according to Gomme, the Athenians had few lightly
armed men or none at all, because these had to be trained. All the same,
there is something of decided value in Gomme's reasoning.

[16] The translation 'body-slaves' (Loeb, *op. cit.*) is misleading and suggests
personal care.

surplus wealth they got from their slaves, most well-to-do Athenians
with political power would have fallen below the level of affluence
at which they could afford to devote most of their time to politics
and war and the whole system would no longer have worked. There
was no comprehensive supply of hired labour de Ste. Croix insisted,
and many of the hired hands who were available either worked in
the mines or else were probably slaves[17].

Jones can also not have been right when he said that those who
had their land worked by slaves could have hired slaves without
owning them. De Ste. Croix emphasized how few sources of labour
there were, so that even a large farm worth half a talent could not
have provided more than 350 drachmae per year interest.[18] In the
fourth century, this would hardly have provided for the needs of a
small family which did not work its own land.

The only valid comment on the difference of opinion between de
Ste. Croix' and Jones is that there was certainly no hiring of slaves
from farm to farm, since all the farms would have needed labour
simultaneously. If indeed slaves were hired, it can only have taken
the form of those who kept slaves for regular work letting them out
in slack times to farmers. Those who let them out need not necessarily have been farmers. No doubt city dwellers too hired them
out to farmers for seasonal labour. We cannot know whether this
method was used extensively or not, but it is important to note
that it cannot have been the farmer who let them out in slack times,
since, he was the one whose labour needs were seasonal.

Slaves as opposed to Free Men

It is true to say that slaves could not be distinguished in many
cases by their clothes. This is also borne out by Greek comedy. The
Old Oligarch also complained about it. (1. 10 ff). It applied especially to certain trades and to seamen. On the other hand, there was
also a saying, 'Dress as a slave', showing that there might have been
differences in clothing. The Megarian *chlamiskidion* and the *katonaké*
were garments worn above all by slaves. They were different from
the *chlainai* of fine wool. The *exōmis* and the *kynē* were also worn
by slaves, but may have been taken up also by the poorer citizens.

Slaves were treated differently at different periods. Their treat-

---

[17] De Ste. Croix, *CR* (1957), p. 59, who based his evidence on Pseudo-
Dem. 53. 20-21.

[18] See IG II², 2496; Isaeus 11. 42-43; compare these with IG II², 1241.

ment also differed according to their masters and their tasks. Mine slaves were generally badly treated, many trying to run away. Slaves on the whole did not live as splendidly as the Old Oligarch claimed.[19] There are many references in Greek comedy to tyrannical treatment of slaves and to their being beaten. To kill one's own slave was perhaps not regarded as a crime in the eyes of the law, but it did incur religious defilement (Antiphon 6. 4). Slaves were treated better after the Peloponnesian War had broken out, because it was feared that they would run away. Once again, however, mine workers continued to be badly treated and still tried to escape.

In all this there is one generally accepted dogma of which I for one am doubtful. It is that the slave-owner had a right to kill his slave. The widely accepted opinion can be found in Ehrenberg.[20] Ten Berge, however, in his commentary on Antiphon [21] gives a different and more acceptable view, which would account, for example, for the law against crimes of violence quoted by Dem. 21. 47, expressly including slaves. The killing of one's own slave could indeed be punished by a γραφὴ ὕβρεως. It should be noted in this context that ten Berge also emphasizes the importance of religious impurity in Athens. The possibility of punishment again is also clearly suggested by Antiphon.[22] Ten Berge clearly believed that charges of this kind did not occur very often. Tradition has nothing very much to tell us on this question and in view of the shortage of data we must regard it as probable that ten Berge was right. What is quite certain, however, is that slaves were beaten and that they were also the victims of their masters' moods. They were also tortured before the court. It should not be forgotten, however, that torture was accepted in Greek and Roman law and was not always exclusively associated with slavery.

Generally speaking, the Athenian court was active when a man was murdered, whether slave or free (see Euripides, Hecuba 291 ff;

---

[19] Apart from Lauffer, R. J. Hopper has also dealt with the mine slaves in 'The Attic Silvermines in the Fourth Century B.C.', *B.S.A.* 48 (1953), pp. 200ff. V. Ehrenberg has also discussed the treatment of slaves in *The People of Aristophanes*, p. 184 ff.

[20] V. Ehrenberg, *op. cit.*, p. 180.

[21] H. M. ten Berge, *Antiphon's Zesde Rede*, Dissertation at Groningen University, Nijmegen (1948), pp. 91-92.

[22] 6, 4: Instead of οὐκ ἔστιν ὁ τιμωρήσων. The text gives μὴ ἔστιν ὁ τιμωρήσων. 'Even if a man slays one who is his own chattel, and if the victim has none to avenge him' ... See G. R. Morrow, *The Murder of Slaves in Attic Law*, *CPh* (1937), p. 216 ff, especially p. 222.

Antiphon 5. 48). But we must none the less conclude that Athens
was not a paradise for slaves and that the freedom of speech attributed to slaves by comic sources has been greatly exaggerated by
scholars who wanted to show Athens in a favourable light.

Must it still be stressed, however, that the culture and economy
of Athens were not based on slave labour? The point has been made
emphatically by Ehrenberg, Jones, and several others.[23] Athenian
free men always bore in mind the danger formulated by Euripides
in Fragment 1019: δούλοισι γάρ τε ζῶμεν οἱ ἐλεύθεροι, 'We free men
live by the slaves'. This is to be understood—so it is alleged—as a
warning rather than a mere statement.

The argument is a weak one and even if it may possibly be true,
there is at least one solid fact that can be presented as a counter-
argument. Xenophon shows us the real situation (Mem. 2. 8, 1-5).
In this text, Socrates asks an unfortunate Athenian who has lost
his property and has to earn his living by manual work what he
would do if he were no longer equal to the work physically. Socrates
suggests that he should become a supervisor in a rich man's business.
The man refuses to consider this, however—he does not want to be
a slave: 'I positively refuse to be called to account by anyone'.
This Athenian of the lowest class in Athenian society did not object
to hard work. He had lost his foreign property, which suggests that
his father, one of the many who did not possess land in Attica, had
emigrated to a *klērouchia* in allied territory. What he did object to
was serving another man. That was also why he did not want
regular employment. That is also why such extremely responsible
functions as that of chief supervisor of a mine or bank director were
carried out by slaves or men who had been freed by their owners.[24]

Slaves were employed as domestic servants, in agriculture, and
above all in business and industry. Generally speaking, the latter
were small in Greece. The few larger industries that are mentioned
in Greek literature, such as the factory belonging to Demosthenes'
father, cannot be included, because they were exceptional. No evidence has ever been found as to whether the Greeks—and especially
the Athenians—were able to live without slaves and at the same
time keep their heads above water economically and carry out their
political and military tasks. The Athenians treated their domestic
slaves humanely, and this may well have been exceptional by the

---

[23] See also the viewpoints mentioned on pp. 207-208 (above).
[24] See Xenophon, Mem. 2. 5, 2; Demosthenes, 36. 28-29, 43.

standards of the time, but they never abolished slavery. We therefore have no evidence whether their relatively high standard of
living could have been maintained without slaves.

I would, however, accept A. H. M. Jones's argument here. Supposing that all slaves, both men and women of all ages, were set
free, the result would not have been catastrophic. The well-to-do
ladies of Athenian society and their daughters would have had to
do more in their homes for themselves. A very small number of
wealthy people who had invested all their money in slaves—this is
something that hardly ever happened, since most people bought
land rather than slaves—would have been reduced to poverty and a
larger number—but still a small minority—would have had to accept
a reduction in income. (This reduction in income would have been
brought about by the loss of slaves working in industry and agriculture). They might have had to let off their farms. Many artisans
might have lost their apprentices and hired men. The great majority
of citizens, however, would have experienced no serious disadvantage as a result of the abolition of slavery in their small businesses
and industries.

This argument has no bearing on the condemnation of slavery
as a phenomenon. It is simply an attempt to envisage slavery in
Greek society. It should also be borne in mind that we can learn
nothing at all from it about what the slave himself thought about
his own situation, in which he was without freedom. What is clear
from the above argument is that the slave certainly longed for freedom. The idea that the slave felt protected and that he was therefore happy to remain with his master has been suggested from time
to time, but it is something that appears nowhere in the Greek
sources themselves. I belief that it should be firmly rejected.

The Nature of Reporting about Slaves and the Lower Classes

Many scholars lament the fact that we have so little traditional
information about the lower levels of Greek society. There are two
possible attitudes here among modern scholars. The majority simply
accept the shortage of data on the 'lower classes' as inevitable and
try to relate the few data to what they know. This attitude is not the
result of class prejudice or an unconscious aversion to the 'little
man', but rather the outcome of an awareness of the kaleidoscopic
nature of the tradition itself. All that the scholar can do is to relate
a piece of papyrus here to an inscription there or a fragment of text

elsewhere and in this way build up a kaleidoscopic picture which is in any case distorted, because pieces from different periods in history are joined together indiscriminately and given equal value. The silence or near-silence that has prevailed for so long in connection with the lower classes in Greek society is understandable, but it cannot be excused.

Naturally most attention has been given to slavery, and those scholars who belong to the second group (which is now becoming more numerous) are no exception. Their attempts have been directed to a thorough investigation of the more abundant material concerning free citizens of the lower and middle classes of Greek society, in order to overcome the predominantly one-sided picture provided by the sources, which reflect only the attitudes of the upper classes. Traces of this new approach are to be found in M. I. Finley's treatment of the economy of classical antiquity, but he is not the only one. Ramsay MacMullen is the real spokesman of this second group of scholars in what is undoubtedly a pioneering book, especially valuable for the material collected in its footnotes.[25] In the socialist and communist countries, on the other hand, there are many historians working in this field. Yet the fruit of their researches is poor. It can hardly be anything else since, as we have seen, the sources give little information and their work also is in many cases checked for its Marxist purity. This situation should not, I think, be regarded as permanent. In an excellent discussion of Barker's book on social and political ideas in classical antiquity, Elias Bickerman provided a list of desiderata that even twenty years later has received serious consideration only in part. This is a fault that must be rectified by modern historians. Some of Bickerman's points in this list of desiderata deserve to be mentioned again, partly in his own words.[26]

1. The treatment of Roman imperialism by its victims cannot be based exclusively on the well known passage of Calgacus, despite its brilliant Tacitean rhetoric. A better impression can be got by study of the opposition of the people in territories dominated by

---

[25] R. MacMullen, *Roman Social Relations: 50 B.C. to 284 A.D.*, New Haven and London, Yale University Press (1974). See also my discussion of this book in *Mnem.* 28 (1975), pp. 455-460.

[26] Elias J. Bickerman, *AJPh* 78 (1957), pp. 325-327, where he discussed E. Barker's *From Alexander to Constantine. Passages and Documents Illustrating the History of Social and Political Ideas, 336 B.C.-A.D. 337. Translations with Introductions, Notes and Essays*, Oxford (1956).

the Romans. This opposition has been expressed, for example, from Egypt (POxyr. 22, 2332) and in the Alexandrian invectives against the Caesars handed down in the so-called Acts of the Pagan Martyrs.[27]

2. Greek, Roman, Jewish, and Christian authors were constantly criticizing the greed and covetousness of the propertied classes. So far as I know, no complete collection of all the data in ancient literature on this subject has yet been compiled. Only one passage, from Cercidas, was quoted by Barker.[28] Social conflicts and the friction to which they gave rise were regarded by those in authority as 'sedition'.[29] This is entirely in accordance with what we know about *stasis* and *seditio* from the viewpoint of the ruling class.

3. For the 'middle class', we have to go to inscriptions such as the funeral inscription from Mactar in Tunisia, which tells of a young man who was originally poor, but who became wealthy and famous by his industry and thrift.[30]

4. The attitude of these middle class people towards their fellow-men is clearly expressed in the frequently occurring words *neminem laesi* ('I have harmed no one').[31] Bickerman has called this a golden rule of paganism under the Empire which should be given more attention than the commonplaces of Pliny's *Panegyricus*.

5. When discussing slavery, it is not enough to confine ourselves to statements made by Roman jurists. It is also important to try to discover what the slaves themselves thought. An example of this is the slave's expectation of reasonable treatment. Westermann has collected a number of data referring to this.[32] In this context too, there is the epitaph of a certain Narcissus: debita libertas iuveni mihi lege negata, morte immatura reddita perpetua est.[33] "The words of Phaedrus, words of a freedman, that the fable was an invention of 'submissive slavery' to express feelings which could not be made known openly are no less characteristic".[34]

---

[27] See H. A. Musurillo, *The Acts of the Pagan Martyrs* (1954).

[28] E. Barker, *op. cit.*, p. 58.

[29] E. Barker, *op. cit.*, p. 60.

[30] The text has been discussed by M. Rostovtzeff in *SEHRE*, p. 292 and can be found in Buecheler, *CLE*, 1238.

[31] Greek equivalents can be found in M. N. Tod, *ABSA*, 46 (1951), pp. 182-190.

[32] See W. L. Westermann, *Slave Systems* (1955), pp. 64, 117-118.

[33] See Buecheler, *CLE*, 1015.

[34] Bickerman has pointed here to E. M. Shtaerman's very instructive article on the ideological tendencies in the Roman Empire, *Symbolae R. Taubenschlag Dedicatae = Eos*, 48, 1 (1956).

6. The Church and slavery. Barker has expressed a fairly widely accepted opinion, that the Church had a cautious and conservative attitude towards slaves. Bickerman has correctly countered with the fact that there is nothing cautious about the exhortations in Paul's letters (Col. 3. 22 ff; Eph. 6. 5) and the Didache 12 Apost. 4. 11. In these texts, the slave is exhorted to work hard for his master as 'an image' (*typos*) 'of the Lord', thus drawing a parallel between the slave-owner and the deity. This is something completely new, hitherto unknown in Jewish or pagan thought. It is significant that many scholars who have discussed the 'Social Gospel' have neglected these Christian texts. It is also amusing that many Soviet historians, who have spoken endlessly about slavery, have also tended to disregard these texts until Bickerman mentioned them in 1957. These scholars have been and indeed still are to a great extent victims of Marxist formalism and this has given them a false vision of slavery. Marx after all regarded slavery, in accordance with the thinking of his own times, in terms of Roman jurisprudence.[35] It is only fair to agree with Bickerman that Westermann's work, which has been widely criticized, 'for the first time opens the way to the understanding of the manifold character of slavery in Antiquity'.

7. The Greeks can be contrasted with the Romans in an example provided in the letter sent by Philip V of Macedon to Larissa (*SIG*[3] 543. 27 ff): 'in which he supports his instruction to fill up the citizen-body, with an elaborate, if inaccurate, account of Roman policy in founding colonies and awarding citizenship'.[36] Rome awarded citizenship to all ex-slaves after manumission (and that is true). The Romans, so it is alleged, sent them also as full citizens to the *coloniae*. And this is, to put it mildly, inaccurate. There are, however, situations, or political opinions, in which the historicity of what had been done or said to have been done, is less important than the opinion of the informant. This is the case here. The majority of our sources depict the Romans as barbarians.[37] Positive

---

[35] So far as I know, Marxist historians are still not aware of this fact. Cf. one of the recent publications 'Marxism and the Classics', *Arethusa* 8 (1975) 7-225, with good bibliography (pp. 211 ff). D. Konstan, who comes very near to a more objective evaluation of Marxism and slavery in his valuable contribution 'Marxism and Roman slavery' (*op. cit.*, 145-169), ignores this source of inspiration for Marx's own views.

[36] F. W. Walbank, *Philip V of Macedon* (reprint 1967), p. 67, note 6.

[37] J. Deininger, *Die politische Widerstand gegen Rom in Griechenland 217-86 v. Chr.*, Berlin-New York (1971) offers a picture in which the Romans as barbarians are central. This book is one of the best examples of the many.

reactions, however, deserve more attention in modern studies, in which the complaints and condemnations of Roman behaviour are central. The bias is understandable and probably more in harmony with the feelings of the Greek contemporaries. Different reactions have been preserved. They have to be collected and explored.

Party Conflicts

I should like in this section by two examples to throw some light on the hopeless partisanship of modern treatments of the question of ancient slavery. G. Thomson criticized A. W. Gomme's discussion of the slave population in his well-known book, *The Population of Athens in the Fifth and Fourth Centuries B.C.* with the words: 'The whole subject will be re-examined by someone who is prepared to take the ancient evidence seriously and is free from the suspicion of seeking to minimise the extent of an evil which casts a sinister shadow over the glory that was Greece'.[38] The second example is a statement by J. H. Thiel (in 1951): 'We should not forget that slavery was not abolished in Christian America until 1863 A.D. Even now Christian Americans regard it as one of their human rights to lynch free negroes, the descendants of negro slaves, as a pastime. Even now, the Transvaal Boers, with the Bible in their hand, call the Kaffirs "creatures", but not fellow human beings. We should therefore be careful not to throw stones at the Greeks of the fifth and fourth centuries B.C. for owning slaves, especially if it is also true that in Greece and above all in democratic states such as Athens, slaves also benefited from the generally humanitarian environment and the treatment of slaves, with the exception of the mine slaves, was reasonable, much more reasonable than that of countless poor people in the East at the same period'.[39]

Both of these statements by classical scholars are too emotional. In the case of the first, we are bound to recognize that an ethical accusation in a society that is simply unaware that any issue exists, is rather cheap and of no historical value. Against that, we must equally admit that the writer of the second quotation is clearly not on easy terms with Calvinistic Christianity, which he quotes for the sake of the white Americans and Afrikaners. His emotional outburst does not further research into ancient democracy and slavery. We must therefore bear two points in mind:

---

[38] *Oresteia* I, p. 70, note 1.
[39] *Het oudste Christendom en de antieke cultuur*, I, (1951), pp. 4-5.

I. Judgements about ancient slavery must be related to the standards of morality obtaining in the ancient world.

II. The unity of all men was a concept unknown to ancient humanism. *Homonoia* was the equality of all citizens. Human rights were civil rights.[40]

In addition to these historical affirmations, a few further points must also be made:

1. Greek business and industry was on a small scale.

2. Slavery was not cheap, in the first place because it took time to bring up slave children; the mother was eliminated for a shorter or longer period. Slaves therefore had not often been bred as such. Meno's slave (Plato 81 b) was an exception. By far the greater number of slaves were purchased.[41] This means that they had known freedom. Slaves were only 'bred' when they were scarce and therefore expensive to buy. Because they had known freedom, there was always a risk that they would run away. This risk was greater in their case than in the case of those who had been born into slavery. Again, in the case of slaves who had been purchased and were relatively expensive, there was a risk of illness and death. Because of this risk, small industries—and all industries were small in ancient Greece—had to bear a disproportionately heavy burden.

3. Slave labour was never cheap, with the result that there was always a place for the free worker in Greece.[42]

These points give rise to the suspicion that slavery was not in fact the material basis of Greek society. But if we are to make our argument convincing, we must go a little more deeply into the whole question. To be satisfied with these three points alone would do nothing to explain the continuing profound difference of opinion

---

[40] See Antiphon, above p. 64 and C. J. Classen in *Lampas* 8 (1975), p. 356 ff. There is a good deal of conflict with W. W. Tarn about this. For the early literature, see M. Mühl, *Die antike Menschheitsidee* (1928) and J. H. Waszink's inaugural address *Humanitas*, Leiden (1946). For Tarn's speculations about brotherhood among mankind on the basis of the fatherhood of God, see E. Badian, '*Alexander the Great and the Unity of Mankind*' (1958), reprinted in G. T. Griffith, ed., *Alexander the Great, The Main Problems* (1966), especially p. 426 ff.

[41] The origin of the slaves can sometimes be ascertained from their personal names. A man with the name Carion would, for example, come from Caria and a man with the name Syrus would come from Syria. See Ehrenberg, *op. cit.*, p. 171.

[42] Although H. Bolkestein was outspokenly left-wing in politics, his views are in agreement with these three points, *Economic Life in Greece's Golden Age*, Leiden 1958, pp. 74 ff.

among scholars and the apparent hopelessness of reconciling their divergent views.

For the time being, then, we may draw the following conclusion. There is no agreement concerning the chronology, the extent, the causes, and the consequences of slavery, or even the way in which it was operated. It is not even possible for scholars to agree about the two components of the slavery business itself—the citizen of the city state and the slave. Some scholars regard the city state as a class society with the different groups sharply distinguished by levels of wealth. Others see the city state as a fairly homogeneous community in which citizens, slaves, freedman and metics associated with one another—in sharp contrast to the modern state, with its clear division between capital and labour. This second viewpoint is more attractive. We may go further and say that, as far as the expense of slavery is concerned, some scholars believe it was more expensive, while others think it was less so than free labour. Opinions also differ regarding the treatment of slaves—some think that it was hard, others that it was humane. Some again think, as Aristotle did, that slaves were stupid, others that they were intelligent. There can be no doubt that slaves were intelligent, often trained workers, especially in the case of those who had previously been free.

How can we escape from this Labyrinth?

It is perhaps possible to find our way out of the maze by beginning at the point of human experience that most slaves were aliens who had known freedom. The consequences of this for the Greek slaveholders state were important. Slaves were often unmotivated and unskilled. They worked mechanically at manual work of a purely physical kind, without the help of technical aids. Slavery also called for heavy capital investment, especially to start with. Workers were, in other words, not hired, but purchased. Whether the initial expense was justified by much lower expenses in the long term depended on many factors—sickness, running away, rebelliousness, and so on. For this reason, the small Greek businesses did not invest in slaves without thought. The risk was too great. It was possible to 'breed' slaves, but this depended on circumstances. If we think of slavery in America, we should not forget that there were slave producing and slave consuming districts. In the case of slavery

in general, if transportation is difficult from the country where the
slaves originate or if there is a general fear that the death rate
among imported slaves will be high because of the change in climate,
for instance, there will then perhaps be 'breeding' of slaves on a
commercial scale, as was indeed the case.

In periods when the supply was low the conditions of slavery
were favourably affected, and slaves could only gain from a state of
disorder or war, unlike free men. Slaves formed a rebellious element
in the state. They were aliens and therefore formed no friendships
with their masters. We may say that under special conditions
slavery drove out free labour for three reasons. A number of men
were taken away from free labour for supervision and national defence. There was a general aversion to manual work of the kind done
by slaves and free men left the trades and forms of employment
that could be carried out by slaves. There was thus a class of citizens
which by its steady decrease endangered the stability of the Greek
community. The situation has often been compared with that of
the poor white in South Africa during the first half of the twentieth
century. The whole subject has moreover been analyzed by a prominent economist, J. E. Cairnes, in his book *The Slave Power*, (1862)
and this seems to me to provide a very good point of departure.

One of the first questions that we have to ask is about the numbers of Greek slaves, but here we are bound to admit that very little
is known, partly because the sources always juggle with figures.
(This applies not only to numbers of slaves, but also of course to
the strength of armies, as for example in the Persian wars). Gomme
has shown how little even men of high reputation are to be trusted
with figures, in connection with the population of London in the
seventeenth century. According to a statement made in 1636, this
was 700 000, a figure which included more than 100 000 Dutchmen
and Frenchmen. But according to an account given in 1661, there
were then two million more Londoners than before the plague of
1625. Yet in actual fact we have enough material to be able to
estimate the population of London before 1650 at about 175 000.[43]

---

[43] A. W. Gomme, *The Population of Athens in the Fifth and Fourth Centuries B.C.* (1933) and *JHS* (1946). Gomme's calculations are supported by
the data collected by S. Dow in *Hesperia*, Suppl. 1 (1937) and Westermann in
the *Harvard Studies*, Suppl. Vol. I (1940), pp. 451-470. V. Ehrenberg has
also reproduced these data, without adding to them, and placed them in a
wider context in *The People of Aristophanes*, p. 168.

The Data for Greece

In Athens, Zimmern calculated that there were 100 000 slaves
in a total population of 250 000, Gomme came to a different conclusion. He calculated that there were 115 000 slaves in a total population of 315 000 before 431 B.C. and, before 425 B.C., after the
great epidemic in which so many Athenians died, there were altogether 228 000 inhabitants, of whom 81 000 were slaves. In 323
B.C., that is approximately a century later, again according to
Gomme there were 104 000 slaves in a total population of 356 000.[44]
Since Gomme, other estimates have been made which hardly change
the picture at all. They all fluctuate slightly about a proportion of
one third slave and two thirds free in the population of Athens in
the fifth and fourth centuries.

We should also take into account the different slave statistics in
different parts of Greece. On the island of Chios, for example, there
were more slaves than in any other state with the exception of
Sparta, at least according to Thucydides (8. 40, 2). As in Sparta,
most of them worked on the land, but for the rest we can deduce
nothing.

The picture provided above is extremely incomplete, but we have
to be satisfied with it. If we now ask what place the slave occupied
in Greek society, we are, I think, bound to take into account the
difference between skilled and unskilled slaves. From the economic
point of view, it is reasonable to assume that the untrained slave
had a harder life than the trained slave and indeed that he was no
more valuable than an ox used for ploughing. We may also assume

---

[44] *Op. cit.*, p. 26. The basis that Gomme has taken for his calculation is
rather primitive, but so far no better one has been found. The number of men
between the ages of 18 and 59 who were liable for military service is known to
us in those cases when a mass levy of troops was necessary, in other words, at
critical times. The numbers obtained in this way have been multiplied by
four to get a total citizen population. We know with a fair degree of certainty that there was an excess of births over deaths in Athens between 480
and 430 B.C., which means that it can be compared with certain modern
countries. The multiplication factor 4 has been applied in demographic
studies over periods before the development of modern techniques and
modern medical science and has proved fairly reliable.

The estimates that have been made of the population in later periods—
Hellenism, the Roman republic, and the imperial period—are less certain.
For the period of the Roman republic, see P. A. Brunt, *Italian Manpower,
225 B.C.-A.D. 14* (1971), pp. 121-130; for the imperial period (in various
areas), see R. Duncan-Jones, *The Economy of the Roman Empire* (1974),
pp. 272-273, 347-348.

that the trained slave had the prospect of advancement and even of acquiring freedom, whereas the untrained slave did not.

Again from the economic point of view, the most important aspect of the slave's attitude is that he had no reason for working or even for living, because he and the whole of his family belonged to someone else. It is from this fact that all the evil results of slavery came. What then were the circumstances?

We can put ourselves in the position of the slave-owner or rather the slave-dealer who has bought a cargo of slaves. What does the cargo consist of? Mainly of young men and boys, young women and girls. The men who are able to fight have for the most part been killed and the women who have lost the freshness of youth and are therefore less qualified to follow the oldest profession in the world are quickly eliminated. The slave-dealer has to separate the less marketable wares from those more marketable. It should be noted that I am not making a distinction here between 'chattel' and 'apprentice', as Zimmern does; my distinction is simply between usable goods and those that were less so, between skilled and unskilled slaves. Many of the young men when they were sold as slaves were given a kind of contract which held out the possible prospect of freedom. Both Xenophon and Aristotle noted that slaves who had a prospect of freedom were more employable.[45]

The slave, then, had no legal security, that the arrangement governing his employment would be observed, but he did have the 'security of custom'. It was also in the interest of both parties that the arrangement should be carried out. It was above all in the interest of the slave-owner that the agreement should be for a short term or that, if the slave proved satisfactory, the term could be shortened as a reward for work. This, of course, had many advantages. In the first place, a floating population of slaves meant that there was less likelihood of civil disorder. Secondly, the slave population was not a community of interests in such a situation. Solidarity was more difficult to achieve among slaves with very different interests. A slave with a short term to serve had far more to risk if he joined forces in a rebellion with slaves who were bound

---

[45] This can be compared with the condition of a prisoner detained for a certain time, whose term can be increased if he transgresses the rules of his captivity or reduced if he behaves well under detention. The inscriptions concerning emancipation are mostly to be found in I.G. II², 1553-1578. See also p. 237 below.

for a longer period. There were, in other words, no repercussions in such a situation. There was no unrest of the kind related by Thucydides (8. 40) as having taken place on Chios.

There were also disadvantages, of course. The slave-owner would want to keep a skilled slave working for him as long as possible. There were consequently provisions allowing a slave who had been set free to remain bound to his previous master. These provisions were often financial. We know nothing, however, about the length of such a term of slavery. It probably depended on the age of the slave in question. Younger slaves had longer working hours, but these cannot have been too long, since slaves must always have had time on their own when they were able to offer themselves, if young enough, on the free labour market.

It was also possible to bind trained slaves by offering them an opportunity of marriage although this possibility did not prove worth while in the case of those who were less well qualified. We may therefore assume that small families of slaves were permitted and that exposure occurred as seldom in the case of slaves as in that of the free.

The Control of Slaves

Slaves were forced into obedience by the threat of being sent to the mines. (This is clear from examples in Greek comedy). We do not know whether the threat was in fact carried out. We can only be sure that it had a disadvantage for the slave-owner in that his slave's value would be reduced. Corporal punishment was frequent. (We know this from Greek comedy, especially Aristophanes). Mutual arrangements were also made between different city-states concerning runaway slaves who had to be handed back to their original masters. In the case of corporal punishment, we are bound to point out that no objections would have been raised in the ancient world to the use of such punishment—ethical scruples of the kind encountered in the modern world did not then exist. We can have a good idea of the contents of the treaties concerning the handing back of slaves to their masters from the fact that 2000 slaves who fled from Athens during the period when Decelea was occupied were bought and sold at the slave market in Boeotia. All this points to the fact that there was a fairly accurate and efficient control of slaves.

Contracts

The slave was able to buy his freedom with money that he had earned during his years of slavery and had been able to keep. Thus the emancipated slave was often in an unenviable position, because he had to hand over the money that he had saved throughout his working life when he was already at an advanced age. As a result of this, his position was one of dependence. Yet, because he had once known freedom, he never ceased to long for it during slavery. In states such as Athens, where slaves were dressed like poor citizens, the equality (that had once existed) was stressed. The Old Oligarch, for instance, complained that slaves pushed ordinary citizens aside in the streets. There were also feasts which were intended exclusively for slaves, but there were certainly many points of contact between citizens and slaves in ordinary life, which also meant that the slave never lost his desire to be free. The slave-owner, on the other hand, did all that he could to obliterate the slave's feeling of belonging to a different community in which he had once been free. It was again and again impressed on him that it was a glorious thing to become a free 'Hellene'.[46]

The Situation of Slavery seen from the Slave's Point of View

The slave always had the possibility of promotion on merit. He was also able to gain his freedom by hard work. This made him self-seeking and individualistic and, because of this, less dangerous to the state; he seldom or never joined forces with other slaves who were in a different situation. He was also the product of natural selection based on his economic value. The slaves who reached the top and were given their freedom were therefore those with an intellectual and physical capacity that was well above average. The consequence was that both the emancipated slaves and those who were heading for it formed an élite group. There was also a select group of skilled men among the slaves. They probably did not dominate and they did not determine the appearance of slavery. They were very closely linked to the slaves who were in a less favourable position because of their absence of freedom, but they were never linked to other slaves in one great association which might have constituted a danger to the state and have perhaps led to rebellion.

---

[46] Jason's address to Medea in Euripides' drama (335 ff.) has an extremely irritating effect on most modern readers.

Finally, slaves tried to influence their masters' feelings so that their term of duty might be as short as possible. There were frequent intrigues against other slaves, favours, various forms of flattery, and so on. One of the commonest tactics of slaves aiming at freedom was to make themselves indispensable to their masters and in this way to have greater influence on their masters' domestic affairs. They often became confidants in their masters' houses and even familiar with their masters' secrets. This might even result in blackmail—an aspect that frequently figures in later Greek comedy.

Other, non-economic influences suggest that the distinction between skilled and unskilled slaves may not have been very deep. As we have already said, slaves belonging to the first group could be transferred to the second by way of punishment. The household —the οἰκία with its inmate the οἰκέτης—was a place in which both kinds of slave were found and where the owner took care to move slaves up the status ladder as well as down it.

There were also differences among the men who possessed οἰκίαι. Some worked and had their own business. Of these, some employed the lower category of slave, others the higher and more expensive. The difference was often simply a question of how the slaves were treated. The pedagogue was frequently in very much the same position whether slave or free.[47] In the patriarchal household the relationships were less sharply defined. The treatment of the slaves, Eurycleia, Odysseus' nurse, and Eumaeus, the swineherd in the Odyssey, shows that the position of the slave in that great family was bearable. Many of these earlier relationships persisted in the sphere of the οἰκία. Above all the nurse who brought up the children of a free man was of privileged status.

Differences in Special Places and Special Circumstances

Helots cannot be included in the framework that we have been discussing above. These slaves in Sparta are still a subject of controversy, but to go into the question here would take us too far from our main point.[48] We may summarize the situation by saying that there are two opposite points of view. According to the first, the helot was a peasant who was to a varying extent dependent on the citizens of Sparta and the campaigns against whom were really

---

[47] Zimmern, op. cit., p. 134; see also R. Boulogne's dissertation, De plaats van de paedagogus in de Romeinse literatuur, Utrecht (1951).

[48] I refer to the sensible summary of Finley, The Ancient Economy, 63 f.

initiation rites undergone by the young male citizens of Sparta.
According to the second group of scholars, the *krypteia*, which kept
the peasant members of the native population under control, was a
form of state police that went to work quite arbitrarily, with young
men violating peasant girls simply because they belonged to the
'master race' of the Spartiatae.[49]

In colonies of Greek citizens abroad, the natives were treated as
serfs bound to the soil, employed agriculturally on plantations. The
Dorian territories such as Sicily were notorious for this praedial
slavery, whereas the democratic city states seem to have operated
the plantation system much less extensively, though appearances
may be deceptive. In Greece proper, with the exception of such
districts as Laconia and Thessaly, praedial slavery disappeared before the fifth century B.C. In Attica, Solon's reforms improved the
situation of peasants and tenant-farmers without much capital. The
distances in Attica made it necessary for the larger landowners to
rely on their workers. The so-called Hectēmoroi (paying a sixth of
the yield were after all Greek and it was thought wrong to treat
them as completely dependent and subordinate, even though the
Thessalian merchants did not hesitate to enslave Greeks if it suited
them.[50]

Whatever the situation may have been with regard to praedial
slavery, it was given little opportunity of expansion in the Greece
of the historical period. It occurred nowhere but in agricultural
districts. If we were asked to classify the serfs we should have to
say that they were skilled rather than unskilled workers, since the
need in such districts was for men who were capable of performing
agricultural duties with little or no supervision.

Activities

What can we learn from the texts about the activities carried out
by slaves? They were to be found in almost every trade and profession, from the humblest to the most esteemed. They were active
in the arts and sciences, in trade and industry, in farming and
mining, in medicine, teaching, innkeeping, shopkeeping, domestic

---

[49] For a recent discussion, see J. Ducat, *Le mépris des Hilotes, Annales,*
E.S.C., 29 (1974), p. 1451 ff., who has amplified an article by H. Jeanmaire,
La cryptie lacédémonienne, REG 26 (1913), pp. 121-150. Jeanmaire applied
his theories to universal anthropology in his great work *Couroi et courètes*,
Paris (1939). Ducat's most recent contribution in *Ancient Society* 9 (1978),
5-46. See also p. 154, n. 11 (above).

[50] See Ehrenberg, *op. cit.*, p. 169.

service, secretarial duties, the police, prostitution, and many other occupations. They were often treated as favourites and confidants. They were liable to all kinds of personal treatment and their work was evaluated in many different ways. It is precisely because of this great diversity in the evidence available that opinions are so sharply divided about the position of Greek slaves.

There is, however, one reliable touchstone. Were free men also working in the same trade or industry, doing the same work for the same remuneration? If so, this was a form of slavery with a higher degree of freedom and independence. If not, then the activities concerned were assigned to the lowest kind of slaves. The building workers were an example of the first and the mine slaves an example of the second.

We must, however, correct this picture somewhat and be prepared for some great surprises. Lauffer, for example, pointed out that in the beginning free men too were employed digging ore in the mines.[51] The work was carried out in shafts that were sometimes 80 m. deep and galleries of 100 m. or longer, supported by wooden props. The work was usually done by unskilled slaves, who were cheaper to employ. They were strictly supervised, frequently by a skilled slave. (Slaves were often the hardest taskmasters towards other slaves). They were also often shackled and worked day and night in groups.[52] Ardailon assumed that there were at a given time 20 000 slaves employed in the mining industry. According to the author of *De Vectigalibus*, the purchase price of a mine slave was 158 drachmae, but it should not be forgotten that this price was not constant and that the quality of the slave employed played a part in determining the price. According to Demosthenes, the price was 150 drachmae (see his 37th speech); this would be about 100 drachmae in the fifth century. Other kinds of slave at this time cost between 160 and 200 drachmae. The mine slave, then, was cheaper and of inferior quality. These prices, however, must be treated with the greastest caution, because the data are of casual origin and the prices naturally tended to fluctuate according to supply and demand. Wars and piratical raids usually meant an in-

---

[51] Lauffer, (1956), 929: 'Jedenfalls hat die Sklavenarbeit während des 5. Jahrhunderts die freie Arbeit im Bergbau fast völlig verdrängt'.

[52] Among the earlierworks on this subject, I would draw attention to that by E. Ardaillon, *Les mines du Laurion* (1897). Among the later works, I would mention those by Hopper and Lauffer (see pp. 213, n. 19. and 239 below). Data drawn from Greek comedy will be found in Ehrenberg, *op. cit.*, p. 181.

crease in the supply of slaves and a lowering of prices. The same system applied to mining as to plantation work—the workers were paid according to the demand for the product. Silver was almost the only material with an international market and an unlimited demand. The supply of slaves fluctuated and their prices accordingly.[53]

Another form of slavery was found in the building industry. If the data relating to the fifth century are compared with those from the fourth century, it is not difficult to detect certain differences and these have been emphasized by some modern scholars.[54] It made a difference if the job was one for skilled workers, as was possible in the case of building contractors employing slaves.

Free men and slaves did practically the same kind of work in the building trade. From the Erechtheum building inscriptions (IG², I, 373-4; 409-7 B.C.) we know the status of 86 workmen; 24 were citizens, 42 metics, and 20 slaves. All the slaves were skilled and were only employed in major trades, as masons or carpenters. Skilled workers had always to be engaged for this trade sometimes from abroad. It would seem, then, that the building industry was sometimes affected not by unemployment, but by a shortage of skilled workmen.[55] This situation can be compared with that of

---

[53] The commentaries on the *Poroi* of Xenophon are important in this context. Two outstanding editions are J. H. Thiel's dissertation, Amsterdam (1922) and Mme G. Bodei Giglioni, *De Vectigalibus*, in Biblioteca di studi superiori, vol. 57, Florence (1970). Commentary by Ph. Gauthier (Genève-Paris (1976).

[54] Gomme, *The Population of Athens in the Fifth and Fourth Centuries B.C.*, Oxford (1933), repr. 1967, especially p. 40, note 2, is a good example of this.

[55] For the Erechtheum workmen, see R. H. Randall, Jr., *AJA* 57 (1953), p. 199 ff. The data contained in the building inscriptions have recently been briefly but clearly discussed by M. Finley in *The Ancient Economy*, London (1973), pp. 74, 79 and 192, note 32. In this note, Finley provides an important modern bibliography. Some of the authors and titles mentioned are: G. Glotz, 'Les salaires à Délos', *Journal des Savants* 11 (1913), pp. 206-215, 251-260; P. H. Davis, 'The Delos Building Accounts', *Bulletin de correspondance hellénique* 61 (1937), pp. 109-135. See also A. Burford, *The Greek Temple Builders at Epidauros*, Liverpool (1969), especially pp. 191-206; *The Economics of Greek Temple Building*, Proceedings of the Cambridge Philological Society, New Series 11 (1965), pp. 21-34. Similar details for Rome are not available. Finley points out that a difference was made in these contracts between work for free men and work for those who were not free, but at the same time notes that slaves were not extensively employed in this form of building because trained workers from the homeland were preferred. This, however, calls for further research. Randall, for instance, thinks it conceivable that a large number (of the metics), even a majority, were journeymen (*op. cit.*, 202). Finley, however, asserts: 'Enterprises hiring free men ... are

Solomon, who obtained labour from Hiram for the building of the temple of Jerusalem, and the mention of a staff shipyard agent with the task of importing the necessary labour in the Epidaurus inscriptions. Free foreign workers were certainly not hired because they were cheaper than skilled slaves.[56] The question arises: why did the skilled slave not replace the skilled free worker? Why did the aversion (attested by our aristocratic sources) to the work performed by slaves not prevent free men from doing it?

If we are to answer this double question, we must pay attention to a number of points, including the floating nature of the slave population (skilled slaves), the handicaps of the slave dealer with regard to the regular supply of slaves and so on. Among the difficulties encountered by the slave-traders were wars, expeditions, risks at sea, fluctuating prices, difficulties on the local market because of the absence or slowness of information, changes in the political situation in the Greek cities and in the purchasing power of the local inhabitants and finally the risks involved in dealing in such an unsafe article as human beings, many of whom needed a lengthy period of training.

All this goes to explain why trained slaves never completely ousted free workers. The desire was there, but it came to nothing, because the trained slave, who was paid the same and had a prospect of freedom, was once again accepted into the life of the city state: 'It is sometimes said that slavery destroyed the City State life. It would be truer to say that City State life destroyed slavery' was Zimmern's optimistic conclusion. We hardly need to point out that this is not something that would be emphasized by anyone who realized how extremely bad the position of many slaves was, especially those who worked in the mines. In my view, however, Zimmern's conclusion is valuable as far as the work in the building industry was concerned.

The fact that from the economic point of view free men and slaves—with the exception of the mine slaves and a few other groups —were so closely connected can be explained by the relative poverty

---

not found in the sources' (*op. cit.*, 74). He adds that 'public works reveal certain nuances differentiating them from private enterprises'. He admits 'distorting factors' from which it is not clear that they (or part of them) did not occur in private enterprises.

[56] For wages in the building trade and the cost of living in late fifth-century Athens, see Randall's summary (*op. cit.*, 209).

of this civilization and the generally low standard of living.[57] Another explanation is the limited nature of commercial life and the fact that it was not possible to buy everything. We only have to consider the opposite for a moment—in modern society, it is possible to build a factory anywhere, anything can be bought for money and if one has the means one can acquire machinery, a factory, labour, experts, and even patents and licences. In the earlier society, certain secrets remained within the family or 'guild', with the result that the latter, whether it was free or not, came to possess a kind of solidarity.

The only conclusion that can clearly be drawn is that Zimmern and other scholars of his generation at the beginning of the present century regarded the social position of slaves as favourable. This view of slavery was, in their opinion, confirmed by the evidence of Greek comedy. Even after the Second World War, Ehrenberg thought the same and emphasized it in his work.[58] Other scholars have also placed an exaggerated emphasis on the industrialization that took place in Greece in the fifth century. Despite this, however, what is above all important is that the slave had known freedom. He was originally an alien and that determined his position in Greek society as the victim of a 'peculiar institution'.[59]

Technology and Morality

It is frequently claimed, probably correctly, in discussions about slavery in Greece, that the Greeks were not very inventive with regard to technology. One of the reasons suggested for this lack of inventiveness is that it was not necessary for the Greeks to concern themselves very much with technical inventions because they had sufficient relatively cheap labour in the form of slaves. We are bound to ask in this context whether this charge can really be made against slavery. It is, of course, extremely difficult to find evidence for and against, but it cannot be denied that technology had a great influence on Greek society and that, in one way or another, morality was also influenced by it. What is significant, however, is that this influence has never been studied as a special subject.[60]

---

[57] See Zimmern, op. cit., pp. 153-155 and especially his book The Greek Commonwealth, 5th Edn. (1931).

[58] Ehrenberg, op. cit., pp. 184-188.

[59] See M. I. Finley's article in the Times Literary Supplement on 2 July 1976, p. 819; see above, p. 207.

[60] See Addendum 2, p. 240 below.

It is clear from the work of Sambursky that Greek ideals and especially those of the Stoics were closely connected with the development of technology, with the result that morality and technology were clearly related to each other (even though the relationship was more primitive than that existing today).[61]

The Greeks were inventive, but this inventiveness did not extend to the technical control of the means by which life could be lived more pleasantly. This observation has been well summarized by Hans Lamer in a lexicon that was very successful before the Second World War; in one article he made fun of modern man's often astonished question: 'Did they *already* have that too in antiquity?'[62] It would be much more sensible to turn the question round and ask how far we *still* possess and use certain appliances of a technical kind acquired by humanity in very early times. It must surely have affected mutual relationships among the workers if both slave and free were dependent on their own hands and muscles. The solidarity of a small peasant family employing one or two workers (who might or might not have been slaves) would be a case in point.

In the case of trade, it must be borne in mind that on board ship a certain solidarity must have resulted from the dependence of all hands on the elements. The ship itself was dependent on the wind for its motion. We may therefore say that it was not until the coming of the steamship that really radical changes were made in transport and trade and that it was the telegraph that made commercial traffic possible over great distances. Diels has written about a form of telegraph signals in time of war.[63]

It is significant, however, that a similar form of signalling for the quick transmission of messages was never developed and put into service for peaceful ends, except in such great world empires as that of the Romans. The Roman problem was above all one of defending frontiers. It is certainly correct to speak, as Bolkestein did, of war-

---

[61] S. Sambursky, *Physics of the Stoics*, London (1959).

[62] H. Lamer, *Wörterbuch der Antike mit Berücksichtigung ihres Fortwirkens;* see especially the article *Auch schon* ('also ... already').

[63] H. Diels, *Antike Technik*, Berlin (1920²), p. 77 ff. For the rapid transmission of messages, see W. Riepl, *Das Nachrichtenwesen des Altertums* (1913). See also W. L. Westermann, 'On Inland Transportation and Communication in Antiquity', *Political Science Quarterly* 43 (1928), p. 364 ff. For the Roman postal system, see C. W. J. Eliot, 'New Evidence of the Roman Internal Post', *The Phoenix* 9, 2 (1955), pp. 76-80. See also, for general information, L. Friedländer, *Sittengeschichte Roms* I¹⁰ (1922), p. 333 ff., and L. Casson, *Travel in the Ancient World*, London 1974 (review by H. W. Pleket, *BiOr.* 33 (1976). 9 ff.).

fare as the only form of major industry in Greek antiquity. Tele-
graphy, signalling over long distances, indirectly confirms his point
since it was consistently used only for military purposes. The low
level of technical development was connected with the level of needs.
If the demand could be met by already existing means, no thought
was given to improving those means.

This was certainly so in the case of siege techniques. Here there
was undoubtedly a need of technical apparatus and if the Greeks
had been a military people they would probably have applied their
resourcefulness to developing new techniques to a greater extent
than they in fact did. Yet they continued to use primitive methods
of killing, although there were many ingenious forms of apparatus
applied to the war business in antiquity.[64] For a long time the
techniques remained at a low stage of development because of the
cruder methods by which walls could be attacked. Siegecraft
(πολιορκία) did not really develop until later during the Hellenistic
period and among the Romans. It remained at an undeveloped
stage in the heyday of Greek civilization. The surname of Demetrius
'Poliorcetes', one of the Diadochi, is explained as a nickname, first
given him in derision, undoubtedly not because he took towns but
because he besieged them for months without taking them. He was
no *Ek*poliorketes.[65]

As we have already seen, those of lower social status, including
slaves, were given a decent burial when they were killed or died in
the service of their masters during wartime. It was also clear that
war widows who had been married to free men were taken care of
when they had children. The war business therefore certainly had a

---

[64] E. Marsden, *Greek and Roman Artillery. Historical Development*, Oxford
(1969), has written well about this subject. See also the *Times Literary
Supplement*, 18 June 1970. A recent summary of technology in classical
antiquity has been provided by M. I. Finley in 'Technical innovation and
economic progress in the ancient world', *Economic History Review*, 2nd ser.,
no. 18 (1965), pp. 29-45; *idem*, 'Aristotle and Economic Analysis', *Past and
Present* 47 (1970), pp. 3-25, especially p. 20 ff (= *Studies in Ancient Society*,
London (1974), 26-52). A survey of modern problems illustrated from
situations in Antiquity: M. A. Wes, *Tussen polis en technopolis*, Inaug.
lecture, Leiden (1974).

[65] This comment was made by A. W. Gomme, *Commentary* I, p. 17, note 1.
It was disputed by E. Marsden in a conversation that I had with him about
this question in 1968. As far as I know, however, he has published nothing on
the matter. Since then I have found evidence against this modern theory in
Diodorus 20, 92 where the name *Poliorkētēs* is explained as a name of honour.
Also Plut. *Dem.* 42, 10: *Arist.* 6. 2.

connection with various forms of legislation in which ethical tendencies were expressed. This does not mean, however, that technology here had a direct influence on lived morality. The 'batmen' of the heavily armed warriors played a useful part in establishing personal relationship between master and servant. Edifying stories about slaves saving their masters and masters their slaves were quite common.

The other side of the coin is, of course, that slavery was unquestioningly accepted in a primitive community and this was a burden which subject peoples had to bear. This circumstance must be borne in mind in considering the relationship between technology and morality.

Our ignorance here is very great, partly because we know nothing about the fluctuations that took place in the populations of the great centres. Higher birth rates or lower death rates—or both—may have occurred in periods about which we have a good deal of information, such as the period between 500 and 430 and that between 400 and 320 B.C. in Athens. Every time that we question the material, however, it proves to be so meagre that we are unable to find answers to even the most elementary questions. We know even less about the birth and death rates in the different classes of the population or about housing at different levels of the population. Because of this, no sociological study of Athens can ever be written and, if this is impossible in the case of Athens, it is also impossible in the whole of the Greek world. Our data about Rome are similar. An example of this can be found in the legionaries. For a period of three hundred years at least, we have to rely on data that do not exceed the figure 3000; these data are, moreover, in many respects very formal and are, for example, often derived from funeral inscriptions found in places where Roman legionaries were buried.[66]

Even in principle it would be impossible to undertake an investigation of this kind into the situation in other Greek states apart from Athens, however many questions we may ask. Some sociologists suggested a pattern of research which could also be applied to antiquity, above all in its reference to inscriptions, the stage (and comedy in particular) and proverbs. Certainly there are

---

[66] In the case of classical Athens, scholars had been hoping for new data to be revealed by the American excavations in Athens. As A. W. Gomme was obliged to state in *JHS* (1946), these data were not, however, forthcoming.

aspects of social life brought to light in comedy, but the latter is extremely free, exaggerated, heavily charged with political nuances and so on. It is therefore very dangerous to use comedy as a source unless it is possible to use other sources as a check—and these corrections can seldom or never be found.

The value of the material derived from inscriptions should also not be overestimated, because such inscriptions are often stereotyped in the language that they use or reflect in a very concise— literally 'lapidary'—form an official view which is open to suspicion. Although there has been a considerable increase in the results—I would point in this context especially to the work carried out by Rhodes and Davies [67]—we have not progressed sufficiently with demographic investigation into the ancient Greek world for a social history or a sociological study of classical antiquity to be written. We are bound to agree with what Gomme said in 1946: 'We cannot even attempt (perhaps never shall be able to attempt) a tithe of a true Social Structure of Athens, such as is done for modern countries'.[68]

Town and Country [69]

Bearing in mind what has been said above, we must now consider whether there are any data concerning the relationship (and fluctuations in the relationship) between the populations of the towns and those of the country districts such as Attica. To judge by the numbers of councillors found in the inscriptions at the time of Cleisthenes, the population of Athens was much less than one third of that of the three great component parts of Attica (the coast, the interior and the city).

1. During the heyday of fifth century Athens, most of the noble families belonged to the city demes. In the fourth century, however, there were few men who played a part in public life who came from the city and many who came from the interior and the coast. This was not because the country party had become more powerful, but rather because many families had moved from the country into the city, but were still named after the country district from which they had come and still registered there.

---

[67] P. J. Rhodes, *The Athenian Boule* (1972); J. K. Davies, *Athenian Propertied Families* (1971).

[68] Gomme, *JHS* (1946), p. 48.

[69] Gomme, *Population*, p. 37 ff.

2. It is clear from the inscriptions on buildings that citizens from every district took part. The metics, it will be remembered, were attracted to the city and it may therefore be assumed that the same applied also to many of the citizens living in the country and on the coast.

3. We may conclude from the inscriptions relating to manumission (I.G. II², 1553-1578, covering the years 340-320 B.C.) that most of the slave-owners who had urban occupations belonged to the town-demes. All owners who were metics lived in town-demes. We may also assume "that the majority of citizen owners belonging to inland and coast demes were living in Athens or Peiraeus".[70]

4. The same diversity of all the demes, however small and remote they may have been, can be found on the tombstones in Athens and Peiraeus.

5. In the inscriptions dealing with leases or mortgages or sales of land and houses, 'it is rare to find a man owning or leasing property in his own deme, comparatively common to find the reverse'. The mine owners of Laurium came from all over Attica. (24 came from inland demes 13 from the town 18 from the coast; of these last only 12 came from a district near to the mines).

A few literary data are worth discussing separately, because they are found scattered throughout Greek literature generally. Demosthenes reports (57. 10) that the *Halimousioi* lived to a great extent in their own demes in the middle of the fourth century. It was in a town district and it did not have an urban character. According to Xenophon (Hellenica, 2. 4, 8-9; 26), very many of the Eleusinioi and Aixoneis lived in their own demes at the end of the fifth century. In the introduction to his History, Thucydides says that, even after the *synoikismos*, the Athenians to a great extent lived outside the city and continued to do so until the Peloponnesian War.

Despite these literary data, which only show that Athens remained mainly agricultural, there was certainly a movement towards the city in the fifth century. It is possible to agree here with Gomme, from whose work the above is largely taken,[71] that about a third of the citizen population in 430 B.C. lived in the town (that is, about 60 000 people) and that a hundred years later half that population, in other words, 50 000 people, lived there. Including

---

[70] Gomme, *op. cit.*, 43, and for the following conclusions, *ibid.* pp. 45 and 46.

[71] Gomme, *op. cit.*, p. 47.

the metics and slaves, this means that more than half the population of Attica was concentrated in the town area in 430 B.C. and
almost two-thirds lived there in 330 B.C. However conjectural these
data may be, and difficult to confirm except approximately it is
true to say that Gomme's results in this sphere have not—or have
hardly—been challenged throughout the past thirty years.

Our ignorance here is, however, very great, because we know
nothing about the causes of the increase in the population of the
city between 500 and 430 B.C. and 400 and 320 B.C. We can only
repeat what we have already said, namely that the sociology of
Athens can never be written. It is a gap in our knowledge which we
may regret, but which we have to accept.

It would be very interesting to know more about Sparta in this
context, since it was in practice a more important state than Athens.
It may seem strange, but it has to be said that Sparta occupied a
greater place in history than Athens both in antiquity and later.
It is plausible of course, that this military community always made
a greater appeal to the imagination.[72] Thucydides, for example,
complained about the fact that the Spartan constitution was
hidden.[73] This complaint can be extended to include not only the
constitution, but also the whole of Sparta's social life as such, which
was kept hidden by the Spartans. The reasons why they did this
are clear enough. They had to be constantly on their guard against
the subjugated population and alert to the support that the latter
might receive from outside and because of this they kept what
happened in their own house secret.

The secrecy, then, was the result of fear. We cannot here discuss
the question as to whether other states were equally reluctant to
disclose social data. In the whole of ancient society, it was not so
much a question—as it was in Sparta—of a desire to keep certain
things secret, but of giving too little attention to the structure
of that society in practice and as a whole. The situation was accepted as it was. This explains why the most famous ancient historians did not trouble to mention certain data that *we* find important. There is a very good section in Gomme's commentary on

---

[72] F. Ollier, *Le mirage spartiate*, 2 volumes (1933 and 1943); N. E. Tigerstedt, *The Legend of Sparta in Classical Antiquity*, Stockholm (1965 and
1974); E. Rawson, *The Spartan Tradition in European Thought*, Oxford
(1969).

[73] Thuc. 5. 68. 2: διὰ τῆς πολιτείας τὸ κρυπτόν. 'The secrecy with which
their affairs were conducted' (Warner).

Thucydides, in which he speaks of 'what Thucydides took for granted'. This was much more than many modern historians would regard as permissible.

Dissatisfaction with the Scarcity of Data

It is not surprising that many scholars, who were preoccupied with their own special view of social questions, have made up for the great scarcity of data from their own opinions. Almost always, morality in such cases depends on the inventiveness of the scholar concerned. G. Thomson has suggested, in his *Studies in Ancient Greek Society*, that the Greeks evolved socially from barbarians to civilized people. This theory is in accordance with something that the Greeks themselves are believed to have acknowledged, through the mouth of Thucydides, in the following words: 'The Greeks once lived as the barbarians now live'. This was reputedly a materialistic tradition. The opposite view was that the Greeks were superior to the barbarians. Plato was, according to this theory, the chief apostle of the second view, which gradually displaced the first tradition originally proposed by Democritus and perpetuated by Epicurus.

The difference postulated by Thomson is unhistorical. It never existed. The Greek view that they were superior to the barbarians (and they were) may well have co-existed with the idea that they had also been barbarians. From the social point of view, however, it is more important that this feeling of superiority applied above all to the Greek political system of the democratic city state and the freedom of the citizen. This is a Greek achievement that Thomson cannot take away from them. To consider only the citizen and not the slave can hardly be grounds for recrimination. We have again and again found good reasons for regarding a view of this kind as anachronistic.

Addendum 1

There is still a shortage of good collections of material. Valuable information can be extracted from certain works, particularly in specialized fields. F. Bömer's *Untersuchungen über die Religion der Sklaven in Griechenland und Rom*, four volumes (1957-1963) is an example. A valuable source concerning our topic of morality and religion in the context of slavery is J. Vogt, *Sklaverei und Humanität im klassischen Griechentum*, in the *Akademie der Wissenschaften und der Literatur, Abhandlungen der geistes- und sozialwissenschaftliche Klasse* (1953-1954). K. Latte's *Griechentum und Humanität* (1947) is also useful, as are S. Lauffer, *Die Bergwerkssklaven von Laureion*, Mainz, *Abhandlungen* (1955), 12; (1956), 11; P. Ducrey, *Le traitement des prisonniers de guerre dans la Grèce ancienne*, Paris (1968) and O.

Mischnat, *Studien zur Kriegsgefangenschaft und zur Sklaverei in der grie-chischen Geschichte*, I, *Homer*. The collected studies of A. H. M. Jones. *The Roman Economy*, ed. P. A. Brunt (1974), are also important and the index of his book should be consulted. All that can be found on this subject also in his *Later Roman Empire* (1964) is of inestimable importance. It hardly needs mentioning that the later Roman Empire is currently at the centre of interest. As examples we may mention such scholars as E. A. Thompson, A. Grenier, and J. Percival.

The position of slaves changed with changing circumstances; cf. Y. Garlan, *Les esclaves en temps de guerre, Actes du Colloque d'histoire sociale*, Besançon University (1970), Paris (1972). For the history of slavery during early Christianity, see the recent detailed study of the earliest data on this subject in the *New Testament and the early Christian sources* by H. Gültzow, *Christentum and Sklaverei in den ersten drei Jahrhunderten*, Bonn (1969).

T. R. S. Broughton's *New Evidence on Temple Estates in Asia Minor. Studies in Honor of Allen Chester Johnson* (1951), pp. 236-250, is very valuable.

Without listing all the titles in detail, apart from those referred to already we may cite the series *Forschungen zur antiken Sklaverei*, Mainz, which includes also a number of foreign publications mainly by Russian authors, but of very unequal content.

There is also a great deal of controversy on this topic in the West, as is clear from Finley's discussion (*TLS*, 14 November 1975, p. 1348), entitled *The Necessary Evil*; its subject is the translation of J. Vogt's *Sklaverei und Humanität* (2nd. edn., Mainz 1972) into English: *Slavery and the Ideal of Man* (Oxford, 1974). See also Finley on 'Progress' in Historiography, Daedalus, 106. 3 (1977), particularly on the role of slavery in ancient society, as interpreted in some modern general works on Greek history (p. 133 ff).

Research still to be done on slavery in Hellenistic Egypt and elsewhere is discussed by H. Heinen, *Zur Sklaverei in der hellenistischen Welt*, I and II, in *Ancient Society* 7 and 8 (1976 and 1977), especially 8 (121-154).

Addendum 2

Various works have recently appeared in England and Italy which have a bearing on technology in classical antiquity. A good summary will be found in H. W. Pleket, 'Technology in the Greco-Roman World: A General Report', *Talanta* 5 (1973), 6-47. Among the earlier publications on this subject, I would mention those by A. Rey and B. Farrington, but only *honoris causa*. I have myself listed a number of studies in *TvG* 84 (1971), p. 382, note 6. Among the English works, I would like to mention especially two by G. E. R. Lloyd, *Early Greek Science: Thales to Aristotle*, and *Greek Science after Aristotle* (1973). Various studies of tools and instruments available in clas-sical antiquity are also worth consulting. K. D. White has written about the implements used in agriculture; see especially his *Agricultural Implements of the Roman World* (1967) and *Farm Equipment of the Roman World* (1975). Various Italian authors have written about the ideological aspect of the development of technology. Recent Italian works include those by M. I. Parente, *Techne, Momenti del pensiero greco da Platone a Epicuro*, Florence (1966); G. Cambiano, *Platone e le Tecniche*, Turin (1971). Other works worth consulting in this context are: A. Rey, *L'apogée de la science technique grecque*, Paris (1946) and another work by the same author stressing thought rather than action: *La maturité de la pensée scientifique en Grèce*, Paris (1939). The historical materialist B. Farrington, who has an entirely different approach to the subject has written four brilliant though one-sided studies: 1. *Greek Science. Its Meaning to Us (Thales to Aristotle)*, Harmondsworth (1944, repr. 1966); 2. *Head and Hand in Ancient Greece. Four Studies in the Social Relations of Thought*, London, The Thinker's Library (1947); 3. *Science and Politics in the Ancient World*, London 1939; 4. *Science in Antiquity*, The Home University Library London (1969 [2]).

CHAPTER ELEVEN

WOMEN IN RELIGION AND MORALITY

In ancient society, there is no reference to the sanctity of marriage, a doctrine that arose in Western civilization as a result of Jewish traditions and the Roman Catholic sacrament of matrimony. The institution of marriage in paradise was a biblical tradition and, according to Christian morality, 'marriages are made in heaven', the key-stone of the orthodox Christian teaching about marriage being: 'What God has joined together, let not man put asunder'.

Before discussing the place of marriage in the community in ancient Greece, I must refer to one aspect of such discussions that has often been noted. It is that they are influenced by modern notions of the man-woman relationship and that between people general as reflected in current literature. Present-day authors often judge the past by modern standards, and especially do they do this in the case of ancient Greece, where the modern ethos of marriage is allowed a great say. This is common in all the humanities and in classical studies even more than elsewhere it seems inevitable.[1]

There have been many studies of the position of women in ancient Greece and especially Athens. It has generally been described as lamentable. More than a quarter of a century ago, Kitto called Gomme's study of the position of women [2] the only exception to this general rule. Since that time, several good books have appeared on the market. I think especially of Flacelière, *L'amour en Grèce* (1960), but there is also Chantraine's edition of Xenophon's *Oeconomicus* (1949) and an article by Martin.[3] Kitto's and Gomme's works are certainly the most penetrating that have appeared in the last half century.

---

[1] There is a good record of modern writing about the place of women in classical antiquity in the *Histoire mondiale de la femme I: Préhistoire et Antiquité*, in which R. Flacelière deals with Crete and Greece, and P. Grimal with Rome. See also the recent bibliography by K. Thraede in his article 'Frau' in *RAC* 8 (1972), pp. 197-269.

[2] A. W. Gomme, *The Position of Women in Athens in the Fifth and Fourth Centuries B.C.* (1925), pp. 1-25 (= *Essays in Greek History and Literature*, 1937, pp. 89 ff); H. D. F. Kitto, *The Greeks*, Harmondsworth (1951).

[3] J. Martin, *Bulletin of the Association Guillaume Budé*, 39, p. 18.

A different note is heard, however, in the most recent publications. The data have been re-examined in the light of the modern movement for female emancipation, of which 'women's lib' is the most notable representative. The result has been an even deeper revulsion against the position of women in classical antiquity and a sense of indignation about their slavish lack of freedom and absence of rights. In other words, women are represented as an oppressed minority in a male society by challenging and conscientious modern research.[4] And yet, apart from an often disconcerting lack of understanding of historical relativity, the picture is not satisfying. Why is this?

The results are offered in a modern setting but the answers are not new. On the contrary, it is certain that before 1925 most studies on the position of women provided a gloomy picture, with Ischomachus' wife, Neaeria and the Vestal Virgins in the focus of almost exclusively male attention to their lamentable position. This then prevailing view was vigorously attacked by Gomme and others after him, especially Kitto. We are now half a century on from the year in which Gomme's article was published.[5]

The view then attacked to which so many scholars have now returned is represented in the journal *Arethusa*, which devoted two complete volumes to 'Women in Antiquity'.[6] The arguments of the opposing camps can be briefly summarized.

Unfavourable

First, Greek literature reflects a 'male society', family life playing no part at all. Only men featured in early comedy, with the exception of such extravagances as the *Lysistrata* and the *Parliament of Women*, Aristophanes' two most famous comedies about the relations between men and women. Only men take part in Plato's dialogues and Xenophon wrote exclusively about men. (A small exception must be allowed in Plato's case—the figure of Diotima in the Symposium).

Secondly there is the seclusion of women. The Greek house had rooms for men and separate rooms for women. The women's rooms

---

[4] S. B. Pomeroy, *Goddesses, Whores, Wives and Slaves. Women in Classical Antiquity*, New York (1975).

[5] The above is taken partly from my review of Mrs Pomeroy's book in *Mnem.* 29 (1976), 319 ff.

[6] *Arethusa*, Vol. 6 (1973), with a very important contribution by K. J. Dover, *Classical Greek Attitudes to Sexual Behaviour*, pp. 59-73, and Vol. 11 (1978).

were secluded and barred (see Xenophon, *Oeconomicus*). Women
only left the house under escort except for the special religious
festivals for women. Before marriage, girls never went out and were
always carefully guarded lest they be exposed to injury by the
stronger sex. Antigone and Electra, both young girls, are ordered in
tragedy to go indoors: 'that is your place'. The emancipated Lysistrata comments in the comedy: 'It is difficult for the married
woman to escape from home'. Even shopping was no reason for a
woman to go out into the streets for it was done by the man who
would have slaves to carry his purchases. Menander's young men
could meet a girl only at a festival and nowhere else.

Thirdly, there is frequent reference to homosexuality between
men and to its harmful effect on the relationship between men and
women. It has been pointed out that Plato only becomes lyrical and
tender when he is speaking about the relationship between an older
man and a beautiful adolescent boy.[7]

Marriages were concluded by the parents. The standard example
of this is Ischomachus, in Xenophon's *Oeconomicus*. His wife was
ignorant and he instructs her himself in what she needs to know.
This thirty-year-old husband (who may have been older) had no
spiritual contact with a child-wife of fourteen and so he sought it
with strangers, the *hetairai*, one of whom was a certain Neaera.
In this context, a statement by Demosthenes is quoted: 'Mistresses
we keep for our pleasure, concubines for our day-to-day physical
well-being, and wives in order to beget legitimate children and to
have trustworthy guardians of our households'.[8]

This has been compared with Xenophon's *Oeconomicus* (3. 12):

---

[7] For a correct assessment of homosexuality, we are bound to have
reservations about many views, but would point to a recent account in K.
J. Dover's *Greek Homosexuality*, London (1978), and an earlier summary
in *Greek Popular Morality in the Time of Plato and Aristotle*, Oxford (1975),
pp. 213-216.

[8] Dem. 59. 122. Dover, *op. cit.*, p. 14, has correctly pointed out that 'this
gives us not, as has been alleged, the "fourth century view" of women, but
one view which was possible, was judged by the speaker unlikely to offend,
and was absolutely necessary for the argument ("Neaira passed herself off
as Stephanos' wife") which he is developing in that part of his speech'. Kitto
explained the passage from Demosthenes, with a clear reference to the
charge that he was levelling against modern scholars who condemned the
Athenian attitude to women in the following way (*op. cit.*, p. 231), namely
that *hetairai* and slave girls were quite all right, but when it was a question
of the continued existence of the city of Athens, to whom should men go?
To their wives.

'To whom do you entrust serious matters and with whom do you
have less need of argument? Your own wife'. The translation implies that there was co-operation between man and wife as partners
and that their mutual attachment did not have to be immoderately
expressed. According to Kitto, both Demosthenes and Xenophon
were far from expressing scorn—they were paying a great compli-
ment. The lawful spouse, who was a citizen, was always higher in
status than the stranger or alien. Yet Kitto was using Xenophon's
text for his own ends. The crucial words are: Ἔστι δὲ ὅτῳ ἐλάττονα
διαλέγει ἢ τῇ γυναικί; This means: 'With whom do you need fewer
words than with your wife'? This does not necessarily indicate trust
or confidence—it could also have expressed an authoritarian attitude. Similar texts have been summarized by Van Leeuwen *ad*. Ran.
1044, who translates the words as 'Quis cum uxore sua confabula-
tur?'. Van Leeuwen's edition is very valuable here, as it so often is
in other cases. Chantraine translated the words as 'Et y-a-t-il des
gens avec qui tu aies moins de conversation qu'avec ta femme'?
Some aspects of Kitto's conclusion are therefore, I believe, vulner-
able to criticism and to say, as he does on p. 231, that the whole is
in accordance with the vases is to depart from what he said on p. 228
about the vases. (Clearly the interpretation of the vases is hazar-
dous).

Every account quotes Pericles (or the words attributed to him by
Thucydides) and Aristotle. The well-known words from the funeral
speech: 'The greatest glory of a woman is to be least talked about
by men', gives nothing about husbands—the point being that no
man *outside* the household must talk about the wife;[9] the other
notorious remark comes from Aristotles' *Politics*: 'Man is by nature
superior to woman'.

If we look at the position of women in Homer—the girl Nausicaa
was to some extent free—and in a military community such as that
of Sparta, where women were also relatively free, then it is an obvious next step to compare Athens unfavourably as the centre of a
culture where women enjoyed no special rights or proper regard for
their human dignity.

It is sometimes suggested that this view of the matter is con-

---

[9] As in tribal Islamic society today, where you must not even ask about
your host's wife health. If a wife's name is bandied about owing to some
action *of the wife* it is of course a terrible disgrace (as in Victorian England).
See above, p. 33-34, and p. 248 below.

firmed by the very laws of Athens, where women had no vote and could not be elected to any public office. They could not own anything or transact any business that was recognized and protected by the law. From the cradle to the grave, every woman was under the guardianship of her next of kin or her husband and she enjoyed legal rights only through him. Her 'guardian' married her off and gave her a dowry, and if there was a divorce the bride and the dowry were returned to the guardian. The male next of kin could claim the heiress by marrying her, if the father had left no will. If he was already married, he could divorce his wife in order to marry the heiress.[10]

The having of children was certainly not esteemed for the psychological satisfaction it gave. A married man who was childless did not adopt a young child, but an adult man, such as his brother-in-law.[11] Isaeus tells us (or rather he tells his audience, which is not necessarily the same thing) that many men divorced their wives in order to marry an heiress. But we must recognize that the wife equally could divorce her husband. In this respect law was not partisan. A childless marriage could, for example, be dissolved on the insistence of the wife's relatives. All that we must notice is that the official application for dissolution of the marriage was not submitted by the wife herself.

Favourable

We have considered the arguments of those who take an unfavourable view of the position of women and the practice of marriage in Athens. We now turn to those who defend the Athenians. What are their arguments? Here too Kitto, using Gomme's findings, throws valuable light on the whole question.

In the first place, we have to remember that we are foreigners to the world of Athens and ancient Greece. Our remoteness may even be increased by interpretations and generalizations based on our own modern travel impressions. Historians are by nature prone to generalization, as I have demonstrated in a study *Greeks and the*

---

[10] It should be borne in mind here that, according to Athenian law, marriage was permitted between an uncle and a niece or between a half-brother and a half-sister. If this did not happen the male next of kin became the heiress's guardian and had to marry her off with a suitable dowry.

[11] See Kitto, *op. cit.*, p. 22: 'For the purpose of the adoption was not to indulge a sentiment or cure a psychosis, but to leave behind a proper head of the family to continue its legal existence and religious rites'.

Greeks (see p. 129 above), with a number of different examples. Kitto and Gomme, despite their criticism of the manner in which other scholars generalize, are themselves not entirely free of this habit, when it comes to their beloved Athenians.

It is misleading to suppose that if no traces of a given situation are to be found in the literature the situation itself did not exist. The situation we are considering concerns family relationships. Here it is particularly dangerous to rely on the argumentum e silentio but it would be even more so to conclude that a thing the sources are silent about did in fact exist. And this does happen. There is in Greek literature no real description of domestic life. In Homer, there are references but no background. The dramatists too where they mention the subject have nothing to say about the realities of marriage and life together in families. Their accounts are 'constructional' rather than 'representational'.[12] Almost the only informal work of literature that we have is Xenophon's *Memorabilia* and even this does not provide an intimate biography of Socrates, but deals with him as a philosopher. This is, of course, one reason why Socrates' wife Xanthippe has been so variously interpreted by modern scholars. In the *Oeconomicus* the peasant Ischomachus is an unromantic figure, but what are we to expect? He is described in a context which has nothing to do with intimate married life, but concerned with running a farm and all the anxieties that go with it.

An extremely bad practice, which even the modern defenders of Athenian customs have tended to follow, is to assemble quotations unconnected with one another, regardless of the context in which they occur. I would classify in this category the noble woman in the Symposium, Diotima, and such young women as Antigone and Electra, who are certainly described in life-like terms, but have pathetically little to say about the relationship between man and wife. This is, of course, because the direction in which the individual is facing in the literary context is quite different. It is not that of a relationship with a man or a male society, but of the individual

---

[12] There is a modern parallel in a discussion between S. Dresden and A. Romein-Verschoor about the novel as a source for knowledge of social life. Dresden argued that the worse the novel, the more significance it could have for ordinary life. Mrs. Romein, however, preferred to seek it among the peaks of literature. Once I had a similar experience in Venice, where on the Lido ordinary Italian life seemed to be not much in evidence, despite its being the scene of Thomas Mann's *Death in Venice*. To a knowledge of ordinary every day life Mann has less to contribute than Mrs. Courths-Mahler.

responsibility of a wife or other member of a family towards her relatives and society. History can very soon be distorted if human relationships in general are discussed on the basis of such literary examples, in other words, if a particular literary situation is generalized.

We have already discussed Pericles' address to the widows of those who had fallen in battle.[13] It has been said that fame is good for one who is unknown. This is quite true and recognizes that woman too may be ambitious. It is, however, the very thing missing from the Pericles speech. He rejects women. Why? Like Kitto, I can imagine that what we have here is a certain male prudery about women. As Kitto says, 'But suppose Gladstone had said, "I do not care to hear a lady's name bandied about in general talk, whether for praise or dispraise", would that imply disdain, or an old-fashioned deference and courtesy'? [14] The answer that Kitto is clearly expecting is, of course, the second. And this possibility must be left open. We must, however, realize that such a solution would come more easily to a nineteenth-century writer. Pericles after all does not ask the question that Kitto here attributes to Gladstone and the one he does ask about the 'natural disposition' of women is not asked by Gladstone.

What is most important is to avoid anachronism in discussing the question and not compare the Athenian woman of the fifth century with women in a modern industrial city or country district. In the ancient world the family was more important than the individual and not only the woman but the man also were part of that family.[15] The man in addition had to subordinate all his activities to the demands of the community. If well to do, for instance, he had tax liabilities, the liturgy. He must pay his share whether it suited him or not.

Finally, in the matter of anachronism, we must remember that the undeniable physical differences between men and women had a different significance in ancient Greece from that which they have

---

[13] See above, p. 33-34.

[14] Kitto, *op. cit.*, p. 224.

[15] Kitto, *op. cit.*, p. 226: 'We think that it is normal to regard society as an aggregate of individuals. This is not normal from the historical point of view: it is a local development. The normal view is that society is an aggregation of families, each having its own responsible leader. This conception is not Greek only: it is also Roman, Indian, Chinese, Teutonic'. See the same author's comment on p. 225 of his book.

today. In antiquity, the importance of physical strength in actual combat made men the natural protectors whose role of authority derived from their fighting skill. It is, of course, true that the woman had an enormous task in farming communities where work on the land and its management was added to their labour of having children and running the family. But the general pattern of man as the protector and fighter was different from today. Even in the case of the working class, as it used to be called, forms of work have developed requiring skill without sheer physical strength so that women are as well able to perform them as men.

Thus the physical differences between men and women which were of such significance in antiquity and indeed until not very long since in modern times are no longer so decisive today. Their different physique and work performance may in fact be the real reason why the need was never felt in antiquity (leaving aside for the moment the priestly functions, which will be discussed later) to grant definite rights to women in society, such as at Athens membership of the Council, the Assembly, or the jury courts. The woman's duties were quite separate and so all-embracing that they left her no opportunity to take part in politics and law. If this was the argument, it is not very convincing. For the territory over which government operated was much smaller than today and both men and women knew the districts by political and judicial experience. They could judge for themselves. Thus no reason for discrimination between men and women can be sought on such lines. On the contrary, they ignored the very need of an explanation. I would therefore not be so prone as Kitto to argue that the discrimination between men and women in antiquity was because the government of the country was better in men's hands because of their experience. Kitto has commented: 'One reason why women have the vote today is that in many matters of current politics their judgement is likely to be as good as a man's, sometimes better, where in important matters their ignorance is not likely to be greater'.[16] This, for Kitto, was a clear distinction from the situation in antiquity. But I would disagree. I think the situations then and now are indeed comparable in this respect. I see no reason to suppose that women won equal rights in modern times through having their attention drawn to politics. I believe that in classical antiquity both men and women

---

[16] Kitto, *op. cit.*, p. 225.

engaged in discussion on matters of state, on politics, and even on military questions and that it was especially between married men and their wives that this happened. There is, however, no source material to prove it. All we have is notion of human behaviour in the intimacy of conjugal living which we presume has remained constant through the ages. There is no sense in speculating further about it.

I would now like to come back to the well-know passage from Demosthenes (59. 122),[17] devoted to Neaera, the hetaira of the demi-monde, whose children, acquired citizen rights if they were born of an Athenian father, and a claim on their father's property. The plaintiff turns to the jury and says (translated freely): 'when you get home, your wives will ask you how it went and if you have to say: I have acquitted that slut, then the fat will be in the fire'. This sort of saying means that women certainly had an influence but that they exerted it, as always, from the living room and not in a public place. And they never had any clear right to it. In Xenophon's *Symposium* we read of a man coming home from a feast and trying to avert the suspicion that he has been in female company, because he is afraid of his wife. All that can be said about this passage is that it supports my notion of a pattern of male predominance but does not indicate a definite moral position—at most a practical trend. At this point vase paintings are always brought in. What do they show? The man and the woman behaving politely to one another (or so it seems). But they tell us nothing about the position of women in the community or as defined by the moral code. The situation of Andromache in the Iliad is not really relevant here, nor is that of the man and wife who go through life 'thinking alike in all their thoughts' in the well-known verse in the Odyssey (6. 183). Nor do the heroines of Greek tragedy have any contribution to make to our understanding of the general pattern.

What is more interesting, however, is the segregation of women. The fact is attested by the sources and cannot be disregarded. Its purpose presumably was practical and social, a necessary measure of protection of women from the many different dangers that could threaten them if unaccompanied. In a time of violence ourselves, we sadly have no difficulty in understanding such a situation. It is important that the segregation was broken during the women's

---

[17] See above, p. 244 ff; below p. 255.

festivals, when they were all together and therefore less endangered.[18] Another factor, which, however, had nothing to do with averting the danger of violence, was that women had a great deal of work to do and were for that reason alone prevented from appearing much in public. Even the wish to play a part in public life, it may be argued, would have been absent if their time was so taken up in the home. There is also the further factor that women married young and child marriages—they can certainly be called this, since girls were married at fourteen or thereabouts—have always been an obstacle to any form of emancipation.

The segregation of women was certainly not so universal a practice as has sometimes been suggested. We reiterate that it was intended to be a protection rather than a curtailment of rights. If for example we ask whether women were allowed to go to the theatre, we are bound to answer that they were. The evidence all clearly points in that direction. Kitto mentions some pieces of evidence. Plato's opposition to poetry in general and tragedy in particular is, in Kitto's opinion, a kind of manifesto addressed to boys, women, men, slave and free, without distinction.[19] According to the *Life* of Aeschylus, which was preserved in antiquity, the chorus of the Erinyes in the *Eumenides* was so terrifying that boys died of fear and women had miscarriages. This story is of course absurdly exaggerated but the man who told it 'obviously saw that women did attend the theatre'. It has been suggested that they were not allowed to go to the comedy, just as children were excluded from that type of drama, because the performances were too coarse. This, however, is not true. What is more, they would not have been spared the coarseness even if they had been confined to tragedy since tragedies were performed in tetralogies with a satyr play at the end, and that was certainly not decent.

Intermediate Standpoint

In the preceding sections, we have had several opportunities of making corrections to the two extreme standpoints that we have

---

[18] Kitto, *op. cit.*, p. 234, quotes the case of a Syracusan who was visiting Alexandria, but this example is not relevant for several reasons. First, the city state in all instability no longer existed. (Kitto himself noticed this.) Secondly, Theocritus the poet came from that part of Greek society known as Dorian and in the Dorian part, to which Sparta also belonged, the attitude towards women may have been different. In Sparta, women were also freer.

[19] Kitto, *op. cit.*, p. 233.

discussed. Now that we have reached the point where we can evaluate both these points of view, especially that which defends the Athenian position, we must make certain allowances in favour of the Athenian male, now under attack from so many sides.

I distinguish three aspects of the problem—legal, social, and general. In this I follow both Gomme and Kitto. I first mention Gomme's remark that the social position of slaves was not so very different from that of their masters, differing less than the poor from the rich today. But slaves in Greece had no political rights. We know too that they were disrespectedly treated. It can be argued of course that this treatment was no different from the contempt with which women were regarded, but a sweeping statement of this kind is not an argument, and I for one think that such a comparison between slaves who were an external minority, and women, who though downtrodden were necessary members of Greek society will not help us.

In France, women have fewer rights than women in England, but this difference is of no account in a general appreciation of the position of women in both countries. Even though this has been stated frequently in the past by many people—and seems a truism— we can certainly repeat it and agree with it.

There is, however, the personal aspect of the problem and this has been overlooked by Gomme and those who support his arguments. Women are often called 'childlike and not yet grown up' and were so called also in antiquity. Such an attitude has always been fatal to the advancement of women.

Those who defend the liberal attitude of the Athenians towards women have nothing to say about the legal aspect of the question for the simple reason that there is no disputing the fact that their rights were so restricted. It must be added, however, that the law did also give women a considerable degree of protection, regardless of any considerations of personal morality. It is after all possible to be so concerned with the legal position as even to exaggerate the view of Athenian women as 'childlike and not grown up'.[20] The

---

[20] In his rather old-fashioned, but otherwise excellent book, K. Kuiper (*De Atheensche vrouw*, 1920, p. 43 ff), gives a fairly full summary of the legal position of women. We need a modern popular book on this subject. It is remarkable that, in the Netherlands, we still turn to foreign publications. Yet Kuiper's book is there for the asking and surely it would, in the meantime, be worth reprinting. In England W. K. Lacey's *The Family in Classical Greece*, London (1968), can be suggested. One of the new scholarly works

apologists of Athens—and they can certainly be called that—place too much emphasis on the general aspect of the problem. Such general views, however, are confined mainly to women in Greek tragedy or to women such as Helen in epic. If we say, for example, that women were not appreciated or even despised, then any general view to the contrary must be emphasized and it is quite appropriate to mention Helen or Antigone in such context. In the appreciation of women, in love of them or admiration of their beauty and charms, men have never been slow to respond. They responded also in ancient Greece and moreover valued and praised firmness of character and courage in women. Here I readily agree with the apologists of Athens, but would like to say a little more about the social and personal aspects of the problem. These directly confront us with the question of social morality.[21]

From the social point of view, what Xenophon has to say in his *Oeconomicus* about the peasant Ischomachus and his wife is of the greatest importance. A woman's place was in the home, by the hearth. The man worked outside the home. In it the woman ruled, brought up the children, gave the slaves their tasks, and cared for them when they were sick. (This is what Chantraine called a *détail touchant*). Xenophon's tone is certainly like that of a schoolmaster, but it is not lacking in tact. If his child-wife does not do everything properly, Ischomachus makes excuses for her. Her place is like that of the queen-bee in the hive—honoured but troublesome. Ischomachus does not, for example, allow his wife the freedom that cultured Athenian ladies might expect to enjoy. Nor does a Dutch peasant allow his wife the freedom of a townswoman and the peasant's wife would not like her daughter to enjoy the freedom of a girl student in Leiden. There was, of course, more unity in views and attitudes in ancient society than there is in the modern world, but none the less there were differences which must be noted. Ischomachus' wife, for instance, was no Aspasia. We must bear the

(not on a par with G. Glotz or N. D. Fustel de Coulanges) is A. R. W. Harrison, *The law of Athens. The Family and Property*, Oxford (1968).

[21] See G. Rudberg, *Socrates bei Xenophon* (1939); R. Lallier, *De la condition de la femme dans la société athénienne*; Chantraine, Edition of the *Oeconomicus*, p. 14; Kuiper, *op. cit.*, p. 65. W. E. Higgins, *Xenophon the Athenian*, Albany (1977), 28 ff,—for the position of Ischomachus—. 'Athenian girls came of age when they were fourteen', has sometimes been said. It might be better to speak, not of coming of age in this context, but rather of reaching marriageable age. For Athens see Lacey, *op. cit.*, 106, 162; for Thasos, see Pouilloux, *Thasos* I. 377.

beehive image in mind. In a community of bees, everything follows strict rules and the individual is subordinated to the interests of the community. I have already made this point and now underline it most emphatically. The woman had her function as mother of the legitimate children and therefore as the one who kept the community in existence. Love, it has been said, was outside that framework and the result was damaging to the personal standing of women. It cannot be denied that this may have been so, but we must not generalize. There were also marriages in Athens which were good—we have ample evidence. If we acknowledge that the wife of Ischomachus was not positively free, but add that Xenophon was not writing about marriage, but rather about domestic economy,[22] it is not the whole story. It does, however, tell us a great deal about the meaning of marriage—that it was a social event, an institution of economic importance, with military significance (male offspring), and a future insurance against old age (protection by the children). It was hard on the woman and sometimes humiliating. The fact that she regarded it as normal does not mean that her position was enviable, but that she submitted to the inevitable.[23]

We can perhaps advance further in our understanding of the situation if we do not identify all Athenians with *the* Athenians. Athens was not always what it has been made out to be by modern accusers. Cleisthenes, Themistocles, and Cimon were all sons of foreign mothers. The resistance to 'mixed' marriages, however, was very great. The law of 451 B.C. is a clear indication—it limited citizenship to children born of marriages between citizens.[24] It was

---

[22] See above, Kitto's argument.

[23] Chantraine, *Xenophon's Oeconomicus*, p. 13, goes too far in a positive direction, but there is some truth in his statement about Ischomachus and his wife: 'The correctness of Ischomachus' tone and his delicacy when he is telling his young wife what to do have rightly been admired. He reproaches her for her untidiness and she blushes. Instead of becoming irritable with her, he makes excuses for her for not knowing what he wrongly did not teach her. On another occasion, he rebukes her tactfully for using too much make-up in an attempt to please him'.

[24] See Jacoby, *FGrHist. Philochoros*, 328, fragment 119, and Gomme's criticism in *CR* (1956), p. 26, claiming that the Athenians are not to blame for what Jacoby imputes to them. 'Anything less like Athenian history it is difficult to imagine'.—It is remarkable that, even as recently as 1956 the controversy still went on between prominent scholars specializing in the study of Greek history. What Gomme here offers can hardly be called to produce an argument. It is more like a prejudice based on affection. And this is precisely why these questions have to be discussed again and again—in order to remove such prejudices.

clearly a retrograde step,[25] since it not only lowered the status of
the foreign wife, but also restricted the female citizen to her own
sphere as the mother of children in the home, while the foreign
woman became the man's mistress. It is only in this way that the
bitterness of Athenian women can be explained. This is a general
observation which I cannot wholly endorse, since it could equally
well be regarded as an honour for the wife and mother to know that
she had a unique place. This is not my suggestion—it was made by
Mrs Werre-de Haas, whose ideas on this subject centre round the
thought that the wife and mother was proud of her motherhood and
that it was a matter of secondary importance to her whether or not
she was loved by the man who had married her. He could slip away
from home unnoticed and she would not mind, but he would come
home again because he knew that she had borne his legitimate
children.[26]

Whatever the case, woman's reaction to male infidelity in the
ancient world has not or hardly been recorded. The type of woman
who is reported as complaining most about her fate is the courtesan
who has lost her lover. And this can hardly be ranked with the
complaint of a legal spouse in a society where the marriage bond
was held in respect.

To have legal rights and to be generally appreciated as a mother
were for some women a source of keen satisfaction if they no longer
wanted her husband as a lover. It should not be forgotten that
sexual life had an entirely different rhythm at a time when people
became old at an earlier age than they do now. We are therefore
bound to take seriously the passages that Zimmern has quoted from
such tragedies as the Medea, the Bacchae, the Hippolytus, and the
Heracleidae,[27] but not so seriously that we come to regard them as
historically and universally true.

We should therefore do better to leave conjecture alone and
return to the law of 451 B.C., which decreed that the only legally
valid marriages were those between citizens. We may now go further
and say that, such a measure in the age of Pericles was ill-considered
in its consequences for women of all sorts. It made the lawful wife an

---

[25] A. E. Zimmern, *The Greek Commonwealth*, 5th edn., p. 339, is excellent
on this question.

[26] Mrs. M. Werre-de Haas, in an unpublished paper for her degree in
Ancient History, Leiden (1960). See also K. J. Dover's quotation, above
p. 244, note 8.

[27] *Op. cit.*, p. 336.

indispensable instrument in the τεχνοποιία and it also made her a housekeeper. This was, in all fairness, not exactly an honour for the woman as citizen. But it must have been intolerable for women from outside when what had previously been a perfectly legal relationship was suddenly declared illegal and the mother of children was reduced to the status of concubine and her children declared illegitimate.

I believe that the law of 451 placed women of both kinds—citizens of Athens and foreigners—in an impossible situation. The bitterness of the woman whom I gave as an example above may well have been general. At a later period in history, it is possible to speak of a crisis in marriage—in the fourth century, for instance—but in the fifth century the law of 451 set something in motion that did no good at all to social relationships both inside and outside marriage. It brings us to a question that has often been discussed in this connection, the emancipation of women in antiquity, and especially at the end of the fifth century. The bitterness of which I was speaking above is thought to have furthered this emancipation. It is believed to have occurred at the end of the fifth century B.C. and Chantraine has summarized it in the following way: 'At the end of the fifth century, the feminist question was the order of the day'.[28] As Chantraine assumed, Pericles' well-known words in his funeral oration may actually have been a reference to an emancipation movement that had already begun. But, before we go into this, we should be wise to enquire whether it is really possible to speak of emancipation in this context.

Emancipation? [29]

I must say here quite deliberately that we must look carefully at

---

[28] *Op. cit.*, p. 14.

[29] See I. Bruns, *Frauenemanzipation in Athen*, an oration delivered on the emperor's birthday in 1900 in Kiel. This work was later republished in *Vorträge und Aufsätze*, Munich (1905), p. 157. There has been no lack of objection to this presentation of the issue. Wilamowitz criticized Bruns in an article in *Hermes* 35 (1900), p. 551. A protracted controversy developed between the two scholars and it is always worth recalling in such cases how the disagreement first arose. In this one we have a guarantee from the standing of the two coryphaei, Bruns and Wilamowitz, that the debate began at a high level. The discussion between them still attracts attention and we must note with regret that hardly any new data have been added to the subject since its conclusion. J. Vogt's article on sexual equality, *Von der Gleichwertigkeit der Geschlechter in der bürgerlichen Gesellschaft der Griechen*, *Akademie der Wissenschaften und der Literatur in Mainz, Abhandlungen der geistes- und sozialwissenschaftl. Kl.* Wiesbaden (1960), 2, pp. 211-255, shed no really new light on the subject.

the period from which the data are derived. I would not say that mutual affection between men and women did not occur.[30] I would point to the *social* tensions that arose after 450 B.C., with the later result that Aspasia, the wife of Pericles, was one of those rejected. She was, after all, a foreigner. It also meant that the son of Pericles and Aspasia was not treated on an equal footing with Pericles' two sons by a previous, legal marriage, although the later son was granted the rights of citizenship later, as an exceptional case, on the death of the first two. The apprehension felt by female citizens spread to their husbands, who were sometimes dominated by their wives. In addition to Pericles and Aspasia, there is also the case of the sculptor Praxiteles and his model Phryne, whose golden statue was consecrated at Delphi and who had her image placed beside that of Aphrodite in the temple at Thespiae. This same Phryne was also shown to the jury and spectators in the court either naked or with the upper part of her body revealed by her lover Hyperides, who was defending her in the trial.[31]

Plato was clearly on the side of modern thinkers, according to many scholars (Laws 841). He declared that he would like to forbid sexual relationships outside marriage, but that concessions had to be made and the politician ought therefore to permit relationships that would be rejected by the moralist, so long as they took place in private.[32]

In my opinion, it is time that scholars ceased calling Plato an advocate of female emancipation. He did not advocate it at all. The most that we can claim is that he accorded women, in his ideal state, the position of second-rate men. In that state, women are admitted to positions in government when they reach the age of forty, men when they are thirty. This may be called an adaptation

---

[30] Glotz in this context referred to Aristotle, *Nicomachaean Ethics* 8. 14, 7-8; *Eudemian Ethics* 6. 10, 7; 7. 9, 4: Aristotle, *Oeconomica* 1. 4, 1-3.

[31] Paus. 9. 27, 5; 10. 15, 1; Athen. 13. 7 (559 a-d). See also Menander and Glycera, Diphilus and Gnathaina. For Socrates and Theodote, see Xenophon, *Mem.* 3. 11. In the case of Socrates, there was a sharp contrast between Xanthippe's attitude on the death of the philosopher and that of Socrates himself. We are bound to ask whether Socrates was as individualistic in this respect as he pretended to be in so many others.

[32] Whether or not this justifies Zimmern's statement is another question. Zimmern said: 'In the last quarter of the fifth century Athens witnessed the rise of a movement for the emancipation of women which, because it won the heart of the arch-Conservative Plato, has left an undying mark upon the literature of the world' (p. 336). Kuiper has written well about this problem, *op. cit.*, p. 70.

to practical life—women are considered only when they are too old to bear children. Plato's point is supported by a passage concerning women and military service. Here too there is a difference between men and women—the former must be available between the ages of twenty and sixty, whereas women are regarded as capable of performing suitable tasks in wartime when they are past the age of childbearing and have not yet reached their fiftieth year. There is no question of female emancipation in the sense in which modern authors understand it—as equality between men and women. In this case of service in wartime, women are to be used simply to supplement the armies when reduced in strength. Thus it was a practical military measure, presumably inspired by the losses of Athenian troops in the Peloponnesian War.[33]

The circle of the Socratics (the name is a vague one and for this reason open to suspicion) is always mentioned in this context as the outstanding group that was working towards emancipation. In my opinion, however, this community never had emancipation as one of its aims. It can be argued that the theoretical formulations defining various tasks for women of a more advanced age are at least evidence of a concern to find suitable activities for this group of older women. I would admit this possibility but am bound to point out at once that the position of women was not practically speaking at all changed by it. How could it be otherwise in a closed group of men who, in reflecting on the consequences of bad behaviour by a man during this life, suggested that, when born again, he would return to earth as a woman.

Certain Greeks, as for example Euripides, eloquenty defended women, but there was never any question in Athens of their being regarded as the equals of men in public life and they certainly had no say in the matter themselves. Aristophanes' comedies about women—the *Ecclesiazusae* is especially important in this context—have a Utopian character even when they are taken very seriously (and this is, of course, not in accord with the nature of comedy as such).[34]

Some of the philosophers attempted to put their ideas about the state on a 'scientific' basis. Plato, for example, (Laws, 806d) de-

---

[33] One of the best treatments of this question was provided more than fifty years ago by K. Kuiper in *De Atheensche vrouw*, Haarlem (1920), p. 70 ff.

[34] See W. J. W. Koster, *Naar aanleiding van het communisme bij Aristophanes en Plato*, Groningen (1955), especially p. 7 ff.

clared a preference for the Spartan state and for the position of
women in Sparta, where however the greater freedom enjoyed by
women was dearly bought. In Sparta, the men went out on raids or
to war and it was thus the women who looked after the homebase.
It is of course possible that the plays of Aristophanes played their
part in spreading the idea of 'freedom' for women (the older ones,
at least) but in my opinion they could not have been decisive because his work was too limited to his own period, and conditioned
by it, that is by the Peloponnesian War and its aftermath.[35]

Some of the Sophists, who were then at the height of their influence, believed in the equality of men and women. But there was
no question of any kind of woman's lobby in existence agitating
for emancipation. Wilamowitz has given a sober and useful opinion
on this question.[36] He has also correctly pointed out that the *Medea*
was not written by Euripides as a play about female emancipation,
but as a plaint for woman's lot—'death by poison was the only thing
for her (Medea), woman that she was'.

What, then, was the real position and influence of woman in
Greek society? To answer this question, let us first go back to
Neaera and look more closely at the quotation from Demosthenes
59. 110-111: 'And when each of you goes home, what will he find
to say to his own wife or his daughter or his mother, if he has
acquitted this woman? when the question is asked of you, "Where
were you"? and you answer, "We sat as jury". "Trying whom"? it
will at once be asked. "Neaera", you will say, of course, will you
not? "because she, an alien woman, is living as wife with an Athenian contrary to law, and because she gave her daughter, who had
lived as a harlot, in marriage to Theogenes, the king, and this
daughter performed on the city's behalf the rites that no one may
name, and was given as wife to Dionysus". And you will narrate
all the other details of the charge, showing how well and accurately
and in a manner not easily forgotten the accusation covered each
point. And the women, when they have heard, will say, "Well, what
did you do "? And you will say, "We acquitted her". At this point
the most virtuous of the women will be angry at you for having
deemed it right that this woman should share in like manner with
themselves in the public ceremonials and religious rites; to those
who are not women of discretion you point out clearly that they

---

[35] The Lysistrata is dated 411 B.C. and the Ecclesiazusae 392 B.C.
[36] Wilamowitz, *Hermes* 35 (1900), pp. 551-553. Cf. Eur. *Med.* 407.

may do as they please, for they have nothing to fear from you or the laws. For if you treat the matter with indifference or toleration, you will yourselves seem to approve of this woman's conduct'.[37]

Here, then, we at last have a connection with religion. The accusation is clear. Theogenes had a function with which the old title of king was linked. It was a priestly function. His wife was the *basilinna* or queen. She too had a religious function. What then did the accusers say to the jury in the passage from Demosthenes? They said: 'As judges and sworn members of the jury, you are faced with a very great decision. The woman is not an Athenian. She is an alien and her marriage is therefore not legitimate. Her daughter is not legitimate and this woman is therefore—if she is not legitimate and has a husband—living as a harlot and the marriage with Theogenes is not a legal marriage. She is therefore never able to fulfil her priestly functions and, if you acquit her, you are giving permission to all women who lack steadiness to go out in search of adventures'.[38]

What is striking about this of course is the argument based on spurious virtue that is used to convince the members of the jury. Yet we must suppose that it was effective and this at once brings out the tragic situation of Neaera and her daughter and at the same time the great power wielded by the women without emancipation.

The whole presentation of the problem in this speech is susceptible to grave ethical objections and I would add, as Kitto has done, that 'it is precisely what would happen today'. The daughter, mother, or woman at home was able to determine the attitude of judge and jury on such questions, at least in part and perhaps for the greater part. All this is characteristic of the influence exerted by women, and it cannot be said that it was exaggerated in this literary source. What it tells us agrees with a universally human pattern and is so probable that it has to be accepted as historically true, a development that actually took place, although in saying this we risk being called credulous and uncritical of the sources.

In this case the proverbial gossips whose slander provoked the prosecution were the more intelligent women, the wives and daughters who did not 'go on the loose' but stayed at home. Their privileges as citizens might be had for the asking by the first woman who came along from outside Athens if Neaera were acquitted. Any means were justifiable to prevent this happening, including an ap-

---

[37] Translation *LCL*. See also pp. 244, 250 f. above.
[38] I agree with Kitto in this detail.

peal to the worst feminine instincts of the wives of the jurymen. It is significant that Kitto does not mention the mothers in his discussion of this passage. He may have found the wives and daughters more likely to stimulate interest in his comparison and the mothers not modern enough. But the fact remains that the mother in this case represented the earlier tradition and she could also tyrannize very harshly over her daughter and granddaughter.

We may therefore conclude that women in Athens had a weak legal position—much weaker, for example, than women in Sparta— but that their competence at law to act in contract matters could be more considerable.[39] Women also were held generally in great esteem—this is clear from Greek drama—but the complaints of women in drama must also be taken into account.

There are quite different *social* aspects, which were taken for granted:

1. The difference between two kinds of women, both free and both possibly respectable—female citizens and the wives of metics. The latter had no rights.

2. The complete disregard of widows (see above), who formed a considerable part of the adult female population. This contrasts sharply with the treatment of other women.

---

[39] All this is very much in accordance with the situation that prevailed in the Dutch legal system before the most recent revision of the Civil Code in 1956. For the possibilities open to Greek women, see Kuiper, *op. cit.*, p. 45 ff and especially p. 49 ff; L. J. T. Kuenen-Janssens, *Mnem.* III 9 (1940) 199-214. See also G. E. M. de Ste. Croix, 'Some Observations on Property Rights of Athenian Women', *CR* 20 (1970), pp. 272-278. For the whole question of women in Greek private law, see S. B. Pomeroy's short summary of the books and articles available in her 'Selected Bibliography on the Women in Antiquity', *Arethusa*, 6, 1 (1973), pp. 127-157, especially pp. 138-140. The study that is generally speaking of the greatest importance is R. Flacelière's book, *La vie quotidienne en Grèce au siècle de Périclès* (1959) and the same author's contribution to the great collection of writings on the history of women, *Histoire mondiale de la femme I* (see above, p. 242, note 1).

For 'feminism' and emancipation, see S. B. Pomeroy's bibliography, *op. cit.*, pp. 141-144 (see also above, p. 243, n. 4); see also J. Vogt, *op. cit.*, pp. 211-255 (see above, p. 265, note 29) and R. Flacelière, 'D'un certain féminisme grec', *REA* 64 (1962), pp. 109-116. Vogt's ideas, which suggest an out and out feminism, are somewhat toned down by Flacelière, who nevertheless assumes that a movement of this kind existed.

The best summary of prostitution as a social phenomenon can be found in two publications by H. Herter: his article 'Dirne' in *RAC* III (1957), p. 1154 ff. and his article 'Die Soziologie der antiken Prostitution im Lichte des heidnischen und christlichen Schrifttums', in *Jahrbuch für Antike und Christentum* III (1960), pp. 70-111.

The case of widows, however, should not surprise us, since as such they could play no further part in childbearing and could therefore be passed over. If a woman was lucky enough to be still young when she was widowed and therefore able to remarry, she had security and could once again play a part in childbearing. If on the other hand she was older, but was lucky enough to have adult children, she would have been provided for by the children, who had a duty to support her. If, however, she was neither a young marriageable widow nor an older widow with grown up children, she would have been thrown back on her own resources even if she had been a war widow.

Here too, however, it is quite wrong to compare the Greek widow with her modern counterpart. In our case too the widow's pension is of recent date and it has until quite recently been very small. We should therefore not compare their situation in Greece with that in our own countries today. It is unfruitful and subject to error. There is no point in comparing what is not comparable.

It is important to bear in mind that the Greek state made provisions of which women as such could not take advantage. They could obtain financial help only as mothers of children, in particular small children whose upbringing had to be provided for. The mother did not receive maintenance in her own right. If she had grown up children they were taken into account. Otherwise, she had to fend for herself.

School Education

The Greeks had boys' schools, but they were different from ours. The emphasis was on physical exercises and gymnastics or self-expression and much less on the intellectual subjects that play such an important part in our present day schools. There are several references in tradition to girls' schools, but none for Athens and too few altogether to furnish a general picture.[40]

---

[40] See M. P. Nilsson, *Die hellenistische Schule*, and B. A. van Groningen's review of this book in *Gnomon* 28 (1956), p. 501, where he deals especially with the concept 'school'. Kitto slides rather easily over this almost complete lack of education for girls in school. (It was not absent in Sparta!) He claimed that girls learned everything from their mothers and 'if we say "house-work" it sounds degrading, but if we say "Domestic Science" it sounds eminently respectable' (p. 232). This strikes me as a case of 'special pleading'—Kitto claims all the arguments for himself. Reasoning as he does, we should inevitably be forced to the conclusion that all the modern world needed was a reversion to the time when girls learned everything from their mothers!

This is, of course, a phenomenon that can still be observed in modern times—the boys study while the girls help their mothers at home. I therefore hardly think the modern world therefore has much to boast about compared with the Greeks. As far as education in schools is concerned, we have not progressed much further than they, at least in many places. I would not at all agree, however, with any attempt to make light of or explain away the fifth-century Athenian practice of denying a school education to girls.

Being of one mind or saying 'we'

In Graeco-Roman society, the relationship between man and woman was often determined by the intimate association of feelings and thought not necessarily expressed in words, and an attitude of mind resulting from mutual intimacy over a number of years. Traces of this have been preserved from antiquity and have been collected in a good article by F. Zucker entitled *Socia unanimans*.[41] 'Being of one mind' here does not merely refer to the relationship between man and wife, because the term also occurs in Plautus' *Truculentus* in connection with a *hetaera*. In those texts where it refers to the relationship within marriage, however, what this term really emphasizes is the solidarity existing between the partners. Both have duties towards each other, but those duties do not always have to be explicitly emphasized, and we are made to feel that the relationship is based on a deeper feeling of affection between man and wife and of mutual trust. This was often expressed by the word *koinōnia*.[42] The normal patterns of behaviour of the husband towards his wife and the wife towards her husband—τὸ προσῆκον, τὸ πρεπόν, το δέον, rendered in terms that can be translated as 'what is fitting', 'what is suitable' or 'what is polite'—can be found expressed in the spheres of education and marriage itself and are illustrated in the various plays that have come down to us from antiquity.

The force of what is implied in these three terms becomes clear as soon as we consider the consequences. There is only one case known to us in ancient literature in which a father takes his married daughter back home. Legally, this was permitted in Greek society. The fact that we hear so little of it may perhaps indicate that it did not happen very often that a father took such a drastic step. If it had been a frequent and striking occurrence, arousing a great

---

[41] F. Zucker, 'Socia unanimans', *Rh. M.* 92 (1943), pp. 193-217.
[42] See *koinōnia* above, pp. 177, 244, 253 f.

deal of interest, it would have featured more often in comedy as a subject of intrigue. Yet we find no traces of it at all.[43]

The father in this case took the drastic step of taking his daughter home because her husband had gone away on business and nothing had been heard of him for two years. This was in conflict with the behaviour expected of a husband towards his wife. It so often happens that we have insufficient information about normal situations and that the only sources we have concern special situations, such as this case of deliberate desertion of a wife by a husband.

Because of their *koinōnia*, the wife was her husband's dutiful servant. This may provoke our indignation today, but we have to admit that one result of this relationship in ancient Greece was that in many cases man and wife formed a unity. They were entirely fused with one another, συντέτηκε as it is called in Sophocles' Oedipus. The union of marriage was a partnership for the whole of life (κοινωνία παντὸς τοῦ βίου). Because of this close union, the husband was able to educate his wife and instruct her in many things. This is not surprising when it is remembered that a girl might marry at the age of fourteen and that her husband was often twice as old as her. The terms used in education for this process were: to become equal to men, make common cause with them, be in agreement with them, or reach the same level as men: κοινωνεῖν παιδείας τοῖς ἀνδράσιν.[44]

There are frequent references in Greek philosophy to the fact that, unless they are of one mind, husband and wife cannot make a good marriage, but this is, as far as we are concerned, a commonplace and we need discuss it no further. For the Greeks, marriage was based not only on this solidarity, but also on friendship and this friendship was also a form of solidarity which might lead to love. It is, however, very significant that friendship was often the more prominent.[45]

A serious limitation in Zucker's sources (and therefore in his arguments) is that he can discern the wife's faithfulness as her husband's companion only in cases where this solidarity was called into question and threatened. The fault was usually the husband's.

---

[43] The only case in literature that should be mentioned in this context is Demosthenes, *Adv. Spud.* 4; see Zucker, *op. cit.*, p. 204.

[44] Plutarch, *Coniugalia praecepta*, c. 48, 145 D; see also Zucker, *op. cit.*, p. 212.

[45] Aristotle, *EN* I, c. 3. 1165a, 36 ff; later in Stoicism: St. VF 3, fragment 724. See also Zucker, *op. cit.*, p. 214.

It is, however, a serious gap in our knowledge that examples of ordinary harmonious marriages are nowhere or hardly to be found in the extant literature, including also that of the Greek theatre. Comedy has always been based much more on relationships between men and *hetairai* in Greece, or on marital quarrels with a comic aspect than on ordinary everyday life, which is apt to be monotonous and uninteresting. Zucker's paper dealt with later Greek comedy and this in itself was a limitation. We can learn from it something about the development of ethics and even more about what took place in practice outside the various philosophical sects, but it can tell us nothing, or very little at most, about the warmth of ordinary human life in marriage. This is a complaint that can be made about most modern writing.

The Protection of Women

In the preceding sections, we have already mentioned the measures taken to accompany women on the streets. These may have been necessitated by the threat of violence and robbery, but does not necessarily indicate a danger of seduction or rape.

We have a striking example of the protection of women without restricting their freedom in the institution of the *gynaikonomos*. It was connected with the *paidonomos* and the *gymnasiarchos*.[46] They are also known to us through the work of J. Pouilloux.[47] They had to guard, for example, against unrestrained demonstrations of mourning. The situation here can be compared with that in Athens and the measures attributed to Solon (see Plutarch's *Solon* 21. 5). This institution was above all a moral police force in a centre of trade visited by a great number of foreigners.[48] According to Pouilloux,[49] both historians and theoreticians agree that it was an aristocratic institution. I have my doubts, though I cannot disprove it. It was found in coastal towns, whatever their constitution. The argument that has been put forward in favour of an aristocratic origin of the *gynaikonomos* is that the institution is not mentioned in democratic cities until the fourth century B.C. But what does this really mean? Is it not a mere lack of evidence either way?

---

[46] See, for example, Busolt and Swoboda, pp. 493-496; *RE* 7, col. 1089 (Börner).

[47] See his studies of Thasos in *Recherches sur l'histoire et les cultes de Thasos* I (1954), p. 407 ff.

[48] See R. Martin, *BCH* 68-69 (1944-5), p. 160.

[49] *Op. cit.*, p. 410.

Certain scholars, on grounds as shaky as these, have asked whether conservative tendencies did not arise on Thasos, after the excesses that occurred at the end of the fifth century, in a government which must be described as a moderate democracy.[50] Plutarch also has references to protectors of women and to the segregation of women, for their security, not for their control.

In his well-known article on the Greek woman in the fifth and fourth centuries B.C. Gomme made a comment that should not be forgotten. He admitted that his failure to include the orators was a weakness in his position, since evidence from that source was against him. Their handling of cases involving women seemed all to emphasize their dependence, whereas Gomme himself had argued for their relative freedom in Greece.

Clearly he was speaking in honest awareness that the sources were at variance. I do not find this surprising. In Greek legal literature, the law was always in dispute by unscrupulous guardians, by those who sought to exploit the later strict legislation regarding marriage with alien women and the possible difficulties experienced by children of a father's first marriage. It cannot be denied that women sometimes give the impression of being completely defenceless, at the mercy of men out to lay snares for them in their material future. I must therefore insist on the point which I have already made several times, that the position of women in Greek society was not always correctly interpreted by the judges. Despite the admiration I have for legal treatises on the position of women I believe that these studies often overshoot the mark. Legal experts have a great deal to learn here from K. J. Dover's excellent book, *Private Morality in the Time of Plato and Aristotle* (1975), in which the legal arguments used at a period that was dominated, so we believed, by two great philosophers are seen to be central to everyday life.

As an epilogue to this incomplete review of a perennial subject, I should like to note two different interpretations of a famous cautionary tale about female modesty in Herodotus (1. 8).

When Gyges protested strongly against Candaules' suggestion that he should show his beautiful wife naked to his servant (Gyges) to convince him of her beauty, he said: 'A woman puts off her shame with her tunic'. The dispute is about the interpretation of

---

[50] See Cicero, *De Legibus* 2. 26 and Demetrius of Phaleron, for similar laws.

the Greek word αἰδώς (shame). Some have argued with success that rather than the obvious 'sense of shame', 'self-respect', it should be interpreted passively to mean 'the respect of others', 'the consideration due to her'.[51]

In this way, Herodotus' well-known words are given quite a different slant. The woman who shows herself naked forgoes her right to the consideration and respect of men. However attractive this view may be, we have no definitive proof that it correctly understands the passage. But the fact that Plutarch was in favour of the traditional view (*Coniugalia praecepta* 139 C,10) is an argument against it: 'Herodotus was not right in saying that a woman puts off her modesty along with her undergarment. On the contrary, a virtuous woman puts on modesty in its stead'. The moralist Plutarch was obviously of the opinion that the whole relationship between husband and wife in marriage depended on the wife's 'modesty', because the passage continues: 'and husband and wife bring in their mutual relations the greatest modesty as a token of the greatest love'.[52]

It is hardly possible in this treatment of the morality of marriage to avoid discussing the way in which sexual intercourse between man and wife was regarded in antiquity. Generally speaking, we are bound to say that it was seen from the point of view of the man and the satisfaction that he obtained. There are, however, signs which point in another direction.[53] We are told that the satisfaction of both partners was also discussed in antiquity. According to tradition, it was a woman who first wrote on the subject. She was called Astyanassa and she was one of Helen's servants. Her name, which means 'ruler' or 'mistress of the city', may be an indication of the importance that the author, writing in the second century A.D., who named—or invented—this female writer attached

---

[51] R. Harder, *Kleine Schriften* (1960), pp. 208-211 (= *Studies Presented to D. M. Robinson* II, 1953, pp. 446-449). Godley, whose translation of Herodotus was published in the Loeb Classics, has a similar rendering: 'With the stripping of her tunic a woman is stripped of the honour due to her'. This can be compared with Harder's 'in demselben Augenblick, wo eine Frau das Gewand ablegt, entgleitet ihr zugleich die schützende Hülle der Achtung'.

[52] This translation of Plutarch is by F. C. Babbitt, *LCL*, *Plutarch's Moralia* II, p. 305. Babbitt has correctly pointed here to *Moralia* 37 D, where the active meaning of 'shame' (αἰδώς) is emphasized in connection with the same passage in Herodotus. See also Jerome, *Adversus Iovianum* 48 (Migne, *Patrologia Latina* II, p. 292).

[53] See my *Eros en Amor*, The Hague (1962), p. 41.

to the subject. It is significant that he gave her a place in the retinue of the fair Helen. In addition to Astyanassa, the same author also refers to other women who had written about the pleasures of love. It can hardly be a matter of pure chance that only women are named in this context. These women were the first to show the man the way in a territory in which he had been in the habit of going his own way, high-handedly and thoughtlessly.

The information about Astyanassa and her fellow-authoresses happened to find its way into a later lexicon and was thus preserved for posterity.[54] This information shows once again how capricious the tradition was and how meagre our knowledge is. There is no reason for us to doubt that manuals such as the one that is here ascribed to Astyanassa existed in antiquity. Ovid's *Ars Amandi* was an enormously popular book, but there must also have been popular books on the subject before his. It would, however, seem to have been in conflict with the traditional image of the woman in antiquity that a work about sexual intercourse and the man's and the woman's pleasure in sex should have been written by a woman. Yet a woman may have been able to speak more freely about such matters in antiquity than in later periods of history, and if this was the case, why should she not also have been able and permitted to write more freely about them?

Conclusions

1. We have very few data at our disposal relating to the social history of antiquity. This also applies to the subject of women and there is consequently a tendency on the part of many contemporary scholars to generalize.

2. An important part is played by the time factor, that is, the particular period in which a particular view of woman prevails. Women of an earlier period did not necessarily behave in the same way as women of a later period. We may therefore say that the only important period is that in which a given statement originated.

---

[54] *RE*, see under Astyanassa, refers to Suda, which tells us: 'a servant of Helen, Menelaus' wife'. She was the first to experiment with various positions for coitus (κατὰ κλίσεις) and attitudes in sexual intercourse (σχήματα συνου-σιαστικά). If Cohn (*RE*, *s.v.*) is right, Astyanassa was an invented woman, born in the imagination of Ptolemaios Chennos, who wrote in the first quarter of the second century B.C. For this author, see *RE*, under Ptolemaios (77). This indication of the period, of course, is of no importance in the dating of the phenomenon.

3. Greek women did not always live in the same social environment everywhere and throughout classical antiquity. This applies not only to periods far removed from each other, but also to the same period in the same Polis.

4. Finally, there was also a considerable difference between the position of women living at the same time in two states of completely differing social structures. There is little similarity between the Spartan and the Athenian attitudes towards women and marriage. I have confined my comments in this chapter almost exclusively to these two states, because they are the only ones in ancient Greece about which we have a reasonable number of facts at our disposal.

Ancient Greek society was a male society. Our knowledge of women is therefore restricted to what men wrote about them. When we speak about 'man and woman', we are really only speaking about the position of women viewed in different aspects. *Generally* speaking: there was considerable appreciation of women in antiquity. Greek poets praised her beauty, courage, readiness to sacrifice, and her love of her husband and children.

From the *social* point of view, women were more important and the degree of co-operation between man and woman was greater in Sparta than in Athens. The Spartan state was more completely militarized in the historical period than Athens. During the summer, almost all the men were on active service with the army. The women had the task of working on the home front. They had to attend to the harvest and be ready in case of attack. The education of Spartan girls was completely adapted to the demands that were made of women. Generally speaking, Spartan girls married later than Athenian girls. They had greater responsibilities and these made it necessary for them to marry only when they were thought to be in a position to be able to do so. This obligation did not exist in Athens and therefore girls married when they were much younger, sometimes before they were fifteen. Spartan men were also strictly bound to do military service and, if they were married, they had to care for their offspring. Later in life, this task replaced that of the soldier. One of the consequences of this was that bachelors were exposed to certain punishments. The women of Sparta witnessed these punishments and this promoted their freedom. Outside Sparta, Spartan women were notorious for their 'immorality'. Modern scholars attach little importance to this accusation, but tend to explain it by appealing to the differences between Sparta on the one hand and other states, especially Athens, on the other with regard to social structure. From the *legal* point of view, Spartan women were in a more favourable position than Athenian women. This is not surprising in view of the social significance of women in the two states. The Spartan woman's competence at law to act as a party to contracts was greater than that of women elsewhere in Greece, but this does not mean that her status should be measured by this.

Women in the Greek city states had no direct *political* importance. They could not be elected to offices and had no active right to vote. Indirectly, however, they had considerable importance, because they could become the mothers of legitimate children. In states such as Sparta, where concubinage played no part, alien women did not claim legal rights and there were consequently no problems. In Athens, on the other hand, the position of the female citizen was always threatened by alien women who had come from outside Athens and had settled in that great trading centre. In the Athenian lawcourt it was stated plainly: Mistresses we keep for our pleasure, concubines for our day-to-day physical well-being, and wives to beget legitimate children'.[55] In Pericles' law of 451 B.C., foreign women were excluded from legitimate marriage by the citizens of Athens, who wanted to keep the empire for the city. This brought about a lowering of the position of women, including that of the Athenian woman herself.

It sometimes causes surprise that a Greek man could be in love with his wife. What is striking is that terms relating to *eroticism* in the strict sense of the word are used far more frequently in classical literature in the context of illegitimate relationships than in connection with legitimate relationships. If, however, the data were subjected to detailed research, this would undoubtedly prove to be the case all over the world.

We may therefore say in conclusion that the position of women in ancient Hellas was more subtly varied than many people think. We live in a society that we often think is unique in its complexity and we believe that in the past everything was much simpler. We ought therefore to realize that simpler forms of society cannot be understood if they are not seen to be more varied and complex than a superficial examination might reveal. The object of historical

---

[55] See above, p. 244.

study is man, a being whom we no longer try to cut to one particular pattern, thanks to the insights of modern psychology. The relationship between two people—and this includes that between man and woman—is even more complicated than man alone. Ancient Greece is no exception to this rule.

CHAPTER TWELVE

ABORTION AND FAMILY PLANNING

Abortion [1] was almost without exception regarded as wrong in ancient Greek society. Only later do we find reports of legal measures against abortion, but in each case these are attributed to great lawgivers. Lycurgus and Solon, the lawgivers of Sparta and Athens, are quoted as politicians who opposed abortion, but this is probably a later attribution to lawgivers living in the remote past.

Greek philosophers did not concern themselves with the problem until later. Plato was in favour of abortion (Republic 461 C) if a birth threatened the ideals of political development. Aristotle would permit abortion if the birth rate was too high, but only at a stage 'before life and sense had begun in the embryo' (*Politics* 7. 16. 10). The Stoics did not regard the embryo as a living being and did not think that abortion was murder. The later Stoics, however, condemned the practice.[2] In the same way, the Roman jurists regarded abortion as an unlawful action, although the only legal enactments that are known to us date back to a later period, that of the Roman

---

[1] A summary of the various views about abortion that existed in classical antiquity can be found in J. H. Waszink's article 'Abtreibung', *RAC* (1950), pp. 55-60. The most important contribution made up to 1950 is by F. J. Dölger, 'Das Lebensrecht des ungeborenen Kindes und die Fruchtabtreibung in der Bewertung der heidnischen und christlichen Antike', *Antike und Christentum* 4 (1934), pp. 1-61. In recent years, a very great number of books and articles have been published on this topic. A recent summary of the literature about women in classical antiquity has been published by Sarah B. Pomeroy in the journal *Arethusa* 6, 1 (1973), pp. 127-157, and p. 147 lists the modern references to abortion under this head. E. Nardi's book *Procurato aborto nel mondo greco romano*, Milan (1971) is also discussed by Mrs Pomeroy in the same number of *Arethusa*, pp. 158-166. See also John T. Noonan Jnr., *An Absolute Value in History, The Morality of Abortion*, Cambridge, Mass., Harvard University Press (1970). To complete the picture, we must also mention a study of the Caesarean section by J. P. Pundel, *Histoire de l'Opération césarienne*, subtitled *Etude historique de la césarienne dans la médecine, l'art et la littérature, les religions et la législation. La prodigieuse évolution de la césarienne depuis l'antiquité jusqu'aux temps modernes*, Brussels (1969).

[2] See R. Crahay, 'Les moralistes anciens et l'avortement', *AC* 10 (1941), pp. 9-23. In *RAC*: Beseelung (Waszink). On Aristotle, recently J. M. Oppenheimer, 'When sense and life begin: Background for a remark in Aristotle's Politics (1335 b 24)' (= 7, 16), *Arethusa* 8 (1975) 331-343.

Empire. In Greek medical circles there was strong opposition to abortion. There is a clause about it in the Hippocratic oath.

Generally speaking, the Romans were opposed to abortion. This is clear from a review of their literature (as summarized by Waszink, for example). From the legal point of view, abortion was not regarded in Rome as a crime, as the unborn child was not seen as a person.[3] But what was not forbidden by the law could still be felt to conflict with morals. We have already seen that the abandonment or exposure of children was checked by a kind of popular feeling.[4] But even this check did not prevent abortion from taking place frequently. Waszink has pointed to texts which show that abortion was widespread in the imperial period, but we cannot even guess numbers. We can no more know the percentage of abortions in antiquity than we can in later periods of history. Our ignorance is not simply due to a shortage of data—it is also because of a lack of precise terminology. The word *abortus* was often used for miscarriage and *abortus provocatus,* both for a deliberate abortion on medical grounds and for other abortions done for different reasons. The word φθορίη occurs many times in the *Corpus Hippocraticum* with the meaning of miscarriage or the interruption of pregnancy on medical grounds. It is in connection with these cases that many abortions are mentioned in ancient medical writings, which were almost exclusively intended for specialists or future specialists. This should not, however, be regarded as a sign that abortions were frequently carried out on medical advice or for such reasons as the desire to preserve the woman's beauty or because of economic objections to the birth of a (new) child. In the whole of the *Corpus Hippocraticum* there is, as far as I know, only one case of abortion by a doctor for reasons that were not medical. This is the case of a dancing girl whose owner thought her so valuable as a professional dancer that an abortion was arranged for her.[5] It is probable that

---

[3] Dig. 35. 2, 9, 1; cf. 25. 4, 1, 1; 38. 8, 1, 8, but the administration of means of abortion were regarded as *mala medicamenta*. The prevalent morality was very much opposed to abortion for non-medical reasons. Strict practitioners always rejected abortion, however. See the Hippocratic oath; L. Edelstein, *The Hippocratic Oath*, Baltimore (1943), p. 10 ff. For medical reservations, see W. A. Krenkel, 'Erotica I. Der Abortus in der Antike', *Wissenschaftliche Zeitschrift der Universität Rostock* 20 (1971), pp. 443-452, especially p. 451.

[4] See above, p. 135 ff.

[5] Abortion took place seven days after conception by means of 'jumping exercises'. This is a unique case and the operation is attributed to Hippocrates

such cases as this occurred quite often, but it is also likely that the operation was frequently performed by unqualified practitioners and that the consequences were disastrous.

As in later periods of history, it was the women who were blamed. Plutarch can be taken to represent the many men in classical times who blamed the women in this way: 'After the manner of licentious women who employ drugs and instruments to procure abortion for the sake of enjoyment of conceiving again'.[6] The translation here is less bitter than the original Greek text, in which a coarse word for sexual intercourse is used—'to be stuffed' and experience pleasure. This use of words may possibly be the author's way of describing the woman's orgasm.[7]

There is a striking contrast between the fate of the poor woman who bears a child and the rich woman who has an 'easy' abortion in a passage in Juvenal: 'These poor women, however, endure the perils of childbirth and all the troubles of nursing to which their lot condemns them; but how often does a gilded bed contain a woman who is lying in? So great is the skill, so powerful the drugs of the abortionist, paid to murder mankind within the womb'. The woman in this case had obviously not been faithful to her husband, for the satirist goes on: 'Rejoice, poor wretch; give her the stuff to drink, whatever it be, with your own hand; for were she willing to get big and trouble her womb with bouncing babies, you might perhaps find yourself the father of an Ethiopian; and some day a coloured heir, whom you would rather not meet by daylight, would fill all the places in your will'.[8]

Greek doctors and physicians are better sources of information about abortion than philosophers and satirists, because they can tell us about the cases in which they permitted it. In this connection I would refer especially to Edelstein's study of the Hippocratic oath. As we have already seen, all abortion is rejected by this oath, but there must clearly have been exceptions, defined by the circle

---

himself as the doctor in charge. See Galen, *De sem.* 1. 4, vol. 4, p. 525. It is also mentioned elsewhere. See also Krenkel, *op. cit.*, p. 447, *sub* 5. 1.

[6] *Moralia* 134, translated by F. C. Babbitt in *LCL*.

[7] Plutarch, *Moralia* 134, above: καθάπερ ἀκόλαστοι γυναῖκες, ἐμβολίοις χρώμεναι καὶ φθορίοις ὑπὲρ τοῦ πάλιν πληροῦσθαι καὶ ἡδυπαθεῖν. For πληροῦν in comedy, see J. Henderson, *The Maculate Muse*, New Haven (1975), p. 176.

[8] Juvenal 6. 592 ff., translated by G. G. Ramsay in *LCL*. The context has been excellently described by G. Highet, *Juvenal the Satirist* (1954), p. 101.

or sect of physicians for whom the oath was valid. Edelstein himself has said: 'Medical writings of all periods mention the means for destruction of the embryo and *the occasions on which they were to be applied*'.[9]

Soranus, who has rightly been called the greatest ancient gynae-cologist,[10] certainly had little patience with the fundamental objections raised by his colleagues to abortion, as Edelstein has correctly observed. Soranus 'lived in the first century A.D., was philosophically a convinced Epicurean, in other words a supporter of the kind of teaching that is usually called materialistic, and rejected faith in the gods . . . What he said about the education of midwives . . . is perfectly acceptable nowadays . . . Soranus quotes the Hippocratic oath and observes that some physicians appeal to Hippocrates and say that it is essential to medicine to preserve and take care of what is produced by nature. Others, however, have reservations and permit artificial abortion in certain cases—not if a woman wants to conceal the consequences of a slip or does not want to spoil her beauty, but if there is for some reason a danger to life if the child should be born. Soranus is in agreement with the second opinion and gives indications as to when and how an operation may take place. He ends this chapter in his treatise with the advice that conception should as far as possible be prevented in cases of this type. It is important to add that this physician also fundamentally rejects the practice of periodic continence and the use of contraceptives'.[11]

---

[9] See R. Hähnel, 'Der künstliche Abortus im Altertum', *Archiv für Geschichte der Medizin* 29 (1937), p. 224 ff. This has been taken over by Edelstein, *op. cit.*, pp. 11-22. The italics in the quotation from Edelstein are mine. For other books and articles on this subject, see Edelstein, *op. cit.*, p. 11, note 31.
A pioneer in the field of assessing the different points of view taken by doctors and physicians in classical antiquity was J. Ilberg, 'Zur gynäkologischen Ethik der Griechen', *A.f.R* 13 (1910), pp. 12 ff. Hähnel was wrong in believing that Ilberg suggested that Greek physicians did not use abortion. See my review of P. Salmon, *Population et dépopulation dans l'Empire romain*, Brussels (1974), in *Gnomon* 49 (1978), 86-88.
[10] Translation of his *Gynaeceia* by O. Temkin, Johns Hopkins Press, Baltimore 1956. See also A. Preus, 'Biomedical Techniques for Influencing Reproduction', *Arethusa* 8 (1975) 237-263, with interesting passages from Soranus.
[11] This picture of Soranus was drawn by H. J. Drossaart Lulofs, 'De eed van Hippocrates', *Voordrachtenreeks van de Nederlandse Vereniging van Psychiaters in dienstverband*, Series 24 (1965). The quotation will be found on pp. 130-131.

Soranus therefore clearly ruled out the woman's self-interest as ground for abortion, confining himself to medical indications. The woman's self-interest after all, was often no more than that of her lord and master. A horrifying example was that of Domitian, who forced his niece and mistress Julia to have an abortion.[12] Ovid also testified to the possibility of dangerous consequences for the woman.[13]

It is also a matter of course that even in the earliest period the practice of abortion was forbidden by Christian ethics. Debate on the subject was always introduced by what might be called the 'crown of creation' argument, in other words, that violence was done to a creature in God's image when an abortion took place. Abortion was immediately condemned by ecclesiastical law. Waszink has quoted a testimony from monastic literature giving a good example of the Church's attitude. A shepherd murdered a pregnant woman. After a long period of penance, he was forgiven his sin of murdering the woman (this was revealed by a vision from heaven), but not that of murdering the unborn child she was expecting. It should also be mentioned in this context that there does not seem to have been any decrease in the number of abortions in the Christian period, despite the Church's anxiety to condemn it. It is clear from the repeated resolutions made at Church councils and from references in the apocalyptic literature, in which abortion was discussed at length, that the phenomenon persisted in the early Church.

It is also interesting to note that the stage at which a pregnancy could be terminated might then as now be considered in connection with an abortion. We do not know for certain but it seems that a distinction may have been made, in the case of an embryo soon after conception, between aborting one which was already complete in its form' (*quo forma completa est*) and one which was not. The formulation is Tertullian's (De anima 37. 2), in connection with Exod. 21. 22-23. In other patristic writings, however, there is no reference to a discrimination between the embryo when it attains its final form and before that stage. As far as I know, there is no trace of a debate on this question in antiquity, nor is it likely that

---

For a discussion of the general behaviour of doctors and physicians, see R. Etienne, 'La conscience médicale antique et la vie des enfants', *Annales de démographie historique* (1973), pp. 15-16.

[12] Suetonius, *Dom.* 22; Pliny, *Epist.* 4. 11, 6; Juvenal, 2. 29-33.

[13] Ovid, *Amores* 2. 13 and 14. See also Krenkel, *op. cit.*, p. 448, and W. J. Watts, 'Ovid, the Law and Roman Society on Abortion', *Acta Classica* 16 (1973), pp. 89-103.

such a debate could have taken place, since officially the prohibition was absolute, so that the Church authorities would seldom if ever have been consulted about the possibility of aborting an embryo. If the Church learned that a woman had been raped and become pregnant and in consequence had an abortion, she might possibly have been punished and excommunicated. It is difficult to say whether this was so at all periods of the Church's history, but it was certainly characteristic of Church opinion at the time of the Synod of Elvira, when excommunication of the woman was laid down as the penalty for abortion. It is also noteworthy that the practice of abortion and the use of contraceptives were thought of as equivalent crimes, at least according to certain early documents.[14]

Women themselves are seldom mentioned in connection with abortion and contraception problems and this is probably connected with the very early age at which they married in classical antiquity.[15] We must agree with A. J. Toynbee that the best way to prevent women from growing up is to marry them very young. Generally Greek and Roman girls were married very young indeed —at thirteen or fourteen.[16] Unfortunately our information about the age of *menarche* is confused by differing accounts in our sources, chiefly between texts concerning the history of law and medical texts.[17] There is nothing surprising of course about a difference between the ages of legal and physical maturity. It is noticeable, for example, in the initiation rites which were performed in men's clubs and associations as soon as boys became physically mature. The age of physical maturity in boys has been estimated at fourteen to fifteen. But it was not till they were eighteen, that they were fully initiated into male society, an age of course when they became due for military service.

There was also a great desire and need for offspring in the ancient

---

[14] This has been pointed out by M. K. Hopkins in 'Contraception and Abortion in the Roman Empire', *Comparative Studies in Society and History* 8 (1965), pp. 124-151.

[15] See above, p. 34 ff. for the position of the woman in fifth century Athens. Cf. also chapter XI.

[16] See M. K. Hopkins, 'The Age of Roman Girls at Marriage', in *Population Studies* 18, 3 (1964-1965), pp. 309-327; Lacey, *op. cit.*, 71, 162. A. J. Toynbee, *Some Problems of Greek History*, London (1969), p. 363.

[17] The medical sources have been investigated by D. W. Amundsen and C. J. Dieis, in 'The Age of Menarche in Classical Greece and Rome', *Human Biology* 41, 1 (1969), pp. 125-132; see also *idem*, 'The Age of Menopause in Classical Greece and Rome', *Human Biology* 42, 1 (1969), pp. 79-86.

world, as a provision against old age, to ensure the continuous existence of the community, the transmission of the land from father to son, and uninterrupted tendance of the gods with regular sacrifices. As soon as the tendance of the household gods was threatened, families had recourse to adoption.[18] It is scarcely possible to lay down an order of priority among all these reasons for adoption, so general and instinctive were the arguments for large families in communities at a certain stage of development. Recently research into this question has concentrated more on the need to provide against old age. Studies of the Third World today, however, have more and more come to see large families as an economic necessity of such a self-evident kind as to need no explanation. 'A large family is the only preventive against starvation'—is now the slogan. The economist J. Tinbergen has dealt with the question in a recent publication. It is not simply a status symbol or a stupid habit to have many children (especially boys), Tinbergen insists, but an economic advantage for the whole family, certainly in the short term and within the established pattern of a given country. Tinbergen has calculated that a small peasant in Java obtains a higher production per head in a large family than in a small one. This is certainly the case before the peasant in question becomes old and has to fall back on his own, self-won provision for old age. The large agrarian family, then, has an economic cause. Such people are not poor because they have large families—they have large families because they are poor.[19] It is possible to think, as the present writer does, that the attitudes and practices of modern developing countries are illustrative of those in western antiquity. It is also possible to understand—taking classical antiquity as a point of departure—why voluntary childlessness or a limitation in the size of the family is often not accepted or only with great reluctance.

The tendance of the household gods—or, in more general terms, the religious factor—surrounded the cohabitation of man and wife with all kinds of tabus, not all of which were calculated to assist their fertility.

---

[18] See L. Wenger's survey 'Adoption', in *RAC*.

[19] J. Tinbergen in a publication by the Foundation 'Maatschappij en Onderneming' (1976). Taking the well understood need of agrarian workers for a large family as his point of departure, Tinbergen suggests that this need should be overcome by the introduction of an internationally financed general provision for old age. Cf. J. Tinbergen *et al.*, *Reshaping the International Order* (Report 1976).

A recent report by a young doctor on his experiences in Central Africa throws interesting light on these possibilities.[20] He found that in obstetrical cases the mother very often died two or three days after a normal and successful birth, without any previous medical indication (or so it appeared from his preliminary investigation). After observing dozens of cases of this kind in a relatively short time he discovered that the death of the mother was in each case connected with a violent and acute liver complaint. He therefore set out to investigate the phenomenon in the villages.

Gradually the following picture emerged. A feature of the religion of this people was their reverence for water (and blood, which was equated with water). If in the opinion of the midwife or the dry nurse insufficient blood and water were shed at the time of a delivery, an infusion of herbs would be given to the mother in order to 'release' more blood and water. These herbs were so harmful that the mother's liver in each case became infected and the process was so rapid and violent that she died within a couple of days.

The western doctor had to go to great lengths to obtain his information, because everything connected with childbirth was the 'secret' of a small number of women in the community. He was from time to time taken to the dead mother but could of course do nothing. He had to be extremely cautious in asking his questions. If he asked: 'Were herbs used'? he was always given a firmly negative answer. But if he asked indirectly and unemphatically: 'When were the herbs used'? he was sometimes able to obtain a reply without any trouble: 'Yesterday' or 'The day before yesterday'. The herbs, he found, were always given very soon after delivery.

I suggest that there were communities in antiquity in which midwives and dry nurses continued to exert a major influence, greater than that of doctors and physicians. Medical science was developing hesitantly at times, more rapidly at others and its practitioners complained at the time of the prejudice and stupidity of male and female witch-doctors. If this suggestion is correct, search for truth about the distant past is bound to be almost hopeless. We only need consider how much trouble it costs even a modern doctor to obtain information on the spot (like our young doctor himself).

I believe there is a similar parallel in the case of female fertility.

---

[20] For understandable reasons, the young doctor did not want the name of the place to be known. I thank him for supplying me with the information for the purposes of my study.

I am told by modern doctors that young women between the ages of fourteen and nineteen have low fertility, that the peak is between nineteen and thirty, that there is a decline between thirty and thirty-five and that complications may arise after the age of thirty-five.[21]

In antiquity, it was known that there was a greater chance that such complications would develop in pregnancies after the age of forty than in the period between adolescence and adulthood. The number of years during which a woman could conceive and bear children was less than is often thought. The fact that girls married at an early age did not mean that they bore more children. In general, quite apart from the youth or the advanced age of the mother, there was also a relatively high death rate of babies, both new-born and at the breast, and of mothers during confinement, although we lack detailed information.

We cannot learn much from the remains of small children in burial places because their skeletons have all turned to dust. All that we can discover about older people comes from inscriptions and this must be treated with caution. What emerges in general from these inscriptions is that women died young, between the ages of thirty and forty. Of course, there was always a chance of longer survival individually and older women dominated the realms of motherhood as dry nurses and midwives.

The man remained completely outside this world. But it was he, of course in this male-dominated society, who was required to recognize the child and this gave him a powerful hold over his legitimate wife. It was he who presented the child to the community and had it entered in the list of citizens (the register of 'births, deaths and marriages'), at least at a later period, when ancient society was more advanced. Entries in the register were consulted whenever there were legal proceedings regarding inheritance and the right of succession.

Such cases took place in Attica in the demes, not centrally in Athens. The intention was clear. The local people knew their demes or local centres where the people lived and of course they knew when children were to be born, they knew the parents and, once born,

---

[21] See J. Dankmeijer's oration (*De speurtocht naar de normale mens*), as rector at the University of Leiden (1966); these data were confirmed by A. A. Haspels' research according to oral information from the anthropologist J. D. Speckmann.

they knew the children. This meant that they had the means of checking on new citizens. It was rare for an illegitimate child to be smuggled into a deme. It is clear from legal documents that Greek citizens had many ways of contesting the legitimacy of a child, but we need not go into this question here, as it lies outside the scope of our discussion. What is indisputable is that the father played a central part in recognizing the child as legitimate.

But I must at once make a correction. Reliance on purely legal testimonies to determine the position of the woman in such vital decisions on the legitimacy of a child may lead us badly astray. We must not forget the importance of the 'curtain lecture', which no doubt influenced two vital decisions. First, man and wife must decide whether to have children (a much more important decision in classical antiquity than today). Secondly, the mother who wanted her child recognized must consider whether it was possible and what pressure she could put on her husband.

The position of a woman in classical antiquity, then, was not determined simply and solely by the law but also by character and situation of the woman herself.[22]

Another factor that makes it difficult for us to know much about the cohabitation of man and wife in antiquity (and indeed at all periods of history) is our lack of knowledge about the development of male fertility and changes in it. It was (and always has been) accepted as a matter of course that the woman was to blame if the marriage was childless, even if the man was unable to begat offspring in successive marriages.[23] There was (and has always been) a close association felt between the fertility of the crop in the field, of the livestock in the barn, and of the people in the home. In a rural environment, little distinction is made between man and livestock. The ox and the ass are juxtaposed with the neighbour's wife in the Ten Commandments and the phenomenon is not confined to Mosaic Law.

I have mentioned the fertility of the man as something about

---

[22] A novel by Jane Austen can tell us more about the power and influence of women in pre-Victorian England than a hundred treatises in the style of Simone de Beauvoir.

[23] G. Hawthorn has written a general work on fertility: *The Sociology of Fertility*, London (1970); see especially the Appendix: *Components of Natural Fertility*, p. 120 ff. In what follows, I have drawn on my own 'Demography in Roman History: Facts and Impressions', in *Mnem.* 26 (1973), pp. 29-46.

which very little has been written in history. The same applies to female fertility. On the basis of comparable situations in the modern world, we may assume that the same level of female fertility did not persist throughout antiquity. (See above, p. 280). This is borne out by a modern example. In the Second World War, situations arose that can be compared with situations in antiquity. When South-East Asia was liberated from Japanese occupation, all kinds of articles were flown to Indonesia and special consignments were sent to women's camps in which the women and small children had suffered a great deal. Among the articles dropped from aeroplanes in large quantities were sanitary towels, but these proved unnecessary as most of the women had ceased to have normal menstruation during the period of captivity. It was only when they had enjoyed proper food for some time that the normal cycle gradually returned.

I do not wish to suggest, of course, that only women who have good food are fertile. There are women who live with hunger for generations and whose fertility remains unimpaired by a generally atrocious nutritional situation. This is not, however, the central question. The women who were imprisoned in these Japanese concentration camps were upper and middle class women who had never before experienced poverty and severe hunger and who during the war had been suddenly transported to an unfamiliar situation. Their new circumstances exposed them to a violent change in their way of life. I venture to suggest that people, in the very fertile parts of Italy for example, have not always been able to cope positively with such sudden natural disasters as rain, storm, drought, and the consequences of these—bad harvests, livestock epidemics, and so on. It is a commonplace that early communities were often very weak economically because they did not plan and had inadequate reserves and supplies. There is, however, an important reality in this very general truth and so I would assume that the average peasant woman had periods of good food, during which her children were conceived and born, followed by periods when she had little or no food to eat. During the latter periods, I imagine, nature compensated in a special way for this lack of food, as it did in the case of the women in the concentration camps and in countries suffering from food shortages because of military occupation.

I think that my analogy is more meaningful than those that are so often found in demographic studies, based on conditions in France since the Middle Ages or conditions in modern Italy.[24] I do not regard these parallels as without value, but I think that the circumstances that were unfavourable to female fertility also occurred in antiquity and that modern and fairly recent experience can also tell us something about them in antiquity. It is especially clear from the slave population that man in antiquity was well aware of the risks involved in bringing new children into the world. Children were born to female slaves, begotten either by the masters or by the male slaves, but generally speaking this risk was not taken, especially at times when slave labour was expensive.

Ancient literature is silent about the way men and women behaved together in their intimate life. It is most striking that there is no evidence at all in literature of the use of *coitus interruptus* in pagan Italy, although it must have occurred. Indeed, there is confirmation in medical texts that this type of practice apparently did occur and that it was known how to prevent pregnancy by all kinds of means, including lotions, ointments, and magic formulae. Courtesans were familiar with certain techniques, many of which are discussed by J. T. Noonan.[25] Poor peasants knew that there was a risk when a child was conceived. They needed their wives as workers on the farm and birth control was therefore absolutely necessary and partly sanctioned to protect life. Peasants therefore usually lived monogamously, and if they made use of a slave girl in case of great sexual need, it may be assumed that they were extremely careful because of the capital value of a slave girl in their business.[26] Sexual promiscuity was never popular among the rural population, since peasants have always been more concerned to preserve the

---

[24] Recently in the fourth fascicle of the Annales E.S.C. 32 (1977), 287 (for France since the 17th century). For our subject, abortion, the paper of M. Laget on 'Pratiques des accouchements et attitudes collectives en France aux XVIIe et XVIIIe siècle' illustrates a painful mistake, quite often made in studies on the subject. Under 'avortement' she mentions 80 cases (p. 870), but only four in which the mother also died. If that were true, abortion would have been a surprisingly successful practice. Apparently Mme Laget did not distinguish between miscarriage and abortion, between 'fausse couche' and 'avortement'. The Greek word φθορά means both, likewise Latin *abortus*.

[25] J. T. Noonan, *Contraception. A History of its Treatment by the Catholic Theologians and Canonists*, (1965).

[26] See also T. P. Wiseman's parallels from sources on the sexual behaviour of fourteenth century Italian peasants; for example: 'They join themselves in lust with the beasts whom they feed and keep', *J.R.S.* 59 (1969), p. 73, note 122, where references are mentioned.

life already brought into the world. The most important priority in the peasant's programme in antiquity was undoubtedly the care of the cattle and other livestock. It was often regarded as better to safeguard the existence of the living by aborting children or killing them at birth, although this was only done when contraceptive means had failed. It has to be emphasized once again that the small peasant was always very careful because of the danger to his wife, who was usually his helpmate in the business. I would also stress again that the abandonment or exposure of children depended on the will of the parents and that the lives of normal children were generally speaking spared, while deformed children and unformed, humanly almost unrecognizable, or strange embryos or births were done away with, as we have already seen. In general then people in antiquity tried, whenever their difficult economic circumstances and the fragility of their economic equilibrium made it necessary, to prevent pregnancy and we have seen that they had many ways of doing it, being familiar with a great variety of techniques.

It is moreover clear that an increase in the poor peasant population took place as soon as they felt protected but that when it began to look as if easier circumstances would continue, they resisted having large families. Easy circumstances did not (and do not) necessarily promote large families.

The complexity of the problem with which we are concerned here was brought out by the great congress on world population of 1974 in Bucharest. The discussions did not indeed reveal anything new. Concern was expressed about the continuance of the human race, population problems at different social levels were discussed, and the need for birth control was reiterated.

Large families, it seemed, were regarded as a sign of prosperity at every level of society but especially at the lower. They were seen not only as a form of insurance, providing for the maintenance of the parents in old age, but also as a living demonstration of the family's capacity to keep going. Recent calculations and accounts of the 'population explosion' and its dangers made no impression at all on those living in great or comparative poverty. The people of the Third World felt that the richer countries in urging the need for smaller families were simply proposing trivial remedies. The same story was heard all over the Third World, from India to Bolivia. Bad though their circumstances were in every case, they all rejected planned families and the use of contraceptives. It was very simple, they argued, to prescribe smaller families for the great majority of the world's population, while the minority lived in luxury and enjoyed what was denied to the rest. The rich minority might often have compelling reasons for the use of birth control, but they could decide for themselves whether to have a large or a small family. Why must this freedom be denied to the poor—in India or Bolivia whose situation, I would add, was not much different from that of the ancient Greeks and Romans? According to a manifesto published a few years ago in Bolivia (1972), the peasants and workers of that country were of the opinion that they would not make progress and that there would be no increase in their prosperity or improvement in their legal position if they refrained from having children. They were increasingly aware of the fact that, if they limited the size of their own families, they would simply increase the prosperity of others rather than their own. I believe that this statement is correct and that, as I have suggested, it applied equally to classical antiquity.

In most of the foregoing no account has been taken of slavery. Yet it does have something quite useful to tell us. Slaves could apparently find sexual satisfaction wherever they liked in the slaves' quarters—characteristically, only male slaves are considered in this —but it was very difficult for them to found families. The reference to a slave family sometimes receives emphatic mention in the case of young slaves born into the larger family of the lord and master and we have a distinct impression that it was uncommon and somewhat abnormal.

The same picture, however, does not emerge at all periods in ancient society. This is quite understandable if it is remembered that an abundance of slaves might come on to the market as a result of war and that at such times, when the supply was abundant, they were not so expensive. It is moreover necessary to distinguish between various categories of slaves. There were, for example, less common types of slave used for special kinds of work—it was possible to buy a wet nurse to suckle the children of a lady of high social standing. Such a slave and her own child could be sure of loving care in the family and there are many examples, which cannot be dismissed as unhistorical, of foster brothers who went through life together as free lord and slave but in brotherhood and affection. There are other examples of the emancipation of foster brothers who were originally slaves. There are also many instances recorded of the free child's affection for the slave whose milk he or she had drunk. Where the free child was prosperous in later life, such a slave could expect to be cared for when she was old.

During the imperial period of ancient Rome, when there was a less plentiful supply of slaves on the market, because the Pax Augusta had put an end to the great wars, the breeding of slaves became more common, although it is not known how widespread it was.

All these questions have often been discussed. In the gibe of a modern English scholar, they are like stale tea-leaves used in pot after pot.[27] Hardly any new facts come to light, but the fact remains that slaves were not free. However well they might be treated here and there—Athens is the example always quoted—the absence of freedom was the painful perpetual thorn in their flesh. Moreover, even in the case of Athens the mine slaves of Laurium in south Attica should not be forgotten. It is incomprehensible that, even in the most recent writings on the subject, including those about slavery in America, it is again and again stressed that the lot of slaves was not so unfavourable, that they were fed and clothed and able to lead their own lives and develop their own culture. Despite all the great gifts they received, however, freedom was not among them. It is strange that it should be necessary to recall this simple fact, but necessary it is.

Slaves presumably did not regard the having of children as important for their advancement. Probably they would wait for a time when a considerable number of slaves were given their freedom so that they themselves could contract a marriage as free men. Even then, however, they were likely to be cautious about having children. The emancipated slave, married to an emancipated slave woman or possessing a female slave whom he could make his wife, had to be careful about the number of children born to him, because he was often set free at an age when it was not advisable to have young children. Since it takes so long for a young child to grow into an adult, if a slave was thirty-five when he was set free he could not reasonably expect the 'life insurance policy' that he had, as it were, taken out by begetting a son to 'mature' before his fifty-fifth birthday. Nor could he be sure that the child begotten would be a son, and if it were a daughter, the 'policy' would be of doubtful

---

[27] See p. 205 above.

worth. In case of a son, he must be fifty-five before he could hope
to benefit and few could count on reaching what was then an advanced age if they belonged to this lowest level of society. The
average length of life over all, throughout the whole of classical
antiquity was thirty years. This is, of course, a rough calculation
but cannot be very far from the truth. A man of thirty-five who
begot children in certain circumstances almost undoubtedly exposed
his wife, the mother of his children, to a hard life, that of a widow
with children of whom she would be one day the sole supporter.
It may therefore be assumed, and this is confirmed by such scanty
information as we have, that emancipated slaves did not have large
families and that in many cases their marriages were childless.

An exception, of course, can be made of the Spartan case. The
Spartiatai, the men of the highest class in Spartan society, also
tended to marry late. In classical antiquity, as now, the age at
which a man decided to have children and found a family depended
on his own income and prospects. Even now, the older a man mar-
ries, the greater the risk. This is clearly shown today by the provisions of life insurance policies, the rate of premium, the benefits
to widows and orphans, and so on, where the age of the insured
plays a decisive part. It was no different in antiquity.

At certain times and places in classical antiquity, as for instance
in Italy at the beginning of the second century A.D., the maintenance of the orphans of deceased citizens was provided for by a
grant of imperial *alimenta*. A distinction was made between boys
and girls, girls being supported by the state for a shorter period
than boys, partly because as we have already seen girls generally
married much younger than boys.[28]

Despite these *alimenta* provided by the central government and
financial support from private persons who were not altogether
happy at the depopulation of residential districts around their estates, prosperity did not return to Italy. Whatever the support
from private and state welfare the decision to have children (or
another child) meant a very heavy burden for the parents. This is
illustrated by a statement like the following: 'For when poor men

---

[28] All modern studies of the *alimenta* have recently been overshadowed by
R. Duncan-Jones' fundamental treatment of the subject, *The Economy of the
Roman Empire* (1974), *Government Subsidies for Population Increase*, p. 288 ff;
see especially pp. 291-303. See also M. I. Finley, *The Ancient Economy*
(1973), pp. 40, 104 and 200, note 26.

do not rear their children it is because they fear that if they are educated less well than is befitting they will become servile and boorish and destitute of all virtues; since they consider poverty the worst of all evils, they cannot endure to let their children share it with them, as though it were a certain disease, serious and grievous'.[29]

There was a scale of possibilities leading to abortion. The argument quoted is one of them. The extent, however, to which abortion was practised in Greek and Roman society is a mystery which will probably never be fully elucidated. We do not have this knowledge in the case of our own society today because of the unreliability of the surveys into this question, nor do we have the knowledge with regard to antiquity, because there are too few data.

---

[29] Plutarch, *Mor.* 497E (*De amore prolis* 5).

SELECTED BIBLIOGRAPHY [1]

Ardaillon, E., *Les mines du Laurion*, Paris, 1897.
von Arnim, H., *A. Didymus' Abriss der peripatetischen Ethik*, Akademie der Wissenschaften in Wien, Phil.-hist. Klasse, Sitzungsberichte, 204. Band, 3. Abhandlung, 1926, 3-161.
Badian, E., 'Alexander the Great and the Unity of Mankind', *Historia* 7 (1958), 425-444.
Baker, H., *The Dignity of Man*, Cambridge Mass., 1947.
Barker, E., *From Alexander to Constantine, Passages and Documents illustrating the History of Social and Political Ideas, 336 B.C.-A.D. 337*, Translations with Introductions, Notes and Essays, Oxford, 1956.
——, *The Politics of Aristotle*, London, 1968.
Bauer, W., ὀρφανός, Sp. 1155, *Wörterbuch zu den Schriften des Neuen Testaments*, Berlin, 1958.
——, χήρα, Sp. 1743, *Wörterbuch zu den Schriften des Neuen Testaments*, Berlin, 1958.
Beins, J. F. A., *Misvorming en verbeelding*, Diss. Groningen, Amsterdam, 1948.
Berman, H. J., *The Interaction of Law and Religion*, Cambridge Mass., 1974.
Bernays, J., *Grundzüge der verlorenen Abhandlung des Aristoteles über Wirkung der Tragödie*, 1857.
——, *Theophrasts Schrift über Frömmigkeit*, Berlin, 1866.
Bertholet, A., *Die Stellung der Israeliten und der Juden zu den Fremden*, Freiburg i.B.-Leipzig, 1896.
Bloch, R., *Les prodiges dans l'Antiquité classique*, Paris, 1963.
van Boekel, C. W., *Katharsis, een filologische reconstructie van de psychologie van Aristoteles omtrent het gevoelsleven*, Diss. Nijmegen, Utrecht, 1957.
den Boer, W., *Laconian Studies*, Amsterdam, 1954.
——, *Eros en Amor*, Den Haag, 1962.
——, *Grieken en de Grieken*, Diescollege, Leidse Voordrachten nr. 24, Leiden, 1957 (= 'Greeks and the Greeks', *International Review of Social History* 4 (1959), 91-110.).
——, 'Aspects of Religion in Classical Greece', *Harvard Studies in Classical Philology* 77 (1973), 1-21.
Bolk, L., *Mythologie en Teratologie*, Jaarboek Kon. Ned. Akad. van Wetenschappen, 1928-1929, 194-202.
Bolkestein, H., *Wohltätigkeit und Armenpflege im vorchristlichen Altertum*, Utrecht, 1939.
  Reviews by: Heichelheim, F., *Erasmus* 2 (1949), 470-474 Thiel, J. H., *Tijdschrift voor Geschiedenis* 55 (1940), 300-302.
——, 'Iets over de begrippen "menschheid", "menschenliefde" en "menschelijkheid" bij de Grieken', *Hermeneus* 2 (1929), 67-69.
——, 'Almosen' (Nichtchristlich), *RAC* I, Sp. 301 f., Stuttgart, 1950.
——, 'Armut' (Vorchristlich. 1. Griech.-römisch.), *RAC* I, Sp. 698 ff., Stuttgart, 1950.
Bolkestein, J. C., Ὅσιος en εὐσεβής, Diss. Utrecht, Amsterdam, 1936.

---

[1] See also bibliographies for Slavery and Technology, located on pp. 239-241.

Breitenbach, H. R., *Historiographische Anschauungsformen Xenophons*, Freiburg, 1950.
Bremer, J. M., *Hamartia*, Diss. Amsterdam, Amsterdam, 1969.
de Buck, A., *De godsdienstige opvatting van den slaap inzonderheid in het Oude Egypte*, Inaugural address Leiden, Leiden, 1939.
Calhoun, G. M., *Athenian Clubs in Politics and Litigation*, Austin, Texas, 1913. Thesis (Ph.D.), Univ. of Chicago, 1911.
Carcopino, J., *Histoire Romaine* II, *La République romaine de 133 avant J.-C. à la mort de César (44 avant J.-C.)*, Paris, 1950-1952.
Childe, V. G., *History*, London, 1947.
Cohn, M., 'Jüdisches Waisenrecht,' *Zeitschr. für vergleichende Rechtswissenschaft* 37 (1920), 417-445.
Conner, W. R., *The New Politicians of Fifth-Century Athens*, Princeton, 1971.
Dankmeijer, J., *De speurtocht naar de normale mens*, Oration, Leiden, 1966.
David, M., *Adoptie in het oude Israël*, Med. Kon. Ned. Akad. van Wet., afd. Letterkunde, N.R. 18, 4 (1955), 85-104.
Davies, J. K., *Athenian Propertied Families 600-300 B.C.*, Oxford, 1971.
Deininger, J., *Die politische Widerstand gegen Rom in Griechenland 217-86 v.Chr.*, Berlin-New York, 1971.
Delcourt, M., *Stérilités mystérieuses et naissances maléfiques dans l'Antiquité classique*, Liège, 1938.
De Ste. Croix, G. E. M., 'The Character of the Athenian Empire', *Historia* 3 (1954-1955), 1-41.
Deubner, L., *Attische Feste*, Berlin, 1932 (reprinted in Darmstadt, 1966).
Diels, H., *Sibyllinische Blätter*, Berlin, 1890.
——, *Die Fragmente der Vorsokratiker*, hrsg. von W. Kranz, Berlin, 1951-1952 [6].
Dieterich, A., *Mutter Erde*, Leipzig, 1906.
Dihle, A., *Die goldene Regel*, Göttingen, 1962.
Dirlmeier, F., *Die Oikeiosis-Lehre Theophrasts*, Philologus, Supplementband 30, Heft 1, Leipzig, 1937.
Dodds, E. R., *The Greeks and the Irrational*, Berkeley, 1951.
——, *The Ancient Concept of Progress and Other Essays on Greek Literature and Belief*, Oxford, 1973.
Dorjahn, A., ὀρφανοί *RE* XVIII [1], Sp. 1197-1200, Stuttgart, 1939.
Dörrie, H. A., *Leid und Erfahrung. Die Wort- und Sinnverbindung* παθεῖν-μαθεῖν *im griechischen Denken*, Mainz-Wiesbaden, 1956.
Dover, K. J., *Greek Popular Morality in the Time of Plato and Aristotle*, Oxford, 1974.
Drossaart Lulofs, H. J., *De eed van Hippocrates*, in: Voordrachtreeks van de Ned. Ver. van Psychiaters in dienstverband, Leiden, 1965, p. 105-136.
Duncan-Jones, R., *The Economy of the Roman Empire*, Cambridge, 1974.
Edelstein, L., *The Hippocratic Oath*, Baltimore, 1943.
Ehrenberg, V., *The People of Aristophanes*, Oxford, 1951 [2].
——, 'Zaleucus', in: *OCD* [2], Oxford, 1970.
Eliade, M., *Cosmos and History: the Myth of the Eternal Return*, New York, 1959.
Endenburg, P. J. T., *Koinoonia en gemeenschap van zaken bij Grieken in den klassieken tijd*, Diss. Utrecht, Amsterdam, 1937.
Fichtner, J. and Greeven, H., πλησίον, *ThWNT* VI, 310-316, Stuttgart, 1959.
Finley, J. H., *Thucydides*, Cambridge Mass., 1942.
Finley, M. I., 'Was Greek Civilization based on Slave Labour?' *Historia* 8 (1959), 145-164.

——, 'Athenian Demagogues', *Past and Present* 21 (1962), 3-24, (= Studies in Ancient Society, London, 1974, 1-25).

——, *The Ancient Economy*, London, 1973.

——, 'A Peculiar Institution?', *Times Literary Supplement* July 2 1976, 819-821.

Frings, H. J., *Medizin und Arzt bei den griechischen Kirchenvätern bis Chrysostomos*, Bonn, 1959.

Frisch, H., *Xenophon, The Constitution of the Athenians*, a Philological-historical Analysis of Ps.-Xenophon's Treatise *De re publica Atheniensium*, Kopenhagen, 1942.

von Fritz, K., *Die griechische Geschichtsschreibung* I, 2 vols., Berlin, 1967.

Gagé, J., *Recherches sur les Jeux Séculairs*, Paris, 1934.

Gelzer, K. I., *Die Schrift vom Staate der Athener*, Hermes, Einzelschriften, Heft 3, Berlin, 1937.

Gomme, A. W., 'The Position of Women in Athens in the Fifth and Fourth Centuries B.C.', *C.Ph.* 20 (1925), 1-25 (= Essays in Greek History and Literature, Oxford, 1937, 89-115).

——, *The Population of Athens in the Fifth and Fourth Centuries B.C.*, Oxford, 1933.

——, *A Historical Commentary on Thucydides*, Vol. II, Oxford, 1956.

——, *More Essays in Greek History and Literature*, Oxford, 1962.

Guthrie, W. K. C., *The Greeks and their Gods*, London, 1950.

——, *History of Greek Philosophy*, Vol. III, Cambridge, 1969.

Händel, P., 'Prodigium', Sp. 2283-2296, *RE* XXIII ², Stuttgart, 1959.

Hands, A. R., *Charities and Social Aid in Greece and Rome*, London, 1968.

Harder, R., *Studies presented to D. M. Robinson on his seventieth Birthday*, Ed. by G. E. Mylonas, Vol. I, St. Louis, 1951, 446-449 (= Kleine Schriften, München, 1960, 208-211).

Harrison, A. R. W., *The Law of Athens, the Family and Property*, London, 1968.

Hauck, F., πλοῦτος, *ThWNT* VI, 318-330, Stuttgart, 1959.

——, πένης, *ThWNT* VI, 38-40, Stuttgart, 1959.

——, πτωχός, *ThWNT* VI, 885-888, Stuttgart, 1959.

Hönn, K., *Solon: Staatsmann und Weiser*, Wien, 1948.

Hopkins, M. K., 'The Age of Roman Girls at Marriage', *Population Studies* 18, 3 (1964-1965), 309-327.

——, 'Contraception in the Roman Empire', *Comparative Studies in Society and History* 8 (1965-1966), 124-151.

Jacoby, F., *Die Fragmente der Griechischen Historiker*, Berlin, 1923-1930, Leiden, 1940-

——, *Atthis, the Local Chronicles of Ancient Athens*, Oxford, 1949.

Jaeger, W., *Paideia: the Ideals of Greek Culture*, 3 Vols, Oxford, 1944-1945.

Jones, A. H. M., 'The Economic Basis of the Athenian Democracy', *Past and Present* 1 (1952), 13-31 (= Athenian Democracy, Oxford, 1957, 3-20).

de Jong, H. M. W., *Demonische ziekten in Babylon en Bijbel*, Amsterdam, 1959.

Kamerbeek, J., '"La dignité humaine", Esquisse d'une terminographie', *Neophilologus* 41 (1957), 241-251.

——, 'Le titre de "La condition humaine" dans sa perspective historique', *Le Français Moderne, Revue de Linguistique français* 38 (1970), 440-446.

Kern, O., *Die Religion der Griechen*, 3 Bde, Berlin, 1926-1938.

Keuls, E., *The Watercarriers in Hades, a Study of Catharsis through Toil in Classical Antiquity*, Amsterdam, 1974.

Kitto, H. D. F., *The Greeks*, Harmondsworth, 1951.
van der Kolf, M. C., 'Neleus', *RE* XVI ², Sp. 2274.
Kristensen, W. B., *Het leven uit den dood*, Haarlem, 1926.
———, *De antieke opvattingen van dienstbaarheid*, Med. Kon. Ned. Akad. van
   Wet., afd. Letterk., 78, Series B, nr. 3, Amsterdam, 1934 (= Verzamelde
   bijdragen tot de kennis der antieke godsdiensten, Amsterdam, 1947,
   201-230.).
———, *Symbool en werkelijkheid*, Arnhem, 1954.
———, *The Meaning of Religion*, Lectures in the Phenomenology of Religion,
   The Hague, 1960.
Lacey, W. K., *The Family in Classical Greece*, London, 1968.
Latte, K., *Römische Religionsgeschichte*, München, 1960.
Lauffer, S., *Die Bergwerksklaven von Laureion*, Mainz, Abhandlungen (1955),
   12; (1956) 11.
Lietzmann, H., 'An die Römer', *Handbuch zum Neuen Testament*, Tübingen,
   1933 ⁴.
Linforth, I. M., *Solon the Athenian*, Berkeley, 1919.
Lipsius, J. H., *Das attische Recht und Rechtsverfahren, mit Benützung des
   attischen Prozesses*, von M. H. E. Meier und G. F. Schömann dargestellt,
   Band 1-3, Leipzig, 1905-1915.
Lloyd-Jones, H., *The Justice of Zeus*, Los Angeles, 1971.
Loenen, D., *Eusebeia en de kardinale deugden*, Med. Kon. Ned. Akad. van
   Wet., afd. Letterk., N.R. 23, nr. 4, Amsterdam, 1960.
MacMullen, R., *Roman Social Relations: 50 B.C. to 284 A.D.*, New Haven,
   1974.
Mathieu, G., *Isocrate, Discours*, Tome III, Paris, 1950.
McCartney, E. S., 'Greek and Roman Lore of Animal-Nursed Infants',
   Papers of the Michigan Academy 4 (1924), 15-42.
Meerwaldt, J. D., *Vormaspecten*, Den Haag, 1958.
Mehwaldt, J., 'Das Weltbürgertum der Antike', *Die Antike* 2 (1926) 177-189.
Merlan, P., 'Alexander the Great or Antiphon the Sophist?', *C.Ph.* 45 (1950),
   161-166.
Momigliano, A. D., *Jacob Bernays*, Med. Kon. Ned. Akad. van Wet., afd.
   Letterk., N.R. 32, nr. 5, Amsterdam, 1969.
———, *Quinto contributo alla storia degli studi classici e del mondo antico*, Roma,
   1975.
Mühl, M., *Die antike Menschheitsidee in ihrer geschichtlichen Entwicklung*,
   Leipzig, 1928.
———, 'Die Gesetze des Zaleukos und Charondas', *Klio* 22 (1929), 105-124,
   432-463.
Murray, G., *The Rise of the Greek Epic*, Oxford, 1911 ².
Nenci, G., 'La filobarbaria di Ecateo nel giudizio di Eraclito', *Riv. Filol.
   Class.* 77 (1949), 107-117.
Nilsson, M. P., *Griechische Feste*, Leipzig, 1906.
———, *Cults, Myths, Oracles, and Politics in Ancient Greece*, Lund, 1951.
———, *Geschichte der Griechischen Religion*, München, 1955-1961 ².
Noonan, J. T., *Contraception, a History of its Treatment by the Catholic
   Theologians and Canonists*, Cambridge Mass., 1965.
Ollier, F., *Le mirage spartiate*, 2 Vols, Paris, 1933-1943.
Opstelten, J. C., *Sophocles en het Grieksche pessimisme*, Diss., Leiden, 1945.
Otto, R., *Das Heilige*, München, 1936 ²³⁻²⁵.
Paschoud, F., (ed.), *Zosime, Histoires Nouvelles*, Paris, 1971.
Pickard-Cambridge, A. W., *The Dramatic Festivals of Athens*, Oxford, 1953.

Pighi, I. B., *De Ludis Saecularibus Populi Romani Quiritium Libri Sex,* Amsterdam, 1965 [2].

Poe, J. P., *Heroism and Divine Justice in Sophocles' Philoctetes,* Leiden, 1974.

Pötscher, W., *Theophrastos' Περὶ εὐσεβείας,* (Philosophia Antiqua 11) Leiden, 1964.

Pohlenz, M., *Geschichte einer geistigen Bewegung,* 2 Bde, Göttingen, 1948-1949.

Pomeroy, S. B., *Goddesses, Whores, Wives and Slaves. Women in Classical Antiquity,* New York, 1975.

Popp, H., 'Zum Verhältnis Athens zu seinen Bündern im attisch-delischen Seebund', *Historia* 17 (1968), 425-443.

Pouilloux, J., *Recherches sur l'histoire et les cultes de Thasos,* 2 Vols, Paris, 1954-1958.

van Proosdij, B. A., *Der sogenannte orientalische Despotismus, Symbolae ad iura orientis antiqui pertinentes Paulo Koschaker dedicatae,* Leiden, 1939.

Pusey, N. M., 'Alcibiades and τὸ φιλόπολι', *Harvard Studies in Cl. Philology* 51 (1940), 215-232.

Radke, G., *Die Bedeutung der weissen und der schwarzen Farbe in Kult und Brauch der Griechen und Römer,* Inaug. Diss. Berlin, Jena, 1936.

Rawson, E., *The Spartan Tradition in European Thought,* London, 1969.

Reesor, M. E., *The Political Theory of the Old and Middle Stoa,* New York, 1951.

Reijnders, H. F., *Societas Generis Humani bij Cicero,* Diss. Utrecht, Groningen-Djakarta, 1954.

Rhodes, P. J., 'Bastards as Athenian Citizens', *Classical Quarterly,* N.S. 28 (1978), 89-92.

——, *The Athenian Boule,* Oxford, London, 1972.

Robert, L., *Etudes épigraphiques et philologiques,* Paris, 1938.

Ruschenbusch, E., *Solonos Nomoi, Die Fragmente des solonischen Gesetzeswerkes mit einer Text- und Überlieferungsgeschichte, Historia,* Einzelschriften, Heft 9, Wiesbaden, 1966.

Sauppe, H., *Oratores Attici,* Zürich, 1839-1843.

Schäfer, M., *Ein frühmittelstoisches System der Ethik bei Cicero,* Inaug. Diss., München, 1934.

Schmid, W. and Stählin, O., *Geschichte der griechischen Literatur,* in: *Handbuch der Altertumswissenschaft* VII. 1. 2, München, 1934.

Schwartz, E., *Charakterköpfe aus der antiken Literatur,* Berlin, 1919 [3].

——, *Über das Verhältnis der Hellenen zur Geschichte, Gesammelte Schriften* I, 47-66, Berlin, 1938.

——, *Ethik der Griechen,* Hrsg. von W. Richter, Stuttgart, 1951.
   Review by: Verdenius, W. J., in *Erasmus* 6 (1953), Sp. 804-807.

Schwenn, F., 'Die Menschenopfer bei den Griechen und Römern', *RGVV* XV, 3 (1915).

Seesemann, H., ὀρφανός *ThWNT* V, 486-488, Stuttgart, 1954.

Sikkema, R. K., *De lening in het Oude Testament* (Bijdrage tot de kennis van het vraagstuk van schuld en aansprakelijkheid), Diss. Leiden, Den Haag, 1957.

Sinclair, T. A., *A History of Greek Political Thought,* London, 1951.

Sokolowski, F., *Les lois sacrées des cités grecques,* Paris, 1969.

Sprague, R. K., (ed.), *The Older Sophists,* Columbia S.C., 1972
   Review by: Kerferd, G. B., in *Classical Review* 25 (1975), 231-232.

Stählin, G., 'Das Bild der Witwe', *Jahrbuch für Antike und Christentum* 17 (1974), 5-20.

Stählin, G., χήρα, *ThWNT* IX, 428-454, Stuttgart, 1973.

Stroud, R. S., 'Theozotides and the Athenian Orphans', *Hesperia* 40 (1971), 280-301.

Syme, R., *Tacitus*, 2 Vols, Oxford, 1958.

Tarn, W. W., *Alexander the Great and the Unity of Mankind*, Proceedings of the British Academy 19 (1933), 123-166. (= Griffith, G. T. (ed.), *Alexander the Great, The Main Problems*, New York, 1966, 243-286).

Temkin, O., *The Falling Sickness, a History of Epilepsy from the Greeks to the Beginnings of modern Neurology*, Baltimore, 1945.

Terstegen, W. J., Εὐσεβής en "Οσιος in het Grieksche taalgebruik na de IVᵉ eeuw, Diss. Utrecht, Utrecht, 1941.

Thiel, J. H., 'Themistocles (een polemiek)', *Tijdschrift voor Geschiedenis* 64 (1951), 1-39.

——, 'De geschiedenis van het Hellenisme', in: *Het oudste Christendom en de Antieke Cultuur* (eds: Waszink, J., van Unnik, W., de Beus, Ch.), Haarlem, 1951, 3-39, 53-74.

Thomson, G., (ed.), *Oresteia*, 2 Vols, Cambridge, 1938.

——, *Studies in Ancient Greek Society, the Prehistoric Aegean*, London, 1949.

Tigerstedt, E. N., *The Legend of Sparta in Classical Antiquity*, 3 Vols, Stockholm, 1965-1978.

Toynbee, A. J., *Some Problems of Greek History*, London, 1969.

van der Valk, M., *Zum Worte* ὅσιος, Mnemosyne, T.S. 10 (1942), 113-140.

Verdenius, W. J., *Hector*, Groningen-Batavia, 1947.

——, Κάθαρσις τῶν παθημάτων in: *Autour d'Aristote, Recueil d'Etudes de philosophie ancienne et médiévale offert à Monseigneur A. Mansion*, Louvain, 1955.

van de Waal, H., 'Rembrandt en wij', *De Gids* 119 (1956), 40-44 (= *Steps towards Rembrandt*, Amsterdam, 1974, 7-13).

Wagenvoort, H., *Studies in Roman Literature, Culture and Religion*, Leiden, 1956.

——, *Varia Vita, Schets van de geestelijke stroomingen in Rome en Italië van omstreeks 200 vóór tot 200 na Chr.*, Groningen, 1952 ⁵. (= Varia Vita, a sketch of Philosophical and Moral Ideas in Rome and Italy between 200 B.C. and A.D. 200).

Walbank, F. W., *Philip V of Macedon*, Cambridge, 1940.

Waszink, J. H., *Humanitas*, Inaugural address, Utrecht, 1946.

——, 'Abtreibung', *RAC* I, Sp. 55-60, Stuttgart, 1950.

Wegner, M., *Untersuchungen zu den lateinischen Begriffen Socius und Societas*, Hypomnemeta, Untersuchungen zur Antike und ihrem Nachleben, Heft 21, Göttingen, 1969.

Wenger, L., 'Adoption', *RAC* I, Sp. 99-112, Stuttgart, 1950.

Westermann, W. L., *The Slave Systems of Greek and Roman Antiquity*, Memoirs of the American Philosophical Society, Vol. 40, Philadelphia, 1955.
    Review by: De Ste. Croix in *Classical Review*, N.S. 7 (1957), 54-59.

Will, E., 'Fonction de la monnaie dans les cités grecques de l'époque classique', in: *Numismatique antique, problèmes et méthodes*, Annales de l'Est, publiées par l'Université de Nancy, II, Mémoires no 44 (1975), 233-246.

Willetts, R. F., *Aristocratic Society in Ancient Greece*, London, 1955.

Wülker, L., *Die geschichtliche Entwicklung des Prodigienwesens bei den Römern*, Leipzig, 1903.

Wüst, F. R., 'Zu den πρυτάνιες τῶν ναυκράρων und zu den alten attischen Trittyen', *Historia* 6 (1957), 176-191.

Zimmern, A. E., *Solon and Croesus*, London, 1928.

——, *The Greek Commonwealth*, Oxford, 1931 ⁵.

Zucker, F., 'Socia unanimans', *Rheinisches Museum* 92 (1943), 193-217.

GENERAL INDEX

INDEX OF MODERN AUTHORS